The Institutionalization of Science in Early Modern Europe

Scientific and Learned Cultures and Their Institutions

Editor

Mordechai Feingold (*California Institute of Technology*)

VOLUME 27

The titles published in this series are listed at *brill.com/slci*

The Institutionalization of Science in Early Modern Europe

Edited by

Giulia Giannini
Mordechai Feingold

BRILL

LEIDEN | BOSTON

The Library of Congress Cataloging-in-Publication Data is available online at http://catalog.loc.gov

Cover illustration: A meeting of the Accademia del Cimento, fresco by Gaspero Martellini (1785-1857), Tribuna di Galileo, Florence, 1840ca.
Photo credit: Saulo Bambi - Sistema Museale dell'Università degli Studi di Firenze (Italy)

Typeface for the Latin, Greek, and Cyrillic scripts: "Brill". See and download: brill.com/brill-typeface.

ISSN 2352-1325
ISBN 978-90-04-41686-4 (hardback)
ISBN 978-90-04-41687-1 (e-book)

Copyright 2020 by Koninklijke Brill NV, Leiden, The Netherlands.
Koninklijke Brill NV incorporates the imprints Brill, Brill Hes & De Graaf, Brill Nijhoff, Brill Rodopi, Brill Sense, Hotei Publishing, mentis Verlag, Verlag Ferdinand Schöningh and Wilhelm Fink Verlag.
All rights reserved. No part of this publication may be reproduced, translated, stored in a retrieval system, or transmitted in any form or by any means, electronic, mechanical, photocopying, recording or otherwise, without prior written permission from the publisher.
Authorization to photocopy items for internal or personal use is granted by Koninklijke Brill NV provided that the appropriate fees are paid directly to The Copyright Clearance Center, 222 Rosewood Drive, Suite 910, Danvers, MA 01923, USA. Fees are subject to change.

This book is printed on acid-free paper and produced in a sustainable manner.

Contents

Preface VII
Giulia Giannini
List of Contributors IX

PART 1
Research in Institutional Setting

1 Between Teaching and Research: The Place of Science in Early Modern English Universities 3
 Mordechai Feingold

2 The Academization of Parisian Science (1660–1789): Review Essay on a Spatial Turn 20
 Stéphane Van Damme

3 Asymmetries of Symbolic Capital in Seventeenth-Century Scientific Transactions: Placentinus's Cometary Correspondence with Hevelius and Lubieniecki 52
 Pietro Daniel Omodeo

PART 2
Founding and Shaping Scientific Institutions

4 An Indirect Convergence between the Accademia del Cimento and the Montmor Academy: The 'Saturn dispute' 83
 Giulia Giannini

5 The Edifying Science. Academies, Courtly Culture and the Patronage of Science in Early-modern Portugal (1647–1720) 109
 Luis Miguel Carolino

6 The Paris Observatory in the Early Modern Ecosystem of Knowledge (1669–1712) 138
 Dalia Deias

7   The Early History of the Paris and London Academies: Two Paths
    Towards the Institutionalization of Science   174
    Aurellien Ruellet and François Mallet

PART 3
Making and Reporting Experiments: Scientific Styles and Publishing Policies

8   Professionalizing Doubt: Johann Daniel Major's Observation
    'On the Horn of the Bezoardic Goat', Curiosity Collecting, and
    Periodical Publication   199
    Vera Keller

9   Experiments on Collections at the Royal Society of London and the Paris
    Academy of Sciences, 1660–1740   236
    Michael Bycroft

10 The Uses of Licensing: Publishing Strategy and the Imprimatur at the
    Early Royal Society   266
    Noah Moxham

    Summarizing Commentaries – 'Institutions and Knowledge Systems:
    Theoretical Perspectives'   292
    Jürgen Renn and Florian Schmaltz

    Index   297

Preface

Giulia Giannini

The emergence of the first European scientific societies in the seventeenth century has attracted scholarly attention, at least since the publication in 1928 of Martha Ornstein's *The Rôle of Scientific Societies in the Seventeenth century*. Ornstein and her successors considered the foundation of scientific academies as a fundamental step towards the establishment of modern science in Europe. Such a phenomenon became possible owing to the gradual shift – during the second half of the seventeenth century – from a social system of knowledge based on patronage networks to organized institutions sponsored by a public authority. This shift created the conditions for the emergence of collaborative scientific organizations based on experimentation, which complemented existing university associations, and which were connected to political power (either verbally sponsored or financially funded by princes and kings). This process institutionalized, promoted and prescribed specific scientific practices, alternative processes of legitimization, as well as new protocols of argumentation and communication. Important studies have highlighted the influence that academies such as the *Royal Society* or the *Académie Royale des Sciences* had exerted on the emergence of this new scientific practice. But the extent and the complexity of the phenomenon continue to expand the boundaries of research. Moreover, certain aspects of this pivotal shift remain obscure – for example, the historical dynamics that engendered the almost simultaneous appearance, in different parts of Europe, of public institutions based on collaborative and experimental research. Nor had sufficient attention been given to the relations of the new scientific organization with existing learned institutions, or to the informal and formal ties between the various academies and private scientific circles within and without the universities.

The present volume aims to contribute to a better understanding of the scientific and institutional context that gave rise to the first European academies – especially the *Accademia del Cimento* in Florence' the *Academia naturae curiosorum* in Schweinfurt; the *Royal Society* in London; and the *Académie Royale des Sciences* in Paris. The several essays attempt to provide a novel framework that would account for the foundation and the activities of these new forms of scientific organization – in Portugal and Poland as well as in England, France, and Italy – a framework that also encompasses traditional institutions of higher learning. For too long the emergence of scientific academies has been explained as an organizational shift that derived exclusively from new intellectual demands – especially as a reaction to the 'stagnating' environment of the universities. However, as this volume will attempt to demonstrate, the relationship between the new forms of scientific organization and traditional institutions was far more complex. On the one hand, as recent research has already established, the course of studies at many universities proved spacious enough to include the teaching of the old and new learning – including experimental science. On the other hand, not only were the promoters of the new sciences educated in the universities, many members of the various European academies actually held university positions throughout much of their careers. Furthermore, the existence of a large number of learned academies since the late fifteenth century, suggest that this organizational model had been designed with a more expansive vision of intellectual activities in mind. Thus, the emergence of scientific acadmies cannot be explained exclusively as a response to the new climate produced by the *new* science; rather, that scientific practice accommodated itself to an already existing organizational model.

I would like to express my gratitude to the institutions that have supported this project from its inception: the Alexander Von Humboldt Foundation (Berlin); the Max Planck Institute for the History of Science (Berlin); and the University of Bergamo (Italy). Special thanks are owed to Jürgen Renn, Florian Schmaltz, and Paolo Galluzzi.

Contributors

Michael Bycroft
is Assistant Professor of the History of Science and Technology at the University of Warwick. He is co-editor, with Sven Dupré, of *Gems in the Early Modern World: Materials, Knowledge, and Global Trade, 1450–1800* (Palgrave Macmillan, 2019). He is writing a monograph on the role of precious stones in the physical sciences in early modern Europe. He received his Ph.D. from the University of Cambridge in 2013 before taking up postdoctoral positions at the Max Planck Institute for the History of Science and the University of Warwick.

Luís Miguel Carolino
is an assistant professor of history at the Instituto Universitário de Lisboa (ISCTE-IUL), where he is also a researcher affiliated with CIES. His main research interests concern history of science and its institutions, history of astronomy and cosmology, and social, political, and cultural relations of science, areas in which he has published extensively.

Dalia Deias
received her training in astronomy and history of science at the University of Bologna and the Centre Alexandre Koyré in Paris. Her doctoral thesis 'Inventer l'Observatoire: sciences et politique sous Giovanni Domenico Cassini (1625–1712)' reexamines the foundation of the Paris Observatory during the Grand Siècle as the result of Louis XIV's imperialistic ambitions and the transfer of observational practices from Bologna by the Italian astronomer Giovanni Domenico Cassini. Her research topics, which have led to several publications in French and in English, include early modern correspondances, the first generation of royal academicians during the Grand Siècle, catholic astronomers, places and practices of observation of the sky in 16th to 18th century Europe and women in observatories.

Mordechai Feingold
is the Van Nuys Page Professor of History at Caltech. He is the editor of the journals *Erudition and the republic of Letters* (Brill) and *History of Universities* (Oxford). He is the author of a number of books, including *The Mathematicians' Apprenticeship: Science, Universities and Society in England, 1560–1640* (1984); *The Newtonian Moment: Isaac Newton and the Making of Modern Culture* (2004); and *Newton and the Origin of Civilization* (2013), written with Jed Buchwald.

Giulia Giannini

is Associate Professor of History of Science at the University of Milan (Italy). She is the principal investigator of the ERC Consolidator research project TACITROOTS – The Accademia del Cimento in Florence: tracing the roots of the European scientific enterprise (2019–2024). She worked at the Centre Koyré in Paris and at the Max Planck Institute for the History of Science in Berlin. Her research interests focus on the history of experimentation, and on cultural, political and social studies of science in Early Modern Europe.

Vera Keller

is Associate Professor of History at the University of Oregon. In *Knowledge and the Public Interest, 1575–1725* (Cambridge, 2015), she reconsidered the Scientific Revolution from the perspective of the history of knowledge. Her second book, now under review, is *The Interlopers: Cornelis Drebbel (1572–1633) and early Stuart Science on the World Stage*. Her current book project explores Johann Daniel Major's transformation of the *Kunstkammer* into an academic research institution.

Francois Mallet

is a lecturer in English literature in Nice (French CPGE). Previous work includes research into the discourse of natural history in the first half of the seventeenth century, with particular focus on the redefinition of genre and rhetoric in botanical writing as a reflection of changing identities and social dynamics.

Noah Moxham

is a postdoctoral researcher in the history of science at the University of Kent. His recent research focuses on the histories of scientific institutions and cultures of communication in early modern Britain and Europe. He has published widely on these topics, and is the co-author of a forthcoming study of the *Philosophical Transactions*, the world's first scientific periodical, and the editor, with Joad Raymond, of *News Networks in Early Modern Europe* (2016). He is currently part of a Leverhulme Trust project exploring the sites, spaces, and cultures of science in seventeenth- and eighteenth-century London (*Metropolitan Science*).

Pietro Daniel Omodeo

is a cultural historian of science and a professor of historical epistemology at Ca' Foscari University of Venice (Italy). He is the principal investigator of the ERC Consolidator research endeavour 'Institutions and Metaphysics of Cosmology in the Epistemic Networks of Seventeenth-Century Europe' (Horizon

2020, GA 725883). He authored *Copernicus in the Cultural Debates of the Renaissance: Reception, Legacy, Transformation* (2014). Among recent and ongoing projects, he is co-author, with Jürgen Renn, of *Science in Court Society: Giovanni Battista Benedetti's* Diversarum speculationum mathematicarum et physicarum liber (Turin, 1585) (2019), he is the editor of *Bernardino Telesio and the Natural Sciences in the Renaissance* (2019) and is completing for publication the monograph *Political Epistemology: The Problem of Ideology in Science Studies*.

Jürgen Renn
is Director at the Max Planck Institute for the History of Science in Berlin and currently serves as Chair of the Humanities Section of the Max Planck Society. His research projects focus on long-term developments of knowledge while taking into account processes of globalization. His research projects have dealt with the historical development of mechanics from antiquity until the 20th century. In this context he also investigates the origins of mechanics in China, the transformation of ancient knowledge and the exchange of knowledge between Europe and China in the early modern period. A main focus of Renn's research is the history of modern physics, investigating the origin and development of general theory of relativity, and of quantum theory in particular. Recently, he has taken on the challenges of the Anthropocene in investigating the history of knowledge and science.

Aurélien Ruellet
is lecturer in early-modern History at Le Mans Université. He is the author of *La Maison de Salomon: histoire du patronage scientifique et technique en France et en Angleterre au XVIIe siècle* (Presses Universitaires de Rennes, 2016). His current research focuses on the cultural and social history of 'short memories' from the Renaissance until the modern age, on the way they were medicalized or triggered attempts at educational reform.

Florian Schmaltz
is the Research Program Coordinator of the Research Program History of the Max Planck Society at the Max Planck Institut for the History of Science (Berlin). He is historian of contemporary history and history of science. In his research he focuses on the historical epistemology of scientific institutions. He investigates the history of the relations between science, the military, and industry in case studies on chemical warfare research and aeronautical research. Recent publications include Sören Flachowsky, Rüdiger Hachtmann, and Florian Schmaltz (eds.): Ressourcenmobilisierung. Wissenschaftspolitik

und Forschungspraxis im NS-Herrschaftssystem (Göttingen 2016) and Friedrich, Bretislav, Dieter Hoffmann, Jürgen Renn, Florian Schmaltz, and Martin Wolf (eds.): One Hundred Years of Chemical Warfare: Research, Deployment, Consequences (Cham 2017).

Stéphane Van Damme
is professor in history of science at the European University Institute. Specialist of early modern French History of science, his recent publications include *A toutes voiles vers la vérité. Une autre histoire de la philosophie au temps des Lumières* (Le Seuil, 2014) and he co-edited *L'histoire des sciences et des savoirs de la Renaissance aux Lumières* (Le Seuil, 2015); with Hanna Hodacs and Kenneth Nyberg, eds., *Linnaeus, Natural History and the circulation of Knowledge* (Oxford: Oxford University Studies in the Enlightenment, 2018).

PART 1

Research in Institutional Setting

CHAPTER 1

Between Teaching and Research: The Place of Science in Early Modern English Universities

Mordechai Feingold

Most scholars today would acknowledge the shortcomings of a once dominant historical tradition that damned (so to speak) early modern universities as bastions of scholasticism, inimical to new ideas. A growing body of evidence attesting to the teaching of the mathematical sciences, and to the diffusion of new philosophies – either through books or in the lecture hall – belies such a sweeping generalization. Nevertheless, while conceding that the bleak portrayal of the universities has been overstated, many scholars persist in their reluctance to credit the institutions of higher learning with making meaningful contributions to the scientific revolution. As one scholar articulates the modified view:

> the university was the environment within which scientific learning was typically transmitted and disseminated and scientific interests aroused in the early modern period. It was perhaps indispensable for the emergence of sufficient quantum of the scientifically literate to generate transformations in scientific activities. This is not to say that the university was the perfect environment for the advancement of science. This is surely proved by the fact that most blueprints advanced at this time for the ideal scientific milieu envisaged activity not within the university or seminary, but in some sort of more specialized, self-contained, independent institution.[1]

Another scholar is even more emphatic:

> Although it would be wrong to discount the role of the universities in the scientific revolution, it is important not to overstate the case. It should be borne in mind that, throughout this period, the function of the university

---

1 Roy Porter, 'The Scientific Revolution and Universities', in *A History of the University in Europe, vol. 2: Universities in Early Modern Europe*, ed. Hilde de Ridder-Symoens (Cambridge, 1996), 531–562, at 548.

was to teach. The sites for new research were the courtly Academies, the Royal Society, or the private house of a dedicated individual, whether a wealthy grandee like Tycho Brahe or Robert Boyle, or a more humble seeker after knowledge, like Andreas Libavius ... or Antoni van Leeuwenhoek.

The academies, he concludes, 'developed as arenas for advanced, innovative work', indeed as 'proto-research institutes, at a time when universities were merely teaching organizations'.[2]

The basis for such an assessment – like the earlier assessment of the universities' curricula – is rooted in the seeming failure to locate the familiar features of the 'modern' research university in sixteenth- and seventeenth-century Oxford and Cambridge. And just as twentieth-century scholars still embrace the claims of Victorian critics concerning the pernicious effects of obsolete statutes on the Oxbridge curriculum during the early modern period, so the nineteenth-century portrayal of the mission of universities as circumscribed by their role to train gentlemen and clerics, is assumed to hold valid for the earlier period as well.

To a certain degree such a perception is justified. Early modern Oxford and Cambridge were thoroughly humanistic institutions, which offered what came to be known as a liberal education – in addition to serving as vocational centers for the ministry. Nevertheless, the early modern version of such a program was more comprehensive than the one it would later evolve into, the ideal of the university's mission far more inclusive than its iteration in the nineteenth century. The quintessential exponent of the Victorian position was Cardinal Newman who opened his *The Idea of a University* positing the university as a 'place of teaching universal *knowledge*'. This implies, he continued, 'that its object is, on the one hand, intellectual, not moral; and, on the other, that it is the diffusion and extension of knowledge rather than the advancement. If its object were scientific and philosophical discovery, I do not see why a University should have students'. Such a conception, Newman hastens to add, ought not to be interpreted to mean that the university 'sacrifices Science'. There exist many scientific societies – 'the sort of institution, which primarily contemplates Science itself, and not students' – which are far better suited to undertake such a narrower task:

> The nature of the case and the history of philosophy combine to recommend to us this division of intellectual labour between Academies and Universities. To discover and to teach are distinct functions; they are also distinct gifts, and are not commonly found united in the same person. He, too, who spends his day in dispensing his existing knowledge to all

---

[2] John Henry, *The Scientific Revolution and the Origins of Modern Science*, 2nd ed. (Basingstoke, 2002), 48, 46.

comers is unlikely to have either leisure or energy to acquire new. The common sense of mankind has associated the search after truth with seclusion and quiet. The greatest thinkers have been too intent on their subject to admit of interruption; they have been men of absent minds and idiosyncratic habits, and have, more or less, shunned the lecture room and the public school.[3]

To underscore that no antagonism to science is implied – that he simply expressed a genuine conviction concerning the complementary tasks of the two domains – Newman cites approvingly Cardinal Hyacinthe Sigismond Gerdil's late eighteenth-century expression, according to which 'there is no real opposition between the spirit of academies and that of Universities, but only different points of view. Universities are established to teach the sciences to students who wish to develop themselves there; Academies aim at carrying out new research for the development of the sciences. The Universities of Italy have furnished men who have done honor to the Academies; and the latter have given to the Universities Professors who have filled their posts with the greatest distinction'.[4] What Newman fails to mention is that Gerdil's statement was taken from the statutes he had drawn up for a certain scientific society, and as such it represented an apologia common to founders of academies, aimed at assuring existing institutions of higher learning that the projected institution posed them no harm.[5] Newman, therefore, cites Gerdil out of context to suit his own agenda: to defend his position that advanced scientific research has no place in a university.

Newman, of course, was not the first to maintain such a position. Already in the early years of the nineteenth century, several Oxbridge dons had attempted to counter a growing chorus of critics – who charged the universities with an exclusive devotion to the classics, as well as with failure to incorporate new ideas and novel teaching methods – by aplauding the intrinsic value of liberal education and by defending the maligned tutorial system. Responding in 1810 to the brutal censures of Oxford and Cambridge by several contributors to the *Edinburgh Review*, for example, Edward Copleston contended that public lectures by illustrious professors may have indeed enlightened the 'few, through whom the royal blood of philosophy shall descend in its purest channels', but

---

3 John H. Newman, *The Idea of a University Defined and Illustrated*, 8th ed. (London, 1888), ix, xii–xiii.
4 *Opere edite ed inedite del cardinale Giacinto Sigismondo Gerdil*, 20 vols (Rome, 1806–1822) 3: 353.
5 See Mordechai Feingold, 'Tradition versus Novelty: Universities and Scientific Societies in the Early Modern Period', in *Revolution and Continuity: Essays in the History and Philosophy of Early Modern Science*, eds. Peter Barker and Roger Ariew (Washington DC, 1991), 45–59.

not 'the unschooled multitude'. The tutorial system catered best to the needs of the entire student body, 'according to their several measures of capacity'. Consequently, the universities 'do a greater and more solid good to the nation' in forming the minds of the many, than 'if we sought to extend over Europe the fame of a few exalted individuals or to acquire renown by exploring untrodden regions, and by holding up to the world ever ready to admire what is new, the fruits of our discovery'. Not that he discouraged 'speculation', Copleston averred; he only insisted that 'it is not, and it ought not to be the business' of the institutions. 'Individuals may engage in the task of discovery', and experiments may be tried in 'some corner of the farm'; but such activity should not engross the minds of all students.[6]

Distinguished scientists themselves acquiesced to such an assessment. Consider Thomas Young's 1810 defense of the English system against the criticism of the *Edinburgh Review*:

> it must be remembered that the *advancement* of learning is by no means the principal object of an academical institution: the *diffusion* of a respectable share of instruction in literature and in the sciences among those classes which hold the highest situations and have the most extensive influence in the State is an object of more importance to the public than the discovery of new truths.... We think that we have observed numerous instances, both in public life and in the pursuit of natural knowledge, in which great scholars and great mathematicians have reasoned less soundly, although more ingeniously, than others, who, being somewhat more completely in the possession of common-sense ... were still far inferior to them in the refinements of learning or of science.[7]

This line of reasoning became more difficult to sustain in subsequent decades as the superiority of the new German research model became increasingly manifest. Only then did defenders of Oxford and Cambridge become more explicit in their efforts to exclude the advancement of learning – especially by students – from the expressed mission of the universities.[8]

---

6 Edward Copleston, *A Reply to the Calumnies of the Edinburgh Review against Oxford* (Oxford, 1810), 149–151.
7 Thomas Young, *Miscellaneous Works*, eds. George Peacock and John Leitch, 3 vols (London, 1855) 1: 236.
8 John R. Davis, 'Higher Education Reform and the German Model: A Victorian Discourse', in *Anglo-German Scholarly Networks in the Long Nineteenth Century*, eds Heather Ellis and Ulrike Kirchberger (Leiden, 2014), 39–62; John R. Davis, *The Victorians and Germany* (Oxford, 2007), and references there cited.

For their part, critics pinpointed the source of the malaise affecting Oxford and Cambridge: the statutes of the universities and the colleges which remained in effect for centuries. The mathematician George Peacock argued forcefully that the Elizabethan statutes that still regulated teaching at Cambridge militated 'against the introduction of those amendments in the academical constitution and administration which might adapt them to the changes, which the lessons of experience, or the advancement of knowledge, might render necessary or expedient'. On the individual level, he further observed,

> A tutor of superior attainments wants the stimulus which a large class of hearers supplies, and his spirits are exhausted by the weary and uninteresting labour of teaching pupils, who are frequently unable to appreciate the value of what is taught: whilst a pupil, whose difficulties are thus smoothed over without labour or research, is too frequently enervated by this perpetual pampering of his appetite for knowledge, without the necessity of digesting that less palatable food which original inquiry must perpetually present to it.[9]

It took but a small step for nineteenth century critics – and university historians ever since – to conclude that those very statutes must have exerted similar deleterious effects on innovative teaching and research in the early modern period, too.

Curiously, the purported sorry state of the early modern English universities has been contrasted by Lawrence Brockliss with the seeming vibrant conditions of an earlier era: 'the idea that teaching and research might be separated was completely foreign to the medieval mind'. In contrast, he claims, the early modern universities 'became increasingly professional schools dedicated to maintaining theological and political orthodoxies, so they generally ceased to be centres of active inquiry in the metaphysical and moral sciences'. By the eighteenth century a new low had been reached: 'it was universally accepted that the university was a teaching institution tout court. Virtually all the exciting and often anti-establishment developments in philosophy, theology and natural science occurred outside its walls'.[10]

---

9   George Peacock, *Observations on the Statutes of the University of Cambridge* (London, 1841), 58–59, 154.
10 L.W.B. Brockliss, 'The European University in the Age of Revolution, 1789–1850', in *The History of the University of Oxford, Vol. VII: The Nineteenth-Century, part 1*, eds. M.G. Brock and M.C. Curthoys (Oxford, 1997), 77–133, at 104.

Small wonder, therefore, that even those who have sought to argue for the vitality of the early modern universities fall back on apologias. Case in point is Mark Curtis's *Oxford and Cambridge in Transition*. While maintaining that mathematics and natural philosophy were an integral part of the body of knowledge imparted by early modern tutors at Oxford and Cambridge, Curtis finds it expedient to concede that *research* was not considered at all necessary. 'Of the several functions which universities today perform', he writes, 'two perhaps can be considered their fundamental missions: first, to preserve knowledge inherited from the past, perpetuating and refining it through teaching and scholarship; and second, to add to the inherited store of knowledge and wisdom by providing facilities and leisure for research into the unknown. Of these two functions only the first was thought to be an essential one for Oxford and Cambridge' in the early modern period. 'Indeed the idea that knowledge could be advanced, that there was an America of learning and understanding beyond the horizons of the classics, ancient philosophy, and the teachings of religion, was still in those years new and strange'. Only few visionaries even contemplated the possibility of such advancement and their schemes did not consider the universities as sites for such activity.[11]

If accepted at face value, any such admission proves fatal to any claim for the role of universities in the Scientific Revolution, as do earlier charges regarding the injurious effects of the scholastic curriculum. For if the universities did not engage in research, why not marginalize them? Regard the preoccupations of most of their members as amateurish? The universities may have educated most of the architects of the Scientific Revolution, and provided residence and teaching positions to some of them – at least temporarily – yet their creative work had little to do with such institutions; indeed, it was often carried out elsewhere. Floris Cohen is a typical representative of such a dismissive view. In his historiographical survey of the Scientific Revolution he readily admits that even though the universities retained their scholastic veneer, they were neither 'crudely dogmatic' nor actively recalcitrant to the new science. Nevertheless, he insists, it is one thing to show that the universities had assimilated some of the products of the Scientific Revolution; quite another to credit them with making a positive *contribution* to it. At best, early modern universities – or at least Oxford and Cambridge – exhibited 'greater flexibility than they have previously been credited with'. But though 'virtually all protagonists of the Scientific Revolution were rooted in the science of their own time, which was largely that of the university curriculum', the fact remains that 'what makes these men stand out is precisely the degree to which they

---

11   Mark H. Curtis, *Oxford and Cambridge in Transition 1558–1642* (Oxford, 1959), 227.

managed to *transcend* these origins'. In fact, all the 'modernizing' tendencies in the curriculum reflect practices on a plane altogether different from the relentless search for a new truth that provided the powerful, ultimate drive for the unique movement embodied in the Scientific Revolution'.[12]

Clearly, then, the underlying assumption for Cohen and like-minded historians is that the presumed failure of university men to measure up to the likes of Galileo or Newton is tantamount to a mental failing. It assumes both that these men were incapable of relentlessly, and successfully, searching after truth, while at the same time negating the likelihood that they were capable of contributing meaningfully to the researches of scientists of the first magnitude. Constraints of space prevent me from elaborating on this assumption; I will only comment that a hero-centered focus is hardly conducive to a serious examination of lesser mortals – both as regards to their own labors and to the degree to which they collaborated with, or influenced, their more celebrated contemporaries. But to return to the issue at hand. To what extent might it be argued that 'original research' had become intrinsic to the university by the turn of the seventeenth century? How should we interpret the perceptible absence of institutional sponsored research? And what are we to make of the censorious voices of critics of the universities? Obviously, more than an article is required to properly address such questions. Here, I can only highlight a few features of institutional-sponsored research, as well as of individual initiatives, in the hope that they encourage future investigation.

Before proceeding, however, I find it necessary to draw attention to a serious methodological blindspot. Whereas scholars have a pretty good idea of what constitutes 'research' in the modern university, virtually no attempt has been made to ponder what 'research' might mean in an earlier context. To complicate matters, 'research' is invariably understood in terms of scientific investigation – of the 'big science' type especially. I contend that such a perception of research is anachronistic; it ignores a marked difference, both in degree and kind, between early modern and modern science.

So what encompasses research? According to William Clark, at the core of the 'modern metaphysics of research' one finds 'a cool, objective, meritocratic, professional self', which 'suppresses the passionately interested, collegially motivated, nepotistic, old-fashioned, traditional academic self'. Whereas the pre-modern site of learning amounted to a 'juridico-ecclesiastical sphere of knowledge', modern research 'forms part of the politico-economic sphere'. Before the eighteenth century, Clark elaborates, scholars 'did not seek originality in the modern sense of novelty' but rather in the sense of returning *ad fontes*.

---

12   H. Floris Cohen, *The Scientific Revolution: A Historiographical Inquiry* (Chicago, 1994), 207.

Only with the advent of the German research seminar did 'the Romantic ethos of originality [take] hold of academics' – including graduate students. Moreover, it was owing primarily to the bureaucratization of academic life that 'academic labor' morphed into 'research' by ensuring the triumph of the seminar style, and thereby enshrining 'the pursuit of research as an activity demanded of advanced students and, indirectly in the seminar, of professors too'.[13] A 'new ethos of disciplinary specialization' was another important element, according to Clark, as was the bureaucratization of the academic enterprise – both in terms of the appointment and the evaluation of professors, and of the control of budgets, the very lifeline of research: 'The directorate's access to and ability to allocate a budget made the seminar a site of research, while the tutorials in the endowed Oxbridge colleges did not in fact become such sites, regardless of the occasional brilliant scholar they produced. In the German Protestant system, the decisions about scholarships came directly from the seminar directors. They eventually did not make such decisions on the basis of need in the first instance. Academic merit became the first and the crucial test'.[14]

The above conceptualization of institutionalized research is rooted, I contend, in several misguided assumptions. First, and foremost, that the tutorial system was the embodiment of the collegiate university. Second, that merit hardly mattered before the eighteenth century and that early modern scholars were not concerned with novelty. Third, that being part of the ecclesiastical 'sphere of knowledge' necessarily vitiated objective research. All these assumptions are belied through a careful analysis of the structure and the content of intellectual activity in early modern Oxbridge, as I shall attempt to elaborate briefly below.

First, however, I should like to return the issue of anachronism. As stated above, one should not expect to find in the early modern period the autonomous, professional, and state-supported research that became the hallmark of German (or French) science in the course of the nineteenth century. This holds especially true for England, which never adopted the centralized bureaucratic system that distinguished its Continental neighbors. Also, in view of the fact that prior to the late eighteenth century science could scarcely demonstrate its utility, there was little incentive for any government to invest large sums in its furtherance. Equally to the point, the actual cost of carrying out scientific research was still (for the most part) within the reach of the average researcher; and in England, in particular, science was expected to be carried out privately. Jeremy Bentham's utilitarian frame of mind is telling about this ethos: 'Among

---

[13] William Clark, *Academic Charisma and the Origins of the Research University* (Chicago and London, 2006), 7, 68, 141–142, 161.

[14] Clark, *Academic Charisma*, 171, 181–182.

rich and prosperous nations, it is not necessary that the public should be at the expense of cultivating the arts and sciences of amusement and curiosity. Individuals will always bestow upon these that portion of reward which is proportioned to the pleasure they bestow'.[15] And though we often encounter calls for the public support of science, in tandem with expressions of envy of the allegedly more propitious conditions across the Channel, well into the nineteenth century the English remained proud of their voluntarist tradition and looked suspiciously at governmental efforts to underwrite the cost of research.

Instructive in this regard are reflections made by Thomas Young in his previously mentioned review of the first two volumes of the 'Mémoires' of the Society of Arcueil, which he contributed to *The Quarterly Review*. He began with praise for the 'degree of zeal and emulation at tending the pursuits of a private association' – such as the Arcueil – before contrasting such zeal with 'the stipends of the academicians of the Institute, which are sufficient to induce men of small fortunes and moderate wishes to devote their attention to science, [but which] are by no means calculated to call the most brilliant powers into the strongest action'. Such a juxtaposition prompted Young to further reflect on the creative impulse in England, where little or no encouragement was 'directly held out to genius' – which, Young submitted, had actually turned out to be propitious:

> there is always a prospect, often indeed delusive, that talents may raise their possessor to situations of eminence and dignity, in whatever profession they may be exhibited; and the remote chance of a high prize seems to be more likely to produce extraordinary exertions, than a greater certainty of an inferior one. The advantages which are derived, in some of our colleges, from a moderate degree of success in mathematical and classical pursuits, are somewhat analogous, in their effects, to the encouragements which have been granted to scientific bodies on the continent, by their respective governments.[16]

Second, prior to the eighteenth century, specialization was neither imperative nor particularly desirable for a productive research career. Mathematical 'physicists' (such as Christopher Wren and Robert Hooke) actively engaged in fundamental bio-medical research, while naturalists such as John Ray and Francis Willughby, were proficient mathematicians and natural philosophers. Indeed, what constituted 'big science' in the early modern period – both in

---

15   Jeremy Bentham, *Works*, 10 vols (repr. New York, 1962), 2: 255.
16   Young, *Miscellaneous Works*, 1: 235.

terms of cost and number of practitioners involved – encompassed the domains of the bio-medical sciences, natural history, and alchemy (or chemistry). The dominance of these disciplines has been lost on the many historians who single out the mathematical and physical sciences as constituting the essence of the Scientific Revolution. Consequently, the extent and significance of 'research' in the non-mathematical sciences is only beginning to be recognized. Almost needless to add, numerous mathematicians, physicists, and naturalists, excelled in all these subjects as much as they did in theology; Isaac Barrow, Robert Boyle, and Isaac Newton readily come to mind.

The ability and willingness of most men of science to transcend (and even shun) specialization is predicated on the respect that the ideal of the general scholar still commanded in the early modern period. By the late sixteenth century, the undergraduate curriculum had become the staple offering at Oxford and Cambridge, and it was during this period that the students received their grounding in the entire arts and sciences curriculum. Obviously, educators were not deluded into believing that such a brisk survey of knowledge would ensure mastery of all subjects, or that all students were equally capable of maintaining the pace. Nor did they recommend a superficial grasp of knowledge. All they intended was to present a panorama of all knowledge, rooted in the interconnectedness of its various constituents, and thereby lay a solid foundation upon which the student could proceed to build, independently for years to come. It would be a mistake, therefore, to expect to find undergraduates – aged between fourteen and eighteen upon arrival – to be immediately initiated into advanced research.

Third, notwithstanding the semblance of sameness between the curricular structure during the seventeenth and nineteenth centuries, it is simply not the case that early modern practitioners regarded the relationship of science and universities in the same manner. Most notably, and in sharp contrast to nineteenth-century university apologists, their early modern counterparts certainly did not abrogate advanced research from the university's purview when defending Oxford and Cambridge against their detractors. Quite the opposite. During the Interregnum, when the English universities came under attack from a host of Puritan (and other) critics, John Wilkins and Seth Ward asserted in no uncertain terms that teaching the new science, and advancing the frontiers of knowledge, had been integral to Oxbridge's mission. Furthermore, they pointed out, contrary to the assertions of their critics, the universities were quite successful in doing so. Already in 1652 Ward boasted of his colleagues' engagement in 'inquisitive experiments, the end [of which] is that out of a sufficient number of such experiments, the way of nature in workeing may be discovered'. Two years later, in the course of rebutting John Webster's critique of the universities, Ward amplified: Observations and experiments are 'the only way to the knowledge of nature', and whoever intends to profess either natural philosophy or medicine ought 'to take that course'. Indeed, after surveying the multi-faceted scientific researches carried out at Oxford, Ward concluded by sharpening the distinction between the 'occult' philosophy propounded by Webster and the enterprise that he and his colleagues followed: 'there are not two waies in the whole World more opposite, then those of the L. *Verulam* and D. *Fludd*, the one founded upon experiment, the other upon mysticall Ideal reasons'.[17]

In a similar manner, when the over-zealous rhetoric of certain opponents of the Royal Society engendered tension between that institution and the universities, John Wallis – Savilian professor of Geometry at Oxford, and himself one of the architects of the Royal Society – cautioned Henry Oldenburg to tone down inflammatory rhetoric that posited the designs of the universities and the Royal Society to be mutually exclusive. In particular, he called on the Society's apologists to desist from

> that argument, (which you seem to lay some strokes upon,) that the University doth not meddle with Experimentall Phylosophy. For it is a great mistake, (Experimentall Philosophy being as properly appertaining to the Constitution [of the university] as any other; though, perhaps, in former times it have not been so much in fashion, as it now is here as well as with you:) You should rather say: It is no disparagement to the University, for others to pursue philosophicall studies allso. The other insinuation will do hurt.[18]

Wallis was not a mere hired gun. For roughly a century, from the 1620s to the 1720s, Oxford served as the country's leading scientific research center. It was there that the English school of astronomy sprang up under the direction of John Bainbridge, Henry Briggs, and their students; it was there that the English experimental tradition established itself; and it was in Oxford that the Harveian bio-medical research program took shape. Even after much of the local talent, and research interests, migrated to the Royal Society – which, to a certain extent, must be considered in its earlier years as an extension of, rather

---

17   H.W. Robinson, 'An Unpublished Letter of Dr. Seth Ward Relating to the Early Meetings of the Oxford Historical Society', *Notes and Records of the Royal Society* 7 (1949), 68–70, at 69; John Wilkins and Seth Ward, *Vindiciae academiarum* (Oxford, 1654), 34, 46.
18   *The Correspondence of Henry Oldenburg*, eds A. Rupert Hall and Mary B. Hall (Madison, WI. and London, 1965–1986), 5: 499–500.

than an antithesis to, the university – Oxford men continued to engage in research, advance the frontiers of science, and train future generations of researchers, owing to the efforts of, among others, David Gregory, Robert Plot, Edward Lhwyd, John Keill, Edmond Halley, John Whiteside, John Theophilus Desaguliers, John Freind, and James Bradley.[19]

Nor can the university, as an institution, be said to have merely tolerated the labors of the odd individual. Despite its meager resources, the expenditure incurred by the university in ensuring the provision of suitable scientific facilities proved considerable. Already in the sixteenth century, observational astronomy benefited from the occasional provision of funds for the purchase of instruments. During the seventeenth century, Oxford furnished funds for the fitting of several sites to serve as observatories. The university also made provisions on various occasions to support botanical research. Most spectacular of all, Oxford spent the staggering sum of £4,500 to build the Ashmolean Museum, including a fine chemical laboratory and the appointment of Robert Plot as professor of chemistry.[20] That university officials were fully cognizant of the need to ensure the election of competent researchers to scientific professorships is further illustrated by the willingness of the university to risk, in 1675, the displeasure of their chancellor by proceeding to appoint Thomas Millington as Sedleian professor of natural philosophy – in succession to Thomas Willis – notwithstanding the chancellor's support of the botanist Robert Morison. As vice-chancellor Ralph Bathurst explained the university's action: 'We cannot deny Dr. Morison, to be a knowing herbalist, and very well deserving encouragement in that way. But naturall philosophy is of a farre larger extent: and its late improvements have been so great, that now no ordinary things are expected from the professors of it'.[21]

Such instances of university munificence aside, it is obvious that the early modern university cannot be compared to the modern research university, where the 'laboratory system gave institutional expression to the ethos of

---

19   Robert G. Frank, Jr., *Harvey and the Oxford Physiologists: Scientific Ideas and Social Interaction* (Berkeley and Los Angeles, 1980); Mordechai Feingold, 'The mathematical sciences and new philosophies', in *The History of the University of Oxford, vol. IV: Seventeenth Century Oxford*, ed. Nicholas Tyacke (Oxford, 1997), 359–448.

20   Mordechai Feingold, 'The mathematical sciences and new philosophies'; A.V. Simcock, *The Ashmolean Museum and Oxford Science 1683–1983* (Oxford, 1984); Anna Marie Roos, 'The Chymistry of 'The Learned Dr Plot' (1640–96)', *Osiris* 29 (2014), 81–95; Marcos Martinón-Torres, 'Inside Solomon's House: An Archaeological Study of the Old Ashmolean Chymical Laboratory in Oxford', *Ambix* 59 (2012), 22–48; R.F. Ovenall, *The Ashmolean Museum 1683–1894* (Oxford, 1986).

21   Thomas Warton, *The Life and Literary Remains of Ralph Bathurst* (London, 1761), 138.

learning which had come to dominate the universities'.[22] Nevertheless, there existed an elaborate private system of specialized instruction and research activity – fostered by the universities – which proved instrumental in elevating the English scientific community to the forefront of European science. Often ignored is the fact that the founders of new scientific chairs expected their incumbents to carry on with research as well as to initiate advanced students into their investigations. The duty of the geometry and astronomy professors, Henry Savile stipulated in his statutes – beyond their public lectures and informal teaching of practical astronomy and geometry to any who cared to listen – was to make themselves 'of easy access to the studious who would consult them on mathematical subjects'. Furthermore, not only did he expect the astronomy professor to carry out observations, 'making choice of proper instruments prepared for the purpose' but, Savile hoped, 'the University will liberally contribute all assistance and exertion towards this object, as it is the only true way of establishing or amending the ancient astronomy'.[23] In this, as in all other respects, Savile was most fortunate with his professors throughout the seventeenth- and early eighteenth- centuries. Henry Briggs and John Bainbridge, respectively, the first geometry and astronomy professors, were exemplary in cultivating promising youth and in expanding the boundaries of their respective disciplines. Their successors proved equally successful. Walter Pope attested to the diligence with which Seth Ward 'taught the mathematics gratis to as many of the university, or foreigners, as desired that favour of him', numbering among such scholars both Robert Hooke and Christopher Wren.[24] For his part, Wallis tutored, among others, William, Lord Brouncker, Edward Bernard, and Edmond Halley.[25] A few years before his death, Wallis also recollected how he and Ward, apart from their public lectures and publications, 'instructed gentlemen and others, in their private lodgings' in the various mathematical sciences.[26]

Even Thomas Hobbes recognized the indispensability of mentoring for forming a creative researcher. The most proficient mathematicians at the

---

22   R. Steven Turner, 'The Growth of Professorial Research in Prussia, 1818 to 1848? Causes and Context', *Historical Studies in the Physical Sciences* 3 (1971), 137–182, at 137.

23   G.R.M. Ward, *Oxford University Statutes*, 2 vols (London, 1845), 1: 272–274.

24   Walter Pope, *The Life of ... Seth, Lord Bishop of Salisbury* (London, 1697), 25; Richard Waller, 'The life of Dr. Robert Hooke', *Early Science in Oxford*, 4/1: 10.

25   Thomas Smith, *Vita clarissimi et doctissimi viri Edwardi Bernardi* (London, 1704), 8; William M. Marshall, *George Hooper 1640–1727 Bishop of Bath and Wells* (Milborne Port, 1976), 6; C.A. Ronan, *Edmond Halley Genius in Eclipse* (London, 1969), 29.

26   'Dr Wallis's letter against Mr Maidwell', *Collectanea, First Series*, ed. C.R.L. Fletcher (Oxford, 1885), 271–337, at 320.

universities, he wrote, have 'attained their knowledge by other means than that of public lectures, where few auditors, and those of unequal proficiency, cannot make benefit by one and the same lesson, ... the true use of public professors, especially in the mathematics, being to resolve the doubts, and problems, as far as they can, of such as come unto them with desire to be informed'.[27] Half a century later Edmond Halley articulated the dilemma of many a professor:

> I have oftentimes experienced ... how difficult a thing it is to discourse, especially in mathematical matters, so as to please the learned therein, and at the same time to instruct such as yet want to be taught: The former require nothing but what is new and curious, nor are pleased but with elegant demonstrations, made concise by art and pains: the latter demand explications drawn out in words, at length, least any part of the reasoning not being clearly apprehended, should hinder the evidence of the whole argument, whilst those already versed in mathematics cannot endure such prolixity.

Ultimately, Halley resolved 'to consult, not so much [his] own reputation, as the profit of the auditory: omitting therefore what might make a shew of deeper learning'.[28]

Such a 'shew' could be – and was – made outside the lecture room. And if the university could not offer much in terms of financial support, the collegiate system, unique to England, proved ideal in providing remuneration, along with the equally indispensable conditions of space, leisure, and a community, that proved essential for the advancement of science. Practitioners were obviously eager for more. In 1671 Edward Bernard, Savilian professor of astronomy, bemoaned the absence of better material conditions, which prevented Oxford men from turning the university into a major scientific research center:

> if her children had the good utensils, which adorn the colleges of the Jesuits abroad, the world would not long want good proof of their ingenuity. Patrons and tools are rather wanting than willing and fit workmen. We lack a corporation, a set of grinders of glasses, instrument-makers, operators, and the like, that experiments may be well managed in this place, which otherwise, by reason of our living all, as it were, together,

---

27 Thomas Hobbes, *The English Works*, ed. William Molesworth, 11 vols (London, 1839–1845), 7: 346.
28 Edmond Halley, 'Lectures read in the School of Geometry in Oxford', in John Kersey, *The Elements of that Mathematical Art commonly called Algebra* (London, 1717), appendix, 1.

and our freedom from the intricacies and vexations of the world, is most convenient for such a design.[29]

Neither Oxford nor Cambridge could hope to acquire such a lavish infrastructure; London alone was capable of sustaining this. But then, as I've suggested above, well into the eighteenth century the endeavors of numerous Oxbridge men of science were intricately woven with London science. In addition, the English scientific tradition remained, by design as well as by necessity, distinctly amateurish – which, of course, should not be mistaken for dilettantish! And before the nineteenth century this gentlemanly tradition proved spectacularly successful, in the universities and elsewhere in England.[30]

John Merz pointed out long ago how 'British science through all the centuries since the time of Roger Bacon, and in spite of the efforts of his illustrious namesake, has refused to congregate in distinct schools and institutions or to be localised in definite centres'. In fact, despite the efforts of institutions such as the Royal Society, the Royal Institution, or the British Association, 'everywhere the schemes of co-operation or organised scientific research have encountered the opposition of individual pursuits or of local interests'.[31] An early example of such a disposition may be found in the failure in 1685 to establish a philosophical society in Cambridge on par with the Oxford or Dublin Societies. As Newton informed the secretary of the Royal Society, several candidates were approached, but the inability to find 'persons willing to try experiments' proved insurmountable. He was willing to continue promoting such a design, Newton avowed, but only 'so far as I can doe it without engaging the loss of my own time in those things'.[32]

The Royal Society did not fare much better. The efforts to turn it into a national research institution, as its founding members had envisaged, failed to materialize. What happened instead was a slow metamorphosis into an organization whose scientific work was comprised primarily of the sum total of private endeavors carried out by its members elsewhere. On an institutional level,

---

29   S.P. Rigaud, *Correspondence of Scientific Men of the Seventeenth Century*, 2 vols (Oxford, 1841) 1: 159.
30   D.S.L. Cardwell, The development of scientific research in modern universities: a comparative study of motives and opportunities', in *Scientific Change*, ed. Alastair Crombie (London, 1963), 661–677. Nicholas Tyacke, 'From *Studium Generale* to Modern Research University: Eight Hundred Years of Oxford History', *History of Universities* 30 (2017), 205–25.
31   John T. Merz, *A History of European Thought in the Nineteenth Century*, 4 vols (repr. Gloucester, MA, 1976), 1: 249–250.
32   *The Correspondence of Isaac Newton*, eds. H.W. Turnbull, J.F. Scott, A.R. Hall and Laura Tilling, 7 vols (Cambridge, 1959–77), 2: 415.

the Society became a clearinghouse for information received from English and foreign correspondents, as well as a social club catering to those fellows who resided in London and enjoyed intellectual soirees followed by dinner and drinks. Membership was thus geared to a heterogeneous amalgam of non-specialists who delighted in indiscriminate discussions of physics and antiquities, medicine and astronomy, monstrosities and botany. Such a frame of mind, which prevailed at Oxford and Cambridge as well, explains why nineteenth-century critics bemoaned in tandem the backwardness of the universities and of the Royal Society, and why their calls to reform those institutions included a dismissive, and deliberately misleading, characterization of the early modern universities – a characterization that continues to inform scholars today.

The unique character of the English institutions of higher learning should render inopportune skeptical queries such as: 'how much organized scientific endeavour did the university stimulate?'[33] As institutions, neither Oxford nor Cambridge possessed the kind of resources and control over studies enjoyed by the individual colleges. Consequently, to expect to find sponsored research programs and laboratories in early modern Oxbridge is not only anachronistic but unrealistic to boot – which, however, is not to say that professors and many dons were not committed to high levels of original research commensurate, of course, with the state of contemporary science. Only in one area did English men of science fail to equal their Continental colleagues: publications. But, as I've argued elsewhere, this was owing to the obligation of nearly all college fellow to take holy orders within seven years of graduating MA, an obligation which rendered continuing public preoccupation with secular activities problematic.[34]

As late as 1890, Benjamin Jowett, the septuagenarian master of Balliol College, and patron saint of the reformed tutorial and examination system at Oxford, still scorned the very idea of research as a 'mere excuse for idleness', which 'has never achieved, and will never achieve any results of the slightest value'.[35] Many early modern humanists undoubtedly shared Jowett's disdain of scientific research, but the range of issues involved was quite different. The sciences during the earlier period were still considered to be integral to the shared encyclopedia of learning and capable of being pursued by many humanists. Conversely, scientific practitioners were still unable to demonstrate the kind of intellectual and practical superiority that would earn them universal prestige two centuries later. Consequently, as this article suggests, it is incumbent on us

---

33 Porter, 'The Scientific Revolution and Universities', 547.
34 Mordechai Feingold, 'Science as a Calling? The Early Modern Dilemma', *Science in Context*, 15 (2002), 79–119.
35 Logan P. Smith, *Unforgotten Years* (Boston, 1939), 187.

to avoid applying anachronistic criteria when attempting to determine the place and the meaning of research in early modern universities and scientific academies. Rather, we should strive to become attune to contemporary conceptions of knowledge – scientific or otherwise – and carefully scrutinize the archives in order to determine what constituted research within such a context. The outcome of such an investigation, I submit, would not only shed much new light on the advancement of learning during the early modern period; it would enhance our understanding of the genesis and character of the modern research university.

CHAPTER 2

The Academization of Parisian Science (1660–1789): Review Essay on a Spatial Turn

Stéphane Van Damme

For a long time the history of the Académie des Sciences[1] in Paris adopted the form of a grand genealogical and monographic narrative as part of a process of recognising a great institution.[2] Since the 1970s, historians of science have put the Academy back into its Ancien Régime context, seeking to understand its role through an investigation of three main areas: academic work, relations of rivalry and power, and levels of influence. In the first place, efforts have been made to understand the organisation and forms of scientific work within the framework of a comparative history of scientific academies. The social history of sciences has sought to revisit the institutional approach by focusing on the members,[3] disciplines, sites and locations that characterised the academic form of sociability, as opposed to other forms.[4] However, historians have also been careful to underline the diversity of spatial and social dynamics between different disciplines and places.[5] This general movement has often been described as a great *confinement* of scientific activities driven by an experimental culture.[6] Other historians have traced this movement towards confined

---

1   Throughout the chapter, I keep the French name: *Académie des Sciences*.
2   Ernest Maindron, *L'Académie des sciences* (Paris, 1888); Alfred Maury, *L'ancienne académie des sciences* (Paris, 1864); Joseph Bertrand, *L'Académie des sciences et les académiciens de 1666 à 1793* (Paris, 1869). Guillaume Bigourdan, 'Les premières sociétés savantes de Paris au XVIIe siècle et les origines de l'Académie des sciences', *Comptes rendus de l'académie des sciences*, 164 (1917), 129–134, 159–162, 216–220.
3   David Sturdy, *Science and Social Status: The Members of the Académie des sciences* (Woodbridge, 1995), for a collective portrait of academicians, see also James E. McClellan III, 'The Académie Royale des Sciences, 1699–1793: A Statistical Portrait', *Isis: A Journal of the History of Science* 72 (1981), 541–567.
4   Roger Hahn, *The Anatomy of a scientific institution: the Paris academy of sciences, 1666–1803* (Berkeley, 1971). *Histoire et mémoire de l'Académie des sciences*, eds. Eric Brian and Christine Demeulenaere-Douyère (Paris, 1996); *Règlement, usages et science dans la France de l'absolutisme*, eds. Eric Brian and Christine Demeulenaere-Douyère (Paris, 2002).
5   Alice Stroup, *A company of scientists: botany, patronage, and community at the seventeenth-century Parisian Royal Academy of sciences* (Berkeley, 1990).
6   Maria-Pia Donato, 'Les académies dans l'ancien régime des sciences', in *Histoire des sciences et des savoirs, vol. 1, De la Renaissance aux Lumières*, ed. Stéphane Van Damme (Paris, 2015), 87–109.

science, driven by the requirements of precision and controlled experimental conditions, in relation, for instance, to Lavoisier.[7] In Paris, the establishment of laboratories, observatories, botanical gardens, anatomical theatres and lecture halls reflects a trend towards specialisation and discussion between specialists.[8] Historiography has also identified a second movement driven by a desire to move away from these legitimized spaces. The proliferation of new forms of sociability in Paris (salons, lycée, masonic lodges etc.) allowed knowledge to overflow its natural milieus. Larry Stewart has shown this in relation to London in the years 1700–1720, where a network of new locations was established without reference to the Royal Society, enabling new scientific exchanges in the city's coffee-houses with sailors, traders and mathematical practioners.[9] Dealing with the Académie des Sciences also means dealing with places where the Academy did not count, and recently historians have argued that it is important to locate precisely the power of such institutions within the city.

This chapter proposes to measure the effects of the spatial turn in the research agenda of the history of the Parisian Académie des Sciences over the last two decades. By putting science in its Parisian context, historians of science wanted to address four different issues: urban places of knowledge, urban expertise, cultural representation and urban ways of life. The historiographical shift was clearly rooted in the cultural and spatial turn of the 1990s with a strong emphasis put on places and spaces.[10] From the history of academic organisation to the spatial history of science, investigations of the Académie des Sciences in Paris moved towards an analysis of the sciences in terms of the circulation of ideas at different levels (intra-urban, national and international

---

7   Christian Licoppe, *La formation de la pratique scientifique: le discours de l'expérience en France et en Angleterre, 1630–1820* (Paris, 1996) ; Marco Beretta, 'Between the Workshop and the Laboratory, Lavoisier's network of instrument makers', *Osiris* 29 (2014), 197–214. Beretta, 'Big Chemistry: Lavoisier's Design and Organisation of his Laboratories', in *Spaces and Collections in the History of Science,* ed. M. Lourenço and A. Carneiro (Lisbon, 2009), 65–80.

8   On Anatomical theater, see Rafael Mandressi, *Regard de l'anatomiste: dissections et inventions du corps* (Paris, 2003) and Anita Guerrini, *The Courtiers' Anatomists. Animals and Humans in Louis XIV's* (Chicago, 2015).

9   Larry Stewart, 'Other centres of calculation, or, where the Royal Society didn't count: commerce, coffe-houses and natural philosophy in early modern London', *British Journal of History of Science,* 32 (1999), 133–153. Stewart, *The Rise of Public Science: Rhetoric, Technology, and Natural Philosophy in Newtonian Britain (1660–1750)* (Cambridge, 1992).

10 Adi Ophir and Steven Shapin 'The Place of Knowledge. A Methodological Survey', *Science in Context,* 4 (1991), 3–21. *Science and the City,* eds. Sven Dierig, Jens Lachmund, and Andrew Mendelsohn, *Osiris,* 18 (2003). David Livingstone, *Putting science in its place. Geographies of Scientific Knowledge* (Chicago, 2003). For more recent discussion, see *Barcelona: An Urban History of Science and Modernity,* eds. Oliver Hochadel and Agustí Nieto-Galan (Aldershot, 2016).

or even global). These new historiographical approaches have made it possible to reconsider the forms of spatial organisation governing the 'territories' of the so-called 'modern' sciences in Early Modern Paris.[11] In the last twenty years historians have adopted several concepts to describe the process of the circulation of scientific ideas in Paris, including place, space, network and territory.[12] The cartography of metropolitan institutions responsible for overseas knowledge also reveals that the Academy's global dimension was crucial in colonial expansion.[13]

By denaturalizing the places of knowledge, historians of science displaced and redirected their attention to the multiple strategies with which to transform the city into a living laboratory. By doing that, they more recently have found a common ground with environmental historians at large.[14] The Académie des Sciences appeared as a stakeholder in a new geography of knowledge. Far from being inert, the academic framework also acted to bring specificity to the scientific practices carried out within it. Some contexts encouraged Academicians to intense reflection on their own practices, whether in the period of the Academy's foundation, during the Regency or in the decade leading up to the Revolution.[15] Recognising the central role of Paris, from an ethnographic rather than normative view of the sciences, research has highlighted social, practical and intellectual operations involved in 'making a scientific place', in other words, the degree to which 'knowledge is thus a symbolic object – at once an aspect of identity, a sign of recognition, a currency, an instrument of

---

11 John B. Shank, *The Newton Wars and the beginning of the French Enlightenment* (Chicago, 2008). Shank, *Before Voltaire. Making Newtonians Mechanics in France around 1700* (Chicago, 2018).
12 Stéphane Van Damme, *Paris, Capitale Philosophique de la Fronde à la Révolution* (Paris, 2005). *Capitales, Culturelles, Capitales Symboliques: Paris et les expériences européennes, XVIIIe–XXe siècles*, eds. C. Charle and D. Roche (Paris, 2002); *Le Temps des Capitales Culturelles*, ed. C. Charle (Seyssel, 2010). Bruno Belhoste, *Paris savant. Parcours et rencontres au temps des Lumières* (Paris, 2011).
13 Londa Shiebinger, *Plants and Empire: colonial bioprospecting in the Atlantic world* (Cambridge MA, 2004). James E. McClellan III and François Regourd, *The Colonial Machine: French science and overseas expansion in the Old Regime* (Turnhout, 2011). F. Regourd and J.E. McClellan III, 'French Science and Colonization in the Ancien régime: the "Machine coloniale"', *Osiris* 15 (2000), 31–50. See also *Les mondes coloniaux à Paris au XVIIIe siècle: circulation et enchevêtrement des savoirs*, eds. A. Bandau, M. Dorigny and R.V. Mallinckrodt (Paris, 2010).
14 Antonella Romano and Stéphane Van Damme, 'Science and World Cities: Thinking Urban Knowledge and Science at large', *Itinerario*, volume XXXIII (2009), 33, 79–95.
15 Nicholas Dew, 'Un Colbertisme scientifique?', in *Histoire des sciences et des savoirs*, 431–446.

power and the cement of a community'.[16] The same is true of the re-evaluation of the Academy's publishing activities and its provision of local expertise for the Paris city authorities, which further distinguished the Académie des Sciences. The production and circulation of science in Paris involved particular modes of spatial inscription and territorial praticies[17] which will enable us to better situate the Academy's work. I will argue that this historiographical shift abandoned a definition of the Parisian sciences in terms of disciplines in order to approach the question obliquely by exploring the many ways the process of institutionalization transformed and legitimised the Académie des Sciences in Paris as a new central source of scientific authority. Rather than taking legal and institutional definitions as its starting point, this review essay will seek to see in the most recent research outputs how the academicians' work acted to extend the empire and authority of the Académie. If some particular phases will be highlighted, such as the beginnings of the Académie and the call for a patriotic science before the French Revolution, the essay will adopt a more thematical structure in order to avoid the rise-and-fall narrative.

1   Documenting Academic Foundations (1650–1699)

One of the first avenues of research was to come back to the phase of creation of the academy. After the pioneered works of Roger Hahn and Daniel Roche, new research by David Lux, Alice Stroup, James McClellan and Eric Brian retraced the multi-faceted practices and strategies which led to the transformation of intellectual circles into an official academy. The foundation of the academic institutions in Paris in the seventeenth century reveals another dynamic characterising the convergence of knowledge in one place. In the seventeenth century the proliferation of academies founded by the monarchy created the institutional conditions for new forms of intellectual exchange.[18] The establishment of the Académie Française in 1635, the Académie des Inscriptions et Médailles in 1663, the Académie des Inscriptions et Belles-Lettres in 1663, and the Académie des Sciences in 1666 were followed in the eighteenth century by the Académie Royale de Chirurgie in 1731 and the Société Royale de Médecine

---

16   *Les lieux de savoirs. I, Espaces et communautés*, ed. Christian Jacob (Paris, 2008), Introduction.
17   Ophir and Shapin, 'The Place of Knowledge'; Charles W.J. Withers, *Placing the Enlightenment. Thinking Geographically about the Age of Reason* (Chicago, 2007).
18   Daniel Roche, 'Trois académies parisiennes et leur rôle dans les relations culturelles et sociales au XVIIIe siècle', *Mélanges de l'Ecole Française de Rome. Italie et Méditerranée*, 3/1 (1999), 395–414.

in 1776. Compared to the many pre-existing intellectual groupings in Paris in the years 1640–1670, the creation of the Académie des Sciences established the twin benchmarks of recognised legal status and royal protection.

Natural philosophy was discussed in many circles in Paris before the foundation of the Académie des Sciences in 1666 – at Théophraste Renaudot's *bureau d'adresses*, Abbé Bourdelot's academic meetings, Habert de Montmor's Academy, Richesource's Academy, Thévenot's Company and so on. Many studies have shown the mutation of spaces of scholarly discussion throughout the seventeenth century – including René Pintard's reconstruction of libertine circles[19] and the pre-academic organisation of the sciences described by Harcourt Brown –[20] but they too often have remained prisoners of an analysis based on innovation and tradition and postulated a close link between a place and a doctrine, between the 'scientific revolution' and new forms of sociability. Indeed with a few rare exceptions, historical studies of science in the period 1450–1700 have long uncritically accepted the idea that the change of organisation was brought about by the power of the new scientific ideas.[21] Explanations of the 'new age of academies' (Fontenelle), sought to identify the emergence in preceding centuries of scientific ideas and methods that had fostered this localisation of scientific activity. The evolution of the activity of the universities and court patronage in the direction of scientific networks and private circles is still widely described in terms of a transformation of scholastic natural philosophy into pre-modern science. Yet James McClellan[22] has shown that before the eighteenth century the essential features of the 'organisational revolution' did not coincide with the high points of the scientific revolution, and hence that these transformations cannot be ascribed to intellectual change alone. Academies had, during this first period, to work with other places: dissections and experiments took place in private spaces, as the proceedings of the first meetings until 1687 have recorded.[23] As Anita Guerrini has shown in her book discussing the

---

19   Simone Mazauric, 'Le mouvement académique parisien du premier dix-septième siècle et la constitution de la science moderne', in *La science à l'époque moderne* (Paris, 1998), 71–86.
20   Harcourt Brown, *Scientific organizations in Seventeenth Century France (1620–1680)* (New York, 1934). Jean Chapelain gave a lot of details about the establishment of a new academy in his *Lettres*, ed. Tamizey de Laroque (Paris, 1880–1883), t. II, 140.
21   David S. Lux, 'The Reorganization of Science: 1450–1700', in *Patronage and Institutions: Science, Technology and Medecine at the European Court, 1500–1750*, ed. Bruce T. Moran (Woodbridge, 1991), 185–194.
22   James E. McClellan III, *Science Reorganised: Scientific Societies in the Eighteenth Century* (New York, 1985).
23   MS Paris, Bibliothèque Nationale de France, Fonds Français, NAF, 5147, fol. 118 quoted by J. Schiller, 'Les laboratoires d'anatomie et de botanique à l'Académie des sciences au XVIIe siècles', *Revue d'histoire des sciences et de leurs applications*, tome 17 (1964), 97–114, (105).

relations between anatomists and courtiers, anatomists were spread across different institutions (hospitals, the Faculty of Medicine, the royal college, the king's garden and the Academy of Science). In the late sixteenth century anatomy teachers had started to use bodies from the cemetery of the Saints-Innocents between Rue de la Ferronerie and Rue Saint-Denis on the right bank of the Seine. However, most dissections in the seventeenth century were done on animals, primarily dogs, cats and pigs. An employee of the Académie des Sciences had the job of collecting these from the Châtelet, the inner courtyard of which served as a morgue, while others came from the Hôtel-Dieu. The Faculty of Medicine did not open its anatomy theatre until 1620, subsequently becoming responsible for the administration of corpses. A geography of supply sites then developed, initially located in central Paris but gradually moving to the periphery with the cemeteries in Clamart and Saint-Denis. This coheres with the portrait of the Royal Society as, at its beginning, an open-air institution.[24] The period of the foundation and extension of the academic space in Paris can tell us a great deal about practices that had not yet become routine. This enables us to return to the source of the formation of a learned institution and indicates the many different logics driving the localisation of scientific activity in the city.

The naming of the institution itself was an important issue.[25] At the first meetings of the members of the future Académie des Sciences in December 1666, the group had no specific name other than that of 'company' and no organisation, structure or stated aim. Early records of proceedings show that the first weeks were spent debating questions of procedure and the collective definition of scientific work. With the establishment of an archive for the Académie, not always the case in Parisian intellectual circles, we witness the first stage in the assembly's formalisation. In recording the debates on institutional aspects of the new assembly, the minutes of its meetings embody the scientific community, give it permanence and a definitive existence, both for the royal authorities and, notably, for Colbert, who was able to use the records to monitor the establishment process. The formalization of the Académie was also significant for other Parisian assemblies actively supported by aristocratic patrons, including the Académie Bourdelot in the entourage of the Prince de Condé[26] and the Duc de Liancourt's group, who met in Rue de Seine. Having

---

24 Steven Shapin, 'The House of Experiment in Seventeenth-century England', in S. Shapin, *Never pure. Historical Studies of Science as if It Was Produced by People with Bodies, Situated in Time, Space, Culture, and Society, and Struggling for Credibility and Authority* (Baltimore, 2010), 59–88.

25 Marie-Jeanne Tits-Dieuiade, 'Une institution sans statuts: l'Académie Royale des sciences de 1666 à 1699', in *Histoire et mémoire de l'Académie des sciences*, 3–13.

26 Katia Béguin, *Les Princes de Condé. Rebelles, courtisans et mécènes dans la France du Grand Siècle* (Seyssel, 1999).

representatives of the different elements of patronage converge in one company was also innovative – Gallois and Perrault were Colbert's clients, Carcavi had served Liancourt, Pecquet was attached to Fouquet, Du Hamel was supported by the archbishop of Paris, Bourdelin and Marchant had been in the entourage of Gaston d'Orléans and Cureau de la Chambre was a friend of the chancellor Séguier.[27] When new regulations were edicted in 1699 with the letters patent, we have a new phase of development of the Académie des Sciences which partly reshaped the networks of patrons. Louis II Phélypeaux de Ponchartrain and his nephew the Abbot Bignon occupied a centre position in the scientific network.[28] Bignon took control of the presidency of the Académie and of the Journal des Savants in 1701. By assuming these positions, Bignon became a leading figure in the Royal patronage system, participating in the other academies (the Académie Française and the Académie des Inscriptions et Belles-Lettres). With his position as director of the Bureau de la Librairie and of the Royal Library, he could also influence and direct the publication policy.

2   Parisian Academicians at Work

The second shift followed the motto of the new history of science by studying academicians at work. The phase of emergence and stabilisation of these institutions reveals an effort to create equivalence between writing practices (autobiography, correspondence, founding narrative), editorial practices (cabinet lists, catalogues, etc.), social practices (visits, exchanges of objects, etc.) and institutional practices (statutes, regulations, letters patent, pensions). The circulation of sciences in the city through writing was crucial to the foundation of the academies, since it brought scientists together, established groups over the long term and formed a record of their collective work. In Paris, most academies were not born *ex nihilo* at the Prince's wish, but had often been preceded by informal gatherings and correspondence between several individuals. The Académie des Sciences emerged out of a pre-existing scientific fabric and many of varying degrees of formality.[29] These forms of scientific life were rendered stable by a network of correspondence that became denser in the

---

27   Sturdy, *Science and social status*, 139–140.
28   Sarah E. Chapman, *Private Ambitions and Political Alliances: The Phélypeaux de Ponchartrain Family and Louis XIV's Government, 1650–1715* (Rochester, 2004).
29   David S. Lux and Harold J. Cook, 'Closed circles or open networks? Communicating at a distance during the scientific Revolution', *History of Science*, 36, (1998), 179–211, (192–193). David S. Lux, *Patronage and Royal Science in the seventeenth Century: The académie de Physique de Caen* (Ithaca, 1995).

city and was reinforced by political and social alliances. Paris became a centre for training in dissection when Colbert recruited four major figures: Claude Perrault, Marin Cureau de la Chambre, Jean Pecquet and Louis Gayant. Anita Guerrini has shown how these four physicians owed their rise to their networks of patrons and also to their ability to distance themselves from both the Faculty of Medicine and the Saint-Côme surgeons' guild and, since the mid-sixteenth century, had included well respected anatomists of whom the most famous was Ambroise Paré. Some anatomists, such as Cureau de la Chambre, were central to several institutional networks, thus reducing the potential for rivalries and enhancing the status of the new royal and curial institutions. Reputations were also established through clever publication strategies that saw anatomical knowledge gain much of its prestige from its association with natural history on the market for printed materials. Perrault and Pecquet owed their success to both the Faculty of Medicine and the Republic of Letters. The development of scientific practice received institutional and political support: Guerrini describes the success of anatomist Jean Pecquet as due to his intellectual network and the patronage he received, first from the Condés and then from François Fouquet, who was interested in the new natural philosophy. Threatened by the Faculty in Paris, Pecquet went to Montpellier.[30] Families such as the Cassini, Boudulc and Geoffroy in the eighteenth century became famous in Europe as scientific dynasties. This dynastic transmission is greater when it is in a socio-professional context built around a strong corporate sense. Such networks are observable within socio-professional milieus close to urban institutions, like apothecaries which belonged to the corporation of grocers and provided seven *échevins* during the eighteenth century. Specific groups like Parisian apothecaries are particularly interesting in that they contributed both to promoting forms of knowledge like natural history and pharmacopea and to articulating urban authorities and scientific institutions.

The solidity of these underpinning alliances enabled scientific groups to work together and turned them into an academic institution through royal recognition. Here the notion of durability seems crucial, since it defines the investment in formalization as the 'costly establishment of a stable relationship for a certain duration'.[31] Recognition by letters patent in 1699 was a further benchmark indicating that the activities were becoming stable. These regulations of 1699 were the subject of real veneration throughout the eighteenth

---

30   Anita Guerrini, *The Courtiers' Anatomists. Animals and Humans in Louis XIV's Paris* (Chicago, 2015).
31   Laurent Thévenot, 'Les investissements de formes', *Cahiers du Centre d'études sur l'emploi* (1986), 29, 21–71, (26).

century. Around 1783 the mineraologist Guettard wrote, 'Since then I have always respected the regulations. I have regarded them as established wisely. I have made it my duty to meet them as precisely as I could. And I am increasingly convinced that if efforts were made to observe them and have others observe them, all would happen in good order, peacefully and calmly. Everything there would be heard, understood, weighed and judged in full awareness of the facts and the Academy would retain intact the glory acquired for it by our predecessors. As a consequence of these thoughts, I believe the old regulations are very wise and that they must be adhered to and kept whole and entire'.[32]

The *boundary work* consists also in the organisation of scientific work itself. As Daniel Roche has said, 'the institution was presented as the technical and scientific advisory board to the monarchy'[33] and was closely linked to the administration from the outset. The academisation of scientific work had three effects on the formation of a philosophical arena in Paris. In the first place, unlike the university, it did not choose between different philosophical systems, but allowed them to express themselves through the presentation of studies and personal positions. For instance, Newton was first introduced to the academy through a discussion of his treatise on *Optics*. At the disciplinary level, its architecture was subject to regular reorganisations that reveal the model's great flexibility.[34] Lavoisier advocated the creation of a college of physics, as had been the case before the reform of 1699.[35] In addition to ten seats for honorary members – important persons who were often the company's intermediaries with the government and the court – the regulations of 1699 had established twenty seats for pensioners. Two of these were permanent officers in the form of the secretary and treasurer. The other eighteen were divided into six categories, of which three were for the mathematical sciences – geometry, astronomy and mechanics (in the sense of knowledge of machines and tools), and three for the physical sciences covering the study of nature, defined as anatomy, chemistry and botany. After 1785 and many further modifications, notably in 1759 and 1769, institutional reform led to the updating of disciplinary boundaries to create eight categories: geometry, astronomy, mechanics and general physics in the mathematical sciences; anatomy, chemistry and metallurgy, botany and agriculture, natural history and mineralogy in the physical

---

32 MS Paris, Académie des Sciences, Fonds Lavoisier, dation Chabrol, carton n°2, quoted by Eric Brian, 'Lavoisier et le projet de classe de physique expérimentale à l'Académie royale des sciences (avril 1766)', in *Il y a 200 ans Lavoisier*, ed. C. Demeulenaere-Douyère (Paris, 1995), 162.
33 David Roche, *La France des Lumières* (Paris, 1995), 460.
34 Shank, *The Newton Wars*.
35 Brian, 'Lavoisier et le projet de classe', 151–168.

sciences. These reforms are of more than anecdotal importance and must be taken seriously, since they remind us that the institution under the Ancien Régime was not lifeless but a thinking body whose members were actively engaged in reflection. This sustained thinking over a century reveals adherence to a corporatist model that was not fixed, but could adapt to the evolution of scientific activity and new boundaries between disciplines.

The Académie des Sciences was also highly innovative in coordinating its regular, strictly compartmentalised functioning (sessions, competitions, discussions, agendas) with the promotion of intellectual techniques that extended this system (instruments, herbaria, measuring devices). These tools were intended to enable academicians to pass easily from one sphere of action to another, from the military field to court, from administration to the laboratory. Thus a series of stages was developed that categorised academic work and organised the traceability of people and things. These included maintaining records, writing reports, giving lectures, writing books, keeping inventories and drawing up statistical tables. Vauban among others did much to rationalise political decision-making by seeking to better organise the different tasks incumbent upon him. He was the driving force behind the spread of the technique of the agenda, or small notebook, which was at once a diary, a notebook in which he collected technical (fiscal or military) information, a graphic workspace (portable laboratory) and at the same time the format in which he wrote up *Mémoires* and proceedings addressed to the king, which later served as a basis for decision-making.[36] He was not the only one to do this in the early decades. Other academicians served in the army, including Antoine de Niquet and Nicolas-François Blondel, both military engineers. In Condorcet's entourage, Eric Brian has shown the trajectory of the notes and materials produced by scientific observation and academic discussion, which were gradually distilled into administrative documents.[37] Similarly, in the Paris Observatory the preservation of measurements and observations were used to write journals. Most observations carried out in the years 1666–1682 were preserved in three autograph registers in the library of the Paris Observatory. An element of these (concerning the period 1673–1676) also feature in the 'Journal D'observations Astronomiques, faittes à Paris, dans L'observatoire Royalle…' 'maintained by Etienne Villiard, who was Picard's assistant and student. These observations were printed by Le Monnier in his *Histoire Céleste* published in 1741. These texts

---

36   Michèle Virol, 'Les carnets de bord d'un grand serviteur du roi: les agendas de Vauban', *Revue d'histoire moderne et contemporaine*, 48 (2001), 50–76.
37   Brian, 'Lavoisier et le projet de classe de physique expérimentale', 151–168.

were intended as clean versions of notes taken in the course of observations and subsequently discarded.

3 Scientific Sovereignty: Archiving and Publishing New Parisian Sciences

Regarding the place of scientific activity in which knowledge is produced as a 'system of literary inscription',[38] the academic body opted to promote documentary practices and publishing strategies.[39] It was through the accumulation and standardisation of documents and their preservation in a separate, ordered archive that the records revealed this group – primarily retrospectively.[40] The process of writing down reflects only a collective dimension, in which individual positions cannot be read. This model was affirmed by Perrault: 'What our Records have that is most considerable is this irreproachable witness of a certain, acknowledged truth. For they are not the work of an individual. [Our Records] contain no facts that have not been verified by an entire Company'.[41] Understanding documentary forms in the Académie context sheds light on the creation of a scientific institution as an assemblage of moving laboratories, as a place of sociability and discussion, as an early modern form of knowledge, expertise and administration.[42] During the eighteenth century, disputes came even to oppose learned representatives of institutions competing with the heirs of a particular fellow. Thus, when the naturalist Philibert Commerson died in 1774, a dispute opposed Louis-Guillaume Le Monnier (1717–1799), the first *médecin ordinaire du roi*, professor of botany in the *jardin du roi*, the doctor Clériade Vachier (the executor of the will) and Buffon, intendant of the *Jardin du Roi*.[43] Archival resources in the Académie were no longer considered simply as a passive inventory of sources, but as practices

---

[38] Bruno Latour and Steve Woolgar, *La vie de laboratoire. La production des faits scientifiques* (Paris, 1988), 44.

[39] James E. McClellan, *Specialist Control: The Publications Committee of the Academie royale des sciences Paris (1700–1793)* (Philadelphia, 2003) ; Neil Safier, 'Livres et cultures écrites des sciences', in *Histoire des sciences et des savoirs*, 1:205–229.

[40] Lorraine Daston, 'Introduction: Third Nature', in *Science in the Archives. Pasts, Presents, Future*, ed. L. Daston (Chicago, 2017), 1–16. Geoffrey C. Bowker, *Memory Practices in the Sciences* (Cambridge MA, 2008).

[41] *Histoire de l'Académie des sciences* (Paris, 1733), iii.

[42] *Documents. Artefacts of Modern Knowledge*, ed. Annelise Riles, (Ann Arbor, 2006); Jacob Soll, *The Information Master: Jean-Baptiste Colbert's Secret State Intelligence System* (Ann Arbor, 2009).

[43] Jacques Roger, *Buffon, Un philosophe au Jardin du Roi* (Paris, 1989), 291–293.

aimed at the creation of an intellectual archive, at the recognition of an authority and at the delimitation of the legitimate corpus. Thus, these piles of papers and notes were not merely a dormant archive, but rather could be active in scholarly activity. The constitution of records and possession of unpublished work provided a form of power for the minority of scholars at the Académie who could access the ultimate meaning of natural philosophy by consulting unpublished manuscripts. Collections of scientific manuscripts were also constituted during this period. In 1795, the Library of the Paris Observatory gathered astronomical collections by repatriating Joseph-Nicolas Delisle astronomical papers.[44] He had already acquired the correspondence of the astronomer La Hire Called to Russia, following the journey of Peter the Great in 1717, he established contacts with leading astronomers in this country. Through Danzig, he acquired the manuscript correspondence of one of the most famous astronomers, Hevelius. During his stay in Russia, which lasted twenty years (1726–1747), he continued to enrich its collection of observations, and he bought the correspondence of Nicolas Freret and that of the Jesuit Souciet. He went on to Kepler's manuscripts that were in Vienna in 1736. Back in France, he exchanged all his collections for a pension and the title of Astronomer of the Navy. Thus his collection passed in 1750 to the Depot de la Marine in Paris. This example captures the mobility of these objects, but also the creation of collections for astronomical manuscripts.

The new Parisian sciences managed also to become public through a multifaceted strategy of publication. For instance, as Guerrini recently demonstrated, the success of the practice of anatomy in Paris relates to the research conducted within the Académie des Sciences, which led to the publication of Perrault's natural history of animals in 1671 and 1676. Anatomy was the metaphor for a new scientific method based on description and observation, enabling the centre of scientific interest to shift from natural history to comparative anatomy. Guerrini draws up the intellectual genealogy of the various debates through which anatomical culture was updated in France (primarily the circulation of the blood). In the years 1650–1666, libertine scholars (Sorbière, Gassendi, Patin) who believed in the circulation of the blood added their support to dissection as a legitimate practice, enabling it to become institutionalised when the academy was founded. This strong position provided the first academicians with a joint project around the natural history of animals. Colbert brought the academic circles and those of the king's library together in meetings at his personal residence. The project for anatomical observation

---

44   Guillaume Bigourdan, 'Inventaire général et sommaire des manuscrits de l'observatoire de Paris', *Annales de l'Observatoire de Paris*, série mémoire, 21 (1895).

appears in the minutes from 1667 and materialised in experiments on transfusion in dogs in the same year. But the academy's activities are also reflected in the many dissections conducted in Paris by Gayant and Joseph-Guichard Duverney, and at the royal menagerie established in Vincennes in 1654, and then in Versailles 1663–1664. There was a desire not only to promote the method but also to define animals as thinking, speaking beings, an issue that had been actively discussed in French philosophy since Descartes. The anatomists argued in favour of the singularity of animals. Guerrini gives us a detailed study of Perrault's book, showing the degree to which it constitutes a literary technique of dissection – the description of the practice of dissection becomes an epistemic genre. She also notes the importance of the choice of exotic animals. The natural history of animals and the *Philosophical transactions* thus proposed a set of established facts of nature. The other epistemological shift concerns the mechanistic interpretation of the living world. Focusing on Perrault's association with the anatomist Duverney, she discusses the importance of precision in the work of dissection and of illustrations. Duverney, who was to become tutor to the Dauphin in Saint-Germain and then in Versailles, enjoyed a reputation as the anatomist to the court. In 1682 he became anatomy teacher at the king's garden with the title of demonstrator and operator. Since the 1660s Perrault had wanted to use Cartesian theory in describing how living things operate. For him this was more a matter of method than ontological principle and combined both mechanistic ideas and the corpuscular conceptions promoted by Gassendi. Perrault used Duverney's dissections to ground these theories in the movement of animals. Duverney's experiments included the study of digestion and respiration, using the ostrich and tortoise as examples and the Versailles menagerie as a laboratory. The Indian tortoise was captured on the Coromandel Coast by the East India Company. *L'Histoire des animaux* describes both the dissection and the animal experimentation laboratory and the labyrinthine structure created by Colbert and Louis XIV in Versailles. Guerrini stresses the important role played in this anatomical research by both movement and the senses (sight and hearing), revealing the presence of notions of sensibility in descriptions of animal life well before the eighteenth century. There was a clear attempt to attribute a form of awareness to animals, hence their presence in research into music and harmony. Studies of this kind brought the worlds of court and science closer together, since their objects were present in both. Guerrini considers Duverney's work in the king's garden and shows Colbert's role in his appointment in the context of a study of fishing resources off the coasts of France. Later Duverney was called on to dissect the large animals given as gifts to the king, such as the elephant and crocodile, with the idea of developing the public practice of anatomy from 1680 and creating a skeleton room. But Duverney was not only known as an anatomist, but also as a talented orator, whose lectures and published speeches resembled works of theatrical literature. Guerrini sees these practices as a contribution to the culture of the court and to a 'moral anatomy' echoing La Fontaine's fables and Perrault's fairy tales. By publishing these stories of animals, the royal press ultimately turned the *savants* into literary authors.

The printed publication in 1733 of the first volumes of the *Histoire et mémoires de l'Académie*, covering the years 1666–1699, erased the work conducted by the organisation on itself, retaining only the account of its scientific activity. While the Académie des Sciences published its own *Histoire et Mémoire de l'Académie* in the eighteenth century, throughout that century it also constantly reviewed and promoted collaborative and individual publications thanks to its connection with the Royal Printer. As José Beltran Coelho investigated, at the beginning of the century, naturalists sponsored by the King and sent to the West Indies or to the Levant were published by the Royal press with lavish illustrations.[45] The publication of the book on *Machines et inventions*[46] in 1735 and 1777 with an endorsement from the Académie Royale des Sciences undoubtedly sought to publicise inventions in a more detailed way than was possible in the *Histoire de l'Académie*, but it was also a manifestation of academic polarisation. As Liliane Hilaire-Pérez or Paola Bertucci have shown, Parisian inventors, whether or not they were academicians, were thus given legitimacy, as indicated by the words 'with the consent of the Académie' in the title of their works.[47] Every Parisian academy was actively engaged in publishing, giving it a sense of its own authority and of its own field of knowledge. The spread of the model of sociability focused on publication had an important influence on provincial groupings specialising in scientific subjects. The investigative approach of the history of scientific reading has developed out of the dead ends of classical analyses of reception. Reception in science brings us face to face

---

45   José Beltran Coehlo, 'Nature in Draft. Images and Overseas Natural History in the Work of Charles Plumier (1646–1704)', PhD EUI 2017, Chapter 5. See also Anita Guerrini, 'The King's Animals and the King's Books: The Illustrations for the Paris Academy's Histoire des animaux', *Annals of Science*, 67 (2010), 383–386.

46   *Machines et inventions approuvées par l'Académie Royale des Sciences depuis son établissement jusqu'à présent, avec leur Description et publiées du consentement de l'Académie par M. Gallon* (Paris, 1735 and 1777).

47   Liliane Hilaire-Pérez, *L'invention au siècle des Lumières* (Paris, 2002). Paola Bertucci, *Artisanal Enlightenment. Science and the Mechanical Arts in Old Regime France* (New Haven, 2017).

with the already constituted oeuvres of the academicians. The Académie des Sciences could be therefore be considered as an interpretative community where books are read collectively. For instance, from 1738 to 1769, in the proceedings of the Académies, we find traces of presentations and discussion of Antoine Deparcieux's books on trigonometry or on probability.[48] The circulation of scientific writings could thus create 'textual communities' extending beyond the group of academicians and mobilized across distance through the discussion, acceptance or rejection of a text.[49] J.B. Shank notes that Newtonianism emerged in France via two communities of interpreters, on the one hand experimenters interested in the publication of Newton's treatise of 1704 on *Opticks*, which was an obvious composite of documents and experiment protocols published in the 1690s, and, on the other, mathematicians and astronomers who were readers of the *Principia*. In turn these two communities of readers influenced the republication and transformation of both works. These co-constructions of Newtonianism by its early interpreters in Paris helped shape historiography itself, which later distinguished the eighteenth century's true Newtonians (linked to Newton the theorist) from their false counterparts linked to experimental method.

4 The Academic Network: Sites, Laboratories and Instruments

The transformations in the Parisian space linked to the work of the academies were not confined to the institutionalisation of forms of intellectual exchange. They also show the emergence of collective research facilities in some domains. Without claiming to offer an inventory of these different places, we can consider the gradual invention of the 'laboratory'.

In the narratives of foreign travellers, a visit often included an opportunity to see machines or demonstrations, thereby promoting the visibility of the places of knowledge through their facilities and instruments. With the creation of the Académie des Sciences, a new form of scientific facility had already emerged in the late seventeenth century, characterised by the conduct of experiments and the use of instruments. An entire new literature establishes the identity of these practices in Paris. From Nicolas Lémery's *Cours de chimie* (1675) to Baumé, Abbé Nollet and Macquer's *Dictionnaire de Chymie*, containing the

---

[48] Edited in Antoine Deparcieux, *Essai sur les probabilités de la durée de la vie humaine (1746) addition à l'Essai (1760)* (Paris, 2003), 81–84.
[49] Roger Chartier, *The Order of Books: Readers, authors, and libraries in Europe between the Fourteenth and Eighteenth Centuries* (Stanford, 1994).

entry 'Laboratory of chemistry', the new workspace is minutely described.[50] We can note many characteristic features of this mutation. Firstly the authors describe a functional space entirely devoted to chemistry. It is light and spacious, as described by Baumé: 'there are a lot of barely noticeable phenomena that happen in many operations, which would go unseen if these operations were conducted in a poorly lit laboratory. The light from even a great many candles does not provide the same benefits as natural light'. With the exception of a few doctors and apothecaries or rich individuals interested in the sciences, more or less all the large 'laboratories' were either funded by royal institutions such as the Académie des Sciences, the Jardin du Roi or the manufactures at Sèvres and Les Gobelins, or else belonged to the families of princes, such as the Prince de Condé's Académie Bourdelot and the laboratory of the Duc d'Orléans[51] Beyond normative descriptions, often accompanied by plates of illustrations, what is striking here is the appearance of laboratory papers recording experiments and anatomical dissections.[52] We have Claude Bourdelin's papers describing the experimental programmes of the Académie des Sciences for the years 1666–1699,[53] which take three forms.[54] One element consists of financial accounts containing lists of purchases.[55] Another records chemical experiments carried out in the years 1672–1699. The third comprises three handwritten volumes compiled in 1749 by Duhamel du Monceau, who put the descriptions of experiments by Bourdelin into alphabetical order. Claire Salomon-Bayet has noted the epistemological consequences of the promotion of the laboratory through this archive.[56] In the first place it embodies the collective work of the group in the absence of any shared programme. It also

50   Antoine Baumé, *Chymie expérimentale et raisonnée* (Paris, 1773); Abbé Nollet, *L'Art des expériences ou avis aux amateurs de la physique* (Paris, 1770); Pierre-Joseph Macquer, 'Laboratoire de chymie', *Dictionnaire de Chymie* (Paris, 1777), 2nd ed., 2 :220–231. On Nollet, see *The Art of Teaching Physics: The Eighteenth-Century Demonstration Apparatus of Jean Nollet*, eds. L. Pyenson and J.-F. Gauvin (Sillery, 2002).
51   Claude Viel, 'Le salon et le laboratoire de Lavoisier à l'Arsenal, cénacle où s'élabora la nouvelle chimie', *Revue d'histoire de la Pharmacie*, 306 (1995), 255–266.
52   Jean Schiller, 'Les laboratoires d'anatomie et de botanique à l'Académie des sciences au XVIIe siècle', *Revue d'histoire des sciences*, 17 (1964), 97–114.
53   Christiane Demeulenaere-Douyère and David Sturdy, 'Images versus Reality: the Archives of the French Academie des Sciences', in *Archives of the Scientific Revolution. The Formation and Exchange of the Ideas in Seventeenth-Century Europe*, ed. Michael Hunter (London, 1999), 185–208.
54   MS Paris, Bibliothèque Nationale de France, NAF 5147–5149 and Ithaca, Kroch Library, Cornell University, Annalises Chymiques de Monsieur Bourdelin, 6 vol.
55   Stroup, *A Company of scientists*, chapter 14.
56   Claire Salomon-Bayet, *L'institution de la science et l'expérience du vivant: Méthode et expérience à l'Académie royale des science, 1666–1793* (Paris, 1978).

symbolises their agreement on the experimental dimension of academic work. At the Académie, Bourdelin's laboratory notebooks are more than a simple diary of experiments; they legitimate the new institution in the international academic space by crediting it with a store of experiments on which academicians can base their authority.[57]

The penetration of scientific activity begins with the appropriation of the intellectual space of the city in its phenomenological, conceptual and material dimensions. The places of learned work take on new visibility in the urban space, appearing as hubs with a key role in systems of exchange and travel between urban centres. In the second half of the seventeenth century activities of division, hierarchisation and localisation were accompanied by the relative stabilisation of institutional forms of philosophic activity in academies and schools. Scientific work now became more functional, with new facilities that enabled the culture of observation and experimentation to become established in specific locations in Paris, although itinerant practices were still ongoing outside these places, turning the capital into a laboratory in movement.

5 Performing Science: Royal Visits, Courtly Rituals and 'Courtierisation'

Public ceremonies linked to royal power could be another source of legitimacy, establishing scientific academies simply as royal institutions, as well as institutions of knowledge. Recent historiography has highlighted the role of these displays in the mechanisms of production and circulation of science.[58] Ceremonies were part of court life and made Paris into an extension of the courtly stage of Versailles.[59] The representation of knowledge was not absent from these. It can be observed notably in the extraordinary ritual of visits to Paris by princes or royalty. These were not intended to celebrate the integration of knowledge into the ordinary urban calendar, but created events involving places of knowledge. These events had their risks, since in the seventeenth century the celebration of scientific patronage required princes to make increasing

---

57 Demeulenaere-Douyère and Sturdy, 'Images versus Reality', 200.
58 Two examples of such performances: the reception of explorations in Paris and the spectacles of sciences: Neil Safier, *Measuring the new world: enlightenment science and South America* (Chicago, 2008); Marie Thébaud-Sorger, *L'aérostation au temps des Lumières* (Rennes, 2009).
59 Catherine Arminjon, *Versailles et les sciences* (Paris, 2010); *Sciences & curiosités à la cour de Versailles*, eds. B. Saule and C. Arminjon (Paris, 2010), 24–25.

numbers of visits. Distance and indifference on their part were no longer acceptable.

The episode of the king's visit to the Académie des Sciences in 1681 is well known. While the scientific space of Paris was under the direct patronage of the monarch, it remained hard to maintain the king's visibility in his absence. The royal visit was a form of scientific tour, going from the library to the Cabinet des Médailles followed by the laboratory, 'Where Mr du Clos showed him the coagulation of seawater by oil of tartar, which happened in an instant'. However, as Licoppe notes, the presence of Louis XIV remained external to experimental activity and goes without comment. The king was not a learned prince who could settle academic quarrels in the manner of the Grand Duke of Tuscany, and nor did he play an active part in science and mechanics, as Rudolph II had done in the sixteenth century[60] or Peter the Great did when he visited Paris in 1717.[61] Unlike the Dauphin, who came to the Academy in 1677, the king remained a reader patron who preferred learning from books to experiments. 'Having entered the Academy, Colbert showed His Majesty the books printed by the Academy and some of those that are to be printed. The King paid particular attention to the figures of earthly animals in the manuscripts of M. Perrault, and those of the fish drawn by M. de La Hire [...] Lastly the king saw M. Romer's two machines, which Mr Cassini explained to him and where he paused for a long time. One of these machines is for the calculation of Eclipses and the other for the theory of the Planets'.[62] This ritual visit by the king nevertheless reflects the way that patronage operated under the monarchy. As indicated by the housing of scientists in the Tuileries and Louvre palaces and their presence in the Menus-Plaisirs and Garde-Meuble, the Académie des Sciences had a domestic dimension within the king's household, making academicians servants of the king.[63]

Indeed a 'courtierisation' of scientific life is apparent in some capital cities, in a subtle dialectic between city and court. The very strong presence of the sciences in European courts, at least from the Renaissance, can be seen both in Paris, from the reign of Louis XIV, and in London with the arrival of the Hanover dynasty. Versailles in particular acted as a scientific laboratory through

---

60 Paula Findlen, 'Cabinets, collecting and natural philosophy', in *Rudolf II and Prague: The Court and the City*, ed. E. Fucikova, (London, 1997), 209–217.
61 E. Kniajetskaia and L. Chenakal, 'Pierre le Grand et les fabricants français d'instruments scientifiques', *Revue d'histoire des sciences* 28 (1975), 243–258.
62 Paris, Académie des sciences, Registres de l'Académie royales des Sciences, t. IXb, fol. 81, quoted by Christian Licoppe, *La Formation du discours scientifique*, 73.
63 Natacha Coquery, *L'espace du pouvoir. De la demeure privée à l'édifice public, Paris 1700–1790* (Paris, 2000), 187–189.

the development of technological and hydraulic expertise linked to the water supply and more broadly to the technological challenges of building a city *ex-nihilo*, and also of scientific facilities for natural history (the royal menagerie built in 1662, to which were added the Trianon menagerie developed in 1749–1750, the royal vegetable garden constructed in the years 1678–1683 and Rambouillet's experimental farm, built in the years 1784–1787). These facilities fostered the expansion of naturalist activities including the animal dissections conducted before the young Louis XV by his first surgeon François Gigot de La Peyronie in the 1720s and agronomic research. The Trianon garden housed a plant collection gathered by Philibert Commerson in 1763–1764 where Antoine-Nicolas Duchesne studied strawberry plants. Exotic plants were acclimatised there, and it was catalogued in 1795 by Antoine-Laurent de Jussieu. The king's household was full of health officers, engineers, surgeons and apothecaries. Princes of the Blood such as the Contis, Orléans and Condés possessed well-stocked studies, libraries and even academies, such as the Condés's academy in Chantilly. Philosophers such as Buffon, Emilie du Châtelet and Antoine-Louis Lavoisier were present at court.[64] Fontenelle notes that in the reign of Louis XIV the court became a tribunal of reason to rival the academy in Paris: 'At that time the court brought together a considerable number of illustrious minds, headed by Messrs Racine, Despréaux, de La Bruyère, de Malézieu, de Court and M. de Meaux. They formed a kind of singular society, all the more united for its separation from the Illustrious circles of Paris, which claimed no need to recognise a higher tribunal, nor to submit blindly to judgements, even those cloaked in the grand name of court judgements'.[65] The court was the site of famous experiments and a stage for the representation of innovation, underpinned by the figure of a philosopher king who was master of nature.[66] The decorations in Versailles have left traces of this enthusiasm for science and technology. The court became a place of fashionable demonstrations, such as the chain of electric shocks in the Galérie des Glaces, conducted by Abbé Nollet in March 1746. But Versailles was a quintessential theatre of a constructed nature, entirely fabricated and measured. Having been established over several decades, the environment in Versailles received further attention through the management of its grounds and natural resources linked to problems of supply, overpopulation and pollution. The chemistry of gases that was so fashionable

---

64 *Sciences et curiosités à la cour de Versailles*, 24–25.
65 Fontenelle, *Oeuvres complètes*, Paris: H. Champion, 2013, tome VII, 105, quoted by Simone Mazauric, 'Savants et courtisans vus par Fontenelle', in *Sciences & curiosités à la cour de Versailles*, 53–56, at 55. Antoine Lilti, *The world of the Salons. Sociability and Worldliness in Eighteenth-Century Paris* (Oxford, 2015).
66 Chandra Mukerjee, *Territorial ambitions and the gardens of Versailles* (Cambridge, 1997).

in the 1770s and 1780s was also present in Versailles, while medical concerns led to the monitoring of its ponds.[67]

6 Policing Science by Committees: The Académie des Sciences as a Legal Court

Over two centuries Paris increasingly became a site of expert knowledge at the international level, where scientific experiments were assessed. A new historiography shed light on this issue. The Academy's reputation was established by debates bringing different parties together, at which a stable consensus was established, but it was a tribunal whose actors were required to negotiate constantly on the basis of the ideas submitted to them.[68] The multiplication of commissions between 1760 and 1789 is renforced with 170 commissions each year composed by two academicians.[69] The work of Hugues Chabot on scientific ideas rejected in the period 1750–1835 confirms that the Académie des Sciences played an increasingly important role in these operations.[70] Analysis of the proceedings of the Académie des Sciences has revealed the work of panels appointed to consider an essay or an account of a printed book. The number of panels that met annually to provide written reports varies between 80 and 200. After rising sharply in the early years to around 170 panels appointed in the years 1800–1802, the number suddenly falls below 100, after which the average ranges between 90 and 130 until 1820. The number of academicians involved each year varies between 20 and 90. Different sections were involved to different degrees and associations between them are seen to emerge. For example, the agriculture section frequently interacts with anatomy, botany and, to a lesser extent, medicine and chemistry. The medical section has a strong identity. Conversely, mineralogy seems clearly dominated by physics and most of all by chemistry. Physics appears as one of the least specialised sections, since it is most often found associated with mechanics and mathematics and also with chemistry and astronomy.[71] Based on a sample of 70 negative reports on

---

67   Grégory Quenet, *Versailles une histoire naturelle* (Paris, 2015).
68   For an example of the relationship between Science and Law, Sheila Jasanoff, *Science at the bar: Law, Science and Technology in America* (Cambridge, 1995).
69   Pascale Mafarette-Dayries, 'L'académie royale des sciences et les grandes commissions d'enquête et d'expertise à la fin de l'ancien régime', *Annales historiques de la Révolution française*, 320 (2000), 121–135.
70   Hugues Chabot, 'Enquête historique sur les savoirs scientifiques rejetés à l'aube du positivisme (1750–1835)' PhD, Université de Nantes, 1999.
71   Chabot, 'Enquête historique sur les savoirs scientifiques', 282–283.

the 2,000 products in the years 1795–1835, Chabot shows that the distribution of negative reports according to the origins of panel members reveals that they are preponderantly from mathematics (40%), astronomy (30%), mechanics (15%), physics (10%) and chemistry (5%).[72]

In this context Paris was a magnet for disputes in the Republic of Sciences and acted as sounding board and amplifier for local controversies, which it converted into major causes. By creating a large arena for discussion, the shift from controversy to polemic also led to the extension of the city's short university networks to the long networks of the Republic of Letters. The controversy around establishing latitude no doubt played an active role in reinforcing the position of Paris as the international centre of scientific argument. In the years 1735–1745 the city hosted confrontations between the supporters of Newton, defended by Maupertuis, champion of the Académie Royale des Sciences in Paris, and those of Descartes led by the astronomer Cassini. Another example is provided by the scandal following the publication of Buffon's *Histoire naturelle*.[73] This affair is interesting because it brought all the judging bodies into simultaneous competition – readers, aristocratic networks, religious censors, academic assessors and the encyclopaedist camp. Each had its 'reasons' for criticising the book. The first three volumes of the *Histoire naturelle* were instant bestsellers.[74] The first printing sold out in six weeks. The book was printed at the king's expense and published in quarto at 17 *livres*, followed by a second edition in duodecimo. These editions appeared in April 1750 and Dutch, English and German editions were immediately prepared. The book initially circulated in the short networks of the princely households and salons. Raynal wrote that 'women make a fuss about it'. The Jesuits acknowledged this in the *Mémoires de Trévoux* between October 1749 and May 1750. On 6 February 1750 the Jansenist organ *Nouvelles ecclésiastiques* violently condemned the *Histoire naturelle*. Its arguments included accusations of Pyrrhonism and absolute scepticism and Buffon's confusion of human beings with animals. On 1 April 1751 the Sorbonne waded in. Behind-the-scenes negotiations sought to temper censorship. The censors held back fourteen propositions seen as contrary to religion. Another criticism came from Réaumur, who was Director of the Academy until 1752 and could not accept Buffon's failure to respect academic conventions. In 1751 a debate erupted following the publication of the *Lettres à un Amériquain sur l'Histoire naturelle, générale et particulière de M. de Buffon*.

---

72 Chabot, 'Enquête historique sur les savoirs scientifiques', 290.
73 Jeff Loveland, *Rhetoric and Natural History: Buffon in Polemical and Literary Context* (Oxford, 2001).
74 Roger, *Buffon, un philosophe au Jardin du Roi*, 248–272.

Buffon 'is a member of the Academy, but the frontispiece of his book does not mention it. This is clear proof that either he did not dare give his book to the Academy, or that if he did present it, he did not obtain their vote'. This anonymous book was sponsored by Réaumur. While the criticisms were very diverse, all were agreed on what seemed the most effective condemnation: Buffon was said to contradict 'Genesis on everything'. Another attack came from the philosophers' side, which included Voltaire. The institutional authority of the Academy was no longer enough to validate what was said, since most scientific controversies overflowed into the public domain. The role of Paris as a scientific tribunal was no longer played out solely in academic circles, since the philosophical arena was totally transformed when polemic took the institution's arguments into the 'public space'.

7   Branding Expertise: The Académie des Sciences and the City

The Académie des Sciences also took on a crucial role in providing expert evaluations for properly local issues.[75] The Royal and Parisian authorities increasingly transformed the academies, and notably the Académie des Sciences and the Académie de Médecine, into judging authorities and centres of reference that could decide on local questions from a national or even international perspective. In 1780, Necker asked the Académie to assess different projects on public health. The minister of the Maison du roi, the Baron de Breteuil mobilized the expertise of the Académie regarding inventions in conjunction with different jurisdictions: the Chatelet, the Parlement and the lieutenant of Police.[76] It was particularly visible in several scandals such as that concerning animal magnetism and Mesmer in April 1784. This change in the direction of the circuits of expertise took particular cases rooted in the experience and problems of Parisian expansion and turned them into scientific cases. Now it was not the city's engineers or Parisian scientists who were asked to advise the *corps de ville*; instead the Academy was required to decide and select local projects. The operations involved in this transfer of skills brought about a general increase in knowledge. In moving from the narrow circles of the Parisian developers to the academic arena, the subjects under discussion became general

---

75   By contrast see for London, Rob Iliffe, 'Capitalizing Expertise: Philosophical and Artisanal Expertise in Early Modern London', in *Fields of expertise. Paris and London since 1600*, ed. Chistelle Rabier (Newcastle, 2007), 53–82.

76   Pascale Mafarette-Dayries, 'L'académie royale des sciences et les grandes commissions d'enquête', 4.

themes of scientific research. In addition to being called on by the urban authorities, academicians also used problems posed by the Paris administration to formulate scientific problems.

As has been demonstrated, the Académie des Sciences gradually acquired the role of providing expertise in domains as varied as the lighting of public spaces, the construction of bridges, water supply and public health. In 1765 to improve street lighting, the learned society offered a prize of 2000 *livres* to the best project submitted to Sartine, Paris's Lieutenant General of Police. Lavoisier presented an essay in which he suggested setting lanterns of his own invention alongside two or three others to assess their effectiveness as lights. The Academy also spent a long time on water issues, from projects to build fountains for the royal palaces to others for the purification and distribution of water, fire engines and the improvement of watermills.[77] The problem of drainage and the removal of waste was crucial for the city authorities. In 1533, the Paris parliament had made the construction of cesspits compulsory. Proposals were made to increase the supply of water to Paris, including a project by Deparcieux and Peronnet to divert the waters of the river Yvette or the Bièvre, and another by Fer de la Nouerre and Trouville to divert the Seine (discussed in the years 1760–1789).[78] Problems of public health emerged: in 1789 a panel of academicians including Daubenton, Tillet, Laplace and Bailly intervened on the issue of abattoirs. But this work to redefine the urban space in sites of knowledge was sometimes far narrower. The Académie des Sciences was, for example, involved in mapping the population of Paris.[79] We can follow the work of receiving and sorting projects through the example of the Paris water supply.[80] Lavoisier's role in this debate was to decide between the project submitted to the Academy by Antoine Deparcieux in 1762, which involved bringing the water of the Yvette river in Essonne to Paris by means of an aqueduct, and Chevalier d'Auxiron's project of 1768 to build steam pumps near the General Hospital

---

77 See Isabelle Backouche, *La trace du fleuve. La Seine et Paris, 1750–1850* (Paris, 2000).
78 Sayaka Oki, 'Academicians and Experts? The Académie Royale des Sciences and Hospital Reform at the End of the Eighteenth Century', *Fields of expertise*; S. Oki, 'L'utilité des sciences d'après les discours des secrétaires perpétuels de l'Académie royale des sciences de Paris au XVIIIe siècle', in *Entre belles-lettres et disciplines. Les savoirs au XVIIIe siècle*, eds. F. Salaün and J.-P. Schandeler (Paris, 2011).
79 Eric Brian, *La mesure de l'Etat*, figure 15. Daniel Roche, *Histoire des choses banales: naissance de la consommation dans les sociétés traditionelles (XVIIe–XIXe siècle)* (Paris, 1997), 151–182.
80 Lavoisier, *Oeuvres de Lavoisier. Correspondance*, ed. René Fric (Paris, 1955–2012), II, 1770–1775: Letter from Lavoisier to X, 257–264.

and the Île Saint-Louis to raise the level of the Seine.[81] The Academy appointed Lavoisier to examine the projects. In July 1769, and again in 1771, Lavoisier responded in support of Deparcieux's project as 'the least costly and more worthy of the capital'. Despite a council decree of 30 July 1768 approving the aqueduct project, the other side held firm, particularly as on 7 February the company of the Périer brothers succeeded in obtaining letters patent from the parliament to build at its expense the steam machines perfected by Watt. By 1782 these pumps were distributing water.

Lavoisier's expert input shifted the debate in two different ways. In the first place, it validated the Academy's intervention in this domain. It gave the issue of water all the weight of the scientific approach of a royal institution, taking the debate out of the technological sphere of engineers and into that of the chemists. The appointment of Lavoisier as expert reflected his former concerns. During his mineralogical expedition he had become interested in the composition of spring and river water and had taken samples. On arriving in Alsace in August 1767, he was seen checking the analysis of water produced in Thann by a doctor who had studied with Rouelle, which he judged as apparently a 'lie in almost every respect'. He wrote to his father that 'this circumstance made him pay more attention to the analysis of these waters' and that he had filled enough flasks to have 'on arriving in Paris a complete analysis of the waters of this canton'. In 1769 he used the samples taken on this trip to publish an article in the *Mercure de France* on 'the nature of the waters of part of Franche-Comté, Alsace, Lorraine, Champagne, Brie and Valois'. The following year at the Academy in Rouen he gave a 'Report on the nature of the waters of this city'. Examination of the different projects reveals the irony of having to decide between proposals ranging from the well-founded to the most fantastical: 'M. de Parcieux was not the first to be struck by these goals; before his proposal different projects had been put forward to supply water to the city of Paris. One of the best known is that advanced in 1739 by the architect M. Pinson. It consisted of a hydraulic machine to be built in the middle of the river, opposite Bercy. This machine would bring water to the city and distribute it to the houses from above the roofs. A simple description of this project is enough to give a sense of its ridiculousness'.

Secondly, in adopting a position in this minor debate, Lavoisier sought to make the issue of water a priority in urban development policies. He wanted to divert attention and the analytical techniques used to study mineral waters

---

81   Michel Valentin, 'Lavoisier urbaniste, hygéniste, précurseur de l'ergonomie', in *Il y a 200 ans Lavoisier*, 141–150, on the project, 143. See F. Graber, *Paris a besoin d'eau: projet, dispute et délibération technique dans la France napoléonienne* (Paris, 2009).

towards water held in common, a vital resource for urbanisation and public hygiene. Lavoisier stated: 'While it is interesting for society to know the nature of these health-giving waters, the surprising effects of which have so often been celebrated in the annals of medicine, it is no less interesting to know the nature of those used every day for the requirements of life. For it is on these that the strength and health of citizens depend'.[82] Despite these exhortations, Lavoisier conducted only two campaigns to analyse river water, in the Seine and the Yvette, compared to 160 analyses of mineral waters during his travels in the Vosges:[83] 'I shall not expand on the acknowledged need to supply water to the city of Paris; it is frightening to think that the inhabitants of outlying quarters, in other words the greatest number of the capital's inhabitants, are supplied with water drawn from the river and carried on a man's back or on carts. There can be no doubt that such a dearth of water must lead to a lack of cleanliness in the people and contributes to the unhealthy air of the capital'. This dual shift of focus helped make the Academy into an acceptable tribunal for local problems, best able to decide between projects according to how serious they were. It alone could turn water into a political issue. It is hardly surprising that the technological debate led to a scandal on the eve of the Revolution. The confrontation brought two famous advocates head to head: Beaumarchais for the Compagnie des Periers and Mirabeau Père for their opponents. To get around the obstacle of high cost, the supporters of the aqueduct project suggested to the Academy that water could be taken from the Bièvre rather than the Yvette, a plan ultimately adopted by the king's council on 3 November 1787. However, this proposal encountered hostility from the dyers and tanners of the Bièvre valley and a struggle ensued between the king's council and the parliament, which lasted from December 1787 to April 1789. So Lavoisier's example is valuable for us in understanding the processes of selection, abstraction and amplification of the arguments produced by the decision-making power of the Académie des Sciences in local issues. For some decades now, under the influence of new thinking on 'sustainable cities', the history of the Académie des Sciences has shifted the ground under these old questions, reformulating them from a more environmentalist perspective including waste, air pollution,

---

82 Lavoisier, *Œuvres complètes*, 3 :145.
83 Bernadette Bensaude-Vincent, 'Eaux et mesures. Eclairages sur l'itinéraire intellectuel du jeune Lavoisier', *Revue d'histoire des sciences*, January-June (1995), 48, 1/2, 49–70, (54). Soyaka Oki, 'L'aménagement de la Seine et l'Académie royale des sciences de Paris au XVIIIe siècle', *Aesturia, collection Fleuves et archéologie*, 7, 'La rivière aménagée entre héritages et modernité. Formes, techniques et mise en œuvre', *Esturarium*, (2005), 351–365. Pascale Mafarette-Dayries, 'L'académie royale des sciences et les grandes commissions d'enquête', 121–135.

water.[84] Natural risks (flooding, earthquakes, urban pollution), natural resources (recycling, urban chemistry)[85] are one way to investigate the idea of urban nature. According to recent studies made by Sayaka Oki, or Pascale Mafarette-Dayries, by Patrice Bret on the Régie des Poudres or Thomas Leroux on the industralisation and chemical factories in La Villette Basin and Chaptal,[86] Frédéric Graber on water supply,[87] the picture of an Old-Fashioned institution only driven by polemics (if we think of Lavoisier's Chemical Revolution) is changed. In 1780, Necker asked the Académie to assess different project on public health. The minister of the Maison du roi, the Baron de Breteuil mobilized the expertise of the académie regarding inventions in conjunction with different jurisdictions: the Chatelet, the Parlement and the lieutenant of Police.[88] It was particularly visible in several scandals such as the one concerning animal magnetism against Mesmer in April 1784. This change in the direction of the circuits of expertise took particular cases rooted in the experience and problems of Parisian expansion and turned them into scientific cases. Now it was not the city's engineers or Parisian scientists who were asked to advise the *corps de ville*; instead the Academy was required to decide and select local projects. The operations involved in this transfer of skills brought about a general increase in knowledge. In moving from the narrow circles of the Parisian developers to the academic arena, the subjects under discussion became general themes of scientific research. In addition to being called on by the urban authorities, academicians also used problems posed by the Paris administration to formulate scientific problems.

However, we can also see the event as a a way of reassuring the authority of the Academy on local nature and the administration of natural resources (water, electricity, chemistry, etc). This dual shift of focus helped make the

---

84 André Guillerme, 'Enclosing Nature in the City: Supplying light and water to Paris, 1770–1840', *Construction History* 26 (2011), 79–93.
85 On urban chemistry, see Sabine Barles, *L'invention des déchets urbains: France, 1790-* (Seyssel, 2005).
86 Patrice Bret, *L'État, l'armée, la science: l'invention de la recherche publique en France, 1763–1830* (Rennes, 2002); Thomas Leroux, *Le laboratoire des pollutions industrielles. Paris, 1770–1830* (Paris, 2011); see also Maurizio Gribaudi, *Paris, ville ouvrière, une histoire occultée* (Paris, 2014).
87 Frédéric Graber, 'Inventing needs: expertise and water supply in late eighteenth- and early nineteenth-century Paris', *British Journal for the History of Science*, 40 (2007), 315–332; 'Diverting rivers for Paris (1760–1820)', in *Urban Waters. Rivers, Cities and the Production of Space in Europe and North America*, eds. S. Castonguay and M. Evenden (Pittsburgh, 2012), 183–200.
88 P. Mafarette-Dayries, 'L'académie royale des sciences et les grandes commissions d'enquête', 4.

Academy into an acceptable tribunal for local problems, best able to decide between projects according to how serious they were. It alone could turn water into a political issue. Thomas Leroux in his research on chemical manufacture and pollution in Paris demonstrated the pressure exerted by local and petty groups of interest.[89]

8 Placing Parisian Science in a Global Context

At first the transition from 'forums' of discussion and research open to the Republic of Letters to institutional places established as academies in the city led to the creation of a short institutional network in the Parisian arena, bringing together nearby establishments such as the royal observatory and the king's garden. The trajectory of the Académie des Sciences in Paris pointed out a set of tensions between Paris and the provinces, Paris and the empire or Paris within the Republic of Letters. This geographical dynamism is operated through new instruments of publicity which makes Paris a scientific capital. Putting to one side the national aspects of Paris, new approaches seek to understand the Parisian Enlightenment both in terms of locality and internationality. This approach is to understand both the interplay of scales and the relationship with metropolitan identity. As David Garrioch stated: 'Both the "middling sort" and the noble and wealthy elite of Paris began to aspire to a broader "metropolitan" culture, a shared culture yet one that each group lived and interpreted in different ways'.[90]

In the provinces the Academy also had close links to the Société Royale des Sciences in Montpellier, founded in 1706, which presented itself as an extension of the Paris company.[91] In the course of the eighteenth century this small network, closely linked by intense discussions and the circulation of scientists, instruments, objects and information, became connected to the formation of a global academic network.[92] The movement for the foundation of academies touched all the main European capitals before 1750: London in 1662, Berlin in 1700, St Petersburg in 1724 and Stockholm in 1739. In the second half of the eighteenth century the movement expanded to Göttingen (1752), Turin (1757),

---

[89] Thomas Le Roux, 'Chemistry and Industrial and Environmental Governance in France, 1770–1830', *History of Science* 54 (2016), 195–222.
[90] David Garrioch, *The Making of Revolutionary Paris* (Berkeley, 2002).
[91] On Montpellier, see Daniel Roche, 'Natural History in the Academies', in *Cultures of Natural History*, N. Jardine, J.A. Secord and E. Spary eds. (Cambridge, 1996), 127–145.
[92] *Centres and Cycles of Accumulation in and around the Netherlands during the Early Modern Period*, Lissa Roberts, ed. (Zurich and Berlin, 2011).

Munich (1759), Barcelona (1764), Padua (1779), Edinburgh (1783) and Dublin (1785). In 1789 there were no fewer than seventy academies across Europe, not counting those founded in the colonies.[93] Yet, while an early form of internationalisation emerged, it took many contradictory forms. Far from being a homogeneous and fluid space, the Europe of the academies was characterised by its fragility (dependency on interpersonal relationships and patronage) and fragmentation in space. The institutionalisation of scientific practices through academisation led to competition and comparisons between models of academic sociability.[94] The different academic networks thus functioned as circulatory networks. Natural knowledge featured in the strategies employed to re-scale the city as a powerful and attractive metropolis, an emergence that benefitted from new ways of commodifying, consuming and interpreting nature. This also requires consideration of the capacity of the academy to exploit and diversify its forms of knowledge. By linking the Royal Navy, the Académie des Sciences, the Jardin du roi, the Société d'Agriculture, and the Royal Academy of Medicine, the 'colonial machine' revealed a network of institutions, and a number of problems faced by European colonialism. As Emma Spary or Marie-Noelle Bourguet have shown concerning the Jardin du Roi and the network of French naturalists, to be useful these observations had to be reduced to standardized techniques, classified and carefully stored (as Etienne-Louis Turgot did in his *Instructions*).[95]

The centrality of the Académie des Sciences among the other forms of learned sociability in Paris, in France and in Europe is also constructed thanks to the development of mapping genres to help traveling scholars or learned people to identity places and institutions within the capital city. The knowledge of places (cartography, travel guides, lists of cabinets or amateurs, etc.) served as starting-points for local actors to rethink the urban space in its globality. In 1680, the French writer Pierre Le Gallois published his *Traité des plus belles bibliothèques de l'Europe*. In 1686, Charles Baudelot de Dairval gives his lists of amateurs and curious of Europe. Progressively, a specialization took

---

93 James McClellan III, 'Scientific Institutions and the organization of science', in *The Cambridge History of Science*, ed. Roy Porter (Cambridge, 2003), 90–91.

94 Mario Biagioli, *Galileo, Courtier: The Pratice of Science in the Culture of absolutism* (Chicago, 1993), Conclusion.

95 Emma Spary, *Utopia's Garden: French natural history from the old regime to Revolution* (Chicago, 2000); Spary, 'The nature of Enlightenment', in *The Sciences in Enlightenment Europe*, eds. William Clark, Jan Golinski, and Simon Schaffer (Chicago, 1999), 272–306; Marie-Noëlle Bourguet, 'La collecte du monde: voyage et histoire naturelle (fin XVIIe siècle–début XIXe siècle)', in *Le Muséum au Premier Siècle de son Histoire*, ed. Claude Blankaert (Paris, 1999), 163–196.

place during the eighteenth century. But this process was not neutral or consensual. The practices of comparisons underlie the proliferation of inventories of the size in each city, as well as how scientists thought about the differences between them in terms of intellectual and publishing practice. Numerous printed and manuscript sources which are well known to urban history may be used (for example, newspapers, posters, travel guides, descriptions of the city, etc.). In 1742, Desallier d'Argenville wrote a list of the main collectors of shells and natural history in his *Conchyliologie*. In the same way, the Swiss astronomer Jean Bernouilli published in 1776 his *Liste des Astronomes Connus Actuellement Vivans*. In almanacs or travel guides the motivation was different.[96] Functional utility triumphed over the monumental representation of the city. If at the end of the seventeenth century travel guides targeted the amateurs of Fine-Arts, in the middle of the eighteenth century its ambitions were much more encyclopedic. It tried to deploy an urban totality. The *Almanach parisien en faveur des étrangers et des curieux* (1765) was placed under the influence of the urban government and royal administration. In the same way, philosophy and science had a very important place in the economy of the new genre of *Affiches de Paris*. In the case of scientific knowledge, changing travel practices over the course of the century (e.g., in terms of reception and inventories) between London and Paris encouraged an integration of scientific practices into a metropolitan culture of curiosity and collection. Shopping for instruments, uses of equipment and visits to learned circles allowed the unification of academic practices.[97] Moreover, the mobility of natural philosophers between the two cities effectively led to more travel writing in which London and Paris became paradigms of intellectual sociability and philosophical exchange. The pairing of London and Paris played a major role in establishing ideas about national characteristics in the philosophical discourse of the Enlightenment. The marks of these comparative processes can be seen in the literature of the period. In fact, throughout the eighteenth century, such comparisons were stabilised and perpetuated via symbolic lists represented by the recording of experiments, practices and judgements. Louis- Sébastien Mercier, in his *Parallèle de Paris et*

---

[96] Charlotte Guichard, 'La Coquille au XVIIIe siècle: un objet frontière?', *Technologies et culture* 59 (2012), 2, 150–163.

[97] James E. Bennett, 'Shopping for instruments in Paris and London', in *Merchants and Marvels. Commerce, Science and Art in early modern Europe*, eds Pamela H. Smith and Paula Findlen (New York and London, 2002), 370–395. Liliane Hilaire-Pérez, 'Les boutiques d'inventeurs à Londres et à Paris au XVIIIe siècle: jeux de l'enchantement et de la raison citoyenne', in *La boutique et la ville. Commerces, commerçants, espaces et clientèles*, ed. Natacha Coquery (Tours, 2000), 171–189.

de Londres, provides a paradigmatic example of the commonplace of this comparison between the two capitals in the latter half of the eighteenth century.

The attention paid to polemics and controversies allows us to measure the 'proofs of greatness' that agents and institutions drew up in order to test and compare the two cities and to establish a scientific hierarchy between capital cities in Europe. Within this framework, we will also pay close heed to scientific controversies, spiralling disputes around knowledge, or even various incidents (some of which led to court cases), in which both knowledge, and the links between the learned world and urban powers were evaluated. For example, in the early years of the eighteenth century, a technical controversy existed between Paris and London proponents of a new definition of longitude from Paris. Guillaume Delisle, a geographer, published an article in the *Journal des savants* in 1700 in which he wished to draw up a new map of the capital by aligning it with the Meridian.[98] Paris was supposed to be the middle of the globe contested by the British astronomers in the *Philosophical Transactions*. Thanks to the authority of Dortous Mairan, the debate was temporarily closed in 1732.[99] However, the geodesic competition between French and English cartographers of the Greenwich and Paris observatories in the second half of the eighteenth century attests to the processes of recognition of the value of science in the two capitals. In a brief submitted to the British government in October 1783, Cassini de Thury argued that the triangulation between Greenwich and Paris could give the relative position of the two observatories. Between 1784 and 1803 both teams were in place to carry out the measurements. Each team disseminated its findings, criticizing those of the opposing team. Jacques and Dominique Cassini, Pierre François Méchain and Adrien-Marie Legendre published them in the *Exposé des opérations faites en France en 1787 pour la jonction des observatoires de Paris et de Greenwich*, Paris, 1791. It was not until 1810 that Jean-Baptiste Delambre published all data relating to the measurement of the arc of the meridian according to Ken Alder.[100] A list could be

---

98   'Lettre de M. De Lisle au RP* sur la longitude de Paris', *Journal des Savants* (1700), 243.

99   Guillaume Delisle, 'Examen et comparaison de la grandeur de Paris, de Londres et de quelques autres grandes villes du monde, anciennes et modernes', *Histoire de l'Académie des sciences. Année 1725* (Paris, 1728), 48–57. Peter Davall, 'Some reflections on Mr. De Lisle's comparisons of the magnitude of Paris with London and several other cities, printed in the Memoirs of the Royal Academy of Sciences at Paris for the year 1725', *Philosophical Transactions* (1727–1728), 432–436; and the final reply of Dortous de Mairan, in *Histoire de l'Académie royale des sciences*, MDCCXXX, (Paris, 1732), 562–574. Jacques Dupâquier, 'Londres ou Paris? Un grand débat dans le petit monde des arithméticiens politiques (1662–1759)', *Population*, 1–2, January-April (1998), 311–325.

100 Jean-Baptiste Delambre, *La Base du système métrique décimal, ou mesure de l'arc du méridien compris entre les parallèles de Dunkerque et Barcelone, exécutée en 1792 et années*

drawn of scientific and philosophical controversies, disputes and debates between Parisians and Londoners in order to pinpoint moments of tension and lull. Little by little if academic knowledge became more 'territorialized', it is not only through the constitution of sites of knowledge and equipement within the urban space, but also through the multiple practices of comparison. Similarly a transition can be observed towards the progressive institutionalisation of cultural life through the creation of learned groups around common projects increasingly identified with the defense of local identities and local patronage or local interests. It is necessary to investigate the social networks that sustain them and make it possible, within the urban space, to move from isolated initiatives to aggregated practices localised by the constitution of short networks within the capital. These examples also pointed out the ambivalent role played by the State between intelligence gathering and scientific patronage.[101]

To conclude, in the last thirty years, the Académie des Sciences has been subjected to an important shift from institutional history in a national context to a multifaceted and multi-scaled approach focusing on scientific practices and the production of places and spaces of science in the city. By restaging the Académie des Sciences *in* Paris and *of* Paris, historians of science have paid attention to the many ways scientists strove to build a new Parisian scientific authority. The process of institutionalisation is no more considered as a given but as a result of long and disputed articulation of local expertise with metropolitan and international legitimacy through scientific expeditions and international cooperations. At the beginning of the French Revolution, the Académie des Sciences was stigmatized as an emblem of the Old Regime.[102] While the Académie des Sciences enthusiastically welcomed the announcement of the General States, from November 1789 there was a split in the institution between supporters of the king, such as as Le Gentil and Cassini, and those who wished the tutelage of the Assembly, such as as Bossut and Laplace. Politicization did not spare the scientific coterie and probably new places captured the new scientific

---

suivantes, par MM. Méchain et Delambre (Paris, 1806, 1807, 1810); Sven Widmalm, 'Accuracy, Rhetoric, and Technology: The Paris-Greenwich Triangulation, 1784–1788', in *The quantifying spirit in the 18th century*, eds. Tore Frängsmyr, John L. Heilbron, and Robin E. Rider (Berkeley, 1990) 179–206; Ken Alder, *The Measure of all Things. The seven-Year-Odissey that transformed the World* (London, 2004).

101 Paola Bertucci, 'Enlightened Secrets: Silk, Industrial Espionage, and Intelligent Travel in 18th-century France', *Technology and Culture* 54 (2013), 820–852.

102 Françoise Waquet, 'La Bastille académique', in *La Carmagnole des Muses. L'homme de lettres et l'artiste dans la Révolution*, ed. J.-C. Bonnet (Paris, 1988), 19–36.

energy such as the Linnean Société d'Histoire Naturelle de Paris.[103] The conservatives were denouncing the transformation of the Academy into a political platform, while the revolutionaries saw in this 'last stand' of a rearguard defending aristocracy against utility.[104]

---

103 Jean-Luc Chappey, *Des naturalistes en Révolution: les procès-verbaux de la Société d'histoire naturelle de Paris (1790–1798)* (Paris, 2009).

104 James McCLellan III, 'Un manuscrit inédit de Condorcet : sur l'utilité des académies', *Revue d'histoire des sciences*, 30 (1977), 241–253. A.F. Delandine, De la conservation et de l'utilité politique des sociétés littéraires dans les départements, Paris, 1791, 4–5.

CHAPTER 3

Asymmetries of Symbolic Capital in Seventeenth-century Scientific Transactions: Placentinus's Cometary Correspondence with Hevelius and Lubieniecki

Pietro Daniel Omodeo

'Symbolic capital is a credit; it is the power granted to those who have obtained sufficient recognition to be in a position to impose recognition'.[1] Epistolary correspondence in the early modern period functioned as a powerful means of accreditation, formation and reinforcement of group identity, and evidenced individuals' ranking within the scholarly community. According to Pierre Bourdieu's understanding of social space, relational, social and physical closeness ought to be accurately distinguished from one another. In fact, *immediately visible* interactions within a physical (e.g. geographical) space do not reveal social proximity. The latter depends on shared 'properties' (positions and functions) of agents, i.e. groups or institutions within a topology of (material and symbolic) distribution of resources. Early modern correspondence networks were purposely aimed at making elites' proximity *visible* despite spatial distances. They especially paraded connections between powerful patrons and personalities of high status and recognition. To a historian, indeed, such ostentation has become more visible than the elusive reality of personal 'confabulatory' exchanges, as the former is well documented, while the latter is not.[2] Therefore, the historian's eye reverses the sociological relation of visibility and invisibility. Scientific correspondence and the paratexts of printed books (such as dedicatory letters and laudatory poems) offer direct access to early modern networks (or at least, to their celebration), whilst scholars' immediate environment often disappears. Scholars' collaborators, their families and the people with whom they interacted on a daily basis only fragmentally reappear through indirect sources or archival materials.[3]

---

[1] Pierre Bourdieu, 'Social Space and Symbolic Power', *Sociological Theory* 7 (1989), 14–25, 23.
[2] See Mordechai Feingold, 'Confabulatory Life', in *Duncan Liddel (1561–1613), Networks of Polymathy and the Northern European Renaissance*, ed. Pietro D. Omodeo with Karin Friedrich (Leiden, 2016), 22–34.
[3] The problem of reconstructing the world of those who 'cannot speak' has been addressed many times in historiography. It is the *fil rouge* of Carlo Ginzurg's studies on the Inquisition

Early modern epistolary transactions reveal a particular form of social capital, consisting of scholars' access to and positioning within the learned community, their capacity to benefit from connections for their research (e.g., through exchange and acquisition of data) and the ability to mobilize them for fundraising or dispelling scientific controversies. The exchange of letters was the *symbolic* representation of the *social* positioning on the level of legitimization and recognition. It indeed qualified as an exchange of credit with an economic and cultural bearing.[4] In the system of early modern scholarship, such symbolic capital was unevenly distributed and negotiated within a complex transnational and often cross-confessional system of diplomatic relations, courtly patronage, academic affiliations and university appurtenance.

As a paradigmatic case, Erasmus of Rotterdam fully deployed the symbolic power of correspondence as early as the beginning of the sixteenth century. Deliberately setting himself at the centre of a Europe-wide editorial and epistolary network, the celebrated humanist distributed his letters, advice and cultural credits to powerful people, peers, pupils and admirers. His tireless efforts to weave a web of contacts and relationships was aimed at establishing a *respublica literarum* the appurtenance to which implied adherence to values such as humanist literacy, scientific solidarity and anti-dogmatic tolerance.[5] However, the ambiguity and difficult implementation of such ethos was to sharply emerge from confessional divisions entering late-humanist controversies, from 1550 to 1650, at a time of *Konfessionalisierung* in which learned networks opposed one another.[6] Stability could be granted to networks only by backing up symbolic exchanges through institutionalized hubs, especially in the form of academies. The social power (or, if one prefers, *social capital*) descending

---

and witchcraft in capital works of micro-history such as *I benandanti: Ricerche sulla stregoneria e sui culti agrari tra Cinquecento e Seicento* (1966) and *Il formaggio e i vermi: Il cosmo di un mugnaio del '500* (1976). On the 'invisible' technicians of early modern experimental philosophy, see Steven Shapin, 'The Invisible Technician', *American Scientist* 77/6 (1989), 554–563. On professorial household, see Elizabeth Harding, *Der Gelehrte im Haus: Ehe, Familie und Haushalt als Standeskultur an der protestantischen Landesuniversität Helmstedt* (Wiesbaden, 2014).

4   According to Bourdieu, 'Social Space and Symbolic Power', 21, symbolic capital can be seen as 'economic or cultural capital, when it is known and recognized'.

5   Cf. Christoph Galle, *Hodie nullus – cras maximus: Berühmtwerden und Berühmtsein im frühen 16. Jahrhundert am Beispiel des Erasmus von Rotterdam* (Münster, 2013). Also see Pietro Daniel Omodeo and Enrico Pasini, 'Erasmian Science', introductory essay to 'Erasmian Science: The Influence of Erasmus of Rotterdam on Early-Modern Science', *Journal of Interdisciplinary History of Ideas* 6 (2014), 2:1–2:19.

6   The point is clearly stated in Martin Mulsow, 'Netzwerke gegen Netzwerke: Polemik und Wissensproduktion im politischen Antiquarianismus um 1600', in id., *Die unanständige Gelehrtenrepublik: Wissen, Libertinage und Kommunikation in der Frühen Neuzeit* (Stuttgart, 2007), 143–190, at 148–149.

from connectedness was continued, symbolically, through 'exchanges' of letters alongside books, instruments, data, and – most importantly in this respect – recognition.

In the Gutenberg era, the possibility to publish letters or large epistolary collections offered unprecedented opportunities to deploy strategies of co-optation and exclusion at the corporate level, as well as of self-fashioning and discrediting of adversaries at the level of individual career strategies. Late sixteenth-century printed collections of scientific letters are a clear witness to the double agenda of both disseminating scientific views and of acquiring and conferring prestige in the eyes of the scholarly community. One could suitably mention the Renaissance mathematician and physicist Giovanni Battista Benedetti, who published a miscellanea of scientific epistles as one of the most extensive sections (and the concluding one) of his *Diversarum speculationum mathematicarum et physicarum liber* (Turin, 1585). These letters, known as *Physica et mathematica responsa per epistolas* (*Epistolary Answers on Physics and Mathematics*), constituted a heterogeneous collection on various issues, ranging from geometry to astronomy, meteorology, geography and philosophy. It was organized according to the rank of the addressees: the first letters in the collection were those directed to the Dukes of Savoy, of whom Benedetti was a courtier, as well as to the highest Turin dignitaries, followed by professors, scholars and courtiers whose social position was seen as less important.[7] Another example is the publication of the scientific correspondence by the Danish astronomer Tycho Brahe. In his *Epistolarum astronomicarum libri* (*Books of Astronomical Letters*) (Uraniburg, 1596) his concern with prestige and status recognition is manifest. Coming from a family of noble lineage himself, Brahe gave prominence to epistles directed at aristocrats rather than to those addressing 'simple' professors or courtiers. He allowed his correspondence with the patron of sciences Landgrave Wilhelm IV of Hessen-Kassel to appear prominently, at the expense of acknowledging his *actual* scientific correspondent in Kassel, the court mathematician Christoph Rothmann.[8] Brahe also used this publication to attack adversaries, most notably the imperial mathematician to Rudolph II, Nicolaus Reimarus Ursus, whom he accused of plagiarizing his geo-heliocentric planetary hypothesis. As this famous *querelle* shows, epistles could escape the control of their senders.

---

[7] Giovanni Battista Benedetti, *Diversarum speculationum mathematicarum et physicarum liber* (Taurini, 1585), Book Six. Cf. Michela Cecchini and Clara Silvia Roero, 'I corrispondenti di Giovanni Battista Benedetti', *Physis* 41 (2004), 31–66.

[8] Cf. Adam Mosley, *Bearing the Heavens: Tycho Brahe and the Astronomical Community of the Late Sixteenth Century* (Chicago, 1993). On Rothmann: *Christoph Rothmann's Discourse on the Comet of 1585. An Edition and Translation with Accompanying Essays*, by Miguel Ángel Granada, Adam Mosley and Nicholas Jardine, (Leiden-Boston, 2014).

For instance, at the climax of the polemic, Ursus published a deferential and flattering letter he had received from the young mathematician Johannes Kepler, who was in search of an employment in Prague. The fact that this epistle appeared, without permission of its author, in the opening of a book including a fierce attack against Brahe created many problems for Kepler, as he then had to apologize to Brahe, one of the most prominent astronomers and patrons of astronomy of the time.[9]

The seventeenth century offers a wide range of examples of epistolary webs in which key personalities acted as networkers, promoters and circulators of knowledge, as was the case with figures such as Marin Mersenne, Athanasius Kircher, Ismael Boulliau or Samuel Hartlib, to name only some of the most distinguished. All of them exchanged letters with Johannes Hevelius, whose large correspondence network has not been entirely published and is yet to be adequately studied.[10] Another important correspondent of his, the secretary of the Royal Society, Henry Oldenbourg, developed an editorial project called the *Philosophical Transactions*, which contributed to the transformation of the epistolary genre into the prototype of journal communication. An important accomplishment of his generation was the creation of new platforms for communication, including the *Journal des Sçavants* and the *Acta eruditorum*, both of which were closely related to the activities and exchanges of newly-founded scientific academies. Their transactions were said to have taken place in a sort of *terra Franca* extending over and beyond confessional barriers even during the worst religious wars. Such intentions contributed to the creation of the myth of a literary republic ruled by egalitarian ideals of respect and solidarity in the name of objectivity and impartiality. This myth often disguised or mystified a much less idyllic reality, one that was marked instead by asymmetrical access to and possibility of mobilization of the symbolic capital descending from the appurtenance to this community. In this essay, I will explore such asymmetries exemplified in the epistolary exchanges on the comets of the 1660s that took place between three Polish scholars: the heterodox Cartesian Johannes Placentinus; Johannes Hevelius, who was a professor of mathematics at Frankfurt on Oder, protégé of the Brandenburg Prince; and Stanisław Lubieniecki, a wealthy Gdańsk entrepreneur and astronomer, a member of the Royal Society and an aristocratic Socinian émigré in Hamburg.

---

9   Nicholas Jardine, *The Birth of the History and Philosophy of Science* (Cambridge, 1984), in particular Chap. 1, 'The Circumstances of the Composition', 9ff.

10 For general considerations on the challenges of an edition of Hevelius's correspondence, see Chantal Grell and Patricia Radelet-De-Grave, 'Un projet: L'edition de la correspondence d'Hevelius (1611–1687)', *Archives Internationales d'Histoire des Sciences* 60/2–165, (2010), 423–428.

1 Hevelius's Indiscreet Correspondent, Placentinus

Johannes Hevelius cultivated one of the widest correspondence networks of his time. From the publication of his *Selenographia* (1647) onwards, he kept copies of all of his letters alongside the originals of those he received. Over the years, he gathered an impressive collection of letters to and from the most prominent people of the time, including kings and first-rank politicians, scientists affiliated to the *Académie de France* and the Royal Society, university professors, Jesuit scientists, diplomats and courtiers. About 2,800 epistles are preserved; Hevelius intended to publish them as part of his ambitious scientific and editorial projects, but was hindered by a fire that destroyed his house, observatory and printing press in 1679.

As Chantal Grell has recently stressed, Hevelius's correspondence mirrors a European *réseau* initially directed to secure his contacts with London, Paris and Florence and later re-centred in the Baltic and German area.[11] Hevelius's relations with Paris and the French court were mediated by a loyal friend, Ismael Boulliau. Boulliau introduced him to the '*grand maître des pensions royales*', Jean Chapelain, who in turn won Hevelius the favour of Jean-Baptiste Colbert and Louis XIV. Another Frenchman, Pierre des Noyers – a pupil of Roberval and secretary to the queen of Poland Maria-Luisa Gonzaga – constantly exchanged letters with him and safeguarded his interests in the Polish court. Hevelius's contacts in Tuscany and with the short-lived *Accademia del Cimento* mainly consist of correspondence with the protector of sciences, Leopoldo de' Medici, with whom he exchanged letters from the early 1660s to the mid-1670s. Moreover, he had close relations with many British scholars, especially Henry Oldenbourg, thanks to whom he could steadily publish in the *Philosophical Transactions*. The Polish aristocrat and diplomat Stanisław Lubieniecki in Hamburg was Hevelius's key to the wide Baltic network. In Germany, his Leipzig connections, in particular the mathematician Christoph Pfautz, co-secretary of the *Acta Eruditorum*, secured Hevelius's publications in this learned journal.[12]

Hevelius's epistolary exchange with Johannes Placentinus is only a fragment of his large correspondence, Placentinus being a 'lesser figure'. Throughout the 1650s, this Polish Cartesian from Leszno had struggled to affirm his

---

11 Chantal Grell, 'Hevelius en son temps', in *Correspondance de Johannes Hevelius*, vol. 1, *Prolégomènes critiques*, ed. Chantal Grell (Turnhout, 2014), 75–89.
12 Klaus-Dieter Herbst, 'Hevelius' Correspondence with Scholars in Leipzig', in *Studia Copernicana* XLIV, *Johannes Hevelius and His World: Astronomer, Cartographer, Philosopher and Correspondent*, ed. Richard L. Kremer and Jarosław Włodarczyk (Warsaw, 2013), 201–212.

philosophical views against peripatetic Lutheran censors at the University of Frankfurt on Oder. In 1656 the protector of the university, Friedrich Wilhelm of Brandenburg, had sanctioned Placentinus's *libertas philosophica* by appointing him as court mathematician.[13] Galvanized by such a legitimation, Placentinus started an intense phase of publications and research activity. Regrettably, his career was tragically interrupted at the beginning of 1666, when his mental health was cast into doubt and as a consequence he was placed under house arrest, and his wife and daughters were taken from him. These events excluded him from public and academic life. In spite of these tragic circumstances, as we will see, he still had the will to continue his intellectual activity in the first phase of his reclusion.[14]

The remaining proof of correspondence between him and Hevelius consists of eight letters exchanged between 1659 and 1665. Seven of them are handwritten and preserved in the Paris Observatory. One more letter was printed by Placentinus in a booklet on the stormy winds of winter 1660/1661, *Physicalischer und Astrologischer Bericht von denen erschrecklichen...Winden* (*Physical and Astrological Report on the Frightening... Winds*, Frankfurt/Oder, 1661).[15]

In the first letter (Gdańsk, 3 December 1659), Hevelius asked Placentinus's support in finding a talented mathematician (*ein studiosus mathematum*) ready to move to Gdańsk to help as his assistant. The tone of the epistle is cordial. It begins by mentioning a personal meeting in Gdańsk: 'I remember with *pleasure* the honour and friendship that You once bestowed on me, when You visited me during one of your travels and You offered me Your devoted service'.[16] Acquaintance is the basis upon which a durable connection could be implemented. 'Personal meetings [...] – as has been observed relative to the development of

---

13   Pietro Daniel Omodeo, 'Central European Polemics over Descartes: Johannes Placentinus and His Academic Opponents at Frankfurt on Oder (1653–1656)', *History of Universities* 29/1 (2016), 29–64.

14   The details of these events and the reasons for these extreme measures against Placentinus are obscure in many respects. The most significant documents have been summarized in a recent publication by Andrea Lehmann, '"Nun ist wohl keiner bey dieser Stadt, so den traurigen Zustandt gedachten Placentini nicht von Herzen solte Beklagen". Tragisches Ende der Karriere des Mathematikprofessors Johannes Placentini', *Jahresbericht/ Forschungsstelle für Vergleichende Universitätsgeschichte (Frankfurt/Oder)* 6 (2011), 40–56.

15   Placentinus, *Physicalischer und Astrologischer Bericht von denen erschrecklichen...Winden* (Franckfurt an der Oder, 1661), ff. E3r-E4r.

16   Hevelius to Placentinus (Gdańsk, 3 December 1659), Bibilothéque de l'Observatoire, Paris (from now onwards abbreviated as OP), coll. BO, vol. 4, n. 555, [1r]: 'Ich erinnere mich billig, die Ehr und freündlikeit die er mir erwiesen, wie er eines mahles im durchreisen mich ersuchete, imgleichen der anerbietung seiner willigen dienste'.

scholarly networks in the early-modern period – established the weak ties upon which correspondence could be established'.[17] A scholar like Hevelius, being at the centre of many such 'weak ties', was in the most favourable position for gathering information and disseminating his ideas.[18]

The rest of Hevelius's first letter to Placentinus is devoted to discussing the appointment of a suitable assistant. The candidate is accurately described: He should be a pious and decent person (*der absonderlich eines gutten frommen und sitsamen habens und verhaltens were*) with a clear predisposition to mathematical studies. He should already be well versed in astronomy, be acquainted at least with planetary theory and be able to make astronomical computations of planetary motions. Moreover, the successful candidate should have good eyesight, in order to observe the smallest stars.[19] The position would last for one year, granted the person meets Hevelius's expectations. He would live in the astronomer's house (*behausung*), have a desk (*einen freyen tisch*) and receive a fair salary (*ein billiges honorarium*). He would be introduced to the use of the astronomical instruments in Hevelius's observatory and be free to improve his scholarship to his own advantage. His duty would be to assist the observational campaigns at night (*er sonsten nicht anders würde zu thun haben als des nachts mir helffen observiren*) and make calculations (*rechnen u. calculiren*).

The next handwritten letter was by Placentinus. It was penned on 25 March 1661, according to the old calendar used in protestant Brandenburg (corresponding to 4 April on the Gregorian calendar). He started by thanking Hevelius for sharing his cometary and celestial observations with him. Placentinus added that they had arrived at the moment in which he was publishing a booklet on the stormy winds of 1660/1661. In his opinion, the winds had been generated by the comet that Hevelius had recently observed. Hence, he had taken the opportunity to print Hevelius's letter as a confirmation of his own natural views:

> I would like to thank You, very erudite Sir, in the most devoted manner for the most desired report on the new comet. I received it in the most convenient moment, as the printer was just beginning to print my small

---

17 David S. Lux and Harold J. Cook, 'Closed Circles or Open Networks? Communicating at a Distance during the Scientific Revolution', *History of Science* 36 (1998), 179–211, at 191. The authors draw on Mark S. Granowetter, 'The Strength of Weak Ties', *American Journal of Sociology* 78 (1973), 105–130.
18 Ibid, 182.
19 Hevelius to Placentinus (Gdańsk, 3 December 1659), [1r]: 'insonderheit aber ein gutt gesicht haben in die fern zusehen, damit er die kleinen fixas wol möchte discernieren können'.

treatise on the frightening and unusual winds. Also, this beloved letter reinforces my theory; therefore I printed it in it and hope that my very erudite Sir will have nothing against it.[20]

It is clear that Placentinus tried to take advantage of Hevelius's credit, as one of the most admired astronomers of the time, and exploit the correspondence with him to strengthen his own position and the value of the theses expounded in the booklet *Physikalischer und Astrologischer Bericht von denen erschrecklichen...Winden*. Hevelius's letter (Gdańsk, 2 March 1661) dealt with celestial singularities observed that year: a comet, a nova and a spectacular parhelion ('seven suns'). Placentinus explained to his correspondent that this information was very precious to him, as he had not been able to observe the comet from the very beginning (*weil ich den Comet nicht vom anfang gemercket*) and he had not seen the nova in the constellation of Cetus at all (*die Fixam in Ceto habe auch nicht observiert*). He complained that he had no astronomical observatory but announced that the Electoral Prince of Brandenburg would fund one and endow it with the necessary instruments; but he added a precautionary note: 'whether this will happen, only time can tell' (*ob es aber wird geschehen, lehret die zeit*).

Placentinus also briefly reported his main theses. According to him, the comet had been generated from the nova and this, in turn, provoked the devastating winds of 1660/1661. He reassured Hevelius that his views were firmly grounded in Cartesian principles. Accordingly, he could also foretell that the nova would reappear, although he could not determine its exact position due to the lack of observational data. On this account, he required Hevelius to send accurate data concerning the dimensions of the nova and its exact coordinates.

> I am ready to affirm that the newly disappeared star will reappear, not least because this is in agreement with Descartes's principles and hypotheses. I am of the opinion that the comet originated from this new star. From its motion and duration one can determine [...] when it will reappear, but I am not able to determine where. Therefore, I kindly request You

---

20   Placentinus to Hevelius (Frankfurt on Oder, 25 March/4 April 1661), PO, coll. BO, vol. 5, n. 665, [f. 1r]: 'Wegen der gewünschten Nachricht von newlichem Comet, bedanke ich mich gegen meinen hochgelehrte herrn dienstfreundlichst, welche mir zu rechter Zeit ist wol worden da der buchdrucker hatt angefangen zu drucken mein kleines tractätlein von denen erschrecklichen und ungewöhnlichen winden; und weil im vielgeliebte brief meine Meinung bekräfftiget, habe ich denselben auch dabey drucken laßen, hoffe daß er meinem Hochgehrten herrn nicht wird inwider seyn'.

for more information, in particular on how big the fixed star was and where in Cetus [...].[21]

Placentinus also asked for more details on the parhelion (*wegen der 7 sonnen bitte ich umb einen außfuhrliche bericht*) and he proposed to share his observations of a recent solar eclipse in exchange. His tone is self-assured. He relies on the friendship with Hevelius (*große freundschafft*) and shows interest in Gdańsk's scientific life, asking whether Leurentius Eichsted's former position as chair of mathematics at the Gymnasium had been given to somebody after his death. He himself had attended the school in 1648.[22]

Hevelius found Placentinus's publication indiscreet. Judging from the tone of his response on 5 July 1661, he was irritated. Formally, he was polite; he even apologized for his delayed answer. However, he expressed his disappointment for the decision to publish his letter without permission:

> Although I am grateful to You for the small tract on the winds, nonetheless I would *have not given my consent* to You, my *dear Sir*, to publish my writing immediately after its reception without my knowledge and approval, as I wrote it in a rapid and confuse manner and did not finish it. In fact, if it had been intended for publication, it should have had a different form. Moreover, if I had wished to announce something about the comet or the new star at that point, I would have done it myself. The motto to follow here is 'sat cito si sat bene' [quick enough if well enough], therefore one should better not expose oneself with unfinished things.[23]

---

21 Ibid, [f. 1v]: 'Daß der newe verschwundene stern vom newen widerumb erscheinen werde, gebe ich gerne zu, weil es auch mit denen *principiis* und *hypothesibus Cartesii* ubereinkomt: und halte dafür, daß der Comet auß diesem Nowem stern entstanden, auß deßen *motu* und *duratione* man auch *praeter propter* die zeit zvar aber ich nicht den ort da er wiederumb erscheinen werde derminiren können. Bitte derowegen umb fernere nachricht, wie groß die Fixa gewesen, und wo sie im Ceto gestanden [...]'.

22 *Catalogus Discipulorum Gymnasii Gedanensis (1508–1814)*, ed. Zbigniew Nowak and Przemysław Szafran (Warsaw/Poznań, 1972), 161. Also, see Omodeo, 'The Scientific Culture of the Baltic Mathematician, Physician and Calendar-Maker Laurentius Eichstadt (1596–1660)', *Journal for the History of Astronomy* 48 (2017), 1–25.

23 Hevelius to Placentinus (Gdańsk, 5 July 1661), PO, Coll. BO, vol. 5, n. 666, [f. 1r]: 'Für das tractatlein von den winden bedanke ich mich zwar freundtlich; ich hette mich aber nicht *versehen* gehabt, daß der Herr meinen in aller eyll *confus* geschriebenen Schrift, den ich zu dem ende nicht geschrieben, noch ubergeschickt, solte alsbaldt ohn meine wißen und willen drucken laßen. Den wann er hette sollen gedruckt werden, hette er woll könnnen anders auch müßen sein. Dazu hette ich von dem *Comet*en oder newen stern etwas noch Zur Zeit kundt thun wollen hette ich es woll selbsten vorrichtet; uber dieses drucket mich *sat cito si sat bene*, und mit unfertigen dingen ists besser Zu Hauß geblieben'.

After this complaint about the hasty publication of his letter, Hevelius criticized and even mocked Placentinus's competency and assumptions. He claimed to be completely unsurprised that the latter had not observed the nova: this was certainly due to his rushed methods. He accused Placentinus of looking at ephemerides rather than at the heavens (*coelo Stellato*). The new star shone brightly, he insisted, and no astronomical observatory was necessary to see it, but rather application and sufficient knowledge of the sky. Hevelius stressed to his correspondent that many celestial phenomena pass unperceived if one is not familiar with the stars.[24] He did not address Placentinus's post-Cartesian theory of the generation of comets from stars but assured that he did not agree with it. In later writings on comets, he would argue that comets were generated from the exhalations of the outer planets.[25]

In the last part of the caustic letter of July 1661, Hevelius appeared more conciliatory. He reported that he had observed Mercurius' transit on the solar disc on 3 May and asked Placentinus whether he or anybody he knew had succeeded in capturing this event. Probably nobody, he bitterly remarked, since he knew of no calendar-maker who mentioned it, despite its intrinsic astronomical interest and the fact that it could be easily forecast.[26] Hevelius alluded again to Placentinus's incapability to stand out from the ordinary.

Placentinus and Hevelius's correspondence is two-sided. As can be seen, the exchange could turn either into a form of credit or discredit and into a means of inclusion or exclusion from the learned community. 'Exchange transforms the things exchanged into signs of recognition and, through the mutual recognition and the recognition of group members which it implies, reproduces the group. By the same token, it reaffirms the limits of the group [...]. Each member of the group is thus instituted as custodian of the limits of the group'.[27] Whereas Placentinus seized the opportunity to use his correspondence with Hevelius to gain a better reputation, Hevelius feared that his name could be tarnished if his letters were abusively employed for aims that went beyond his intentions. Hence, Hevelius did not only complain but also made himself a guardian of scientific standards casting doubt onto Placentinus's methods and assumptions. His negative judgment addressed both Placentinus's behaviour and his research activity, thus questioning his credibility. This was a threat to Placentinus's recognition in the *respublica literarum*, of which Hevelius was a

---

24   Ibid.
25   Cf. Donald K. Yeomans, *Comets: A Chronological History of Observation, Science, Myth, and Folklore* (New York, 1991), 82–87.
26   Ibid, [ff. 1r-v].
27   Pierre Bourdieu, 'Ökonomisches Kapital, kulturelles Kapital, soziales Kapital', *Soziale Ungleichheiten*, 2nd special issue of *Soziale Welt* (1983), 183–198, 250.

very reputable member. As a matter of fact, Placentinus was damaged by his own impulsivity: he would not regain Hevelius's respect. His apologetic reply is still extant (a letter from 29 July/8 August 1661), but it is in such bad condition that I was not able to decipher it. Still, it is apparent from the readable fragments that it readdressed the controversial issues: the rushed publication of Hevelius's observations, comets, the position of the nova and his academic duties, which left him no time for regular starry observations.[28]

A few years later, in January 1665, Placentinus wrote to Hevelius again in order to communicate his observations of the presently shining comet, expecting in return Hevelius's data. Placentinus's diagram showing the position and trajectory of the comet along with the table of the positions are preserved with the epistle. With his usual straightforwardness and lack of tact, Placentinus urged Hevelius to procure him a telescope as soon as possible, as he needed it to make closer observations of the phenomenon. He assured Hevelius that his patron, the Prince of Brandenburg, would cover the costs. Moreover, since the fame of Hevelius's *Cometographia* had reached Frankfurt, he requested a copy of the work:

> To my most revered Sir, I send herewith my limited observation of the current comet, which has been taken by means of a quadrant with a radius of six feet [6 *schuh*]. Also, I kindly request You to communicate to me Your observations in return. If possible, would You be able to send me a good telescope [*Tubum Opticum*]? My most serene Lord, the Electoral Prince, will reimburse You the costs. I would be very thankful if You were able to provide a quick response, so that I can continue to observe the comet as I did yesterday.[29]

Before receiving Hevelius's response, Placentinus sent him another message on 30 January/9 February 1665. It contained a revised table of observations and

---

28 Placentinus to Hevelius (29 July/8 August 1661), PO, coll. BO, vol. 5, n. 680.
29 Placentinus to Hevelius (Frankfurt on Oder, 16/26 January 1665), PO, coll. BO, vol. 6, n. 925: 'Meinem Hochgeehrten Herrn uberschicke ich hiemit meine geringe observation des itzigen Cometen welcher verrichtet wurden auf einem quadrante, deßen radius 6 schuh lang ist, und bitte mir auch dessen observationes reciproce zucommunicieren und wo möglich mir einen gutten großen Tubum Opticum zukommen laßen. S. Churfl. Durchl. mein Gnädigster Herr pp. werden die[...] kosten erstatten; Bitte sehr umb schleunige antwort, damit ich ferner im Comet observiren könne welchen ich auch gestern gemachet habe'.

a request to ignore the earlier one, as it contained mistakes. His request for a telescope was reiterated.[30]

Hevelius's response was quick; it was actually a brief note, hastily written on 6 February 1665. It did not meet the expectations of the feverish Placentinus in any respect. Hevelius refused to pass on his observations since he had yet not finished his study of the comet. As to the *Cometographia*, it was still a work in progress. Therefore, Placentinus should patiently wait until its completion. Thirdly, Hevelius made him notice that his time was too precious to construct telescopes for others. If Placentinus wished to buy one, he should look elsewhere:

> Thank You very much for the cometary observations that You, Sir, have sent me. My own are provisional and are not ready to be transcribed, therefore those who desire to see them should wait until my *Cometography* or *History* about this comet is complete. I consider my time too precious to prepare good telescopes of the length of two feet and give them to others. Besides, You can request one from Augsburg, if You have 100 or 150 ducats to spend. I also bought such one.[31]

Far from being applauded by Hevelius, Placentinus had become an unwelcome correspondent and was accordingly marginalized within his own network of correspondents.

2 Hevelius's Precarious Position in the Republic of Letters

Hevelius refused to give Placentinus his observations of the comets of 1664 and 1665 for several reasons. First, he must have been highly disappointed in Placentinus's use of his earlier letter; second, the lack of deference on Placentinus's

---

30 Placentinus to Hevelius (Frankfurt on Oder, 30 January/9 February 1665), PO, coll. BO, vol. 6, n. 927.

31 Hevelius to Placentinus (Gdańsk, 6 February 1665), PO, coll. BO, vol. 6, n. 926: 'Für des Hr uberschickte observation des Cometen bedancke ich mich; meine viel sie steh weitleuffig und verdeißlich abzuschreiben, also müßen die liebhaber sich gedulden biß meine Cometographia, oder Historia zum wenigsten dieses Cometen verfertiget. 2 Fuße lange und gutte Tubos opticos selbsten zuverfertigen und anderen uberszulaßen, dazu habe ich meine Zeit viel zu kostbahr. Unterdessen kan der Hr von Augspurg gar wol einen bekommen, wenn er wil 100 oder 150 ducaten spendiren; dergleichen ich selbsten einen gekaufft'. Hevelius owned an Augsburg telescope made by Johann Wiessl, which went lost in the fire of his house-observatory in 1679.

side did not make him well-disposed toward him; third, he was investing great energy in editorial projects on comet observations and theory in order to secure himself the protection and the financial aid of princely patrons such as the King of France and, to a lesser extent, Leopoldo de' Medici. Moreover, he probably did not want to be associated with Placentinus's speculative approach to cosmology nor with his fervent Cartesianism. His dissatisfaction with Placentinus can be seen by comparing the harsh tone of his reply to Placentinus's requests with the cordial one he used in exchanges with Stanisław Lubieniecki on the same subject.[32]

Lubieniecki was an aristocratic diplomat and Socinian pastor, who had abandoned Poland in the events following the Swedish invasion, particularly the prohibition and ban of his faith from Poland in 1658. He had first sought refuge in Stettin and later in Copenhagen from 1660 to 1662. Hindered by orthodox censors and in search of a place where he could freely practice his religion, he moved to Hamburg and Altona where he was eventually poisoned, probably for his political and religious positions, and died together with two of his daughters. Among others, he also served as a political correspondent to the king of France, informing the king about the events in northern Europe. The appearance of the comet of 1664 inspired him to write to a wide range of more or less prominent scientists of the time in order to gather observations and comments, which he would finally publish in a collected volume entitled *Theatrum cometicum* in 1668.[33]

On this occasion, Lubieniecki also began corresponding with Hevelius. On 9/19 December 1664, he addressed him in an extremely polite manner, starting with a *captatio benevolentiae* and a mention of their common friendship with Boulliau:

> My most sincere congratulations to You, whom I know not only for Your highest repute all over the world but also for Your image and your most distinguished writings (through which You enlighten Astronomy, that loftiest part of philosophy), to which I should add the study of the most humane letters as well as my wide correspondence with erudite friends. Like me, my erudite friends admire your most celebrated virtues, especially your unique humanity alongside your excellence in astronomical science. However, I hope that the epistolary exchange with You, which I

---

32   Stanislai de Lubienietz, *Theatrum cometicum* (Amstelodami, 1668) I 8 'Communicatio Gedano-Heveliana', 361–414.
33   See Volker Weidemann, *Theatrum cometicum: Hamburg und Kiel im Zeichen der Kometen von 1664 und 1665* (Hamburg, 1987), esp. 35–36.

desire and I wish for myself in light of your humanity, will not constitute a burden and an annoyance for You, who are busy with other and more serious enquiries and occupations. You know what ties bind the lovers of the good letters. It must be evident to You, most illustrious man! It could be arranged in such a manner that, as far as Your serious occupations and lofty studies make it possible, You tie with me through the most loyal literary bond – and this will be automatically extended to the very illustrious Ismael Boulliau, a singular and very honest friend of mine as well as Yours. I cultivate a constant correspondence with him (as testified by the transcription of past epistles hereby included). Therefore, if You wish to join this [correspondence] or, as I believe, You already access and practice it, I offer you to take care of the mutual work, an effort that will certainly be most loyal to you.[34]

After this rhetorical introduction, Lubieniecki proposed to act as a mediator between Hevelius and other scholars in Hamburg and elsewhere, in order to establish a fruitful scientific exchange discussing the new comet. The attempt was successful; Hevelius replied positively and started the exchange.

In fact, the growing interest in the comets of 1664 and 1665 among scholars all over Europe, beginning with Lubieniecki and the many publications on the subject, forced Hevelius to anticipate his results and to quickly publish his views on the subject. He had already begun the ambitious composition of the *Cometographia*, a *magnus opus* on comets that was intended to repeat the success of the *Selenographia*. This volume was not complete when the new comets appeared and Hevelius decided to preliminarily publish the introduction of

---

34   Ibid., 361, Lubieniecki to Hevelius (Hamburg, 9/19 December 1664): 'Te mihi non tantum de fama per Orbem clarissima, sed et de facie ac scriptis tuis egregiis (quibus Astronomiam, illam maxime sublimem Philosophiae partem illustras) notum esse, vehementer gratulor. Tibi pariter ut notus fiam, studium literarum humaniorum, sed et commercium amicarum literarum, quod cum doctis hic illic exerceo, facit. Alliciunt et celebratissime virtutes Tuae, praesertim singulari humanitas, cum insigni et excellenti rei Astronomicae scientia, qua itidem delector, conjuncta. Nolim tamen meum literarum Tecum commercium, quod ambio, et Tua Humanitate mihi polliceor, Tibi aliis, iisque gravioribus, studiis et negotiis occupato, negotium et molestiam facessere. Nosti quae vincula viros literarum bonarum amantes conjugant. Patere itaque et Tu, Vir Clarissime! Tibi haec aptari, ut quantum per seria Tua negotia et sublimia studia licebit, mecum fido literarum vinculum jungaris, et sic etiam Clarissimo Ismaeili Bullialdo, Amico meo juxtaque Tuo singulari et integerrimo. Cum quo cum assiduum literarum colam commercium (quod et nuperae epistolae exscriptum exemplum huic adjunctum docet) si et Tu idem desideres vel, quod potius credo, possideas et exerceas, offero Tibi meam qualemcunque in literis mutuo curandis operam, fidam certe te industriam'.

his cometary work. This introduction, entitled *Prodromus cometicus* (1665), was dedicated to Jean Baptiste Colbert, 'councillor of the very Christian King among the most saint ones and highest treasurer of France' (Regis Christianissimi a sanctioribus consilius, summusque Galliarum aerarii moderator). Beginning in 1663, he had received a pension from Louis XIV through Colbert, and this publication aimed to strengthen his ties with his French benefactors. Hevelius's desire to be recognized within the Paris scientific élite is clear from his dedication of the *Prodromus* to Colbert:

> Very Illustrious and Excellent *Sir*,
> My soul has been encouraged to dare offering these modest pages of mine to Your eyes in consideration that You, the most Illustrious and Excellent, showed such great benevolence and singular favour toward me and my Uranic enquiries that goes beyond all merits and even beyond any hope and expectation of mine. You went so far as to kindly recommending me to the very Christian King so that he judges me worthy of being included among those who benefit from the holy royal clemency and protection.[35]

On 13 May 1665, Hevelius sent Lubieniecki a copy of the *Prodromus*, which Lubieniecki welcomed and later summarized in the *Theatrum cometicum*.[36]

The French reactions to the *Prodromus* were not as positive as Lubieniecki's. The mathematician Adrien Azout dedicated an *Ephéméride du comète* (1665) to the King in the hope that he would be appointed among the first members of the *Académie des Sciences*. He and Hevelius had opposing views on the nature of comets. While Hevelius considered comets to be ephemeral phenomena with elusive spiral trajectories, Azout deemed them to be stable cosmic objects endowed with regular and predictable motions. He and his associate Pierre Petit started a polemic casting doubt upon the accuracy of Hevelius's observations. What was at stake here was not only theory. In fact, it was particularly important for Hevelius to gain recognition in Paris during the time of the establishment of the *Académie des Sciences*, when inclusion implied a

---

35 Johannes Hevelius, *Prodromus cometicus* (Gedani, 1665), dedication: 'Illustrissime ac Excellentissime Domine. Summa Illustrissimae Excellentiae Tuae benevolentia, atque singularis benignitas, qua me meaque qualia Studia Uranica, praeter omne meritum, imo spem meam atque expectatione, prosequeris, usque adeo, ut etiam Christianissimo Regi inter eos, quos Sacra Reg. M. Sua Regali Clementia, ac Protectione dignos iudicavit, me intime commendaveris, animo addidit, ut non verear hasce pagellas Tuis sujicere oculis'.
36 Ibid., 388 ff.

'redistribution of credit within a group under the king's direct control'.[37] The institutional shift produced much clamour and fostered competition.

The polemic with Azout developed through letters, publications and articles in the *Philosophical Transactions* and the *Journal des Sçavants*, and involved members of both the London Society and the emerging Paris *Académie*. The polemicists eventually asked for the arbitrage of the Royal Society, of which Hevelius had been a member since 1664. Nonetheless, the verdict – communicated to him by Oldenbourg on 24 January 1666 – dispelled the controversy in favour of the French party. The consequences were fatal for Hevelius: his prestige declined in London and was irreparably damaged in Paris. In contrast, Azout was appointed both as a member of the *Académie* and as a fellow of the Royal Society.[38] Moreover, these events anticipated the most famous polemic with Robert Hook, who castigated Hevelius's observational methods, in particular his refusal to use telescopic pointers for measuring stellar positions.[39]

In the course of the polemics, Hevelius issued a report on the last comet in 1666, *Descriptio cometae anno... 1665 exorti*, alongside an apologetic essay on the comet of 1664, *Mantissa Prodromi cometici*. This double publication was dedicated to Leopoldo de' Medici, whom he addressed as one of his patrons and a protector of the sciences. In the dedicatory letter, Hevelius reminded him of their earlier correspondence and expressed his wishes to be included among the scholars of his entourage:

> Very Serene Prince,
> It has been a while since I noticed that people who are well-known for the glory of their erudition, especially the investigators of the most sublime and abstract doctrines, concurred from all over the world to celebrate and revere Your very serene height. Their tribute was not as much directed to the splendour of the birth as to the outstanding virtues, as

---

[37] Christian Licoppe, *La formation de la pratique scientifique: Le discours de l'expérience en France et en Angleterre (1630–1820)* (Paris, 1996), 72.

[38] Nausicaa Elena Milani, 'The *Prodromus cometicus* in the Académie des Sciences and the Royal Society: The Hevelius-Auzout Controversy' in *Johannes Hevelius and His Gdańsk*, ed. Marian Turek (Gdańsk, 2013), 195–208.

[39] Hooke's *Animadversiones on the First Part of the Machina Coelestis of... Johannes Hevelius* notably appeared in London in 1674 by the printer of the Royal Society, John Martyn. Cf. Voula Saridakis, 'The Hevelius-Hooke Controversy in Context: Transforming Astronomical Practice in the late Seventeenth Century', *Studia Copernicana* XLIV, 103–135. On the epistemological stake, see Ofer Gal and Raz Chen Morris, *Baroque Science* (Chicago, 2013), 101–113.

well as the love and intelligence of the loftiest sciences, which are unusual for a prince and which You have at an incomparable degree, legitimately and according to Your merit. Although I do not belong to those people [gathering around You], I also directed all of my will and enquiries so far to enlighten and possibly augment the astronomical knowledge, therefore I dare to add myself to the other very excellent admirers of Yours by dedicating to Your very serene name myself and that part of my efforts – I mean, my observations of recent comets that I was able to observe with instruments not less apt than others.[40]

In the letter to the reader following the dedication to Leopoldo de' Medici, Hevelius recounted the ongoing controversy over his *Prodromus*. In a sense, he was trying to expand the debate beyond the English-French axis. At that time it was impossible for him to anticipate that Leopoldo's *Accademia del Cimento* would quickly dissolve and could not rival the rise of the London Society and the Paris *Académie*. Hevelius's exclusion from the internal *strong ties* of these new institutions would gradually isolate him from the most important European centres of scholarship from the mid-1660s, throughout the 1670s and onwards. He tried to save his position with the publication of the *Cometographia* in 1668, dedicating it to Louis XIV. In this work, he stubbornly repeated his cometary theory, stressing his distance from the opposing views of the French academicians.

In the course of the following years, Hevelius's private observatory came to be regarded as incapable to accomplish the research that was being conducted at richly funded institutions such as the Paris Observatory (established in 1671) and the Greenwich Observatory (1676). His appointment as a royal astronomer and mathematician to Jan III Sobieski in 1677 did not change his position, nor did it enable him to restore his reputation in the French and British circles. It

---

40   Johannes Hevelius, *Descriptio cometae anno... 1665 exorti* (Gedani, 1666), ff. a2r-v: 'Serenissime Princeps. Jam dudum animarverti, passim Viros eruditionis gloria celebres, imprimis sublimium, et abstrusarum doctrinarum Indagatores, ad cultum et venerationem Serenissimae Celsitudinis Tuae concurrere; non id duntaxat splendori Generis, quam praecipue summis Virtutibus, et sublimiorum Scientiarum amori, aeque ac Intelligentiae, in Principe pene inusitatis, planeque incomparabilibus jure meritoque tribuentes. Quamvis autem ego inter illos recenseri nequeam; cum tamen nec voluntas, nec studium meum illustrandae, et si fieri possit, amplificandae rei Astronomicae hactenus defuerit: audeo jam in eo saltem me adjungere caeteris Excellentissimis Cultoribus Tuis, ut me, atque conatuum meorum partem, observationes videlicet recentiorum Cometarum, quas Organis haud usque adeo inconvenientibus, non minus mihi, quam aliis, feliciter rimari obtigit, Serenissimo Nomini Tuo devoveam'.

was at that time that he shifted the centre of his network to the Baltic and German areas.

The more Hevelius felt marginalized from the French and English academic centres, the more he was compelled to strengthen and emphasize his connections. He had long conceived the project to capitalize these ties on a symbolic level by printing his scientific correspondence. However, in his astronomical works Hevelius seldom named his correspondents. In the *Prodromus* he mentioned a letter by Boulliau on the comet of 1664, in the vain hope that it could help reinforce his connections with the higher spheres in France.[41] Like the *Cometographia*, the *Prodromus* appeared as the product of his own ingenuity and efforts, without much acknowledgment of other contemporary scholars. Thus, although Hevelius strongly relied on his network of contacts and correspondents to promote his research, circulate his works, gather support and acquire patrons, he did not regard the scientific web of the Republic of Letters as fundamental to his scientific achievement. It regarded it instead as an unavoidable measure. In 1679, a fire broke out in his house and observatory, destroying most of his printing house and thus bringing the publication of the correspondence to a halt. Without enough funding or a suitable printer, Hevelius only managed to publish a selection of 197 letters (out of about 2,800 scientific epistles). This was entitled *Excerpta ex literis illustrium virorum* (*A Choice of Letters to Illustrious People*), and was edited by his secretary and relative Johann Erich Olhoff in 1683. It was a sort of '*bouquet de compliments*' comprising letters of gratitude and eulogies by princes, prominent political personalities, diplomats and scientists.[42] It appears more as a form of self-promotion than a scientific epistolary dealing with astronomical matters.[43]

---

41 Id., *Prodromus cometicus*, 42.

42 Grell, 'Hevelius en son temps', 131.

43 Hevelius omitted to mention Placentinus both in these *Excerpta* of his correspondence and in the *Cometographia* – a work that dealt with the comets of 1652, 1661, 1664 and 1665, and comprised theoretical sections on appearances such as color and light, discussed Hevelius's own hypotheses concerning comets' alleged spiral motions as exhalations departing from the outer planets and ended with a chronicle of all comets ever observed by 'historians, philosophers and astronomers'. Placentinus's absence can be ascertained by simply looking at the *Catalogus Autorum quorum mentio fit in hoc Opere* in Hevelius, *Cometogrpahia* (Gedani: Auctoris Typis et Sumptibus, 1668), 'Te mihi non tantum de fama per Orbem clarissima, sed et de facie ac scriptis tuis egregiis (quibus Astronomiam, illam maxime sublimem Philosophiae partem illustras) notum esse, vehementer gratulor. Tibi pariter ut notus fiam, studium literarum humaniorum, sed et commercium amicarum literarum, quod cum doctis hic illic exerceo, facit. Alliciunt et celebratissime virtutes Tuae, praesertim singulari humanitas, cum insigni et excellenti rei Astronomicae scientia, qua itidem delector, conjuncta. Nolim tamen meum literarum Tecum commercium, quod ambio, et Tua Humanitate mihi polliceor, Tibi aliis, iisque gravioribus, studiis et

3   The Inclusion of Placentinus in Lubieniecki's 'Philosophical Senate'

Hevelius's *Cometographia* and Lubieniecki's *Theatrum cometicum* were published in the same year. They discussed the same subject with strikingly different approaches to knowledge. Although the success (or lack of success) of Hevelius's work largely relied on its approval by and circulation within the learned community of the Republic of Letters, he underestimated the epistemic value of this web as the discursive context providing the cometary discourse with its scientific legitimation. Rather than dialogical, his attitude was self-referential, which damaged his reputation. He presented his work on comets (which was almost a thousand pages long) as the autonomous product of his ingenuity and of his own entrepreneur-like research. He was the *owner* of both his observatory and his printing press. The *Cometographia* boldly appeared as his own product, both technically and financially: '*Auctoris Typis et Sumptibus*'. Unlike English and French academicians, Hevelius's work in Gdańsk underwent no peer discussion whatsoever, since his collaborators – if that is what they could even be considered – were his employees. In many respects, Hevelius's scientific production is intentionally reminiscent of Tycho Brahe's model. The latter's castle-observatory in Uraniborg had been ruled as a fief or personal belonging, which produced consequences also on the extension of intellectual property over the ideas of those who visited it.

Lubieniecki's *Theatrum cometicum* is based on a very different perception of the intrinsic scientific relevance of the Republic of Letters. This collection of letters on the comets of 1664 and 1665 is conceived as a mirror that should reflect the interconnectivity of a Europe-wide web. In Lubieniecki's eyes, this network was an epistemic space permitting the exchange, discussion and comprehension of natural phenomena. He did not avoid repetitions, faithfully printing all reports and diagrams by different authors, even if the information appeared redundant. If several scholars offered similar accounts of the celestial phenomena, this was assumed as evidence for the correctness and accuracy of their work. Moreover, differences should inspire inquiry.

Whereas Hevelius's *Cometographia* is a sort of long monologue, Lubieniecki's *Theatrum* reads as a polyphonic encounter of voices that are sometimes

---

negotiis occupato, negotium et molestiam facessere. Nosti quae vincula viros literarum bonarum amantes conjugant. Patere itaque et Tu, Vir Clarissime! Tibi haec aptari, ut quantum per seria Tua negotia et sublimia studia licebit, mecum fido literarum vinculum jungaris, et sic etiam Clarissimo Ismaeili Bullialdo, Amico meo juxtaque Tuo singulari et integerrimo. Cum quo cum assiduum literarum colam commercium (quod et nuperae epistolae exscriptum exemplum huic adjunctum docet) si et Tu idem desideres vel, quod potius credo, possideas et exerceas, offero Tibi meam qualemcunque in literis mutuo curandis operam, fidam certe te industriam'.

dissonant, but mostly consonant or harmonic. Lubieniecki makes his addressees aware that they are the elected members of a Philosophical Senate (*senatus philosophicus*). The themes dealt with in the correspondence are as diverse as his interests. The front page of the work is indicative of such interdisciplinarity: *Opus mathematicum, physicum, historicum, politicum, theologicum, ethicum, oeconomicum, chronologicum*. Compared to this eclecticism, the intention underlying Hevelius's correspondence is the opposite. When describing the editorial project to Pfautz on 20 December 1681, Hevelius stressed the purely scientific character of his epistles, leaving out all political, private and mundane issues:

> These [letters] contain almost nothing private or related to politics and even less on new events occurring in the world. They only deal with issues related to astronomy, geometry, optics, chronology, mechanics or physics.[44]

Moreover, while Hevelius maintained Latin as the language of the learned, Lubieniecki's work was multilingual. It includes excerpts and quotations in French, Italian and German accompanied by Latin translations. Pluralism does not only refer to a multiplicity of views, but also of idioms; knowledge circulation is *inter*cultural as well as *intra*cultural, as the distances to be bridged are not only geographical but they are also the distances separating the learned from the amateur.

The *Theatrum* resulted from Lubieniecki's efforts to collect information from as many scholars as possible. He was able to benefit from his status as a Polish aristocratic émigré and diplomat to intertwine relations and mediate among scholars belonging to different epistemic cultures and confessions, by presenting himself as an interested and clever interlocutor *super partes*. In the name of a humanistic *libertas philosophandi*, he invited his addressees to openly express their opinions and submit them to their peers. Northern centres of knowledge were most frequently represented in his correspondence, in particular Baltic towns such as Gdańsk, Königsberg, Lübeck, Rostock, Stockholm and Hamburg. Among others, he corresponded with Otto von Guericke in Magdeburg, Rudbeck in Uppsala, Wright and Oldenbourg in London, Boulliau

---

44 Hevelius to Pfautz (Gdańsk, 20 December 1681), in Bibilothèque nationale de France, coll. Lat 10349/15, 59, quoted from Harald Siebert, 'De Dantzig à Paris', in *Correspondance de Johannes Hevelius*, ed. by Grell, vol. 1, Chap. 1, 150, n. 6: 'In quibus [literis] nihil fere de rebus privatis, vel politicis, multo minus noviter in orbe gestis occurrit, sed solummodo, quae ad astronomiam, geometriam, opticam, chronologiam, mechanicam, vel physicam spectant'.

and Azout in Paris and the Jesuits Riccioli and Kircher in Italy.[45] Placentinus was also acknowledged as a member of this Philosophical Senate. The section entirely dedicated to him is entitled *Communicatio Francofurto ad Viadrum-Placentiniana*.[46]

Lubieniecki wrote his first letter to Placentinus on the same day he contacted Hevelius, on 9/19 December 1664. He addressed him as '*Vir Clarissime, Doctissime et Humanissime*' and reminded him of their mutual friendship (*amicitia nostra*). Alongside the letter, he forwarded to him reports by others on the comet and asked for Placentinus's advice.

Placentinus did not react immediately; he thought it better to publish first. His *Astronomica et astrologica observatio cometae terribilis… Das ist: Astronomische und Astrologische Observation* appeared in Frankfurt on Oder at the beginning of 1665 as a bilingual booklet in German and Latin. Whereas the introductory and more general parts were written in both languages, the technical sections were exclusively expounded in the language of the learned. On 22 March 1665, Placentinus sent the small tract to Lubieniecki and explained to him the political-providential implications of the heavenly message. He saw the cometary apparition as an admonishment directed at princes and the clergy, urging them to protect and foster the freedom of conscience (*libertas conscientiae*) of their subjects. Particularly, rulers should renounce following the 'satanic' reason of state (*Status rationis*) and lift bans that sent religious minorities into exile.[47] He was obviously hinting at the condition of religious fugitives such as Lubieniecki himself and the Polish Socinians, or that of his own family, who belonged to the Bohemian diaspora.[48]

Lubieniecki highly appreciated these political remarks. As an émigré himself, he was particularly concerned with politics and often acted on behalf of a sort of patriotic pride, which was rather complementary to his philosophical

---

45 For a recent contribution to the study of Lubieniecki's work and network, cf. Maciej Jasinski, *Astronomiczne podglądy Stanisława Lubienieckiego (1623–1675)*, PhD Thesis, Warsaw: Instytut Hisotrii Nauki im. Ludwika I Aleksandra Birkemajerów, 2017, especially Section 2, 'Lubieniecki i *res publica litteraria*'. I am very thankful to Dr. Jasinski for sending me a copy of his thesis.

46 Stanisław Lubieniecki (Stanislaus de Lubienietz), *Theatrum Cometicum* (Amstelodami, 1668), chap. 14, 549–574.

47 Ibid, 549–550.

48 Ole Peter Grell has reconstructed the formation of an international identity among Calvinist refugees, who had shared experiences of persecution and exile from the late sixteenth century up until the end of the Thirty Years War. This was reinforced by economic and familiar bonds. Ole Peter Grell, *Brethen in Christ: A Calvinist Network in Reformation Europe* (Cambridge, 2011). Placentinus and Lubieniecki evidently had a shared experience of religious diaspora in a later confessional and geopolitical setting.

cosmopolitanism. 'Our fatherland can be proud of you' (*habet de quo sibi patria nostra gratuletur, quod Te videat...*); he began his second letter to Placentinus with this emphatic *incipit* (Hamburg, 7/17 April 1665).[49] It was a long and rhetorical text, embellished with classical references and quotations. Lubieniecki fully agreed with Placentinus concerning the respect that was due to '*aurea conscientiarum libertate*' (the golden freedom of conscience). Freedom of conscience should always be protected from violence, and dialogue and teaching should similarly be preferred to coercion or, even worse, murder. His proto-enlightenment position is epitomized in his affirmation of the innate right to freedom of thought: 'And this is the law of nature, according to which everybody is born endowed with a free conscience'.[50] He quoted many classical and modern authors supporting this claim. Among the ancients that gave valuable moral advice to politicians, Marcus Aurelius is an example; among the moderns, there are Erasmus of Rotterdam and Justus Lipsius. As for the state, Lubieniecki called it a modern form of idolatry, though he cautioned Placentinus not to reject politics altogether. Instead, he argued that one should favour an enlightened form of government, although he did not describe what exactly this means in detail.[51]

Before receiving this letter, Placentinus had already written another one to Lubieniecki (Frankfurt on Oder, 19 April 1665). It entailed three *positiones* (i.e. propositions, or theses) concerning the recent comets, which Placentinus intended to communicate to none other than the kings of France, Denmark and Sweden. The first and second theses simply state that the celestial phenomena seen at the end of 1664 and in 1665 are not the same comet but two distinct ones. The third thesis is astrological: 'Not only do comets exert their influence onto these inferior beings, but also affect human minds through the human body and they constitute a sort of premonition signs in the heavens'.[52] In this context, Placentinus expands on the Cartesian theory that comets are generated from fixed stars and are transported through cosmic space by ethereal vortices.

After receiving Lubieniecki's 'political' letter, Placentinus wrote to him again on 18/28 April 1665, signing the letter as P.T.R., that is, as *pro tempore* Rector of the University of Frankfurt. Lubieniecki promptly reacted (Hamburg, 5/15 May

---

49 Lubieniecki, *Theatrum Cometicum*, 550.
50 Ibid., 551: 'Et haec est naturae lex, ut quisque libera conscientia praeditus nascatur'.
51 Ibid., 553–554: 'Alioquin et bona ac legitima Status ratio, quae in bona Reipublicae forma bonum publicum est, datur, et antiquis quoque temporibus inter recti pravique vices tractabatur'.
52 Ibid., 558: 'Cometas non modo in haec inferiora influere, sed etiam mediante corpore humano, mentes humanas afficere, ac in caelo tanquam signa portendentia existere'.

1665), thanking him for both communications and congratulating him on his prestigious academic appointment. It took many more months for Lubieniecki to write a detailed comment in response to Placentinus's cometary views. In this communication (Hamburg, 10 November 1665), he announced his plan to publish the *Theatrum cometicum*. Then, he distanced himself from Placentinus's astrological theses on several accounts, especially concerning the difficult reconcilability between celestial influences and human freedom with the Scriptures. Moreover, he had some reservations concerning the effort of combining of the Cartesian doctrine with astrology, in particular Placentinus's treatment of comets as planets and their inclusion in horoscopes. Finally, since Placentinus hinted at a new form of chiromancy of his invention, Lubieniecki feared that he was going too far and venturing into occult and impious realms:

> As far as the third thesis [*positio*] on the meaning and action of comets, this issue, as you know, is controversial. [...] It is impossible not to find many detractors. I do not dare to recklessly dispel problems that reach beyond my understanding and are far from my studies. Nonetheless I will freely communicate my opinion to you, to which, I hope, you will listen with equanimity bearing in mind the [principle of] philosophical freedom. [...] You are certainly aware of the opinion on chiromancy, *similar constructions* and other astrological doctrines by learned and wise men. If you can achieve more than they did, you are divine. [...] If I do not err, not even astrologers usually mention comets in their birth horoscopes, but only the planets and the other stars. By contrast you affirm that cometary bodies are akin to planets. I leave this undecided. In fact, I know that others bring the origin of comets back to planets and call them false planets. The very illustrious Hevelius shares this opinion.[53]

---

53 Ibid, 563: 'Quod ad tertiam positionem de cometarum significatione et operatione attinet: hac res, ut nosti, non aeque certa est. [...] Fieri non potest, quin multos contradicentes invenias. Ego, ut non ausim temere quidpiam de iis, quae capitum meum excedunt, et a studiis meis aliena sunt, decernere, dicam nihilominus libere apud Te sententiam meam, quam Tu libertatis Philosophicae memor, aequus audies. [...] Quid de chiromantia, et thematum erectionem aliique Astrologicis placitis sentiant Viri docti et cordati, probe noris. Tu si plus caeteris hic praestas, divinus es. [...] Nisi tamen fallor, nec astrologi in struendis genethliacis ullam cometae mentionem facere solent, sed planetarum et aliarum stellarum tantum. At vero tu corpora cometica planetis cognata dicis. Hoc ego in medio relinquo. Scio et alios cometarum originem ad planetas referre, eosque falsos planetas vocare. In qua sententia et amplissimus Hevelius est'.

Placentinus's reply is dated 27 March 1666, after he had already suffered under the medical violence of his adversaries and had been imprisoned as a fool. 'I write to you as ex-Rector, not as Rector anymore' (*tanquam Ex-Rectori, nec qua Rectori*), he cautioned his correspondent.[54] For the same reason, he signed with his original name: Joannes Kolaczek, alias Placentinus. He apologized to Lubieniecki for his delayed reply, due to the abuses he had been a victim of: '[...] the chains, offence, the violence without reason of wicked people (alas!) which I suffered in the last winter time'.[55] His condition notwithstanding, he wished to respond to Lubieniecki's objections. As far as his chiromancy was concerned, he appealed to the authority of his protectors, especially Friedrich Wilhelm of Brandenburg and Elisabeth of Palatinate, praised as 'miracle of this century, who deserves the name of Queen and Empress in the Christian and literary world'.[56] Secondly, Placentinus claimed that his astrology was not a probable or conjectural doctrine. He called it a demonstrative science [*scientia demonstrativa*]. Thirdly, the divergences between himself and Hevelius concerning the origin of comets were traced back to Placentinus's adherence to Cartesianism. Eventually, he offered to send Lubieniecki a fourth proposition on these matters.

On 30 April 1666 Lubieniecki offered Placentinus his sympathy for his condition (*de hac dolui ex animo*). He avoided discussing astrology with him and declared that he shared his correspondent's feelings of admiration towards the Electoral Prince and Elisabeth of Palatinate. As far as Descartes was concerned, he had met him in person and admired his wit but declared himself incapable of judging his cometary theory: 'It is not my task to refute or defend the philosopher Descartes, who is highly reputed in our century and was once a friend of mine, nor to judge the theories of the very illustrious Hevelius. I leave this task to the experts in the field [...]'.[57]

The severity of Placentinus's condition is clear from the first lines of his next and last letter to Lubieniecki (Frankfort on Oder, 30 April 1666): 'My present state is gloomy, alas!'[58] Nevertheless, he had been able to formulate a fourth

---

54   Ibid, 565.
55   Ibid, 567: 'ob vincula, injuriam, violentiam a malitiosis proh dolor! sine causa, praeterito tempore hiemali, mihi illatam'.
56   Ibid, 566: 'Seculi miraculum, quae in orbe Christiano, et literato, nomen Reginae et Imperatricis meretur'.
57   Ibid, 568: 'Cartesium Philosophum nostro seculo celeberrimum, et meum olim amicum, nec refutare nec tueri, ut nec de Amplissimi Hevelii sententia decernere, meum est. Relinquo haec artis peritis [...]'.
58   Ibid, 569: 'Modernum meum statum lugubrem proh dolor!'

thesis (*4. positio*) arguing for a consensus between astrology and the Sacred Scriptures.[59] In the last letter of the correspondence with Placentinus printed in the *Theatrum cometicum,* Lubieniecki thanked him for this additional thesis and agreed that some astrology could be reconciled with faith, but refrained from a full exposition of his views on that matter because, as he stated, this would have made Placentinus upset:

> I am duly thankful to you for the fourth thesis you sent me. I am not the one who should judge it, as I am not the censor of this century and I am aware of my own weaknesses. Even though I could say something on the subject, I do not want to embitter you anymore. I respect your reasons, the more so since the greatest pain has recently been brought to you by the Author of all our lives, who can give us everything and take it away from us at his will [...]. I am very sorry for this crude case and I share your pain: I pray God who made you suffer to reward you.[60]

While Placentinus was par-force excluded from the academic world, with the publication of the *Theatrum cometicum* in 1668 Lubieniecki virtually reintegrated him or at least reminded the literary republic of this heterodox and unfortunate professor of mathematics. The publication of Placentinus's epistles among those of the most distinguished literati of the time, together with declarations of grief for his fate, was a gesture worth of such a gentlemen as Lubieniecki, for whom humanity, tolerance and freedom of conscience were signature traits. The presence in absence of the silenced Cartesian symbolically stressed the endurance of the bonds of friendship and solidarity that were supposed to hold together the citizens of the Republic of Letters. Hence, Lubieniecki's orchestration of a self-representation of this elected community was not limited to abstractly illustrating its interchanges, but also served as a means to establish its values. The social status of a disinterested aristocrat in

---

59   Ibid: '4. Positio breviter probans, quod *S. Scriptura nec Astrologiam veram et genuinam, nec Astrologos minime superstitiosos reporbet, sed eosdem et illam approbet atque concedat*'.

60   Ibid, 573: 'Quod ad positionem tuam quartam attinet, quam mihi misisti, gratiam tibi de ea ago debitas. Non est meum de ea judicare. Non enim censor huius anni sum; imo vero propriae tenuitatis prope mihi conscius. Etsi vero possem aliquid de his dicere: merito tamen molestus tibi amplius esse nolo. Debitam enim Tui rationem habeo, eoque magis, quod te recens maximo dolore affecerit omnium nostrum vitae Auctor, qui pro lubitu dat cuncta aufertque nobis, dilectissima vitae et thori socia vi mortis extincta. Huius acerbum casum doleo, et in partem moeroris tui venio: Deumque qui te contristabit, ut te soletur, precor'.

exile was a symbolic capital giving credit to the scientific and ethical play staged in his *Cometary Theater*.

4 Concluding Remarks

Early modern scientific transactions exemplify the 'production', consolidation and advancement of knowledge through its circulation. In the astronomical debates of the 1660s transfer was not an extrinsic factor but rather an indispensible component of science as a discursive practice. Arguably, 'science in transit' or 'episteme in motion' is not only a cultural phenomenon bridging geographical and linguistic distances;[61] it also concerns the circulation of knowledge among social groups.[62] The early modern debates on comets were famously inter-class and interdisciplinary.[63] Their language was the Latin of the learned as well as the French of the emerging élites and the German of a wide aristocratic and bourgeois readership in the territories of the Holy Roman Empire and beyond, in the Baltic area and in Polish territories. Decentralized and distributed networks of correspondents and of interlinked institutions played an essential role in the processes of science, as they constituted the basis for its mobile stabilization. At once, they guaranteed the endurance of the scientific community, the preservation of its knowledge and its advancement.[64] The *réseaux* of weak ties of the seventeenth-century Republic of Letters promoted communication, secured the transfer and preservation of data

---

61 See James A. Secord, 'Knowledge in Transit', *Isis* 954 (2004), 654–672 and Eva Cancik-Kirschbaum and Anita Traninger, 'Institution – Iteration – Transfer: Zur Einführung', in *Wissen in Bewegung: Institution – Iteration – Transfer*, ed. by Cancik-Kirschbaum and Traninger (Wiesbaden, 2015), 1–14.

62 Augustí Nieto-Galan, 'Antonio Gramsci Revisited: Historians of Science, Intellectuals, and the Struggle for Hegemony', *History of Science* 49 (2011), 453–478.

63 See, among other studies, Tabitta van Nouhuys, *The Age of Two-Faced Janus: The Comets of 1557 and 1618 and the Decline of the Aristotelian World View in the Netherlands* (Leiden, 1998); *Grenzgänger zwischen Himmel und Erde: Kometen in der Frühen Neuzeit*, ed. Christoph Meinel (Regensburg, 2009). Anna Jerratsch, whom I wish to thank for discussing these matters with me, has recently completed a PhD dissertation on the early modern cometary discourse at the Max Planck Institute for the History of Science and the Humboldt Universität Berlin. It will soon appear as a printed book.

64 As has been noticed, a decentered and distributed web is more stable than a centralized one, whereby the dynamic system is entirely dependent on one or a few hubs, and thus its possible collapse might irreparably damage the entire structure and the knowledge it supports. See Dirk Wintergrün, Jürgen Renn, Roberto Lalli, Manfred Laubichler and Matteo Valleriani, 'Netzwerke als Wissensspeicher', *Preprints of the Max Planck Institute for the History of Science* 475 (2015), especially 7–9.

and theories through redundant exchange of information and allowed for knowledge to be tested and to progress. The rise of scientific academies in the mid-1660s created a restructuring of the web and the redistribution of credit and of means. In the case of the *Académie des sciences*, it established *strong local ties* marking the inner and outer boundaries that could hinder or weaken the wider circulation of information and an extensive assignment of credits.[65] Hevelius, for one, happened to be marginalized during this process of institutionalization of a few powerful hubs.

In the debates on the comets of 1664 and 1665, the importance of scholarly networks for the production and advancement of scientific discourse is particularly evident.[66] Access to learned correspondence, a wide range of contacts and participation in the exchanges of the Republic of Letters were all presuppositions for a scholars' activity and recognition. Various actors related differently to this social capital and the corresponding symbolic capital. The Brandenburg mathematician Placentinus tried to make the most of his correspondence with scholars such as Hevelius, who were located in the high spheres of the scientific community. Although his social capital rested more on strong ties with local patrons in Brandenburg-Prussia than on connections at an international scale, his publication of an epistle by Hevelius in his *Physicalischer und Astrologischer Bericht von denen erschrecklichen…Winden* (1661) certainly served to credit his work and theories, but also provoked a negative reaction on the part of his correspondent. In fact, the inclusion of his letter in an unconventional tract interpreting comets and wind tempests through Cartesian and astrological lenses threatened to tarnish Hevelius's status as a learned and Latinized scholar, whose ambition was to enter the graces of kings and safeguard his international reputation. Therefore, Hevelius was quick to distance himself from Placentinus and began to weaken his relationship with him. In his eyes, the symbolic capital of correspondence ought to be exploited to promote his own work, to advertise himself and to obtain royal patronage. Nevertheless, he did not acknowledge the *epistemological* importance of the network and the wide connectivity of the Republic of Letters. Of the three scholars considered here, it was Lubieniecki who most clearly recognized the collective dimension of knowledge production fostered through open confrontation and exchange. Lubieniecki's *Cometary*

---

65   This is the thesis by Lux and Cook: David S. Lux and Harold J. Cook, 'Closed Circles or Open Networks? Communicating at a Distance during the Scientific Revolution', *History of Science* 36 (1998), 179–211.

66   'La correspondence – Chantal Grell remarks ('Hevelius en son temps', 75) – est […] une nécessité pour un astronome qui doit échanger et comparer quotidiennement des observations et des informations et suivre l'actualité des phénomènes célestes. Elle est aussi une arme […] dans cette course à la propriété intellectuelle'.

Theatre was at once the result and the *mise en scène* of an 'epistemic web'.[67] He succeeded in gathering a 'philosophical senate', as he called it, *freely* discussing the celestial phenomena of 1664 and 1665. His attitude was shaped by ideals of openness and inclusiveness that especially valued the multiplicity of theories and opinions. In this *democratic* republic a heterodox thinker such as Placentinus had the same right of citizenship as Hevelius, von Guericke, Boulliau, Riccioli and other reputable intellectuals. From the viewpoint of symbolic capital, in the philosophical senate he presided, he was in the favourable position to distribute and impose recognition. However, in the light of the polemics pitting Hevelius against Paris and London scholars, it is evident that Lubieniecki's humanistic vision was an abstract idealization. In the course of the 1660s and the 1670s, it became clear that it was not individuals but emerging institutions such as the Royal Society and the *Académie des Sciences* – and their organs of communication – to be the major repositories and distributors of symbolic capital, and the most important source of scientific credit.

Acknowledgements

This article is part of a project that has received funding from the European Union's Horizon 2020 Research and Innovation Programme (GA n. 725883 EarlyModernCosmology).

---

67   On the concept of epistemic web mirroring the structures of social networks circulating and producing knowledge at an epistemological level, see Malcolm D. Hyman and Jürgen Renn, 'Toward an Epistemic Web', in *The Globalization of Knowledge in History*, ed. Jürgen Renn (Berlin, 2012), 711–726.

PART 2

Founding and Shaping Scientific Institutions

∴

PART 2

CHAPTER 4

An Indirect Convergence between the Accademia del Cimento and the Montmor Academy: The 'Saturn dispute'

Giulia Giannini

Introduction

The purpose of the present chapter is to examine an indirect (albeit significant) point of contact between the Florentine academy, later known as the Accademia del Cimento, and the so-called Montmor Academy: their role in the 'Saturn dispute'. In particular, this essay intends to demonstrate how, despite fragmentary evidence and often interrupted exchanges, the issue of the planet's strange appearances offers a unique standpoint from which to assess the interests and the ways in which the two societies operated, as well as the nature of their relations.

The two academies were active between 1657 and 1666–7, in Florence and Paris, respectively. The first occasional meetings at the house of Henri Louis Habert de Montmor (1600–1679) can be dated back to the period between 1654 and 1656.[1] However, it is only from 1657 – when the academy approved its own statutes – that the beginning of the Parisian circle can be dated with certainty. The Cimento, on the other hand, never had official rules or statutes.[2] The dating of its meetings can be determined thanks to the diaries kept by its academicians, and also through the only publication produced by the Florentine academy: the *Saggi di naturali esperienze* (1667). This book – signed by the 'accademici del Cimento' and by the 'Saggiato segretario', Lorenzo Magalotti – attested that an 'academy', sponsored by Prince Leopoldo de' Medici (1617–1675), was 'founded in the year 1657'.[3]

---

1 Harcourt Brown, *Scientific organizations in seventeenth century France* (1620–1680) (New York, 1967 (1934)), 69–71.
2 See in particular: Paolo Galluzzi, 'L'Accademia del Cimento: 'Gusti' del Principe, filosofia e ideologia dell'esperimento', *Quaderni storici* 48 (1981), 788–844.
3 '[…] la nostra accademia istituita dell'anno 1657', Lorenzo Magalotti, *Saggi di naturali esperienze* (1667) (Palermo, 2001), 40. English transl. in W.E. Knowles Middleton, *The Experimenters: a study of the Accademia del Cimento* (Baltimore, 1971), 92.

Even less information is available regarding the cessation of their activities. Having never official statutes, the Accademia del Cimento did not have an official closure either. By the time when the *Saggi* was published, the meetings had become sporadic, many of the academicians moved elsewhere, the prince was elected cardinal and thus the meetings simply ceased to take place. The circumstances that led to the disbandment of the Parisian group are equally unclear. In June 1664 – following a long debate on the form that the group should have taken in order to become more robust and better regulated–[4] Christiaan Huygens informed Robert Moray that the Montmor Academy had 'ceased to exist'. On its 'remains' another group activity emerged, spearheaded by some of the members of the Montmor Academy.[5] They met in the house of Melchisedéch Thévenot (c.1620–1692), one of the most active members of the Montmor Academy, at least until the establishment of the *Académie Royale des Sciences* in 1666.

The history of the relations between the two academies – which prior to the foundation of the *Royal Society* and of the *Académie Royale des Sciences* were the two most renowned groups of scholars engaged exclusively in matters of natural philosophy – is difficult to piece together, given that the various attempts to establish epistolary exchange often encountered delays, if not outright indifference. Consequently, the dialogue between the two academies might be better described as a succession of monologues.

1 Fragmentary and Difficult Exchanges

a *Autumn 1658: Michelangelo Ricci, Melchisedéch Thévenot and the First Contact between the Two Academies*

As is well known, the first tentative contact between the two academies was made by Melchisedéch Thévenot,[6] a French diplomat, bibliophile and man of letters, and a collector of travel literature. His language skills earned him the

---

[4] See for instance: Christiaan Huygens to Lodewijk Huygens, 6 April 1663, Christiaan Huygens, *Œuvres complètes de Christiaan Huygens*, Tome IV. *Correspondance 1662–1663* (The Hague 1891), letter n. 1104, 323–324; and Christiaan Huygens to R. Moray, 12 Mars 1664, Christiaan Huygens, *Œuvres complètes de Christiaan Huygens*, Tome V. *Correspondance 1664–1665* (The Hague, 1893), letter n. 1218, 39–42.

[5] 'A Paris il n'y avoit rien de nouveau en matiere de Sciences, sinon que l'Academie chez Monsieur de Montmor a pris fin pour jamais, mais il semble que du debris de celle cy il en pourroit renaistre quelqüe autre, car j'ay laissè quelques uns de ces Messieurs avec de tres bonnes intentions', Christiaan Huygens to R. Moray, 12 June 1664, *Œuvres complètes de Christiaan Huygens*, V, letter n. 1234, 69–70.

[6] On Thévenot see especially: Robert McKeon, 'Une lettre de Melchisédech Thévenot sur les débuts de l'Académie Royale des Sciences', *Revue d'histoire des sciences et de leur*

position of ambassador in Genoa in 1647 and later in Rome, where he had already resided between 1643 and 1645 and where he witnessed the conclave that elected Pope Alexander VII (1655).[7] Although information on his life and activity is scarce, the letters reveal that during his first stay in Rome Thévenot had met with some of the scholars who, from 1657 onwards, gravitated in various capacities around the academy sponsored by Prince Leopoldo de' Medici. He was introduced to Michelangelo Ricci (1619–1682),[8] corresponded with Vincenzo Viviani (1622–1703),[9] and wrote to Carlo Roberto Dati (1619–1676).[10]

In 1658, having long before returned to Paris, Thévenot was also one of the men of letters that attended the regular meetings at the house of Henri Louis Habert de Montmor. In autumn 1658, perhaps inspired by the new statute written by Samuel Sorbière (1615–1670)[11] less than a year earlier, Thévenot wrote Michelangelo Ricci to express his desire to establish a form of 'communication'

---

applications 18 (1965), 1–6; Trevor McClaughlin, 'Une Lettre de Melchisédech Thévenot', *Revue d'histoire des sciences* 27 (1974), 123–126; Id., 'Sur les rapports entre la Compagnie de Thévenot et l'Académie royale des Sciences', *Revue d'histoire des sciences* 28 (1975), 235–242; Jan Swammerdam, *The Letters of Jan Swammerdam to Melchisedec Thévenot*, ed. G.A. Lindeboom (Amsterdam, 1975); Anthony J. Turner, 'Melchisédech Thévenot, the bubble level, and the artificial horizon', *Nuncius: annali di storia della scienza* 7 (1) (1992), 131–145. Nicholas Dew, *Orientalism in Louis XIV's France* (Oxford 2009), ch. 2; as well as Thévenot's sketch of himself in Melchisédech Thévenot, *Bibliotheca thevenotiana* (Paris, 1694). On his relations with Tuscany, see the recent essay by Alfonso Mirto: Mirto, 'Lettere di Melchisédec Thévenot ai fiorentini: Leopoldo de' Medici, Cosimo III Granduca di Toscana e Vincenzio Viviani', *Galilaeana* 12 (2015), 145–191.

7 Details on Thévenot's two stays in Rome can be inferred primarily from his correspondence. The main source of information on the first stay are the letters preserved in the Galileo Collection at the Biblioteca Nazionale Centrale in Florence (hereafter BNCF); as for the second stay, see especially: *Lettres autographes de Melchisedech THÉVENOT au ministre sur les affaires de Rome. (1654–1655)*, Bibliothèque nationale de France, Ms. Français 10729.

8 See for example the letter dated 30 September 1644 in which Michelangelo Ricci informed Torricelli that he had delivered his *Opera geometrica* to Thévenot, among others: *Le opere dei discepoli di Galileo Galilei*, ed. Paolo Galluzzi and Maurizio Torrini (hereafter DIS), I, 'Carteggio 1642–1648' (Florence, 1975), n. 116, 158.

9 The Galileo collection at the BNCF contains six letters between Viviani and Thévenot dating from the summer of 1643 to the summer of 1645, the last of which was written when Thévenot had already returned to Paris: DIS, I, 'Carteggio 1642–1648', n. 51, 54, 56, 88, 96, 106, pp. 62, 70, 72, 117–118, 127–128, 145–146. Furthermore, on 12 May 1646 Thévenot sent a letter to Viviani (now lost) via Ricci: M. Ricci to Viviani, DIS, I, 'Carteggio 1642–1648', n. 199, 293–294.

10 Thévenot also enclosed a message for Dati (now lost) to a letter written for Viviani on 1 August 1643: DIS, I, 'Carteggio 1642–1648', n. 56, 72.

11 On Sorbière and his role within the Montmor Academy see in particular Gregory M. Adkins, *The Idea of the Sciences in the French Enlightenment: A Reinterpretation* (Newark 2014), 9–28.

between the Montmor group and the Florentine scholars. For one of the articles of the *Réglement* – mentioned in a letter that Sorbière addressed to Hobbes at the beginning of 1658–[12] required members to engage in scientific correspondence on behalf of the group.

Michelangelo Ricci, Thévenot's addressee, was not a member of the group that convened at the Granduke's residence and never participated in any of the activities carried out in Florence. In 1658 he was at the service of the papal court in Rome.[13] Nevertheless, he counted among his friends many of the scholars that convened in Florence (such as Giovanni Alfonso Borelli (1608–1679) or Vincenzo Viviani), and regularly corresponded with them as well as with the prince. He was therefore well acquainted with the group's activities, and probably discussed them with Thévenot. Borelli in particular appears to have been an important point of contact between Ricci and the Tuscan court.[14] It is therefore not surprising that the first approach between the two academies was mediated by Ricci and Borelli.

Borelli mentioned Thévenot's initiative in one of his letters to Leopoldo. As the correspondence between Ricci and Thévenot is not extant to date, the exchanges between Borelli and the prince are the only source available to trace back the requests made by the Frenchman and the ensuing response from Florence. This is probably one of the best-known[15] exchanges between the two academies. Divided between the fear that the French could take advantage of

---

12   Samuel Sorbière to Thomas Hobbes, 22 January /1 February 1658, in Thomas Hobbes, *The Correspondence*, ed. Noel Malcolm, 2 vols (Oxford, 1994), 1:491; English translation on 494. The letter is also published in Samuel Sorbière, *Lettres et discours* (Paris 1660), 631–636.

13   On Michelangelo Ricci see especially Fancesco Bustaffa's important doctoral thesis (*Michelangelo Ricci (1619–1682). Biografia di un cardinale innocenziano* (Scuola superiore di studi storici di S. Marino, a.a. 2010–11). (I wish to thank Bustaffa for furnishing me with a copy of his work). See also Luigi Tenca, 'Michel Angelo Ricci', *Atti e memorie dell'accademia patavina di scienze, lettere ed arti. Classe di scienze matematiche e naturali* 68 (1955–1956), 142–158; Teca, 'Michel Angelo Ricci', *Torricelliana* 11 (1960), 5–13; Teca, 'Relazioni fra Vincenzio Viviani e Michel Angelo Ricci', *Rendiconti dell'Istituto lombardo di scienze e lettere. Classe di scienze matematiche e naturali* 87 (1954), 212–228.

14   Formerly a student of Benedetto Castelli like Ricci, Borelli spent the summer of 1658 in Rome to work with Abraham Ecchellensis on the translation of Apollonius' *Conics*. As noted by Bustaffa, after Torricelli's death (1647) records of the relations between Ricci and Florence had weakened to the point of disappearing completely between October 1648 and 1658. As Bustaffa himself points out, the relations between the Jesuit and the Florentine milieus appear to have been rekindled around the time of Borelli's sojourn in Rome. Bustaffa, *Michelangelo Ricci*, 108–109.

15   Middleton, *The Experimenters*, 300–301. See also Françoise Waquet, *Le modèle français et l'Italie savante : conscience de soi et perception de l'autre dans la République des lettres (1660–1750)* (Rome, 1989), 407–412.

the discoveries made by the Italians on the one hand, and the need to be updated on the work that was being carried out abroad on the other, Borelli sought advice from the prince.[16] Ricci, in turn, was concerned with the damage that failure to respond to the letter would cause to the image of the academy and, by extension, of Italy.[17] In any event, Thévenot did not receive an official response until 1660.

b   *Spring 1659: the 'form of government of the new Philosophical Academy in Paris'.*

In the spring of 1659 Borelli received from Ricci a lesser-known report, still unpublished, on the Montmor Academy. The manuscript, probably written by Thévenot,[18] but of which only Magalotti's Italian copy[19] is extant, is mentioned by Middleton as an 'undated and unidentified secretarial copy of part of a letter written to someone in Italy by someone in France', which may have belonged to the correspondence between Ricci and Thévenot.[20] The content corresponds perfectly with the comments sent by Borelli to Leopoldo[21] on 19

---

16 'Ora io godo sommamente, che da quei Signori in Francia si vada con nuove Sperienze, e Speculazioni, promovendo la Natural Filosofia; ma ho anche qualche sospetto e gelosia, che dell'Invenzioni e Speculazioni dei nostri Maestri, e di quelle che abbiamo trovato Noi, se ne abbiano, secondo l'usanza vecchia, a far Autori e Ritrovatori gli Stranieri. Questo rispetto mi fa andar ritenuto, ad attaccar questo Commercio con quei Signori dell'Accademia Parigina, poiché non si può far di meno nello scrivere, di non comunicare loro qualche cosa; e l'istesso dubitare dà campo a quegli Ingegni pellegrini di ritrovar le cose, tratto delle Ragioni, non delle Esperienze. Dall'altra parte parmi che sarebbe pur bene esser informati di quello, che si va operando, e speculando in quell'Accademia, sicché io mi trovo irresoluto; e però ricorro a V.A.S., perché mi comandi come mi debbo portare in quest'affare'. See: Borelli to Leopoldo, 11 November 1658; published in: Giovanni Targioni Tozzetti, *Notizie degli aggrandimenti delle scienze fisiche accaduti in Toscana nel corso di anni LX. del secolo XVII* (Bologna, 1780), t.1, 456; Angelo Fabroni, (ed.), *Lettere inedite di uomini illustri*, 2 vols. (Florence, 1775), 115. English translation: Middleton, *The Experimenters*, 300.

17 '[I]l Sig.r Michelagnelo Ricci mi replica questa settimana, e con moltissime raggioni vive, et efficaci procura mostrare quanto pregiudizio si faccia alla nostra accademia, et all'Italia tutta con il nostro tacere e non scrivere a quei Sig.ri dell'accademia di Francia vorrebbe egli insomma che si palesassero le conclusioni da noi ritrovate, e dimostrate facendo però, et occultando le raggioni, e le dimostrazioni: in questa maniera dice egli potremo esser sicuri che non ci possa esser tolto il primo luogo dell'inventione, preoccupata e palesata da noi'. BNCF, Ms. Gal. 275, c. 130r-131r. English translation: Middleton, *The Experimenters*, 301. See also: Waquet, *Le modèle français et l'Italie savante*, 408–410.

18 The manuscript begins indeed with a reference to an earlier message concerning the Montmor Academy: 'Quell'adunanza di Virtuosi, ò Academia della quale scrissi già a V.S. Illustrissima [...]'. BNCF, Ms. Gal. 293, c. 30r.

19 BNCF, Ms. Gal. 293, cc. 30r-v.

20 Middleton, *The Experimenters*, 299.

21 G.A. Borelli to Leopoldo, 19 April 1659, BNCF, Ms. Gal. 275, cc. 146r-v.

April concerning a report discussing the 'form of government of the new Philosophical Academy in Paris'[22] received by Ricci and which, he added, was enclosed to the letter (now missing).

The report – discussing experiments carried out in Paris and focusing on the group's composition and its code of conduct – was apparently never answered, despite the assurances of the author of the letter of the group's good faith regarding their correspondence with Italy:

> In quanto poi alle difficoltà e sconcerti che veggo accennati nella lettera di V.S. Illustrissima e che arrivarono già in simili occorrenze, pare che la communicazione havendo da passar per via di lettere con la Data e tempo di esse si possa assicurare la fede di tal commercio virtuoso; può ben cader tal mancamento in un particolare che ambisca il principato di una scienza ma difficilmente rendersi commune à tutta un'adunanza di più di quaranta persone, che tanti ordinariamente sono quei virtuosi che convengono in questa nostra Academia, e forse in maggior numero saranno quei di Firenze.[23]

It is possible that this assurance – which would seem to indicate that Ricci had informed Thévenot of Borelli's concerns – contributed to persuading the Florentines to draft a belated response.

c   *Summer 1660: An Experiment Involving Fumes in a Vacuous Space and the Promise of a Speech that was Never Sent*

Shortly after activities resumed at Pitti Palace in early summer 1660,[24] Lorenzo Magalotti (1637–1712) – the new secretary of Leopoldo's academy – wrote to

---

22   '[…] la forma con la quale si governa la nuova accademia de Filosofi di Parigi'. BNCF, Gal. 275, cc. 146r-v.
23   Ibid., c. 30v.
24   Thévenot's letter arrived at the start of one of the longest periods of inactivity for the Accademia del Cimento: no session is recorded between September 1658 and May 1660. In addition to the risk that the French could take advantage of yet-unpublished discoveries (as indicated by Borelli's letter), the fact that the French letters went unanswered could also be explained precisely because academic sessions had been suspended, and many of the Cimento academicians were not in Florence at the time. In a letter to Boulliau dated 24 April 1659, Leopoldo wrote: 'la forza di varij accidenti è stata cagion che molti della mia Accademia sieno stati, e sien separati in diversi luoghi; onde per qualche tempo non si è applicato alle esperienze, et alli Studi incominciati'. BNCF, Gal. 282, 10r.

Ricci about 'a gem recently studied by this Academy' with the purpose to inform 'Mr Thévenot'[25] in France. This is the only experiment that was officially announced abroad before the publication of the *Saggi di Naturali Esperienze* (1667). The experiment in question took place on 12 June 1660, and was related to the smoke that was generated in the vacuum left by the mercury inside a Torricellian tube. The description of the experiment was accompanied by a detailed drawing, and the letter justified the delay with various 'unexpected events' – most notably the prince's indisposition 'on various occasions'.[26] The letter also noted that, besides providing further proof against the Peripatetic hypothesis of positive lightness, the descending fumes clearly demonstrated that the void left by the mercury inside the instrument was far from obvious.

The letter did not make any reference to the composition of the Florentine academy, or to the manner in which the meetings were organsied. For their part, the French responded by merely expressing gratitude for the official commencement of a correspondence with the 'Pisa academy'. Furthermore, despite the fact that the experiment was discussed at a special session held at the

---

25   'Mi comanda il Serenissimo Principe Leopoldo mio Signore che io mandi copia a V.S. come fo con l'aggiunta d'una galanteria nuovamente osservata in quest'Accademia [...] si contenterà VS. di parteciparla in Francia al Sig. Tevenot', Lorenzo Magalotti to Michelangelo Ricci, 4 July 1660, BNCF, Gal. 268, 67r-70r and Gal. 289, 1r-4r (these are two different copies of the same letter, parts of which are published in Fabroni, *Lettere inedite di uomini illustri*, II, 88–90).

26   'Servirà in oltre il comunicarla per far credere a quei Signori vano il sospetto significatoci, che habbia l'A.S. revocato il pensiero del commercio letterario stabilito più mesi addietro, sentendo hora attribuirsi le cagioni del nostro indugio ad accidenti di mera casualità, fra i quali son forse stati i più considerabili alcune indisposizioni in vari tempi occorse all'A.S.; delle quali essendone andate copate per buona parte le sue non mai intermesse applicazioni a questi medesimi studi, e stata S.A. dalla violenza delle congiunture accennate consigliata di quando in quando ad un riposo più forzato, che volontario. Così l'essersi differito l'incominciamento del promesso commercio è stato più, che dalla propria elezione del Sig.r Principe, effetto della lentezza degli accademici in sollecitare l'A.S. a nuove fatiche, sapendo ciascuno per prova con qual fervore poi l'intraprenda, anzi che per l'evidenza di tal verità solo in questo caso haremmo forse men' che volentieri secondato anche l'espressi comandi con gl'atti per altri eternamente dovuti della nostra obbedienza'. Ibid.

Montmor residence, the Cimento[27] never received the 'speech' that Thévenot had promised in his letter of thanks to the prince.[28]

d Spring 1661: Thévenot's List

In April 1661, Thévenot sent Leopoldo a list of 43 observations conducted in Paris in addition to a few experiments from England that were supposedly going to be carried out on the Canary Islands.[29] These involved primarily capillarity experiment: i.e. those phenomena whereby a fluid placed inside a very thin tube – the tube being either one of two communicating tubes, or immersed into a bigger container – reaches a considerably higher or lower level than usual. The experiments probably took place in Paris between November 1660 and February 1661.[30] This subject was pursued avidly by the Cimento academicians.

---

27 On 22 November 1660 Ricci was yet to receive the 'writing' promised by Thévenot: 'La speranza che mi dava il Sig. Thévenot con l'ultime sue, di farmi avere quanto prima una scrittura di que' Signori sopra l'esperienza che a loro inviai, così commandandomelo V. Altezza Serenissima; è stata cagione ch'i'abbia indugiato qualche ordinario a scrivere, volendo supplire nell'istesso tempo a due cose, per non portare V. Altezza duplicato incommodo con le mie lettere. Ma forse le novità devono colà tuttavia durare, et impediscono il radunar l'Accademia'. M. Ricci to Leopoldo de' Medici, 22 November 1660, Fabroni, *Lettere inedite di uomini illustri* II, 106–108.

28 'Hanno poi straordinariamente unita l'Accademia a fine di partecipare l'esperienza graziosissima, come la chiama il Sig. Thévenot, a quei Signori, li quali vogliono provar di nuovo l'esperimento, e quanto prima mandare all'Altezza Vostra Serenissima sopra di quella un Discorso', M. Ricci to Leopoldo de' Medici, 14 October 1661, Fabroni,), *Lettere inedite di uomini illustri* II, 105–106.

29 M. Thévenot to Leopoldo de' Medici, 7 April 1661, BNCF, Gal. 270, cc. 139r-141v, 155r-156r. Published in: Mirto, 'Lettere di Melchisédec Thévenot ai fiorentini'; and Targioni Tozzetti, *Notizie degli aggrandimenti delle scienze fisiche accaduti in Toscana nel corso di anni LX. del secolo XVII* (Bologna, 1780), 2/2: 716–721.

30 Huygens' diary entries suggest that in December 1660 Jacques Rohault (1618–1672) presented his experiments on the 'water ascending small tubes' several times. Henri L. Brugmans, *Le séjour de Christian Huygens à Paris et ses relations avec les Milieux Scientifiques français. Suivi de son Journal de Voyage à Paris et Londres* (Paris 1935). The entry for 7 December notes that 'Rohaut lut les experiences de l'eau qui monte dans les petits tuyaux' at Montmor's residence, and again on 14 December Huygens wrote that 'Rohaut expliquoit des petits tuyaux'. On 21 December Huygens witnessed instead the 'experiences des tubes et des petits tuyaux' at Rohault's own residence. After him, Balthasar de Monconys (1611–1665) – who had met with Torricelli during his stay in Florence in 1646 – read a lecture on the same topic, the 'Discorso sull'Ascensione dell'acqua sopra al suo livello in un tubo stretto' which was commented by Rohault himself as well as Roberval, Adrien Auzout (1622–1691), Jean Pecquet (1622–1674) and Montmor. See: Balthasar de Monconys, *Journal des voyages de Monsieur de Monconys*, 3 vols (Lyon 1665–66), 3: [109–114] 33–38.

From the very first sessions, they had engaged in the observation of the motion of various fluids inside syphons and tubes of different caliber.[31]

Having received Thévenot's list, Leopoldo dispatched a hasty note of thanks; he did not offer any further comments besides apologising for not being presently able to return the courtesy, owing to the impending nuptials between the Granduke's son, Cosimo III de' Medici, and Louis XIV's cousin, Marguerite Louise d'Orléans, which had brought all academic activities to a halt.[32] A few days later Viviani also wrote to Thévenot, intimating that he 'greatly enjoyed' reading about the experiments 'of your illustrious academy', and about 'the other experiments from England that will be carried out on the island of Tenerife'.[33] No other reference to the Parisian observations can be found in the correspondence available to date.

Nor is it possible to determine whether Thévenot's list had been discussed at the Accademia. We do know, however, that once activities were resumed after the wedding of Cosimo III, capillarity continued to be frequently discussed in Florence. Yet the academicians shifted their focus into experiments in a vacuum, wishing to learn whether the same phenomena would occur with or without air. No mention of the Paris list appears in the academicians' diaries either, not even in the entry for 28 November 1661,[34] when the Cimento academicians observed – contrary to the position defended by the French–[35] that cold water does not, in fact, rise higher than hot water. And while the Florentines continued with this course of experiments after 1661, it doesn't appear from Thévenot's list that the Parisian academy even consider the topic. We may concluded, therefore that, having been prompted to return to the topic, the Cimento academicians did not take into serious consideration the observations received from Paris.

---

31 See for example the experiments recorded in the diaries for 22 June, 27 July, 29 July, 7 August and 22 December 1657. BNCF, Ms. Gal. 260, cc. 5r, 28r, 43r, BNCF, Ms. Gal. 262, cc. 5r-v, 21r-22r, 24v, 49v-50r.
32 Leopoldo de' Medici to M. Thévenot, 21 April 1661, BNCF Ms. Gal. 282, c. 50r-v.
33 V. Viviani to M. Thévenot, 6 May 1661, BNCF, Ms. Gal. 252 doc. 37, c. 70r-71v.
34 'Messo un Cannellino nell'acqua fredda, e notato l'altezza, alla quale per esso s'innalza l'acqua, votata per attrazione l'acqua fredda del vaso, e messavene ugual mole della calda, l'altezza di quella che si solleva si mantiene l'istessa'. BNCF, Ms. Gal. 260, c. 172r and Ms. Gal. 262, c. 123v.
35 'Pare che da molte osservazioni possa asserirsi, che l'Acqua Fredda si sollevi assai più della Calda'. Targioni Tozzetti, *Notizie degli aggrandimenti*, 2/2: 719.

2   1658–1661: The Saturn Dispute

An indirect, albeit significant point of contact between the two groups can be found in their involvement in the 'Saturn dispute'. Between 1658 and 1660 the two academies were the main actors in the debate concerning the interpretation of the planet's 'strange appearances' – first observed as triple-bodied, then oval, then solitary, then triple-bodied again. Galileo's descriptions of Saturn that began in 1610 produced a flurry of observations and hypotheses. Those involved included Gassendi (1592–1655), Boulliau (1605–1694), Hevelius (1611–1687), Riccioli (1598–1671), and Grimaldi (1618–1663); and a variety of drawings were published and widely disseminated around the middle of the seventeenth century. The debate on the correct interpretation of the various guises under which Saturn made itself visible was ignited by Christiaan Huygens. In March 1656, the Dutch astronomer published the *De Saturni luna observatio nova*, where he announced the discovery of Saturn's moon – which Huygens had already revealed to some colleagues during his stay in Paris several months earlier – further revealing a new theory to explain the planet's strange appearances. It was his intention to publish a full account shortly thereafter, but in the *De Saturni luna observatio nova* he reduced the hypothesis into an anagram, so as to ensure priority of the discovery.

Hevelius[36] and Roberval[37] immediately responded to the enigmatic announcement by sending Huygens their own theories, but the long-awaited *Systema Saturnium* was not published until the summer of 1659. In the meantime, the meaning of the anagram was revealed only to two close friends, Ismael Boulliau and Jean Chapelain: *Annulo cingitur, tenui, plano, nusquam coharente, ad eclipticam inclinato* (It is surrounded by a thin, flat, ring, nowhere touching, inclined to the ecliptic). And it was owing to the mediation of Chapelain and Boulliau that the issue of Saturn's appearances reached the two academies.

---

36   On 22 June 1656 Hevelius sent Huygens his *Dissertatio de Nativa Saturni Facie*, in which he put forward a different explanation for the Saturn phases. See: J. Hevelius to C. Huygens, 22 June 1656, *Œuvres complètes de Christiaan Huygens* I, letter n. 302, 435. As early as in May 1656 Hevelius delivered to Christiaan Huygens' brother, Philips, an anagram that was later discovered to say simply that the Saturn phases took place over a period of about 15 years. In the same letter he also announced that he was preparing a new treatise on Saturn.

37   Having read Huygens' treatise, Roberval put forward a hypothesis to explain the Saturn phases that was based on the vapour exhalations that would periodically pervade the planet's atmosphere. See: G.P. de Roberval to Christiaan Huygens, 6 July and 4 August 1656, *Œuvres complètes de Christiaan Huygens* I, letter n. 311 and n. 324, pp. 451–452 and 474–475.

Huygens met Chapelain and Boulliau during his first stay in Paris in the summer of 1655.[38] On that occasion he had shared with many his discovery of Titan, Saturn's moon. Chapelain was particularly impressed by it, and his urgings were instrumental in persuading Huygens to publish the *De Saturni luna observatio nova*.[39] After he received the text, Chapelain presented it in some Parisian circles and sent copies to influential acquaintances (including Montmor), later informing Huygens of the enthusiastic reception of his work.[40] Understandably, then, when Chapelain received in March 1658 Huygens's detailed explanation of his hypothesis concerning Saturn's strange appearances,[41] he was very eager to announce it at the sessions taking place at Montmor's house, which he assiduously frequented. Huygens was already informed the new academy, probably by Boulliau,[42] and thanks to Chapelain he had already exchanged a few letters with Montmor – who expressed his strong desire to learn the details of Huygens' discoveries.

On 18 April 1658 Huygens granted Chapelain permission to present his hypothesis on Saturn's ring to the Parisian academy where, twenty days earlier, Roberval had read his own lecture on Saturn's system.[43] As is well known, nothing was left to chance in the organisation of the session. Chapelain and Montmor took every step to produce the greatest possible sensation, by inviting not only renowned Parisian savants, but doctors from the Sorbonne, state counsellors, and even knights of the Order of the Holy Spirit. The outcome exceeded expectations,[44] with the session representing one of the pinnacles in

---

38   On Huygens' first stay in paris see especially: Brugmans, *Le séjour de Christian Huygens*, in particular pp. 23–31. On the relations between Huygens and Chapelain see especially: Albert J. George, 'A seventeenth-century amateur of science: Jean Chapelain', *Annals of Science* 3:2 (1938), 217–236. On the relations between Huygens and Boulliau see especially Robert A. Hatch, 'Between Friends: Huygens and Boulliau', *De zeventiende eeuw: Cultuur in de Nederlanden in interdiscipInair perspectief* 12 (1996), 106–116.

39   See in particular: Christiaan Huygens to J. Chapelain, [March 1656]; Christiaan Huygens to [Cl. Mylon], 15 March 1656; Christiaan Huygens to G.P. de Roberval, [March 1656]; Christiaan Huygens to J. Chapelain, 8 June 1656, *Œuvres complètes de Christiaan Huygens*, I, letters n. 270, 271, 276 and 299, pp. 390, 391, 395–396 and 430–431.

40   See: J. Chapelain to Christiaan Huygens, 8 April 1656, *Œuvres complètes de Christiaan Huygens*, I, letter n. 278, 397–399.

41   Christiaan Huygens to J. Chapelain, 28 March 1658, *Œuvres complètes de Christiaan Huygens* II, letter n. 477, 156–162.

42   A letter to Heinsius dating from February 1658 provides one of the first descriptions available to date of the Montmor Academy. See: Brown, *Scientific organizations*, 77–79.

43   J. Chapelain to Christiaan Huygens, 12 April 1658, *Œuvres complètes de Christiaan Huygens* II, letter n. 480, 165–167.

44   'L'Assemblée estoit nombreuse et de plus de quarente Personnes, entre lesquelles il y auoit deux Cordons bleus le Marquis de Sourdis et Monsieur Du Plessis Guenegaud

the activity of the Montmor Academy: the group achieved fame because it had been chosen by Huygens to announce his important discovery.

Within the academy, Huygens' theory of Saturn's 'ears' was seen as a response to Roberval's earlier lecture, in which the latter explained the different appearances of the planet by connecting them with the vapours generating from the hotter area, akin to sunspots. Chapelain, who at the time had already been made aware of Huygens' theory, had immediately expressed his misgivings, though the real response came from Huygens himself. Roberval, who had previously insinuated that Huygens had plagiarised his own theory, dropped all charges against him, while remaining doubtful of Huygens's hypothesis. His reservations were included in a letter that Chapelain hastily addressed to Huygens. It is not clear whether the responses of the Dutchman was read out verbatim or simply summarized in the Academy. Be that as it may, owing to Huygens's absence, Chapelain became the chief promoter and defender of the young Dutch astronomer in Paris.

Whereas Chapelain played a key role in introducing Huygens' Saturn hypothesis to the Parisian academy, Boulliau played an equally significant role in bringing the *Systema Saturnium* to the attention of the Accademia del Cimento. Following the Saturn debate at the Montmor residence, and also at the insistence of Chapelain – whose support was indeed acknowledged in the final text – Huygens devoted himself to completing the work. During the final writing stages, the Dutch astronomer was charged with an even more aggravating accusation. As noted earlier, before revealing his hypothesis on Saturn, Roberval accused Huygens of having based his theory on the revelations that he himself had shared with the Dutch astronomer during the summer of 1655, when they were both in Paris. It was easy for Huygens to demonstrate that his ring had nothing to do with the vapours theorised by the Frenchman. The research on Saturn went hand in hand with important studies on the application of pendulums to clock. Chapelain and Montmor eagerly advertised these findings – which included interesting applications for the determination of longitudes. In 1658, after two years work, Huygens published his *Horologium*. The publication of this short treatise engendered disputes over prioirty, starting with Leopoldo de' Medici himself, who accused Huygens of having plagiarised one of Galileo's

---

Secretaire d'Estat, plusieurs Abbés de conditions, plusieurs Maitres des Requestes, des Conseillers du Parlement des Officiers de la Chambre des Comptes, des Docteurs de Sorbonne, plusieurs Gentilzhommes qualifiés, des Medecins de reputation force Mathematiciens d'importance et quantité de Scauans lettres', J. Chapelain to Christiaan Huygens, 10 May 1658, *Œuvres complètes de Christiaan Huygens* II, letter n. 484, 174.

inventions.[45] The *Horologium* had reached the prince via Boulliau and it was to him that the prince conveyed his criticism. The two met for the first time in 1645 when Boulliau visited Florence with Nicholas Heinsius, and since then thet two carried out regular correspondence.

It is therefore not an accident that, while Boulliau mediated between the two, that Huygens decided to dedicate the *Systema Saturnium* precisely to Leopoldo de' Medici.[46] While it is not clear whether Boulliau came up with the idea, there is no doubt that he supported it.[47] The text reached the prince from Heinsius in August 1659 via Carlo Roberto Dati, who befriended Huygens ever since the latter visited Florence.[48] Huygens' first Saturn publication reached Florence quite late. Although in July 1656 Vincenzo Viviani was informed of the *De Saturni luna observatio nova* by the mathematician Rasmus Bartholin,[49] the work itself did not reach Florence before July 1658. The news of a 'new planet that revolves around Saturn in 16 days' was welcomed with great interest by Borelli who, having received a copy of the text from Flanders, immediately sent it to Leopoldo 'so that he might be able to see it with the exceptional telescopes of his Highness the Granduke'.[50]

The publication of the much-awaited *Systema Saturnium* generated a new wave of critical reactions. The most critical was the *Brevis annotatio in Systema Saturnium*, co-written by Honoré Fabri and Eustachio Divini – though published with the latter's name only. The two rejected Huygens' theory and proposed a different explanation, according to which Saturn did not have any rings, but instead four satellites, two large and dark ones close to the planet and two, smaller and brighter, farther away. Published at the start of July 1660, the *Brevis annotatio* was also dedicated to Leopoldo, and furthermore it exhorted

---

45 On Huygens, the invention of the pendulum clock, and the ensuing debates see especially: Joella G. Yoder, *Unrolling Time: Christiaan Huygens and the Mathematization of Nature* (Cambridge 1988); Id., 'Book on the pendulum clock' in *Landmark Writings in Western Mathematics*, ed. Ivor Grattan-Guinness (Amsterdam, 2005), 33–45. Cornelis D. Andriesse, *Huygens: The Man Behind the Principle* (Cambridge, 2005).

46 See the dedicatory letter: *Œuvres complètes de Christiaan Huygens* II, letter n. 635, 432–434.

47 I. Boulliau to Christiaan Huygens, 4 July 1659, *Œuvres complètes de Christiaan Huygens* II, letter n. 633, 430.

48 Nic. Heinsius to C. Dati, 14 August 1659, *Œuvres complètes de Christiaan Huygens* II, letter n. 652, 462–464.

49 Rasmus Bartholin to V. Viviani, 26 July 1656, DIS II, letter n.715, 360.

50 '[...] È venuto da Fiandra in stampa un foglio, nel quale si dà notizia di un nuovo pianeta, che circonda Saturno in 16 giorni, del quale ne mando a V.A. la copia, acciochè possa farlo osservare con li telescopij squisiti del Ser.mo G. Duca, perché con telescopij più piccoli tal pianetino non è osservabile [...]'. A. Borelli to Leopoldo de' Medici, 27 July 1658, BNCF Ms. Gal. 275, c. 102r.

the prince to adjudicate which of the two theories was correct: 'facile, ni fallor, iudicabis utri potius habenda fides sit'.[51]

Leopoldo turned to the Accademia for assistance[52] and, in so doing, he followed the suggestions that Boulliau had offered Huygens several months before. At the end of November 1659, Boulliau was finally converted to the theory of Saturn's ring, but at the same time he cautioned his friend that, in order to demonstrate the verity of the theory once and for all, it would be necessary to conduct 'some experiments'.[53] And while it doesn't appears that Huygens did so, the Cimento academicians built models for both hypotheses. Having accurately analysed distance, lighting and positioning, they proceeded to observe such models through various types of telescopes.

Borrelli clarified the decision to test the two hypotheses experimentally in a report, which he wrote for the prince with the aim to have it sent to the authors:

> Noi [...] secondo il costume dell'Accademia di Vostra Altissima Signoria ch'è d'inuestigare il uero, col mezzo di riproue esperimentali, l'abbiamo inuiolabilmente osseruato anche in questo affare, per quella parte però che può ridursi ad esperienza di cose tanto remote da nostri sensi, ed esaminando per ultimo nei congressi tenuti dauanti all Altezza Vostra Serenissima disappassionatamente i concetti del Signor Vgenio, e quei degl' auuersarj che se gli oppongono vi sono cadute alcune riflessioni [...]. [...] Qui s'è scoperta l'incertezza di tal discorso con sensata esperienza, e finalmente quell'aspetto che in Saturno non poteua esperimentarsi, che tra'l termine d'otto ò noue anni, è riuscito a noi artifizialmente di rappresentarlo.[54]

---

51 E. Divini, *Brevis annotatio in Systema Saturnium Christiani Eugenii* (Rome, 1660), 55.
52 On the Cimento's experimental work concerning the Saturn system see especially the seminal work by Albert Van Helden. In particular: Van Helden, 'The Accademia del Cimento and Saturn's Ring', *Physics* 3 XV (1973), 237–259.
53 'Je scay que la nature a pû faire vn cercle autour de ce corps la, & que par la raison qui fait que la terre est suspendue in aëre libero, vn anneau peut aussi y estre suspendu; neantmoins il vous faut encores quelques experiences pour demonstrer absolument ce que vous posèz'. I. Boulliau to Christiaan Huygens, 21 November 1659, *Œuvres complètes de Christiaan Huygens* II, letter n. 684, 510. On this point and on Boulliau's role in the Saturn dispute see also: Robert A. Hatch, 'The Republic of Letters: Boulliau, Leopoldo and the Accademia del Cimento' in *The Accademia del Cimento and its European Context*, ed. by Beretta, Clericuzio, Principe (Sagamore Beach, 2009), 165–180.
54 [A. Borelli] to Leopoldo de' Medici, undated, *Œuvres complètes de Christiaan Huygens* III, letter n. 796, 152–158.

THE 'SATURN DISPUTE'

In addition to the Accademia's general resolution to rely on experiments to study the natural world, the decision to test the two hypotheses by building a mechanical model was owing to a more immediate constraint: the study of all the various appearances that Saturn had shown up to that time would have required eight or nine years of astronomical observations.

This decision found a strong supporter in Michelangelo Ricci, who proved instrumental in managing the 'Saturn dispute' and in disseminating information on the various characters of this episode. On 20 September 1660, having received the first reports from Florence, Ricci wrote to the prince:

> Io per me avendo conosciuto il sistema del P. Fabri essere un ingegnoso capriccio, e quello dell'Ugenio o vero, o che al vero molto s'avvicina, ma col bisogno di più accertate osservazioni per istabilirlo o istaurarlo, poche ore ho consumate nell'uno e nell'altro, differendo questo a miglior tempo, e quello tralasciandolo per attendere a più fruttuose speculazioni. La via dell'esperienze stimata da v.a.s. e con ragione, riesce di maggiore utile e diletto, tanti più a chi ha la perspicacia, l'intelligenza, e l'amore della verità, che in v.a.s. per raro esempio s'ammirano; perché direttamente porta alla verità che si cerca, e bene spesso a caso dell'altre sen'incontrano.[55]

By studying these experiments, the Florence academicians came to the conclusion that Huygens' hypothesis best explained the phenomena at stake.

Interestingly, the dispute was handled in very different ways in the two academies. Whereas the Montmor group became the privileged seat where the announcement of such new astronomical news was made and discussed, the Cimento was the first scientific academy to act as an arbiter of a dispute – doing so by enlisting its members to carry out a concerted experimental effort. And although it is not known whether Florence had been informed of the discussions that took place at the Montmor residence, the Paris academicians were fully informed of the Cimento's involvement and of the conclusions there reached. News of the experiments in Florence reached Huygens in late August or early September 1660 – before he received Leopoldo's response to the dedication of his work, a copy of which he had sent to Florence via Heinsius in August the previous year. In the meantime, Carlo Roberto Dati had informed him in May – as usual via Heinsius – on the publication of the *Brevis annotation*, on Fabri being its co-author, and of its being dedicated to Leopoldo.[56]

---

55 M. Ricci to Leopoldo de' Medici, 20 September 1660, Fabroni, *Lettere inedite* 2:103–104.
56 C. Dati to N. Heinsius, 25 May 1660, 1 August 1660, *Œuvres complètes de Christiaan Huygens* III, letter n. 752, 83.

The *Brevis Annotatio* reached Huygens one month after its publication via Pierre Guisony,[57] who was the first to inform him of Divini's reactions in Rome.[58] Guisony also informed Huygens on the experiments carried out in Florence. On 27 August[59] he wrote that in order to resolve the dispute, the Cimento academicians had built a mechanical model that fully replicated the planet's characteristics as he had described them in the *Systema Saturnium*. By observing the model with two different telescopes, and under different conditions, the academicians had concluded that 'the objections raised by Fabri and Eustachio were false'.[60]

Noteworthy is that not only was Guisony a key intermediary for Huygens during the dispute,[61] but he also maintained important relations with the Montmor Academy. Born in Avignon (France), Guisony was a friend of Gassendi's,[62] and in May 1659 he visited England, where he attempted to establish contact with Hobbes. Guisony' letter to Hobbes reveals his contacts with some of the most prominent members of the Paris academy, such as Sorbière and Du Prat, as well as his participation to a number of its sessions.[63] In August 1659

---

57 P. Guisoni to Christiaan Huygens, 1 August 1660, *Œuvres complètes de Christiaan Huygens* III, letter n. 765, 101–104.

58 P. Guisoni to Christiaan Huygens, 25 March 1660, *Œuvres complètes de Christiaan Huygens* III, letter n. 732, 45–49.

59 P. Guisoni to Christiaan Huygens, 27 August 1660, *Œuvres complètes de Christiaan Huygens* III, letter n. 774, 116–118.

60 'Ces Messieurs pour se conuaincre sensiblement, firent dresser à Florence vn cors artificiel de Saturne & vn cercle à l'entour aueq la proportion de leur diametres & autres circonstances que vous aués décrites; ils le mirent en suite la nuit au milieu de 4. flambeaux en quarré qui l'eclairoient & se mettans dans certaines distances & certains aspects l'obseruoient aueq 2. lunetes, l'une de fû Torricellj & ie ne sáy quelle autre: en sorte que aueq la moins bonne on voioit 3. córs separés, & aueq la meilleure ils uoioient le cercle tout continué. Ils ne furent pas contans de céte ingenieuse experience, mais le lendemain épreuuerent le méme en rase campagne dans un beaucoup plus grand eloignement; & la meme chose leur reüsissant comme la nuit, ils conclurent de la fausseté des obiections du Père Fabry & d'Eustachio'. Ibid.

61 On Guisony's role and, more generally, on Huygens' informants during the Saturn dispute see also: Antonella Del Prete, 'Gli astronomi romani e i loro strumenti: Christiaan Huygens di fronte agli estimatori e detrattori romani delle osservazioni di Saturno (1655–1665)' in *Rome et la science moderne: Entre Renaissance et Lumières*, ed by A. Romano (Rome, 2009), 473–489.

62 See: P. Guisoni to Christiaan Huygens, 1 August 1660, *Œuvres complètes de Christiaan Huygens* III, letter n. 765, 101–104 and S. Sorbière, 'De Vita et Moribus Petri Gassendi', *Opera omnia de Gassendi* I (Lyon, 1658), sig. i3v: 'PETRVM GVISONIVM Cauallionensem, iuuenem in Philosophicis & Mathematicis versatissimum'.

63 'MM. Sorbière and du Prat know how highly I esteem your illustrious name and those fine writings of yours by which all Europe is now instructed [...]. At M. de Montmor's academy M. du Prat led us to hope that you would explain to us the phenomenon of the rising of

Chapelain wrote to Huygens (who had inquired about him) that, although he was not personally acquainted with Guisony, he had indeed lectured on vegetation at Montmor's.[64]

Another Roman informant of Guisony was Michelangelo Ricci, who had informed him of the Florentine experiment on fumes in a vacuous space that was sent to Paris in the hope of establishing a fruitful exchange between the Cimento and the Montmor Academy.[65] It is also very likely that Ricci was the 'Gentilhomme de mes amis'[66] from whom Guisony had received details about the Saturn experiments long before Fabri and Divini, and who had made the Frenchman promise to keep such details secret until such time as the prince would have decided to make them public.

In October 1660,[67] minutes of the experiments, a letter from Leopoldo, and reports by Magalotti and Borelli were sent to Huygens via Heinsius. Huygens

---

water in the small siphon'. P. Guisony to Hobbes, 15 [/25] May 1659, Hobbes, *Correspondence*, 1: 501–502 (English transl. 502–503).

64 'Ce Monsieur Guisoni dont vous me demandés d'estre informé n'est point particulierement connu de moy. Je scay seulement qu'il est de Prouence, et que c'est vn Genie propre aux Speculations Physiques. Il sit vn jour ches Monsieur de Monmor vn Discours de la vegetation apres quelques autres, qui plut sort et qui parut fort sensé. Depuis nestant point venu a l'Assemblée on l'y a trouué fort à dire. Cette experience que vous me dittes qu'il a faitte en vostre presence fut faitte et examinée dans la Compagnie, et il me souuient qu'ayant à mon Auis attribué cette ascension de l'eau dans le petit tube plus haut que dans le grand, a la plus grande impression de la colonne d'air sur le large que sur lestroit, cette pensée eut beaucoup de partisans encore que dailleurs elle fust contreditte'. J. Chapelain to Christiaan Huygens, 20 August 1659, *Œuvres complètes de Christiaan Huygens* II, letter n. 655, 467–470.

65 The news had reached Ricci in order to be forwarded to Thévenot on 4 July 1660. On 1 August of the same year Guisony informed Huygens: 'Il Signor Ricci nobiluomo romano grande esperto in geometria e grande amico, mi ha detto da poco che il granduca è lieto che la sua accademia di Pisa comunichi con la nostra di Parigi e che a questo scopo le ha fatto inviare la seguente osservazione. Se con uno specchio d'acciaio si accende un corpo combustibile, abilmente sistemato nel luogo che nell'esperienza di Torricelli del sifone con il mercurio chiamiamo vuoto, il fumo anziché salire scende sul mercurio secondo la linea parabolica di Galilei. Questi Signori ne concludono contro gli aristotelici che non esiste leggerezza positiva: ciò non convince me che ci sia della pesantezza positive', P. Guisoni to Christiaan Huygens, 1 August 1660, *Œuvres complètes de Christiaan Huygens* III, letter n. 765, 101–104. Huygens was thus made aware of it before he heard from Thévenot himself a few months later, during his stay in Paris: 'Tevenot m'envoya l'observation de Florence de la fumée descendante dans le vuide', 5 December 1660: Brugmans, *Le séjour de Christian Huygens*, 135.

66 P. Guisoni to Christiaan Huygens, 27 August 1660, *Œuvres complètes de Christiaan Huygens* III, letter n. 774, 116–118.

67 C.R. Dati to N. Heinsius, 5 October 1660, *Œuvres complètes de Christiaan Huygens* III, Appendix I to letter n. 793, 149–150.

was about to leave for Paris, where he arrived on 28 October. During the days that followed he met with Chapelain and Montmor and, on 9 November, he attended, probably for the first time, a meeting at Montmor's residence, where Sorbière read a letter from Leopoldo to Boulliau on the 'making of a telescope'.[68] On that same day Huygens loaned 'papers he had received from Florence'[69] to Cosimo Brunetti.

Huygens received the documents piecemeal.[70] It is therefore difficult to know what exactly he was able to show to Brunetti. However, by 19 November Huygens had all the documents,[71] and on the 28th he informed Leopoldo that he had presented the 'most erudite theories of His Highness' Academicians' at a session of the Montmor Academy – making explicit reference to the report written for the Accademia, as well as to reports by Borelli and Magalotti which, Huygens noted, met with widespread approval.[72] On 16 and 28 December he loaned his *papiers de Florence* again, this time to Auzout and Thévenot.[73]

Further confirmation that the Cimento experiments had been met with great success at Montmor came from Thévenot himself. On 18 April 1661 Michelangelo Ricci wrote:

---

68   Brugmans, *Le séjour de Christian Huygens*, 129. Although the letter from Leopoldo to Boulliau is no longer extant, a similar instrument is described by the prince in a letter to Huygens dated 14 September 1660: Leopoldo de' Medici to Christiaan Huygens, 14 September 1660, *Œuvres complètes de Christiaan Huygens* III, letter n. 781, 129–131.

69   Brugmans, *Le séjour de Christian Huygens*, 128.

70   'Quantum ex Dati verbis colligo, eodem tempore omnia isthuc perlata fuere, sed quaedam eorum ipse perlegere voluisti, atque hac ratione a reliquis separata venerunt'. Christiaan Huygens to N. Heinsius, 19 November 1660, *Œuvres complètes de Christiaan Huygens* III, letter n. 809, 182–183.

71   See: Christiaan Huygens to N. Heinsius, 19 November 1660, *Œuvres complètes de Christiaan Huygens* III, letter n. 809, 182–183. On 17 November Huygens marked on his diary: 'M. van Beuningen m'envoya mes pacquets de Florence [...]. Le Pr. Leop. m'exhorta a l'observation de quelque estoile fixe a travers les anses de, ce que Frenicle aussi venoit de me dire'. Brugmans, *Le séjour de Christian Huygens*, 132. Among the missing pieces of the Florence file was therefore Leopoldo's letter: Leopoldo de' Medici to Christiaan Huygens, 4 October 1660, *Œuvres complètes de Christiaan Huygens* III, letter n. 795, 151.

72   'In hac urbe etsi ne unum quidem inveniam qui Astronomiae seriam operam det (Bullialdo peregre ad visendum Hevelium profecto) sunt tamen aliqui qui intelligant, ac Systema etiam nostrum examinarint quibus abhinc diebus paucis apud Illustrissimum Monmorium, ut solent, congregatis, ostendi doctissimas Academicorum Tuae Celsitudinis Diatribas (nam praeter illam Academiae nomine scriptam alias quoque binas Clarissimus Datus mihi impertijt, subtilissimi Borelli et ingeniosissimi Magalotti,) summaque cum approbatione et laudibus exceptas vidi'. Christiaan Huygens to Leopoldo de' Medici, 28 November 1660, *Œuvres complètes de Christiaan Huygens* III, letter n. 817, 195–198.

73   Brugmans, *Le séjour de Christian Huygens*, 138, 140.

Il Sig. Thévenot [...] mi parla di que' Discorsi inviati al Sig. Ugenio da lor altri Accademici con la lode che meritano, mostrando che siano stati molto stimati et approvati. Ammirano ambidue e godono straordinariamente de' progressi che si fanno in Italia, onore che le proviene da lor altri Sig.ri e dalla protezione del Sig. Principe, la cui generosità e virtù innalzano alle stelle [...].[74]

Leopoldo thus publicly reclaimed his role as a European patron of science via the Accademia.

No indication of further Florentine discussions about the experiments sent to Huygens are known to exist. However, the Saturn dispute remained one of the main topics in the exhanges between the two academies in subsequent years. With the exception of information on new and forthcoming books – such as Borelli and Abraham Ecchellensis's translation of Apollonius of Perga's *Conics*[75] and Thévenot's *Relations de divers voyages curieux*–[76] the correspondence between the two academies was dominated by astronomy-related news: about comets as well as information about Huygens' work.

Thus, Huygens' trip to Paris made it possible for the work of the Cimento's academicians to be known to the Montmor academy; and conversely, the trip also created a new channel of communication between Huygens, Rome, and Florence. As early as October 1660 Guisony advised the Dutch astronomer to write to Michelangelo Ricci, whom the prince held in high esteem and whom he used for all his communications with Fabri.[77] What survives of the correspondence suggests that Huygens did not follow his friend's advice before

---

74 M. Ricci to [L. Magalotti?], 18 April 1661, BNCF, Ms. Gal. 283, 154r-v.

75 *Apollonij Pergaei Conicorum lib. 5. 6. 7. paraphraste Abalphato Asphahanensi nunc primùm editi. Additus in calce Archimedis Assumptorum liber, ex codicibus Arabicis M.SS. serenissimi magni ducis Etruriae Abrahamus Ecchellensis maronita in alma vrbe linguar. orient. professor Latinos reddidit. Io. Alfonsus Borellus ... curam in geometricis versioni contulit, & notas vberiores in vniuersum opus adiecit.*, Florentiae: ex typographia Iosephi Cocchini ad insigne Stellae, 1661. See for instance: G.F Marucelli to Leopoldo de' Medici, 28 Ottobre 1661, BNCF, Ms. Gal. 276, c. 146r-147v; Leopoldo de' Medici to M. Thévenot, 10 December 1661, BNCF, Gal. 282, c. 62r; Leopoldo de' Medici to M. Thévenot, 11 September 1662, BNCF, Gal. 282, c. 57r; M. Thévenot to Leopoldo de' Medici, undated, BNCF, Gal. 280, c. 116r-v.

76 M. Thévenot, *Relations de divers voyages curieux* (Paris, 1663). See for instance: M. Thévenot to Leopoldo de' Medici, 7 May 1663, BNCF, Gal. 276, c. 191r-v; Leopoldo de' Medici to M. Thévenot, 8 June 1663, BNCF, Gal. 282, c. 69r-v; Abraham Ecchellensis to V. Viviani, 17 November 1663, BNCF, Gal. 254, c. 261r-262v.

77 'Si vos occupations vous le permettoient, ie crois qu'il seroit à propos que vous écriuissiés une petite lettre de compliment à Monsieur Michel Angelo Ricci gentilhomme de céte uille & le plus grand Geometre qu'il ỳ aye; le Prince qui l'estime beaucoup s'est serui de luy icy dans tous les ecrits, qu'il à receus ou enuoiés au Pere Fabry, & d'ailleurs il est fort uótre

February 1661.[78] The opportunity arose in Paris on 2 February 1661, when Thévenot showed Huygens a letter (now lost) that the former had received from Ricci,[79] in which reference was made to the *Systema Saturnium* and to its author. The correspondence between Ricci and Thévenot had therefore acquired a further scope besides being the primary means of communication between the Cimento and the Montmor Academy: it had now become the preferred channel through which news on Huygens' work crossed the Alps.[80] Via Thévenot the prince was informed in spring 1662, that new observations had led Huygens to change the proportions of the ring surrounding Saturn.[81] It is also possible that the Dutch astronomer himself wrote to Leopoldo around the same time to inform him directly of such changes, together with his criticism of Eustachio Divini's *Pro annotatione sua*.[82] Yet, it was again via Thévenot that in December 1662 the patron of the Cimento solicited updates on Huygens' Saturn system.[83] And it was again via Thévenot that Florence was informed of Huygens' work on dioptrics and that Huygens attempted to find the treatise published in 1660 by Antonio Mancini.[84]

---

ami'. P. Guisony to Christiaan Huygens, 20 October 1660, *Œuvres complètes de Christiaan Huygens* III, letter n. 789, 141–144.

78 See: *Œuvres complètes de Christiaan Huygens* III, letter n. 843, 248.
79 Brugmans, *Le séjour de Christian Huygens*, 149.
80 See for instance: *Œuvres complètes de Christiaan Huygens* III, letters n. 877, 899, pp. 302–303, 346–348; *Œuvres complètes de Christiaan Huygens* IV, letters n. 960, 1026, 1027, pp. 18–19, 160–161, 161–162.
81 'Scrive da Parigi Monsieur Thevenot ch'il Sig. Ugenio per alcune osservazioni fatte di nuovo hà mutata la proporzione della fascia al corpo di Saturno'. M. Ricci to Leopoldo de' Medici, 14 April 1662, BNCF, Ms. Gal. 276, c. 164r. This information had been passed on by Huygens to Chapelain in a letter dated 14 July 1661 (*Œuvres complètes de Christiaan Huygens* III, letter n. 873, pp. 294–296); on 24 June Huygens wrote about it to Moray as well (*Œuvres complètes de Christiaan Huygens* III, letter n. 868, 283–284), who in turn read out the letter at a session of the *Royal Society* on 8 October of the same year. See: Thomas Birch, *History of the Royal Society of London* (London, 1667), 49.
82 See: *Œuvres complètes de Christiaan Huygens* III, letter n. 1087, 286. The letter is not dated and does not mention the recipient. On the basis of a letter written by Huygens to his brother Lodewijk – in which he mentioned that he was planning to send Leopoldo his observations on Divini's latest treatise – the editors of Huygens' correspondence argue that the letter in question was addressed to Leopoldo. According to this theory the letter can only be later than 15 March 1662. See: Ibid, note 1.
83 '[…] ne scriverò in Parigi al Sig. Tevenot, acciò che […] faccia dar fuori al Sig. Ugenio l'altre notizie del suo sistema Saturnio'. M. Ricci to Leopoldo de' Medici, 24 December 1662, BNCF, Ms. Gal. 276, 181r.
84 Antonio Mancini, *L'Occhiale all'occhio, Dioptrica prattica* (Bononiae, 1660). See: M. Thévenot to Christiaan Huygens, 7 May 1661; Christiaan Huygens to M. Thévenot, 21 July 1661; Christiaan Huygens to M. Thévenot, [28 July 1661]; Christiaan Huygens to [M. Thévenot],

3 Some Final Considerations

The Saturn dispute held a fairly marginal place within the Accademia del Cimento. It is not mentioned in the *Saggi di naturali esperienze* (1667), the only work published by the Accademia; and the experimental activity carried out in Florence on the topic came to an end when the reports were sent to the Netherlands and Rome. Nonetheless, the topic was undoubtedly close to Leopoldo's heart, as it was to several academicians. The prince's interest in astronomy, which emerges in his extensive correspondence with Ismael Boulliau, and Borelli's endorsement of the *De Saturni luna observatio nova*, attest to this.

As for the relations between the Cimento and the Montmor Academy, it should be noted that Saturn is the only topic about which neither academy chose to communicate with the other. Thévenot did not inform the Florenitnes about Chapelain's presentation of the Saturn hypothesis to the Paris assembly, while the Parisian academy learnt about the Cimento experiments only through Huygens' own communication.

It should also be pointed out that, by showing and presenting the Cimento reports to the Montmor academy, Huygens probably trespassed or at least pushed the limits imposed by the prince. Indeed, when Carlo Dati sent Huygens the results of the experiments, the reports came with the following warning:

> Appresso auendo io ueduta la uolontà, e il desiderio del Signore Principe, non deuo celarlo a Vostra Signoria che questa scrittura dell'Accademia si mostri, e si legga liberamente a chi che sia non si repugna; ma per ora si desidera che non se ne faccia alcuna mentione pubblica [...].[85]

By granting Huygens permission to show or read the reports freely, it is possible that Leopoldo was simply worried that they might be mentioned in print. But it is noteworthy that after the Cimento academcians had initiated their 'literary trade' with the Paris academy, they did not even contemplate sending Thévenot their work on Saturn. On 4 October 1660, Michelangelo Ricci – perhaps the most enthusiastic supporter of the correspondence with the Montmor Academy – informed Magalotti that he had received the Saturn reports from Florence in addition to a letter from Thévenot, who '*was ecstatic* at

---

[6 October 1661], *Œuvres complètes de Christiaan Huygens* III, letters n. 858, 877, 880, 905, pp. 268–269, 302–303, 306, 359–362.

85 C. Dati to N. Heinsius, 3 Octobre 1660, *Œuvres complètes de Christiaan Huygens* III, letter n. 794, 149.

the news of the literary trade between the two academies'.[86] The Saturn experiments were carried out while the correspondence between the two groups was at its peak, and yet they were completely omitted in the letters until the Cimento reports were discussed at one of the Montmor sessions. Furthermore, the praise and appreciation expressed by Thévenot concerning the reports he heard in Paris were not followed by any further comments, nor were further details shared from Florence.

Even though Thévenot updated the prince on Huygens' activities, in practice the two academies never exchanged direct, substantative information on the dispute. And whilst we may assume a lack of mutual interests in the earlier and later exchanges – which could also explain why the attempts from either side to establish a dialogue failed – the interest and involvement of both groups in the Saturn dispute is manifest.

It is precisely the evidence of a shared and concomitant interest in the dispute that makes this episode in the relations between the two academies particularly worthy of notice. On the one hand, the almost simultaneous engagement of the two academies in the same problem offers a privileged standpoint from which to compare and contrast the methodologies, objectives, and preoccupations guiding the endeavors of the two academies. On the other hand, by ruling out the possibility of either assembly being disinterested in the subject, the withdrawal of information becomes a (more or less) conscious choice.

Regarding the first point, it has been shown that the Paris academy was primarily a site devoted to the exchange of information. Although written reports and letters were often the object of discussion, the primary format adopted was that of oral transmission. As for the Saturn dispute, no evidence survives to indicate that the group carried out observations of the planet. The Montmor salon was, and remained, a salon: a place where contrasting opinions were presented and discussed, but it was never configured as a laboratory. Rather than elaborating new scientific theories, the Paris academy was instead preoccupied with receiving, as early as possible, the most exciting news concerning the physical and celestial realms. Over time Huygens (and others) received several requests to send detailed accounts of their discoveries. Quite revealing in this regard is the account that Chapelain wrote to Huygens, identifying the dignitaries invited to attend the session in which his Saturn hypothesis was presented. Emphasis was placed not only on the attendance of renowned

---

86 '[...] Scrivo con questa occasione al Sig. Principe Serenissimo, e gli mando un piego del Sig. Thévenot, il quale giubila per la nuova del commercio letterario delle due Accademie, che da tutti que' Signori di Francia era tanto desiderato, e mi promette un Discorso et una lettera diretta al Sig. Principe in ringraziamento dell'onor ricevuto, a nome di tutta l'Accademia [...]'. M. Ricci to L. Magalotti, 14 October 1660, BNCF, Ms. Gal. 283, 131r-132v.

intellectuals, but also, and more importantly, on the presence of high-ranking figures within society more broadly. The Montmor academy was effectively an intellectual and social salon, one in which science was simply 'communicated'.

The aims of the scholars that met at Leopoldo's apartments in the Pitti Palace, in contrast, in, were quite different. Reluctant to communicate with the outside world, the Cimento academicians devoted themselves to intense collaborative experimental work. Even though the results of the experiments carried out on the basis of Huygens' and Fabri's hypotheses were never published, the primary scope of this investigation was to produce reliable results which, at least for a certain period of time, were to be disseminated in print. Leopoldo's academy saw itself as a site for the production of knowledge, rather than a salon where to discuss the most recent scientific news.

As for the second point, having ascertained that both groups had an interest in this theme, it is difficult to explain why information was not exchanged; but it is possible to detect what effectively remained unsaid.

In Florence, after the experiments carried out in the summer of 1660, no further significant investigations were conducted. The matter was concluded when Magalotti and Borelli sent their reports to Rome and to The Hague; and despite initial expectations, these reports were never officially published. As the correspondence clearly shows, Saturn's strange appearances were a particularly sensitive topic in light of the relations between the Grand Duchy and the Church. The regime that had so openly supported Galileo was now expected to be particularly cautious with the Copernican implications of Huygens' hypothesis – especially as in the *Brevis annotatio* Divini (and Fabri) argued that one of the main points against the Dutch astronomer's theory was precisely the fact that all Christians were expected to conform to the theory of Earth's immobility. Within the work of the Accademia, this issue is underscored by Michelangelo Ricci, the most influential of the prince's advisors on this matter. In one of his letters to Leopoldo, Ricci wrote:

> A friend of mine sent Divini's tract to Huygens; and I told him that Huygens must apply caution in his writing and not offend anybody, nor mention the Earth's motion, or any other topic that would offer cause to the Rome congregations to prohibit his writings; this would prevent the book from being sold, and would endanger the reputation of the cause itself. I am not sure whether Huygens has been warned, though he must do it, and argue his case by other means.[87]

---

[87] M. Ricci to Leopoldo de' Medici, 13 September 1660, Fabroni, *Lettere inedite* 2: 97.

The letter is dated 13 September 1660. By then, the Cimento academicians had finished their experiments, thus offering their assistance in resolving a dispute that could have had serious consequences for their patron. In an attempt to rescue the cause into which the Cimento academicians got themselves entangled, Ricci – with Guisony's help – tried to convince Huygens to omit from his considerations any reference to Copernicus' hypotheses.[88]

The fact remains that, at least until the reports were sent to Huygens, the Cimento's involvement with the Saturn dispute was shrouded in secrecy. Ricci imposed discretion on Guisony when he informed him of the experiments carried out in Florence; and a few weeks before the reports were sent to the Netherlands, Borelli indicated to Malpighi that the prince did not grant him permission to discuss the question beyond the academic sphere.[89]

Whereas these preoccupations might be sufficient to justify the fact that the Cimento research on Saturn was never published, they do not satisfactorily account for the Cimento's decision not to share the results with Paris. In July 1660, Thévenot did receive of a letter in which Leopoldo presented the experiment looking at the descending fumes which served not only as proof against positive lightness, but also as a demonstration of the real nature of the vacuous space caused by the mercury inside the Torricellian tube. That matter of void was no less sensitive an issue, one that could indeed have suffer ecclesiastical censorship; it is hardly accidental that this experiment is only mentioned in a very descriptive manner in the *Saggi*, with no reference to what motivated it, or to its demonstrative function. What is certain is that this self-censorship mechanism, which influenced the Cimento's activity on numerous occasions, was one of the factors that led to the decision not to share the reports directly with Paris. Yet we have seen how, shortly before that, the Cimento academicians were perfectly comfortable to discuss the issue of the 'void' with Paris.

On the French side, news of the discussion of Huygens' hypothesis at the Montmor residence did not reach Florence before the spring of 1658. What is

---

88 '[...] si vous leur repondiés, prenés garde d'en venir aux iniures & de toucher à la religion, car ce seroit leur soühait & à vos liures un obstacle d'étre ueus en Italie, par ce qu'ils fairoient agir l'inquisition'. P. Guisony to Christiaan Huygens, 27 August 1660, *Œuvres complètes de Christiaan Huygens* III, letter n. 774, 116–118.

89 '[...] Riverisca da parte mia il' Sigr. Mariani, ed il Sigr. Cassini; ed a questo dirà, che qui stiamo occupati intorno l'osservazioni di Saturno con tele[s]copij di e più lunghi forsi, che siano visti, ed à me è toccato nell'Accademia di Sua Altezza di far' le relazioni, e censure delle due operette dedicate al' Serenissimo Principe dall'Eugenio, e da Eustachio intorno all'apparente forma di Saturno, delle quali cose ne parteciperò lor' Sigri., quando però Sua Altezza lo permetta'. A. Borelli to M. Malpighi, 18 September 1660. Marcello Malpighi, *The Correspondence of Marcello Malpighi*, ed. Howard B Adelmann, 5 vols (Ithaca-London, 1975), 1:43–44.

THE 'SATURN DISPUTE'   107

even more striking is the total lack of communications from Paris concerning the debates that followed around the Saturn dispute.

After Huygens had amended the ring's dimensions, Bernard Frénicle de Bessy (c. 1604–1674) had elaborated a hypothesis to explain Saturn's appearances. In August 1661 the Frenchman – a regular attendee of Motnmor's sessions – almost simultaneously informed Huygens[90] and Kenelm Digby (1603–1655),[91] one of the founders of the *Royal Society*, of his theory. Following a discussion of the theory in London,[92] Christopher Wren's (1635–1723)[93] earlier theory was communicated to Frénicle and Huygens, which prompted a brief correspondence between the two.[94]

Frénicle's communications had primarily the features of a private initiative, while the Montmor Academy was more a space for dissemination and debate than a centre for the actual production of knowledge. Thus, in contrast to what happened in Florence, the members' work was the product of individual activity, and was never claimed as the work of the academy as a whole. Nevertheless, the issue was discussed again during the sessions of the Paris group, and both Chapelain and Thévenot strove to persuade the Frenchman of the reliability of Huygens' conclusions.[95] Even though Frénicle argued in his letter to Digby that his hypotheses were based on the observations carried out in Florence and presented in Paris the previous year,[96] no information about it was ever sent to Leopoldo or his academicians.

---

90   B. de Frenicle de Bessy to Christiaan Huygens, 26 August 1661, *Œuvres complètes de Christiaan Huygens* III, letter n. 901, 349–354. In the end Huygens received Frenicle's letter from Thévenot only after he had already been informed by Moray of the discussion of Frenicle's letter to Digby at a session of the *Royal Society*. See: R. Moray to Christiaan Huygens, 16 September 1661, *Œuvres complètes de Christiaan Huygens* III, letter n. 888, 321–322.

91   [B. Frenicle de Bessy] to [K. Digby], 31 August 1661, *Œuvres complètes de Christiaan Huygens* III, letter n. 894, 337–339.

92   See: Thomas Birch, *History of the Royal Society of London* (London, 1667), 43.

93   Upon appointment of the *Royal Society*, Wren enclosed his theories and observations on Saturn in a letter to Sir Paul Neil. Contrary to Wren's requests, the letter was then forwarded to Huygens and Frénicle. See: Chr. Wren to P. Neil, 11 October 1661, letters n. 932, 933, 934, pp. 415–424. See also: Mordechai Feingold, 'Huygens and the Royal Society', *De Zeventiende Eeuw*, 12 (1996), 22–36; Albert Van Helden, '"Annulo Cingitur": The Solution of the Problem of Saturn', *Journal for the History of Astronomy* 5 (1974), 155–174, 166.

94   See: B. de Frenicle de Bessy to Christiaan Huygens, 5 December 1661, *Œuvres complètes de Christiaan Huygens* III, letter n. 927, 401–404.

95   See for instance: J. Chapelain to Christiaan Huygens, 17 February 1662, *Œuvres complètes de Christiaan Huygens* IV, letter n. 982, 61–63.

96   'Ayant veu l'annee passee les observations de florence, qui faisoient voir que l'anneau de ♄ passoit iusques sur le bord de son disque, ie creus qu'il nestoit pas possible que la cause de ces differents aspects, sous les quels il se montre, ne fut que dans le parallaxe, ainsi que

With regard to the communications between the two academies, the Saturn dispute therefore holds a special place. It has often been noted in the literature that the beginnings of various scientific academies are punctuated by a dynamics of competition. The fact that the two groups never had any direct exchanges when it came to an issue in which both had a clear interest, would seem to confirm this theory.

The relations between the two academies reached their peak with Saturn, although this convergence was not the result of an explicit choice. What made it possible was not the activity of the respective secretaries, or the official inception of an institutional exchange; the convergence was made possible by the network of correspondents that gravitated around the individual members and Leopoldo even before the creation of the two groups. It is therefore thanks to this *Republica litteraria*, as Leopoldo called it, composed of Boulliau, Huygens, Chapelain, Ricci and Guisony, that these young scientific academies were able, after many failed attempts, to share something of substance.

Acknowledgements

This article is part of a project that has received funding from the European Union's Horizon 2020 Research and Innovation Programme (GA n. 818098 TACITROOTS)

---

pretend le Seigneur Huguenes de Zulichem dans Son Sistema Saturnium'. [B. Frenicle de Bessy] to [K. Digby], 31 August 1661, *Œuvres complètes de Christiaan Huygens* III, letter n. 894, 337–339.

CHAPTER 5

The Edifying Science. Academies, Courtly Culture and the Patronage of Science in Early-modern Portugal (1647–1720)

Luís Miguel Carolino

1   Introduction

On 8 December 1720, King João V signed the charter of the Royal Academy of Portuguese History (*Academia Real da História Portuguesa*). Established with the general aim of writing the religious and secular history of the Portuguese kingdom, this institution would become a cornerstone of the cultural policy of the Portuguese absolutist monarchy, furthering the image of João V as a munificent and philanthropic king. Physicians and *virtuosi* were among its initial members.[1] Nevertheless, as happened with the Royal Society, the Paris Academy of Sciences and the majority of official learned societies throughout early modern Europe, the origins of the Royal Academy of History actually derive largely from the private gatherings previously held in the capital city. In particular, it stemmed to a large extent from the reputed Portuguese Academy (*Academia Portuguesa*), itself a metamorphosis of the Academy of the Generous (*Academia dos Generosos*), a learned society whose origins had dated back to the mid-seventeenth century. As the English born, French Theatine cleric and pivotal figure in the early years of the Royal Academy of History, Raphael Bluteau (1638–1734) detailed a couple of years prior to the transformation of the amateur society into a chartered, state sponsored institution,

> General acclaim deserved and great success obtained by the inextinguishable Academy of the Generous which, under the insignia of a burning candle and the motto *Non extinguetur* successfully committed itself to keep the immortal light burning. Since its establishment in the year of 1647, it kept alive for more than seventy years and on this day burns even brighter under the same name of Generous, because Portuguese

---

1   The foundation charter, the first statutes and a list of initial fellows of the Royal Academy of History are reproduced in *Collecçam dos Documentos, Estatutos e Memórias da Academia Real da História Portugueza*, 1 (Lisbon, 1721), pages not numbered.

generosity also perpetuates in discretion and just when it seems extinguished, more strongly does it reinvigorate: *Non extinguetur*.[2]

Historians have stressed the great changes that these academies experienced as the seventeenth century progressed. Not only did they increase substantially in number but they also became progressively state-recognized, and in some cases – such as the Royal Academy of History –, state-sponsored institutions. The complex institutionalization process of academies seems therefore concomitant with the emergence of early modern states. The needs of the intellectual community to establish new forms of organization closely matched the demands for increasingly centralized and bureaucratic states. The putting into practice of mercantilist-inspired economic policies that accompanied the political centralization led to new functions for the members of the Republic of Letters, specifically that of consultant on scientific and technical matters to the crown. As this required increasing functional specialization, royal authorities tended to correspondingly encourage specialized academies. In doing so, this process contributed towards shaping the identity of an emergent scientific community. Utility, experimental-based knowledge and inter-pares evaluation gained momentum over more established forms of learning and intellectual authority. The creation of the Paris Academy of Sciences is usually identified as the corollary example of this process of mutual reinforcement between the institutionalization of science and state making.[3]

The Portuguese case, however, apparently challenges this narrative. At the time when general academies devoted to literature and culture were allegedly

---

2 'Mayor admiração merece, e melhor successo teve a inextinguivel *Academia dos Generosos*, que com a empreza de huma vela acceza, e por mote *Non extinguetur*, prometteo, e vay conservando huma luz immortal; porque desde a sua instituição no anno de 1647 ha mais de setenta anos que se perpetua, e hoje torna a sahir mais luzida, com o mesmo titulo de Generosos, porque a generosidade Portugueza tambem na discrição se eterniza, e quando parece extincta, com mais vigor resuscita: *Non extinguetur*'. Raphael Bluteau, *Prosas Portuguesas recitadas em differentes Congressos Academicos* (Lisbon, 1728), 22.

3 See, for example, the classic study by Roger Hahn, *The anatomy of a scientific institution. The Paris Academy of Sciences, 1666–1803* (Berkeley, 1971). Nevertheless, David S. Lux, *Patronage and royal science in seventeenth-century France. The Académie de Physique in Caen* (Ithaca, 1989) has clearly demonstrated that royal patronage was not in itself a sine qua non condition for the success of scientific academies and scientific improvement. Even in England, where absolutism did not take root, there was a relationship between political centralization and the institutionalization of science. As Michael Hunter refers, 'it was in the 1680s, when England came closer to absolutism than at any other time in this period in the reaction that followed the failure of the Whigs, that natural philosophy came nearest to achieving the 'established' position that English scientists had desired ever since the Restoration'. M. Hunter, *Science and society in Restoration England* (Cambridge, 1981), 127.

giving way to specialized institutions, the Royal Academy of History pursued the early model of wide-raging academies devoted to encyclopaedic knowledge. In its sessions, history, poetry and linguistic digressions took place along with scientific excursuses. Even if compared with more general scientific academies, such as the Berlin Royal Academy established by the King of Prussia in 1700 or the Academy of Sciences of Saint Petersburg founded by Tzar Peter the Great in 1724, which included classes of literature and humanities respectively,[4] the Royal Academy of History still appears as a much broader establishment and a type of all-purpose institution.

Nevertheless, the Portuguese state was a centralized state in every means under João V. Furthermore, the state held strong colonial interests with its revenues largely dependent upon its colonial possessions in Africa and America. As recent historiography has pointed out, centralized states with colonial aspirations tended to foster a culture of patronage that promoted 'utilitarian science'. Elizabethan England and sixteenth and early seventeenth century Portugal are cases in point.[5] Further development of the interaction between imperial interests and the organization of a state scientific undertaking emerges in Old Regime France.[6] As in France, practical needs, intimately interrelated with state affairs, for example the demarcation of the borders between Spanish and Portuguese possessions in South America, represented pressing issues for the Portuguese authorities of the eighteenth century. Nevertheless, while still promoting the institutionalization of learned academies in Portugal, the Portuguese king did not enact a scientific assembly. Why did João V opt not to establish an academy of science in Lisbon[7] as Louis XIV, a king João V was always keen to emulate, did in Paris?

This paper argues that, stemming from the previous academic movement, the Royal Academy of History embodied some of its core characteristics. The wide-raging scope of interests covered by the Royal Academy of History drew its precedents from the literary academies of seventeenth century. This feature seemed to fit particularly well with the polymath character of Portuguese academicians but also appeared very appropriate in a context in which science

---

4 James E. McClellan III, *Science Reorganized. Scientific Societies in the Eighteenth Century* (New York, 1985), 68–83.
5 Stephen Pumfrey and Frances Dawbarn, 'Science and patronage in England: 1570–1625: a preliminary study', *History of Science*, 42 (2004), 137–188; Luís Miguel Carolino, 'Science, Patronage, and Academies in early seventeenth-century Portugal: the Scientific Academy of the Nobleman and University Professor André de Almada', *History of Science*, 55 (2016), 107–137.
6 James E. McClellan III and François Regourd, *The Colonial Machine. French Science and Overseas Expansion in the Old Regime* (Turnhout, 2011).
7 The Lisbon Royal Academy of Science was established only in 1779.

was poorly institutionalized and wherein only a meagre scientific community existed. As this paper shall demonstrate, there were very few sources of scientific patronage in early-modern Portugal. Apart from medical specialists and the community of professional astrologers, with the large majority having training in astronomy and medicine, the scientific community included but a few cosmographers and engineers, who made their living as civil servants, and the Jesuit professors of philosophy and mathematics. Whereas the former took place in the seventeenth century academies, the latter generally remained absent from these learned societies.

An academy of history was also closely aligned with the political aims of an absolutist monarchy in the making. Founded in the wake of the coup-d'état that had granted the political independence of Portugal from Habsburg Spain, the academies of the seventeenth century had played a political role. By mobilizing the patronage relations previously supported by the Portuguese nobility and in addition to members of the former academies, the Royal Academy of History furthered the cultural goal of these learned institutions and strengthened their political mission. In the past, noble patrons had endorsed learned academies with the aim of cultivating an ideal of culture modelled on exemplary 'courtesy' literature, in particular on Castiglione's *Cortegiano*. With the establishment of a Royal Academy of History, members of the Republic of Letters would further spur on the advance of an absolutist regime in Portugal. History suited that purpose particularly well.

Yet, in the early modern period, history constituted a literary genre that comprised not only the narrative of human records but also descriptions of the natural world. As Gianna Pomata and Nancy Siraisi point out, 'in striking contrast to the modern use of the term 'history', the early modern *historia* straddled the distinction between human and natural subjects, embracing accounts of objects in natural world as well as record of human action. One may say, in fact, that from the early Renaissance to the eighteenth century, nature was fully part of the field of research called *historia*'.[8] This understanding of history prevailed in the Portuguese Academy of History. Thus, as in the previous seventeenth century academies, there was room to include scientific fields in the new institution.

Portuguese authors perceived the Royal Academy of History as the embodiment of a new model of academy, a comprehensive academy spanning the functions of the extant academies, including scientific academies. In fact, Portuguese Academy of History, like its institutional ancestors, paralleled to

---

[8] 'Introduction' to *Historia. Empiricism and Erudition in Early Modern Europe* eds. Gianna Pomata and Nancy G. Siraisi (Cambridge, 2005), 1–2.

certain extent the academies of Rome. As Maria Pia Donato and others have shown, in seventeenth and eighteenth centuries, a plurality of all-encompassing academies arose in Rome. Reflecting the diversity of competing powers in the centre of the Catholic World, these academies functioned as critical *loci* of sociability for those who aimed at entering the ubiquitous system of patronage that regulated social, intellectual and professional life in Rome. Roman academies were thus attended by a large number of young religious personnel and scholars who aspired to reach the pinnacle of the ecclesiastic structures. From this point of view, Roman institutions tended to diverge from the more specialized academies that succeed in other European cities. Although one can argue that Roman academies legitimized different and competing approaches to the study of nature, their interests went far beyond scientific subjects, giving a special emphasis to issues relevant to the education of the Roman courtiers, such as religious and civil history, antiquarian, poetry and literature.[9] Given the close cultural relationships that tied Lisbon and Rome in the early eighteenth century, it is likely that the example of the Roman academies resonate in the Royal Academy of History. Francisco Xavier de Meneses and Manuel Caetano de Sousa, two of the most active members of the Royal Academy of History, not only sojourned in Rome, but also ordered usually books and manuscripts from Rome.[10] Caetano de Sousa even urged the need to write a history of Portugal along the lines of those being carried out in Roman academies.[11]

The Royal Academy of History was thus based upon prior and contemporary academic experiences. By fostering the multifarious character of the former academies while endowing them with a more political orientation, the Royal Academy of History reshaped the learned society movement in Portugal. Nevertheless, and despite being part of a process of political centralization, this ended up contributing neither to the emergence of specialized academies nor to the formation of any scientific community. Quite the contrary, the foundation of the Royal Academy of History caused the Portuguese academic

---

9   Maria Pia Donato, 'Accademie e accademismi in una capitale particolare. Il caso di Roma, secoli XVIII–XIX, *Mélanges de l'École française de Rome. Italie et Méditerranée*, 111 (1999), 415–430 ; Donato, *Accademie romane. Una storia sociale, 1671–1824* (Naples, 2000); Donato, 'Late Seventeenth-Century "Scientific" Academies in Rome and the Cimento's Disputed Legacy' in *The Accademia del Cimento and its European Context* eds. Marco Beretta, Antonio Clericuzio and Lawrence M. Principe (Sagamore Beach, 2009), 151–164; Federica Favino, 'Beyond the "Moderns"? The *Accademia Fisico-Matematica* of Rome (1677–1698) and the vaccum', *History of Universities*, 23/2 (2008), 120–158.
10 Angela Delaforce, *Art and Patronage in Eighteenth-Century Portugal* (Cambridge, 2002), 72, 78–79.
11 Delaforce, *Art and Patronage*, 79.

movement to diverge from the institutionalization process of scientific academies that was then taking place in Europe. This paper approaches this complex and highly consequential process.

2   Noble Pursuits: The Patronage of Science and Letters

In one of the very last meetings of the Portuguese Academy, held in early 1721, a fellow evoked the modelling role of the founding father of the Portuguese academic movement, António Álvares da Cunha.

> The sciences, mistreated by those who, because of their ignorance, view them with disdain, have found refuge in this very same house of the lord António Álvares da Cunha, whose virtues cannot be sufficiently glorified and praised; who, among many other honours, attained the glory of being the founder of the first academy and the institutor of the second. These chairs, formerly the seat of learned and eminent presidents and erudite and distinguished fellows, and these very same walls, which still echo to the discrete voices of the earlier academicians, encourage us in the pursuit of glory, by following the model of the past.[12]

The Portuguese Academy fellows thus traced the origins of their academy back to the Academy of the Generous established in 1647 by António Álvares da Cunha (1626–1690).[13] The Academy of the Generous started out as an informal academy that gathered at the house of Cunha. In the following decades, this academy alternated between periods of regular activity with phases of presumed inactivity. Despite its initial aims and the official functions of the

---

[12]   'Na mesma caza do Sr. Dom Antonio Alvarez da Cunha, cujas virtudes não só não podem ser encarecidas mas nem ainda cabalmente louvadas, a quem sobre tantas gloriosas congruencias lhe sobra pera occupar a voz da fama o ser instituidor da primeyra Academia, e instaurador da segunda. Pera esta caza parece quer se tem retirado as sciencias maltratadas da rude aspereza de muytos, que as desprezão porque as ignorão. [...] Estas mesmas cadeyras occupadas de tantos igualmente sabios que esclarecidos presidentes, e de tantos eruditos como illustres mestres; e estas mesmas paredes, que com aquella voz que entende bem a veneração parece que repetem ainda os ecchos das discretas vozes dos passados Academicos, são forçosos incentivos da gloria a que nos preparamos nas imitaçoens que pretendemos'. Biblioteca Nacional de Portugal (National Library of Portugal – henceforth BNP), COD. 3181, fols. 64v.-65r.

[13]   In the first couple of years, it was designated simply as the Academy (*Academia*). Elze M.H. Von Matias, 'A Academia dos Generosos. Uma academia ou uma sequência de academias?', *Revista da Biblioteca Nacional*, 2 (1982), 223–241 (224).

Generous and its leading academics, the institution did not contribute towards fostering a consistent endeavour.

Under the patronage of António Álvares da Cunha, the academy stretched out its activities most probably through to 1666.[14] In this period, it functioned basically on an informal and irregular basis, producing very few printed works. Álvares da Cunha was a noble with close ties to the royal court. The son of a higher administrative officer in India and the nephew of the Archbishop of Lisbon, from whom he not only received his education but also the title of Lord of Tábua (*senhor de Tábua*), António served as the royal *trinchante*[15] to the kings João IV, Afonso VI and Pedro II. A member of a family that strongly supported the coup d'état that brought an end to the Spanish Habsburg rule over the Portuguese kingdom in 1640 – the so-called Restoration (*Restauração*) –, he took a full part, along with other noble fellows from the Academy of the Generous, in the Restoration wars against Spain that were ongoing 1640 to 1668.[16] He held other influential posts, including that of supervisor of the Royal archive (*guarda-mor da Torre do Tombo*), a job that played no small role in his activity as a member of the Academy of the Generous and as a historian devoted to genealogy. Cunha's contemporaries considered him as the 'model of the perfect courtier'.[17] He authored a vast poetical *opus*, which remained for the most part in manuscript.[18] Furthermore, Cunha was appointed fellow of the Royal Society in 1668, being the first Portuguese to receive such an honour.[19]

In the mid-1680s, after two decades of apparent inactivity, the Academy of the Generous was reanimated by one of António Álvares da Cunha's sons, Luís

---

14   A very well documented study of the academic movement in the seventeenth and eighteenth centuries academies in Portugal is provided by Elze M.H. Von Matias, 'As Academias Literárias Portuguesas dos séculos XVII e XVIII', PhD. Diss., Universidade de Lisboa, 1988. See also João Palma-Ferreira, *Academias Literárias dos séculos XVII e XVIII* (Lisbon, 1982) and Matias, 'A Academia dos Generosos'.

15   *Trinchante* was the official responsible for cutting the king's food in public ceremonies.

16   Later Cunha authored an extensive and detailed account of the crucial battles that took place in the south of Portugal in 1663. A.A. da Cunha, *Campanha de Portugal pella Provincia do Alentenjo na Primavera do anno de 1663* (Lisbon, 1663).

17   António Caetano de Sousa, *História Genealógica da Casa Real Portuguesa*, quoted in Isabel Cluny, *D. Luís da Cunha e a ideia de diplomacia em Portugal* (Lisbon, 1999), 22.

18   The most comprehensive study on Cunha's biography, his role as institutor of the Academy of the Generous and his literary activities is by Clarinda Maria Rocha dos Santos, 'O Académico *Ambicioso*. D. António Álvares da Cunha e o aparecimento das Academias em Portugal', PhD. Diss., Universidade do Porto, 2012.

19   *The Record of the Royal Society of London for the promotion of Natural Knowledge*, 4th edition (London, 1940), 380.

da Cunha (1662–1749).[20] Following the path usual to second-born sons of Portuguese nobility, Luís received a university education and served in the royal administration. He graduated in Canon Law from the University of Coimbra in 1685 before serving as a judge in the higher courts first in Oporto and then in Lisbon. In the late 1690s, Luís da Cunha embarked on a diplomatic career, which would gain him a great reputation. Cunha served as ambassador to London, Paris and Madrid and was one of the Portuguese representatives to the Treaty of Utrecht (1713).[21]

With Luís da Cunha's long absence from Lisbon, the Academy of the Generous momentarily lost its driving force. However, it soon found a new patron, Francisco Xavier de Meneses (1673–1743), Count of Ericeira and son of a leading minister of King Pedro II. Francisco Xavier continued the family tradition of serving the Bragança monarchy in its higher administrative and military positions. He took part in senior governing councils and served as a high ranking military officer. He was also an active member of the Republic of Letters, writing numerous works on history, poetry and philosophy.[22] There is thus little wonder that he supported Academy of the Generous activities, particularly between 1696 and 1705 and from 1717 to 1721, when the academy was integrated into the Royal Academy of History, an institution in which Meneses was to assume a central role. Throughout those two distinct moments, the academy became known respectively as the Erudite Conferences (*Conferências Eruditas*) and the Portuguese Academy (*Academia Portuguesa*). The academic engagement and intellectual achievements of Meneses were later recognized by the Royal Society, which elected him a fellow in 1736.[23]

This overview description of the patrons of the Academy of the Generous reveals a fundamental characteristic of the patronage relationship established in Portugal. Unlike events in some regions of northern and central Europe, where the consolidation of regional power favoured the emergence of sophisticated forms of scientific patronage which, in some cases, functioned as the kernel of a scientific community, in Portugal, the longest lasting patronage relationships seemed more dependent on the nobility and correspondingly interlinked with the royal court and government. The two main patrons of the Academy of the Generous, António Álvares da Cunha and Francisco Xavier de Meneses, were courtiers and the king's own servants. In fact, these were not at

---

20   Palma-Ferreira, *Academias*, 33; Matias, 'A Academia dos Generosos', 223.
21   On Luís da Cunha's life and career, see Cluny, *D. Luís da Cunha*.
22   Ofélia M.C. Paiva Monteiro, *No alvorecer do 'Iluminismo' em Portugal. D. Francisco Xavier de Meneses, 4° Conde da Ericeira* (Coimbra, 1963).
23   *The Record of the Royal Society*, 405.

all exceptional cases. Historians of the Portuguese aristocracy have long argued that, in this country, the aristocratic elite soon became increasingly dependent on royal graces and favours. The overseas expansion and the founding of the Portuguese empire granted additional revenues to the royal finances that ensured the king did not have to exclusively rely on land-incomes (as happened in most of central and northern Europe) and, consequently, to strengthen the clientage ties binding the noble households to the king and royal interests. By distributing pensions (*tenças*) and offices of governance in the overseas empire, Portuguese sovereigns secured the partnership of the main families of the Portuguese aristocracy. Thus, whereas in central Europe and some parts of Italy, the upper nobility depended on concentrated power, privileges and social prestige on a regional scale, in Portugal, the upper nobility resided in and relied upon the Royal Court.[24] In other words, in seventeenth century Portugal, no 'man of science' found the conditions for patronage similar to those experienced by Galileo in Medicean Florence or Cristopher Rothmann under Wilhelm IV, Landgrave of Hesse-Kassel.

Needless to say, this central feature of the patronage relation bore many effects for the Portuguese academies. Academies highly dependent on the patronage of courtly nobility, such as the Academy of the Generous, tended to have only an intermittent existence. An appointment far away from Lisbon, in all likelihood, meant discontinuing with the academic activities. These were the cases, for example, of Luís da Cunha's appointment as judge to the Porto higher court in 1686, or the nomination of Francisco Xavier de Meneses as governor of Évora in 1705. Periods of Academy of the Generous inactivity followed both these appointments.

Promoted mostly by courtly nobles or the king's senior servants, these academies also tended to become elitist institutions. Their members were above all people of noble extraction but also those dependent on the nobility as well as

---

24   On the Portuguese aristocratic elite, see, among others, Mafalda Soares da Cunha, *A Casa de Bragança, 1560–1640. Práticas senhoriais e redes clientelares* (Lisbon, 2000); Nuno Gonçalo Monteiro, 'Notas sobre nobreza, fidalguia e titulares nos finais do Antigo Regime', *Ler história*, 10 (1987), 15–51; N.G. Monteiro, *O crepúsculo dos grandes. A casa e o património da aristocracia em Portugal,* 2nd ed. Revised (Lisbon, 2003); N.G. Monteiro, *Elites e poder. Entre o Antigo Regime e o Liberalismo*, 3rd ed. (Lisbon, 2012); N.G. Monteiro, Pedro Cardim, M.S. da Cunha, eds., *Optima pars. Elites ibero-americanas do Antigo Regime* (Lisbon, 2005). An overview in English of the historiography of Portuguese aristocracy can be found in N.G. Monteiro, '17th and 18th century Portuguese nobilities in the European context: a historiographical overview', *e-Journal of Portuguese history*, 1 (2003), 1–15 and N.G. Monteiro, 'Nobility and Aristocracy in Ancien Régime Portugal (Seventeenth to Nineteenth Centuries)' in, *The European Nobilities in the Seventeenth and Eighteenth Centuries*, H.M. Scott ed., vol. 1: *Western and Southern Europe*, 2nd edition (Basingstoke, 2007), 256–284.

state functionaries.[25] This would prove an important antidote to the somewhat discontinuous nature of these academies. After periods in which there were apparently no academic meetings, successive patrons took charge of the academy and once again joined together the still active members. Despite the fact that, in some cases, they attributed different titles to these assemblies (in particular, the Erudite Conferences and the Portuguese Academy), continuous generations of patrons and fellows shared both the same academy ideal and the same collective behaviour and ethos, whose origins they were willing to attribute to the first academy launched in the late 1640s by António Álvares da Cunha, deemed the model of the perfect courtier. This strong sense of identity is superlatively embodied in the academy's motto *Non extinguetur*. Successive generations of academicians perceived themselves as the torch bearers of the wisdom that must never perish. As expressed in an academic digression from the late seventeenth century, 'in truth, human life is similar to a torch which a single breath of air can extinguish. However, in the case of the torch of wisdom (which is the *motto* of this academy) neither time will kill it nor will it ever extinguish. *Non extinguetur*'.[26]

The Academy of the Generous sessions consisted by and large of displays of courtly culture. As the extant material produced on those occasions reveals, poetry occupied a central role in the academic sessions in conjunction with laudatory discourses and lectures on historical and literary issues. Usually, the president suggested a topic for each session and a number of academicians composed poetical works or discourses accordingly. The academic compositions cover the usual themes of baroque literature with a particular emphasis placed on moralizing issues. The eulogy of political and civil virtues was also

---

25   The Academy of the Generous was a case in point. In its first meetings, this academy gathered members of the Portuguese higher nobility, including the Count of Ericeira (Luís de Meneses, 1632–1690, father of Francisco Xavier de Meneses, the author of the celebrated book *História de Portugal Restaurado* and an influential minister to Pedro II) and the Marquis of Alegrete. It also comprised the elite of public servants and officials. These were the cases, for example, of the secretary of state, diplomat and writer António de Sousa Macedo and Luís Serrão Pimentel, who, besides being the royal chief-cosmographer and engineer, also served as professor of mathematics and fortification in the Fortification and Military Architecture Class (*Aula de Fortificação e Arquitectura Militar*). The complete list of early members of the Academy of the Generous is provided in Santos, 'O Académico *Ambicioso*', 57–58.

26   'He na verdade a vida humana semelhante a huma tocha que com qualquer assopro se apaga; mas a tocha da sabedoria (que he a diuiza desta Academia) com nenhuma antiguidade do tempo ha-de morrer, nem extinguirse. *Non extinguetur*'. *Primeiras e Segundas Liçoens feitas na Academia de D. Antonio Alueres da Cunha,* Library of Congress, Washington, Portuguese Manuscripts P-244, fol. not numbered [74r.].

CERTAMEN ACADEMICO
Em onze Combates
Na Paleſtra
Dos generosos de Lisboa.
A memoravel Victoria do Canal.

FIGURE 5.1   Frontispiece of a collective work by the Academy of the Generous, with the academy's *motto* 'Non extinguetur' and the respective depiction of the torch of wisdom

commonplace. Events related with the royal family, such as the births and marriages of the few Braganças, also represented a constant source of inspiration.[27] The same happened with the fortunes of the Restoration wars. In one of the few Academy of Generous publications, organized by António Álvares da Cunha to celebrate victory in the battle of Ameixial (8 June 1663), a great number of Generous academicians contributed poetical works exalting the Portuguese king and the nobility that fought in the war.[28] The Academy of the Generous's cultural mission was thus from the outset endowed with a political agenda.[29]

---

27 For exemple, *Varios Versos ao felix nacimento do serenissimo Infante Dom Pedro Manoel. Dos Academicos a que Preside Dom Affonso de Meneses* (Lisbon, 1648) and *Certamen Epithalamico publicado na Accademia dos Generosos de Lisboa ao felicissimo casamento do sempre Augusto e Inuicto Monarcha D. Affonso VI no nome, Rey de Portugal, com a Soberana Princeza D. Maria Francisca Isabel, rainha e senhora nossa,* (Lisbon, 1666).

28 António Álvares da Cunha, *Aplauzos Academicos e rellaçaõ do felice successo da celebre victoria do Ameixal offerecidos ao Excelentissimo Senhor Dom Sancho Manoel, Conde de Villafor, pello Secretario da Academia dos Generosos* (Amsterdam, 1673).

29 The engagement of the founding father of the Generous, António Álvares da Cunha, to affixing the text of the Lyrics of Luís de Camões in a book he dedicated to King Pedro II

However, the Academy of the Generous held a more ambitious goal in aiming not only to delight its fellows with exquisite poetry and erudite discourses but also to offer courtly culture, a culture modelled on the ideal of the perfect courtier. In one meeting of the Academy that took place in António Álvares da Cunha's home, in the late 1660s, the president of the session, Francisco de Azevedo, while presenting the activities that followed, took the chance to recapitulate the ultimate goals of the Academy,

> Here the fruits of sciences grow and here philosophy is instilled in its three branches, Ethics, Economics and Politics, distinguishing between private and public government. Ethics teaches a particular person how to rule one's own life, Economics to rule that particular house and Politics to rule the Republic's own common good.[30]

In fact, the program for that session tried in part to meet such wide-ranging goals. Four speeches addressing history, military science (by the chief-cosmographer Luís Serrão Pimentel), Aristotle's Politics and the Geography of Ptolemy were planned.[31] Decades later, this all-embracing scope of the academy persisted. On 26 May 1717, when the Academy of the Generous was revived as the Portuguese Academy, a set of lections were scheduled to take place in the palace of the academy's patron, the Count of Ericeira, on each Wednesday[32] afternoon throughout the following weeks. The program read as follows:

(Luís de Camões, *Terceira parte das Rimas do princepe dos poetas portugueses de Luis de Camoens* ed. António Álvares da Cunha (Lisbon, 1668)) was probably part of this project for the cultural affirmation of the Portuguese language. Similarly to the Academy of Crusca in Florence, whose goal of supporting the Tuscan language as the literary Italian language led to the elaboration of Tuscan dictionaries in the early seventeenth century,the Academy of the Generous, and particularly Cunha, strove to secure the literary dignity of Portuguese as national language. On Academy of Crusca, see Michele Maylender, *Storia delle Accademie d'Italia*, vol. 2 (Bologna, 1927),122–146, particularly 132–135. See also Eric W. Cochrane, 'The Renaissance Academies in their Italian and European Setting' in *The Fairest Flower: The Emergence of Linguistic National Consciousness in Renaissance Europe* (Florence, 1985), 21–39.

30 'Aqui se sazonão os fructos das sciencias, e aqui se inculcão a philosophia em tres formas, distingue o gouerno particular e o publico em Ethico, e Economico e Politico, ensina o Ethico o gouerno particular de huma pessoa, e o Economico o da Caza particular, e o Politico o comum da Republica'. BNP, Cod. 5864, fol. 31r.
31 BNP, Cod. 5864, fols. 30r-31r.
32 Or Thursday according to Tomás Caetano do Bem, *Memorias Historicas, Chronologicas*, tomb 1 (Lisbon, 1792), 313.

THE EDIFYING SCIENCE   121

    Marquis of Alegrete – the vices of eloquence
    Count of Villamaior – *mathematics proper to gentlemen*
    Viscount of Asseca – the academic paradoxes
    Francisco Manuel de Melo – illustrious women
    Júlio de Melo – panegyric to illustrious men of respectability
    José Soares da Silva – Politics
    Lourenço Botelho – mythology
    Manuel Pimentel – *natural philosophy*
    António Rodrigues da Costa – history
    Inácio de Carvalho – poetics
    Father António de Oliveira de Azevedo – the ethics of modern authors
    Francisco Leitão – the symbolic art
    Jerónimo Godinho – elegiac style and the art of inscriptions
    Manuel de Azevedo Fortes – *Modern logic compared with that of the ancients*
    José do Couto Pestana – maxims of Portuguese kings
    José Contador – *the mathematical paradoxes*
    Father Manuel Caetano de Sousa – moral philosophy
    Father José Barbosa – *dendrology*
    Father Jerónimo Contador de Argote – fables of history
    Father Raphael Bluteau – the excellences and documents of the Christian wise
    Count of Ericeira – *the method of studies*
    Manuel Dias de Lima – jurisprudence[33]

As this list of lectures undoubtedly reveals, a vast field of topics magnetized the interest of the fellows of the Academy of the Generous – Portuguese Academy. Not only did this academy include fellows with different background but its members also embodied the polymath ideal of the early modern savant and courtier, someone whose culture and activities by far exceeded his/her professional area of competence. Raphael Bluteau provided an excellent example of this ideal of a polymath courtier. Author of a quite influential dictionary on the Portuguese language and no few apologetic academic discourses in favour of Portuguese kings,[34] his productions cover unexpected areas such as the cultivation of mulberry trees and silkworms, a topic on which he authored a book

---

33   Bluteau, *Prosas Portuguesas*, 341.
34   For example, R. Bluteau, 'Oração academica Recitada em Palaçio anno de 1721 Dia de annos del Rey de Portugal D. Ioão V E prezença de Vossas Magestades, e altezas pello Pe. D. Raphael Bluteau, clerigo Regular', BNP, Cod. 3181, fols. 9r.-21v.

dedicated to King Pedro II.[35] In the Academy, following the plan established in the 26 May 1717 session, he addressed the topic of the 'excellences' and the proficiencies proper to the Christian wise. Distributed across seven lessons, Bluteau's exposition stretched over disciplines such as logic, physics, metaphysics, politics, cosmography, jurisprudence and theology. A wise man was supposed to hold specific competences in all of these disciplines.[36]

3   Science in the Republic of Letters

Science was among the multiple areas of interest a savant and courtier was expected to command since, as the Count of Ericeira explained, 'sciences are the lights of spirit'.[37] Accordingly, for example, the minutes of the session held on 12 February 1696, in the palace of Francisco Xavier de Meneses, state,

> [The wise of Lisbon] decided to gather, every Sunday, at the library of the Count of Ericeira, whom they elected as Secretary, and agreed to concentrate on scientific matters, in an academic form, exposing in a critical fashion the finest authors in discourses and dissertations, in philosophical questions and mathematical problems, in verses covering various issues, with the whole event in the Portuguese language.[38]

Despite the fact that there are a great deal of indirect references to the scientific activities of the Academy of the Generous, few accounts indeed seem to have survived for contemporary archives and libraries.[39] One of the more

---

35   R. Bluteau, *Instrucçam sobre a cultura das Amoreiras e criação dos Bichos da seda dirigida à conseruação e aumento das manufacturas da seda* (Lisbon, 1679).
36   R. Bluteau, 'Prosas Academicas, Logicas, Fysicas, Metafysicas, Politicas, Cosmograficas, Juriconsulas e Theologicas demonstrativas das virtudes e prerrogativas do Sabio Christão, e manifestadas em sete liçoens na Academia do Conde da Ericeira, D. Francisco Xavier de Menezes' in *Prosas Portuguezas recitadas em diferentes Congressos Academicos* (Lisbon, 1728), 105–183.
37   'Sciencias que são as luzes do espirito', Session of 21 April 1718, BNP. 3181, fol. 1r.
38   '[Os cientes de Lisboa] assentarão juntarse aos Domingos em a Livraria do Conde da Ericeira, a quem elegerão Secretario, e conferirem em materias scientificas, reduzidas a forma Academica, e tratadas em Discursos, e Dissertações na exposição critica dos melhores Authores, em questoens Filosoficas, e problemas mathematicos, em metros a varios assumptos, e sobretudo, em palavras da lingua Portugueza'. In Bluteau, *Prosas Portuguezas*, 1.
39   The palace of the Count of Ericeira, the *Palácio dos Cunhais das Bolas*, was destroyed by the violent earthquake, followed by fire, which struck Lisbon on 1 November 1755. Since the sessions of the Academy of the Generous – Erudite Conferences – Portuguese

interesting examples is the *Primeiras e Segundas Liçoens feitas na Academia de D. Antonio Alueres da Cunha* (The First and Second Lessons delivered in the Academy by Lord António Álvares da Cunha), probably authored by the cosmographer Manuel Pimentel.[40]

The First and Second Lessons address the problematic issues of seventeenth century cosmology and astronomical science. The author goes into some detail on the physical characteristics of celestial bodies and on the rearrangement of the planetary system. Questions such as the presumed fluidity of the heavens and the corruptibility of celestial bodies were set out before the fellows of the Academy of the Generous. The author of *The First and Second Lessons* did recognize that the modern discoveries of astronomy overthrew the foundations of Aristotelian cosmology.[41]

From his point of view, the theory according to which the heavenly region was made up of eight rigid and impenetrable celestial orbs, in which the celestial bodies were incrusted and moved by the actions of the extreme sphere, had been so well received and regarded in the 'Schools' for a period of two

---

Academy took place in the palace's library, a library that counted on over 15,000 volumes in the mid-eighteenth century (Monteiro, *No alvorecer do 'Iluminismo'*, 8), it is most likely that perhaps the bulk of the academy outputs disappeared on that occasion.

40 Library of Congress, Washington, Portuguese Manuscripts P-244, fols. not numbered. The author of these Lessons is not mentioned in the manuscript. Elze Von Matias, 'As Academias Literárias Portuguesas', 31, who was, as far as I am aware, the first scholar to draw attention to this important manuscript, attributed its probable authorship to Friar André de Cristo (previously André de Fróis de Macedo, c. 1617–1689). André de Cristo, despite being a fellow of the Academy of the Generous, expounding on topics such as the poetry of Aristotle, was also professor of philosophy to the Count of Castelo Melhor, Luís de Vasconcelos e Sousa, Secretary of State to King Afonso VI (Diogo Barbosa de Machado, *Bibliotheca Lusitana*, tomb 1, 1741, 142–143). Since these Lessons are bound together with other works, mostly the correspondence and poetry of Manuel Pimentel (1650–1719), chief-cosmographer like his father Luís Serrão Pimentel, Manuel Pimentel most likely authored them. The scientific content corroborates this interpretation. Should this prove the case, these lessons probably date to the late seventeenth century.

41 On the role of astronomical observations in questioning of Aristotelian theories of celestial solidity and perfection, see, among others, E.J. Aiton, 'Celestial spheres and circles, *History of Science*, 19, 1981, 101–103; Miguel Á. Granada, *Sfere solide e cielo fluido. Momenti del dibattito cosmologico nella seconda metà del Cinquecento* (Milan, 2002); Michel-Pierre Lerner, 'Le problème de la matière céleste après 1550: aspects de bataille des cieux fluides', *Revue d' Histoire des Sciences*, 42 (1989), 273–280; Michel-Pierre Lerner, *Le Monde des Sphères. La fin du Cosmos Classique* (Paris, 1997), 21–73; W.G.L. Randles, *The Unmaking of the Medieval Christian Cosmos, 1500–1760. From Solid Heavens to Boundless Aether* (Aldershot, 1999), 80–105.

thousand years that the opposite position was taken as a paradox.[42] And yet the 'modern' astronomical observations proved otherwise. In fact, astronomical phenomena such as the observation of comets in the celestial region, the apparent motion of Venus and Mars around the Sun and the 'satellites' of Jupiter and Saturn, as recently discovered by means of the telescope, pointed unequivocally to the fluidity of the heavens. As the author of *The First and Second Lessons* stated,

> In regard to the planetary region, this theory [arguing for the fluidity of heavens] is demonstrated by such experiences that the thickness and solidity introduced by Aristotle can no longer be sustained. Comets were observed above the Moon crossing the ethereal spaces, a fact which could not happen were those spaces filled by thick and solid spheres. Thus, the planetary region is either completely vacuous or filled up by some fluid and very tenuous body. The planet of Venus was observed as experiencing the same changes as the Moon, with the same periods in which it received more light from the Sun alternating with others in which it received less. This undoubtedly demonstrates that this celestial body moves around the Sun and about its centre, appearing now and again above and below the Sun and now and again on the one and on the other side of it. How could one account for this orbital movement about the Sun if both the Sun and Venus were incrusted in solid orbs without then smashing those orbs into pieces?
>
> In a similar manner, numerous and systematic observations have revealed that four small planets move around Jupiter, like moons, and two other planets (though presenting various forms) do the same around Saturn. These observations prove that the areas in which these planets move ought to be fluid and free to allow for the motion of the small stars that move around them like pages. It has also been observed that Mars, while in the opposite direction from the Sun, is nearer to the Earth than to the Sun itself. If there were solid spheres, one sphere would necessarily cross the other one and break it.[43]

---

42   *Primeiras e Segundas Liçoens feitas na Academia de D. Antonio Alueres da Cunha*, Library of Congress, Washington, Portuguese Manuscripts P-244, fols. n.n [9r-9v.]

43   'Comprouase esta opinião no que toca a região dos Planetas com taes experiencias, que aquella corpulencia e dureza introduzida por Aristoteles não se pode sustentar de alguma maneira. Obseruarãose os Cometas mais altos que a Lua atravessarem os espaços ethereos, o que não poderia succeder se estes espaços fossem occupados com esferas densas, e solidas, de que resulta que aquella região ou he de todo uazia, ou chea de algum corpo fluido tenuissimo. Obseruouse a estrella de Venus padecer as mesmas mudanças que a

The heavenly region hence must be a fluid body. Two further arguments prove that no rigid orbs could exist above the Moon: the apparent lack of refraction and the incapacity of the theory of *primum mobile* to account for the apparent daily motion of celestial bodies as it seemed to slowly retard as the year progressed.[44] This would be difficult to accommodate in a worldview in which only a single mover exists. Furthermore, the mechanical problem of how the *primum mobile* fitted in with the Saturn orb raised additional difficulties to the theory of solid orbs and the usually associated celestial dynamics.[45]

Furthermore, according to the Generous academician who authored *The First and Second Lessons*, these new astronomical observations proved that the celestial region was not only a fluid but also a corruptible body. After refuting the scholastic arguments according to which Aristotle's theory of the incorruptibility of celestial region was based upon the perfection/circularity of the celestial movement and the apparent absence of opposite qualities in celestial bodies,[46] the author of these lessons focused on the astronomical observations that definitely demonstrate that substantial change also occurred in the heavens. The appearance of a new star (*nova*) in 1572 in the constellation of Cassiopeia, diligently observed by Tycho Brahe, left no doubts that the heavens undergo processes of corruption. Further *novae*, such as those appeared in 1600, 1603 and 1638 as well as comets and the sunspots recently observed by means of telescopes, corroborated this theory.[47] As the Generous academician put it, 'these spots that are visible in the Sun suggest that the Sun's body, similar

---

Lua, recebendo a luz do Sol com os mesmos crecimentos e faltas, o que argue infalivelmente que esta estrella gira á roda do Sol, como à roda do seu centro, ficando hora mais alta hora mais baxa, hora por hum lado, hora por outro. E como poderia entender esta giração se o Sol estivesse crauado em huma esfera solida e a estrella de Venus em outra hauendo esta de romper necessariamente aquella e penetralla.

Da mesma sorte se tem obseruado por innumeraueis e constantes experiencias que á roda da estrella de Jupiter girão quatro Planetas pequenos como outras tantas luas; á roda de Saturno outros dous (posto que estes se manifestão em uarias formas), o que argue necessariamente que os campos em que estes Planetas se mouem são liquidos, e que aquelles como pagens que os acompanhão tem á roda de si estendidos espaços liures em que discorrem. Obseruou-se mais que a estrella de Marte na opposição com o Sol fica mais uizinho da terra que o mesmo Sol, e se as suas esferas fossem solidas, huma hauia de cortar a outra ou quebralla'. Ibid., fols. n.n. [10r.-10v.].

44 In fact, stars rise, cross the meridian and set few minutes earlier each day. The original texts reads as follows: 'Aristoteles como os seus sequazes dizem que no mesmo tempo que a suprema leua comsigo uiolentamente as inferiores ou infimas estas fazem algum caminho em contrario resistindo em parte contra o impeto e uiolencia'. Ibid., fol. n.n. [11r.].
45 Ibid., fols. n.n. [10v.-11r.].
46 Ibid., fols. n.n. [17r.-18r.].
47 Ibid., fols. n.n. [19r.-19v.].

to that of Earth, exhales smoke and crass vapours that later dissipate and disappear just like the clouds in our air'.[48]

The heavens and celestial bodies were thus ontologically similar to those of the terrestrial region. Although, according to this academician, the immense distance of celestial bodies should restrain the natural philosopher from making any definitive statement, heavenly bodies were most likely made up of the finest parts of the elements,[49] with the exception of the Sun and stars which were constituted of fire.[50] In other words, the author of *The First and Second Lessons* was clearly at odds with some of the central assumptions of Aristotelian cosmology. He argued that there was not a substantial divide between celestial and terrestrial regions; he understood the heavens to be fluid and corruptible; he recognized that the astronomical observations played a heuristic role in studying nature. Yet, these arguments were not particularly new to Portugal. At the time *The First and Second Lessons* were delivered at the Academy of the Generous, these same positions were being taught in natural philosophy classes at Portuguese universities and Jesuit colleges.[51]

As regards discussions on the planetary systems, a topic which, according to the author, 'was, in the past, a very celebrated question among astronomical controversies, but is most famous in the present times',[52] the analysis clearly reaches beyond the traditional position conveyed in the astronomical and cosmographical classes in Portugal. As usual, the author confronted the Ptolemaic and Copernican theories, also alluding to Longomotanus's theory which attributed the Earth with daily motion, although he did not explicitly present the Tychonic planetary rearrangement.[53] He also did not go into the technical details of these theories, the discussion of the number of epicycles, for example,

---

48 'Estas manchas que se uem no Sol são indicio que do seu corpo bem assim como do da terra se exalão fumos e uapores crassos, e se dissipão, e desapparecem como costumão as nuuens neste nosso ar uizinho'. Ibid., fol. n.n. [19v.].

49 Ibid., fol. n.n. [13r.]. Because of that, they suffer processes of change much more rarely than terrestrial bodies. In any case, again the immense distance that exists between the Earth's surface and the celestial bodies make it impossible for human eyes to perceive ordinary process of coming into being and passing away occurring in the planets and stars (fol. n.n. [18v.]).

50 Ibid., fols. n.n. [82v.-83r.].

51 Luís Miguel Carolino, 'Philosophical teaching and mathematical arguments: Jesuit philosophers *versus* Jesuit mathematicians on the controversy of comets in Portugal (1577–1650)', *History of Universities*, 16 (2000), 65–95; L.M. Carolino, 'Cristoforo Borri e o impacto da *nova astronomia* em Portugal no século XVII', *Revista Brasileira de História da Ciência*, 2 (2009), 160–181.

52 'Foy esta controuersia no tempo passado entre todas as Astronomicas muito celebre, mas no presente he celeberrima'. *Primeiras e Segundas Liçoens*, fol. n.n. [34v.].

53 Ibid., fol. n.n. [35r.].

remained ignored. His attention mostly focused on the heliocentric theory and, particularly, to proving the physical superiority of this theory. By recognizing that the Earth performs both a daily turn on its axis and an annual revolution around the Sun, Copernicans were able to straightforwardly explain a set of astronomical phenomena that Ptolemaic astronomers traditionally justified by artificial means. The apparent 24-hour movement of stars was a case in point. Traditionally, this motion was explained by means of an outermost movable sphere responsible for the east-to-west daily motion of the stars. On recognizing the daily motion of the Earth, there was no need for any such unnatural sphere. In addition, this enabled the astronomer and natural philosopher to discard the difficulty of explaining the process through which stars could cross such a vast area in a short period of time.[54] The annual revolution of the Earth, in turn, accounted for the apparent irregularities in the movements presented by planets, which seem to move forwards, stop and then reverse. The nearer the planets are to the Sun, the faster they move. Thus, seen from the surface of an Earth moving around the Sun, the exterior planets appear from time to time to slow their speed and then retrograde.[55] According to the author of this academic discourse, a further metaphysical argument corroborates this position:

> God is at the centre of every possible thing created in nature; the Sun is a vivid image of God; thus a central position is due to the Sun in order to resemble, also in this way, its archetype.[56]

Furthermore, Copernican theory appeared able to answer successfully all the criticism that its opponents had thus far raised against it. As the Generous academician recapitulates, the Ptolemaic astronomers together with the Aristotelian natural philosophers had claimed that (1) the Earth was made up of the most impure element, that (2) since the Earth was a heavy body and weighty elements tended to move to the centre of the Earth, the Earth itself could not move and, finally (3) if it did move, every mountain and city would collapse as the result of the rapidity of the Earth's rotation. Having previously argued that there was no ontological distinction between the Earth and other planets, the answer to the two first criticisms was found: the Earth could move like any

---

54   Ibid., fol. n.n. [36v.].
55   Ibid., fol. n.n. [37v.].
56   'He Deos o centro de todas as cousas creadas e possiueis; he o Sol hua viua imagem de Deos, pois ao Sol compete tambem o lugar do centro para se parecer tambem nisto com o seu archetypo'. Ibid., fol. n.n. [38r.].

other planet.[57] As far as the third criticism, the author states, 'the Earth is provided with a magnetic virtue through which it gathers together all its parts, both the internal and the external'.[58] Finally, the academician could not avoid the crucial question of the apparent lack of parallax. He did not ignore how in a universe in which the Earth moved around the Sun, the stars were expected to change position in relation to other related stars. According to him, this does not happen because the dimension of the universe was much larger than that usually assumed.[59]

Thus, according to the author of *The First and Second Lessons*, the Copernican theory was superior from the physical point of view. And yet, there was an important caveat: the Bible explicitly contradicted it.[60] As this academician maintained the Biblical text should prevail over physical arguments, he ended up supporting geocentrism. As the case for the large majority of Catholic authors, according to this academician, the literal interpretation of Bible takes precedence over any realistic understanding of the Copernican theory.[61] This seems to be the only reason leading him to abandon Copernicanism.

If the conclusion was not new – quite the contrary – the emphasis on the superiority of the physical arguments is nevertheless noteworthy. Historians have stressed the linkage between the emergence of new forms of social organization of work embodied in the scientific academies and the advocating of ground-breaking theories. Tycho Brahe developed his observational programme and geo-heliocentric cosmological model on the island of Hven, a gift from his patron Frederick II, King of Denmark, before moving to the Imperial Court of Rudolf II, in Prague; Johannes Kepler also lived some of his most decisive and creative years in an imperial court; Christoph Rothmann worked in association with the scientific programme in place at the Court of the German Landgrave Wilhelm IV of Hesse-Kassel; Galileo's major scientific accomplishments took place in the Court of Medici, in Florence.[62] Inspection of the case

---

57   Ibid., fols. n.n [38r.-39r.].
58   'Mas respondesse que a Terra he dotada de huma uirtude magnetica com a qual contem unidas e atadas todas as suas partes desde as intimas ate as exteriores'. Ibid., fol. n.n. [39r.].
59   Ibid., fols. n.n [39v.-40r.]. Yet, on another occasion, the author seems more sceptical about this possibility, considering it improbable, fol. n.n. [99r.].
60   Ibid., fol. n.n [40v.].
61   Among the vast bibliography on this subject, see Pietro Daniel Omodeo, *Copernicus in the Cultural Debates of the Renaissance. Reception, Legacy, Transformation* (Leiden, 2014), particularly 271–321.
62   Mario Biagioli, *Galileo courtier. The practice of science in the culture of Absolutism* (Chicago, 1993); Andrea Bubenik, 'Art, astrology and astronomy at the imperial court of Rudolf II (1576–1612)' in *Tycho Brahe and Prague: Crossroads of European science*, eds. J.R. Christianson *et. al.* (Frankfurt am Main, 2002), 256–263; John Robert Christianson, *On Tycho's*

of the Academy of the Generous or, more broadly, contexts in which science was poorly institutionalized and wherein there was no strong sources of patronage, necessarily nuanced this link. The academies that emerged within this institutional and social framework did not necessarily promote innovative science from the theoretical point of view.

Nevertheless, even in this unfavourable environment, academies still acted as the appropriate stages that regulated controversies, appearing thus as less dogmatic institutions. In fact, not only do the conclusions drawn on Copernican theory at the Academy of the Generous apparently surpass those elaborated in mathematical and cosmographic courses at the universities and Jesuit colleges in Portugal, but this institution also provided the stage for unusual discussions, such as the Giordano Bruno notion of an infinite universe, Gassendi's epicurean ideas or the existence of living beings on other planets.[63] These topics were otherwise systematically ignored whether by professors of natural philosophy in the universities or by their mathematical peers in their classes. Furthermore, the Academy of the Generous, similar to its European congeners, remained open to fellows who supported unorthodox scientific views. In fact, Cartesians featured among the fellows of the Academy of the Generous. Francisco Xavier de Meneses, Count of Ericeira, alluded to them while addressing the academy on the question of study methods, a topic attributed to him – as mentioned above – in the 26 May 1717 session,

> Aristotle reduced the whole of philosophy to a perfect system. I would mention the tributes paid to him by all the savants down through the ages were I not afraid of Descartes's theory of vortexes and of the scandal I would produce among its followers, because some of them are probably listening to us today.[64]

Island. Tycho Brahe and his assistants, 1570–1601 (Cambridge, 2000); William Eamon, *Science and the secrets of nature. Books of secrets in Medieval and Early Modern culture* (Princeton, 1994), 194–233; Paula Findlen, *Possessing nature. Museums, collecting, and scientific culture in early modern Italy* (Berkeley, 1994), particularly 346–392; Miguel A. Granada, Adam Mosley and Nicholas Jardine, eds. *Christoph Rothmann's Discourse on the Comet of 1585. An Edition and Translation with Accompanying Essays* (Leiden, 2014); Bruce Moran, ed., *Patronage and institutions: Science, technology and medicine at the European court, 1500–1750* (Woodbridge, 1991); Victor E. Thoren, *The Lord of Uraniborg. A biography of Tycho Brahe* (Cambridge, 1990); Robert S. Westman, 'The astronomer's role in the sixteenth century: a preliminary study', *History of Science*, 18 (1980), 105–147.

63 The author of *The First and Second Lessons* refutes these positions (fols. n.n [13v., 22v.-28r.,s 29v., 46v., 85v-86r.]).

64 Francisco Xavier de Meneses, *Que sciencia he maes propria de hum Caualheiro, discurso*, Biblioteca Geral da Universidade de Coimbra, Ms. 342, fol. 275r.

Meneses was probably referring to Manuel de Azevedo Fortes, who also delivered a speech at the Academy on *Modern logic compared with that of the ancients*. Azevedo Fortes would later publish a treatise on logics (*Lógica Racional, Geométrica e Analítica*), which supported Cartesian logics and contributed to it spreading widely in Portugal and Brazil.[65] A study on the Academy of the Generous and its fellows thus corroborates a prevalent point of view in historical studies on scientific academies that associates the rise of these institutions with the rejection of theoretical dogmatism.

4 Royal Pursuits: The Academy of History and an Absolutist King in the Making

Every royal academy produced its own historical narrative in which the founder is adequately praised and the aims of the institution amply celebrated. The Royal Academy of History naturally has its own official history, the *História da Academia Real da História Portugueza* (History of the Royal Academy of Portuguese History), authored by Manuel Teles da Silva, the Marquis of Alegrete, and published scarcely seven years after its foundation (1727). In this piece, the foundation of the Royal Academy of History is depicted as the moment of redemption for the academic movement in Portugal.

> The Republic of Letters faced in Portugal the same difficulties of all the political republics in which the imperfection typical of this political genre prevailed. The learned family experienced the abandonment of orphanage; the literary body, the infelicity of being acephalous; the nobility of sciences, of being deprived of court; the confused people of arts, the disregard of an inefficient government. (...) Yet, the blissful moment of transforming this republic into a monarchy has come, in which the professors will give the best of their work without losing their liberty by the relations of vassalage. Having recognized how a history of his reign and domains would contribute to the exaltation of his name (...), the king

---

65 On Azevedo Fortes's Cartesianism and its influence in Portugal and Brazil, see Luís Manuel Bernardo, *O Projecto Cultural de Manuel de Azevedo Fortes* (Lisbon, 2005); Amândio Coxito, *Estudos sobre Filosofia em Portugal na Época do Iluminismo* (Lisbon, 2006), 15–84; *Manoel de Azevedo Fortes (1660–1749)* ed. Mário Gonçalves Fernandes (Porto, 2006); Dulcyene Maria Ribeiro, *A obra 'Lógica Racional, Geométrica e Analítica' (1744) de Manoel de Azevedo Fortes (1660–1749)*, PhD. Diss., UNESP / Universidade Estadual Paulista – Instituto de Geociências e Ciências Exatas, 2003.

decided to take under his royal patronage the whole literary corpus so that it could be ruled by one single head, by one single assembly.[66]

Through the institutionalization of the Royal Academy of History, King João V boosted the incipient clientele relations previously engaged in by some court nobility. Together with the Theatine cleric Manuel Caetano de Sousa (1658–1734), fellow of the Portuguese Academy and seemly the driving force behind the foundation of this institution,[67] the learned court nobility played a key role from the outset. The Count of Ericeira was among the first censors of the Academy and most likely contributed to the redaction of its first statutes.[68] As its first historian explicitly mentioned, this academy specifically aimed to incorporate the previous academies. The Portuguese Academy, which kept the candle of the Academy of the Generous alight, was the first for integration. All of its members would be among the first fifty fellows of the Royal Academy of History.[69] Thus, the former Academy of the Generous, founded back in 1647, to a certain extent continued in this new institution. Nevertheless, with the support of the king, its fellowship followed different rules. Although the courtly networks related to the Academy of the Generous – Portuguese Academy and

---

66 'Achavase em Portugal a Republica das Letras no mesmo estado, em que todas as mais Republicas Politicas se considerão pela imperfeição, que ordinariamente se reconhece neste genero de governo. Experimentava a familia erudita o desamparo da orfandade; o corpo Literario a infelicidade de ser acefalo; a nobreza das Sciencias o damno de não ter Corte, que a Aristocracia não permitte; e o Povo confuso das Artes, a desestimação procedida da inefficacia do governo Democratico. (...) Porém chegou o feliz tempo de se reduzir esta Republica a Monarchia, e as Sciencias, e Artes, sem perderem pela vassalagem a liberdade, principiarão a dar no seu exercicio o melhor premio aos seus professores. Porque reconhecendo El Rey quanto concorreria para a exaltação do seu nome, escreverem-se successos tão memoraveis, como os que acontecerão no seu Reyno, e Dominios (...), determinou tomar debaixo do seu Real patrocinio todo o corpo Literario (...) fosse dirigido por huma só Cabeça, e por hum só Congresso'. Manuel Teles da Silva, *História da Academia Real da História Portugueza* (Lisbon, 1727), 2, 4.

67 Bem, *Memorias Historicas*, tomb 1, 460. On the history of this academy, its foundation and relationship with the state apparatus, see particularly Isabel Ferreira da Mota, *A Academia Real da História. Os intelectuais, o poder cultural e o poder monárquico no séc. XVIII* (Coimbra, 2003).

68 The other censors were Marquis of Fronteira, Marquis of Abrantes and Marquis of Alegrete. Count of Villarmaior was appointed as secretary. 'Proposiçam da Academia' in *Colleçam dos Documentos e Memorias da Academia Real da Historia Portugueza que neste anno de 1721 se compuzerão e se imprimirão por ordem dos censores* (Lisbon, 1721), n.n. [p. 3 of this 'Proposiçam']. According to Isabel Mota, the statutes were written by Manuel Caetano de Sousa, Count of Ericeira and Count of Alegrete. Mota, *A Academia Real da História*, 39.

69 Bem, *Memorias Historicas*, tomb 2, 165.

other literary academies, such as the Academy of the Enlightened (*Academia dos Ilustrados*), were then integrated into the Royal Academy, the latter also comprised a selection of the higher civil servants serving at the Court and the principal figures of the Portuguese Church including a few *qualificators* of the Inquisition. Jesuits, who rarely took part in the Academy of the Generous – Portuguese Academy, also took their seats, a total of six in the newly established institution.[70] The professor of mathematics at the Lisbon College of Santo Antão, Manuel de Campos, was among them. The Royal Academy of History thus mirrored João v's court, political and cultural milieu.

Part of a more comprehensive policy of patronage put into practice by the Portuguese monarchy,[71] the Royal Academy of History contributed to projecting an image of João v as a refined and liberal king.[72] Abroad, the ambitious cultural politics of the Portuguese king had become famous in Rome in the early 1720s. In 1723, in an action that combined politics and diplomacy, king João v was declared the patron of the Accademia dell'Arcadia, donating, a couple of years later, a sum of money to purchase land and build headquarters of this institution.[73] In the same period, João v sponsored the scientific work and publications of the astronomer active in Rome Francesco Bianchini (1662–1729).[74] In Portugal, as in the past, events related with the Royal family led to public meetings of the Academy. These academic sessions took place in the magnificent royal library and were not rarely attended by the king. Furthermore, João v acted in favour of the publication of works by academicians, exempting them from Inquisitorial and state censure.[75] Historical works were particularly praised as their political usage was publicly acknowledged. A normative text entitled *System of Ecclesiastical and Secular History of Portugal* was written by Francisco Xavier de Meneses and Manuel Caetano de Sousa and historical books were published accordingly.[76] *Historia Genealogica da Casa Real Portugueza desde a sua Origem até ao Presente* (Lisbon, 1735) by António Caetano de Sousa is a case in point.

---

70 'Catalogo dos Academicos por ordem alfabetica' in *Colleçam dos Documentos*, 1721, n.n. A sociological study on the first fellows of the Royal Academy of History can be found in Mota, *A Academia Real da História*, 97–111.
71 This comprehensive process is described in detail by Rui Bebiano, *D. João v, poder e espectáculo* (Aveiro, 1987) and Delaforce, *Art and Patronage*.
72 This point is very well made in Mota, *A Academia Real da História*.
73 Delaforce, *Art and Patronage*, 99, 101, 105–106; Donato, *Accademie romane*, 75.
74 J.L. Heilbron, *The Sun in the Church. Cathedrals as solar observatories* (Cambridge, MA, 1999), 155 and 197.
75 Mota, *A Academia Real da História*, 48.
76 'Systema da Historia Ecclesiastica e Secular de Portugal, que ha de escrever a Academia Real de Historia Portuguesa' in *Colleçam dos Documentos*, 1721, n.n.

Nevertheless, according to the academicians of the Royal Academy of History, History comprised not only of the account of human events in the past and, additionally, the encomium of royal affairs of the present, but also the study of nature. The notion that there were close interconnections between the fates of human history and the natural environments in which each people lived paved the way for the inclusion of areas of knowledge such as geography, cartography, chronology, astronomy and natural history. In fact, this point was clearly made in the opening article of the Academy's normative text, *System of Ecclesiastical and Secular History of Portugal*.

> Since Geography and Chronology are the two eyes of History, the entirety of writers need to focus on them, paying attention to the several opinions on which authors disagree concerning the calculations and time ages and the altitudes and locations of places. The academicians destined for geography, in their memoirs, should examine those areas either on the division of ancient Lusitania or on astronomical observations and geographical distances.[77]

Furthermore, as a state institution, all the topics related with sovereign power, such as maps and surveying, could not be ignored. Accordingly, the academicians of Royal Academy of History saw no contradiction in including the natural and mathematical sciences in the wide range of areas of interest of an academy of history. No wonder thus that one of the most active members of the Royal Academy of History was the aforementioned Cartesian-inspired philosopher and professional cartographer and engineer Manuel de Azevedo Fortes who, despite usually participating in the academic sessions while in Lisbon, was actually engaged in surveying the country.[78] Fortes's pedagogical method of cartography *Tratado do modo mais facil e mais exacto de fazer as Cartas Geograficas* (Lisbon, 1722) was published with the Academy's support.[79]

---

77 'Como a Geografia, e a Chronologia são os dous olhos da Historia, he preciso que todos os Escritores se conformen nellas pelas muitas opinioens, em que se dividem os Authores, nos calculos, e epocas do tempo, e nas alturas, e situações dos lugares. Estas devem examinar em todas as memorias os Academicos destinados para a Geografia, assim nas divisões da antigua Lusitania, como nas observações Astronomicas, e distancias itinerarias'. 'Systema da Historia Ecclesiastica' in *Colleçam dos Documentos*, 1721, n.n. [2–3].

78 On Azevedo Fortes's cartographical activities and their relationship with the Royal Academy of History, see João Carlos Garcia, 'Manoel de Azevedo Fortes e os mapas da Academia Real da História Portuguesa' in *Manoel de Azevedo Fortes,* ed. M.G. Fernandes (Porto, 2006), 141–173.

79 On the process regarding the publication of this book, see Mota, *A Academia Real da História*, 85.

Thus, despite the fact that it was not a specialized academy of science, the sessions of Royal Academy of History comprised scientific activities, in the same manner as the Roman learned societies. Furthermore, a fellow of this royal academy, the count of Ericeira, Francisco Xavier de Meneses, received a set of scientific books from the Academy of Sciences of Saint Petersburg, which he then read and commented on. A review of those books was published in the Royal Academy of History's proceedings, wherein Newton and his followers were praised.[80]

> In the Academy of Russia, they rightly followed the principles of Newton, the greatest of the English philosophers, who better than anyone merged [mathematics and natural philosophy] and demonstrated by mathematical principles what in natural philosophy is demonstrable.[81]

Other scientific activities, such as the astronomical observations in which Academy fellows participated, interrelate with the Royal Academy of History's project. This was the case with the astronomical observation of the lunar eclipse carried out in the Royal palace, on the night of 28 June 1722, by Francisco Xavier de Meneses, deploying 'excellent telescopes and other instruments, and rectified pendulums'.[82]

The academicians and their contemporaries recognized the comprehensive character of the Royal Academy of History.[83] Even those who were fully aware of the advancing specialization of the academic movement in Europe, such as

---

80   Francisco Xavier de Meneses, 'Extractos Academicos dos Livros que a Academia de Petersburg mandou à de Lisboa' in *Colleçam dos Documentos*, 1736. On the Meneses's late acceptance of Newton philosophy, see Noberto Ferreira da Cunha, *Elites e Académicos na Cultura Portuguesa Setecentista* (Lisbon, 2001), 71–77.

81   'Na Academia da Russia justamente se seguem os principios de Newton, o mayor Filosofo dos Inglezes, e o que melhor unio, e demonstrou por principios Mathematicos quanto pode ser demonstrável na Filosofia Natural'. Meneses, 'Extractos Academicos', 5.

82   *Gazeta de Lisboa*, 2 July 1722, 216.

83   The exception appears to have been Jacob de Castro Sarmento, a Portuguese physician, member of Royal College of Physicians and fellow of the Royal Society, who went into exile in London in the early 1720s in order to escape from the persecution of the Portuguese Inquisition (he was of Jewish background). In his *Theorica Verdadeira das Mares*, which played a crucial role in the introduction of Newtonian theory of gravitation into Portugal, while praising the foundation of the Royal Academy of History and the its activity in the first 17 years of existence, he argued for the introduction of further branches of 'natural and human knowledge'. J.C. Sarmento, *Theorica Verdadeira das Mares* (London, 1737), ix. I thank Augusto J.S. Fitas for drawing my attention to Sarmento's position.

the ambassador and former advocate of the Academy of the Generous, Luís da Cunha, saw no contradiction in this, indeed, on the contrary. In a long and laudatory letter that Cunha addressed to the secretary of the Royal Academy of History, in which he accepted the invitation to become a supernumerary fellow of the Academy, the then Portuguese ambassador to Paris argued that King João V had established a new academy model, a comprehensive academy which under the label of History would cover a wide range of subjects, including science. As Cunha states,

> Our lord the king, who in the whole of his generous actions not only follows the example of the other monarchs but also exceeds them in such a way that he himself cannot be imitated, has, among many others, the glory of being the first to have conceived and put in practice the great idea of establishing the most needed and most useful academy that has ever flourished in the past and present. As a matter of fact, an Academy of History comprises the most celebrated academies that nowadays enrich Paris and bring prestige upon their founders.[84]

Thus, according to Cunha, the Royal Academy of History epitomized a new kind of academy encompassing the functions already realized by the Parisian academies, namely the French Academy, Academy of Inscriptions and Belle-Lettres, and, of course, the Academy of Sciences.

Yet, despite Cunhas's optimism regarding the innovative character of the Royal Academy of History, the all-encompassing nature of the Portuguese academy is also indicative of a meagre scientific community or, at the least, of a scientific community never in a position to push for the institutionalization of science in this country. João V is usually accredited with the purchase of scientific instruments and books, the majority of them to enrich the Royal library, as well as a benefactor of intellectuals, some of whom entered into his service, such as the Jesuit astronomers and cartographers Giovanni Battista

---

[84] 'El Rey nosso Senhor, que em todas as suas generosas acções [não] só imita os outros Monarcas, em quanto os excede, ou os excede de maneira, que não pode ser imitado, tem a gloria, sobre tantas mais, de que foy o primeiro, que concebeo, e executou a grande idéa de instituir a mais necessaria, e a mais util de todas as Academias, que florescerão nos seculos passados, e vemos florescer no presente; porque huma Academia da Historia compreende as mais celebres, que hoje fazem o melhor ornamento de Pariz, e que grangeàrão tanto nome aos seus Fundadores'. Cunha, Luís da, 'Carta de D. Luís da Cunha em resposta ao aviso que o Secretariado da Academia lhe fez de estar nomeado Academico supranumerario', *Colleçam dos Documentos*, 1723, 88.

Carbone (1694–1750) and Domenico Capasso (1684–1736).[85] These intellectuals did not join the Royal Academy of History. Nevertheless, a study of the Royal Academy of History does demonstrate that, unlike cases such as the Royal Society, the Paris Academy of Science, the Berlin Royal Academy or the Academy of Sciences of Saint Petersburg, the general academy promoted by King João V contributed neither to the institutionalization of a scientific community nor to the gradual specialization of the sciences in Portugal.

5 Conclusion

Michael Hunter has emphatically claimed that 'science and strong government – in England as in Europe – had a natural affinity'.[86] Scientific academies emerged as the main institutions wherein these two dimensions intersected in the early modern period. At the time when an increasingly self-conscious intellectual community kept a sharp outlook for institutionalizing new forms of organization, the increasingly centralized and bureaucratic states of seventeenth century and early eighteenth century, for which technical and scientific expertise was instrumental, provided the chance to bring about a new institutional framework. The complex process of state making in early modern Europe played, therefore, a crucial role in the transition from the general, informal and amateur academies of the Renaissance to the specialized, chartered, and expert academies of the seventeenth century and later periods. While the Paris Academy of Science provides a strong case for this interdependence between state making and the institutionalization of science, the royal-chartered and – supported Berlin Royal Academy and Academy of Sciences of Saint Petersburg also corroborate this interpretation.

Nevertheless, the study of the academic movement in countries in which, despite being politically centralized, there were no eager scientific communities or no official commitment to promoting any such intellectual cluster, necessarily introduces some nuances to the narrative on the specialization of early modern academies. Portugal represents one case in point. At the turn of the century, Portugal was a centralized country in the making, whose king was particularly fond of patronizing culture and science. And yet, as regards the

---

85   Delaforce, *Art and Patronage*, 86–87; Júnia Ferreira Furtado, 'Bosque de Minerva: artefatos científicos no colecionismo joanino' in *Formas do Império. Ciência, Tecnologia e Política em Portugal e no Brasil. Séculos XVI ao XIX*, eds. Heloisa Meireles Gesteira, Luís Miguel Carolino and Pedro Marinho (São Paulo, 2014), 238–249.
86   Hunter, *Science and society*, 135.

institutionalization of academies, King João V did not promote any specialized science based institution, but rather its opposite, an all-encompassing academy. In the Royal Academy of History, scientific activities were pursued alongside the cultivation of history, literature, and with a special emphasis attributed to the political encomiums. Again, the academies and the centralization of power pull in the same direction. However, in this case, the output was not a scientific academy.

A general academy proved more efficient for the king and his political entourage within the framework of building an image of a particularly liberal king and a luxuriant patron of the arts and sciences. From this point of view, the Royal Academy of History suited very well the purposes of a monarchy in the process of advancing towards absolutist rule. The similarity of this academy with the cultural program of some literary academies of Rome, which João V admired and sponsored, also encouraged the Portuguese king to establish such a general institution. Furthermore, the previous experience of academies in Portugal, from which the Royal Academy of History stemmed, also led to the belief that an all-encompassing academy would prove more appropriate to the Portuguese environment. Not only did the polymath character dominate among Portuguese academicians, but also the absence of any strong scientific community, a specialized body autonomous from the universities and Jesuit colleges, discouraged the institutionalization of a specific academy devoted to the mathematical, physical and natural sciences. Unlike northern and central Europe, where the emergence of regional power favoured the inception of autonomous scientific communities, in Portugal, the dependence of the aristocracy on royal revenues and ruling positions in the Portuguese empire did not foster the founding of a strong and self-conscious community of savants. Last but not least, a broad-ranging academy organized under the umbrella of history was believed by early eighteenth-century Portuguese intellectuals to be the latest, the new-fangled kind of academies, where there was room for institutionalizing both science and scientific activities. This proved not to be the case.

Acknowledgment

The research for this paper was partially supported by the FCT –Fundaçao para a Ciência e a Tecnologia through the Strategic Financing of the R&D Unit UID/SOC/03126/2019.

CHAPTER 6

The Paris Observatory in the Early Modern Ecosystem of Knowledge (1667–1712)

Dalia Deias

Introduction[1]

Much has been written on the Paris Académie Royale des Sciences and its Observatoire Royal founded in 1666 and 1667 respectively under Louis XIV (1643–1715). The Observatory in particular, with which this chapter is mainly concerned, was originally built to represent and serve the Academy and, of course, its enlightened royal founder.[2] It is the only edifice devoted to science built by the French sovereign throughout his reign.

One of the Observatory's intended functions according to its original (and only partly-realized) programme was to be a tangible resource for all the Academy's activities, and in particular a venue for its general meetings. Among the most important planned activities that did become a reality was astronomical observation,[3] not least because observation of the sky was the basis for the Academy's vast project to advance the understanding of terrestrial longitude

---

1 I should like to thank all those who have helped me in the writing of this chapter, in particular Kapil Raj and David Aubin; also the archivist of the Missions Étrangères, Brigitte Appavou, and Anne-Sylvie Malebrancke and Dick Nowell for their patient and efficient help in rendering the text into English.
2 On the Observatory, see Charles J.E. Wolf, *Histoire de l'Observatoire de Paris de sa fondation à 1793* (Paris, 1902) ; René Taton, 'Les origines et les débuts de l'observatoire de Paris', *Vistas in Astronomy* 20 (1976), 65–71 ; Guy Picolet, 'Observatoire de Paris' in *Encyclopedia of the Scientific Revolution: From Copernicus to Newton*, eds. Wilburn Applebaum (New-York and London, 2000), 726–728; Suzanne Débarbat, Solange Grillot and Jacques Lévy, *Observatoire de Paris: Son histoire: 1667–1963* (Paris, 1984). On its original functions, see 'Pourquoi et comment l'Observatoire a eté basti', transcribed in *Lettres, instructions et mémoires de Colbert*, 5: 515. See also Dalia Deias, *Inventer l'Observatoire: sciences et politique sous Giovanni Domenico Cassini (1625–1712)* (PhD diss., École des hautes études en sciences sociales, Centre Alexandre Koyré, Paris, forthcoming).
3 By this we mean all studies and disciplines related to observation of the sky at the time. See Deias, Ibid.

as a way to improve French mapmaking.[4] Having the Observatory at the service of the Academy also made it possible to spread Louis XIV's symbolic and practical influence – and indeed pre-eminence – throughout the world.

The Academy and Observatory did not, however, receive their first Rules (*premier Règlement*) and standing orders for the conduct of operations until 1699, a good thirty years after their foundation.[5] By laying down Rules for the internal organization of its membership – far larger at the close of the seventeenth century than in 1666 – and more detailed standing orders of its activities, the king renewed his support for the two royal institutions and established them on a more formal basis. If we follow their work from their foundation, though, we can see that they were scientific institutions right from the start,[6] long before they had any written rules. Many projects were successfully

---

[4] See, for instance: Minutes of Proceedings (*Procès Verbaux* -PV), November 1680, 9: 89^r-92^v; Paris, Archives of the Académie des Sciences (AAdS), 'L'Invention des Longitudes, verifiée par les observations nouvelles de Mr Cassini'and Jean-Dominique Cassini, *De l'Origine et du progrès de l'astronomie et de son usage dans la géographie et dans la navigation* (Paris, 1693), and Deias, *Inventer l'Observatoire*.

[5] Paris, AAdS, PV, vol. 18, from 107^r. The content of the Rules was first discussed by the then Secretary of the Academy in 1699, Bernard le Bouyer de Fontenelle (1657–1757), who transcribed them point by point adding explanatory comments (see Bernard le Bouyer de Fontenelle, *Histoire du renouvellement de l'Académie royale des sciences en 1699, et les éloges historiques de tous les académiciens morts depuis ce renouvellement, avec un discours préliminaire sur l'utilitée des matheématiques et de la physique* (Paris, 1708)). Much more recently specific contributions have been devoted to this subject, including the article by M.-J. Tits-Dieuaide in the *Journal des Savants* for 1998 (Marie-Jeanne Tits-Dieuaide, 'Les savants, la société et l'Etat: à propos du "renouvellement" de l'Académie Royale des Sciences (1699)', *Journal des Savants* 1 (1998), 79–115). That article identifies some of the main reasons why it became necessary in 1699 to grant the Academy its first standing orders to conduct operations. One of those reasons was the situation after the Peace of Ryswick (1697), in which it was realized that a less piecemeal organization and stricter financial control were needed for all state-sponsored institutions after the many wars of Louis XIV. In her chapter (Marie-Jeanne Tits-Dieuaide, 'Une institution sans statuts: l'Académie Royale des Sciences de 1666 à 1699', in *Histoire et Mémoire de l'Académie des Sciences: guide de recherche*, eds. Eric Brian Christiane Demeulenaere-Doyere (London and New York, 1996), 3–13 (5)), Tits-Dieuaide has documented how, while the Academy was under Colbert's protection, the unofficial character of the work and the small number of Academicians were deliberate choices intended to motivate them to work better. On the changes made by the Rules, see also Simone Mazauric, *Fontenelle et l'invention de l'histoire des sciences à l'aube des Lumières* (Paris, 2007).

[6] 'Institution' here meaning 'any form of social organization that links values, norms, models of relations and behaviours, roles', following a description by Georges Balandier (quoted with commentary by Jacques Revel, 'L'institution et le social', in *Les formes de l'expérience*, eds. Bernard Lepetit (Paris, 1995), 63–84 (64)).

launched in those early years without any rules or Letters Patent (*'pas de brevet ni de patentes'*).[7]

The first thirty years of the Academy's life have been the subject of a number of contributions specifically devoted to the period,[8] but most of the literature has focused on the work carried out after 1699.[9] Many of the authors I have cited have been at pains to emphasize how difficult it has proved to investigate these first three decades of the Assembly's activity. Tits-Dieuaide, in particular, has stressed that the Assembly of that day, with its membership of under twenty, nevertheless managed to find some guiding principles and working methods that made scientific advances possible. The most recent literature on these first thirty years has looked primarily at the anatomy of the organization that was given formal shape in 1699, such as the hierarchies among savants, their roles, or the administrative arrangements by which decisions were taken or innovations made. The practical organization of the work of actually carrying out scientific projects in this period has received less attention.

As the literature focusing more on the places and social milieus in which science was done has recently begun to show,[10] the Paris Royal Observatory not

---

7   Philippe Tamizey de Larroque, eds, *Lettres de Jean Chapelain*, (Paris, 1883), 495, cited in Tits-DieuAide, 'Les savants, la société et l'Etat', 87.
8   I already mentioned the papers by Tits-Dieuaide, expecially the chapter in the book edited by Brian and Demeulenaere-Doyere. See also Marta Cavazza, *Settecento Inquieto. Alle origini dell'Istituto delle Scienze di Bologna* (Bologna, 1990); Alice Stroup, 'Royal Funding of the Parisian Académie Royale des Sciences during the 1690s', *Transactions of the American Philosophical Society*, 77/4 (Philadelphia, 1987); Réné Taton, *Les origines de l'Académie Royale des Sciences* (Paris, 1966); John M., Hirschfeld *The Academy Royale des Sciences (1666–1683): inauguration and initial problems* (Chicago, 1981).
9   To mention a few: Brian and Demeulenaere-Doyere, eds, *Histoire et Mémoire de l'Académie des Sciences*; Sturdy, *Science and Social Status*; Stroup, *A Company of Scientists*; Roger Hahn, *The Anatomy of a Scientific Institution, the Paris Academy of Science, 1666–1803* (Berkeley, Los Angeles and London, 1971).
10 A revaluation of the Observatory's contribution using many new primary sources is provided in Charles Wolf's seminal work, already cited, written in the early twentieth century. See also the entire oeuvre of Guy Picolet, in particular Picolet, 'Observatoire de Paris'. We may also mention here the work of Suzanne Débarbat focusing on the scientific results achieved within the early Paris Observatory (Suzanne Débarbat Simon Dumont, 'Les Académiciens astronomes, voyageurs au XVIIIe siècle', *Comptes rendus de l'Académie des sciences*, série II b, 327 (1999), 415–429; Suzanne Débarbat, Solange Grillot and Jacques Lévy, *Observatoire de Paris: Son histoire: 1667–1963* (Paris, 1984); Suzanne Débarbat and Curtis Wilson, 'The Galilean satellites of Jupiter from Galileo to Cassini, Römer, and Bradley', in *Planetary astronomy from the Renaissance to the rise of astrophysics, The General History of Astronomy*, eds René Taton et Curtis Wilson, 3 vols (Cambridge, 1989), IIA, 144–157).

only made geographical and cartographical work possible (in particular due to the correspondence it exchanged with the whole world), but was also central to the Academy's contacts and communication with other countries, circulating and refining information from many circles in and beyond Europe during the latter half of the seventeenth century. It was likewise a catalyst for keeping the Academy visible to Louis XIV and his courtiers, and for its relations with many religious institutions. Here, accordingly, the earlier historical accounts[11] often representing the Royal Observatory as a scientific institution that failed in its original intent (i.e., to facilitate any activity connected with the Academy and its meetings) have proved quite wrong: it was, on the contrary, an important place for the realization of many of the Academy's projects, above all during the period before it was given formal rules.

In this chapter I intend to show, by considering some instances relating to the Observatory's vital importance in the Academy's activities, how a significant number of the informal '*règles de vie*'[12] of the Academy were generated at the Observatory.[13] On the one hand, these unwritten rules were inspired by some original elements of the Observatory project itself (including the representation of royal power), and, on the other hand, by elements based on the social relationships of its *savants* that provided support to other scientific circles and institutions. Specifically, I use the example of the Italian astronomer Giovanni Domenico Cassini (1625–1712), a member of the Royal Academy des Sciences who arrived in Paris from Bologna in 1669 because Louis XIV had asked for his opinion on the Observatory, which was then under construction.[14] The savant remained in France and worked in the Observatory for the rest of his life.

---

11 See for instance Michael Friedjung, 'Cassini and the Paris Observatory', *Journal of the British Astronomical association* 81 (1971), 479–480; Rudolph Radau, 'L'Observatoire de Paris depuis sa fondation', *Revue de Deux mondes* 73 (1868), 740–768.

12 The rules according to which it functioned and did practical work on scientific projects before 1699.

13 Here I shall be using a recent method of investigation in which a number of cases are conceptualized, analysed and explored to reveal patterns that can lead to more general rules. See Jean Claude Passeron, Jacques Revel, eds, *Penser par Cas* (Paris, 2005), and *Jeux d'échelles. La micro-analyse à l'expérience*, ed. Jacques Revel (Paris, 1996).

14 On this topic, see Deias, *Inventer l'Observatoire*; Justine Ancelin, *Science, académisme et sociabilité savante: édition critique et étude du Journal de la vie privée de Jean-Dominique Cassini, 1710–1712* (Diplôme d'archiviste paléographe, École nationale des Chartes, 2011); Anna Cassini, *Gio.Domenico Cassini, uno scienziato del Seicento. Testi e documenti* (Perinaldo, 2003); Paul Brouzeng, and Débarbat Suzanne, *Sur les traces des Cassini, astronomes et observatoires du sud de la France* (Paris, 2001).

Part of my purpose here, then, will be to cast light on these unwritten rules of functioning by looking at some of the Observatory activities before 1699, and accordingly to produce a picture of the ecosystem of institutions which worked closely with it and with the Paris Academy, with the aim to understand how that collaboration was established. What I mean by 'the organization of the work' is, of course, not always to be understood in terms of precise instructions, but also in a broader sense as the milieus supporting the production of science or the reasons why certain choices were made when the rules arrived.

The Observatory's work will be described here by means of a very diverse set of instances and primary sources: a sample of the correspondence between the Jesuit mission to China headed by the Jesuit Jean de Fontaney (1643–1710) and the Academy, and the Observatory in particular, from the time of the mission's arrival in Siam in 1685 until 1699;[15] from this I shall be seeking to deduce the rules (real but implicit) which facilitated exchanges between Asia and France and furthered the work of the Académie des Sciences. Then I shall analyse some scientific connections between the Observatory and the College of Louis le Grand in Paris. I shall then proceed to introduce a course of events which allied the Observatory's work even more closely with the person of Louis XIV,[16] and show how its symbiotic relationship with him was more firmly established and supported by the way it would welcome visits of public importance: here I shall consider the case of the Siamese ambassadors' visit to the Observatory on 27 September 1686. Lastly, referring to some of the precise rules contained in the 1699 *Réglement* and investigating the choices made by various individual Academicians in formally nominating their own correspondents at the end of the seventeenth century, I shall analyse the case of Giovanni Domenico Cassini's appointment of the Italian astronomer Francesco Bianchini (1662–1729) (which was occasioned around 1700 by the project to reform the Gregorian calendar in collaboration with the Vatican Library and other groups within the Vatican), and the role of the Académie des Sciences in that politico-religious project.

In this way, the Paris Observatory begins to emerge as not only a site of fundamental importance for many of the Academy's projects and a research establishment indispensable to it, but also as an example that helps us to understand how the Academy's functioning and projects worked in practice.

---

15   This is not, of course, an exhaustive overview of the correspondence between the Academy and its mathematicians during these years. The sample consists of the letters in Volume 479 of the Archives of the Société des Missions Etrangères de Paris (MEP), a letter in the Biblioteca universitaria of Pisa and letters archived at the Paris Observatory.
16   See also Deias, *Inventer l'Observatoire*.

1   Joining the Jesuit Networks (1685–1699): The Observatory and the Academy seen through a Sample of Letters to and from the Missions to Asia

One instance of the network of information and milieus underpinning science in the seventeenth century is provided by contacts and communications with religious circles and, in the specific case which concerns us here, Jesuit groups and networks in Europe.[17] Long before the birth of the Academy, contact with the Jesuit Order had offered opportunities, mostly through its foreign missions, to reach places and obtain information not only in Europe but throughout the world, at a time when there were no serious alternatives. The whole of the Grand Siècle functioned in part due to the Jesuit networking powerhouse, and more broadly to the institutions whose members included Jesuits.

Around the 1680s, the Académie des Sciences of Louis XIV decided to make use of the Jesuit missions to the East, headed by the Jesuit Fr Jean de Fontaney (1643–1710), to send its royal mathematician correspondents to Asia in a voyage of observation intended to reach China by way of the Cape of Good Hope and Siam.

Here the Academy's interests were one arm of a greater corpus of integrated Asia-oriented policies that characterized the whole of the Grand Siècle, in which various establishments set up by Jean-Baptiste Colbert – trading companies and others – worked together at the service of Louis XIV.[18] The scientific project was designed to satisfy the need to explore Asian lands both commercially and culturally; and the Academy's work was supported by the

---

17 On this topic see *Jesuit Science and the Republic of Letters*, ed. Mordechai Feingold (Cambridge MA and London, 2003); *The New Science and the Jesuit Science: Seventeenth Century Perspectives*, ed. Mordechai Feingold (Dordrecht, Boston and London, 2003); Agostin Udias, *Searching the Heavens and the Earth: the history of Jesuit Observatories* (Dordrecht, 2003); Antonella Romano, 'Entre collèges et académies. Esquisse de la place des Jésuites dans les réseaux européens de la production scientifique (XVIIe–XVIIIe siècle)', in *Académies et sociétés savantes en Europe (1650–1800)*, eds. Daniel-Odon Hurel et Gérard Laudin (Paris, 2000), 387–407 ; Romano, 'Les Collèges Jésuites, lieux de sociabilité scientifique, 1540–1640', *Le Bulletin de la SHM* 3-4 (1997) 6–20; Michael-John Gorman, 'The Scientific Counter-Revolution: Mathematics, Natural Philosophy and Experimentalism in Jesuit Culture', 1580–1670 (PhD diss., Florence, European University Institute, 1998).

18 Examples in the literature include Nicolas Dew, *Orientalism in Louis XIV's France* (Oxford, 2009); Dominique Lanni, *Le rêve Siamois du Roi Soleil (1666–1717)* (Paris, 2004); Ronald S. Love, 'Monarchs, Merchants, and Missionaries in Early Modern Asia: The Missions Étrangères in Siam, 1662–1684', *The International History Review* 21 (1999), 1–27; Glenn Ames, *Colbert, Mercantilism and the French Quest for Asia Trad* (Dekalb,1996); Dirk van Der Cruysse, *Louis XIV et le Siam* (Paris, 1991).

collaboration with trading companies, whose task it was to escort the mathematicians and facilitate the religious missions.

Furthermore, for a number of years the France of Louis XIV had been slowly nibbling away at the Spanish and Portuguese dominance of religious missions, partly through the establishment of the *Société des Missions Etrangères* (Foreign Mission Society).[19] This use of missionaries made it possible in 1685 to have able savants who could verify in practice the method for finding accurate longitudes by observing the moons of Jupiter from locations around the globe and bringing home data from remote regions of the earth, something that was becoming indispensable.[20]

Once the Jesuit Fr Jean de Fontaney had been chosen to lead the mission, he then chose all the other members of the group from within the Order.[21] The six Jesuit mathematicians were officially appointed correspondents of the Academy and 'Royal Mathematicians', a role that, to judge by the correspondence, seems to have given formal priority to their requests from abroad, at least during the years immediately following 1685.[22] As we shall see, despite this group's more formal link to the Academy it was in fact the Observatory's scientists who mostly made the mission effective.

The supreme and ultimate purpose of this mission was, once arrived in China, to set up two sister institutions for the Paris Académie des Sciences and its

---

19   The *Société des Missions Etrangères* has since that time comprised various religious orders; it works in Asia. On the project of Louis XIV in relation to these foreign missions, especially in Siam, see Love, 'The Missions Étrangères in Siam', 1–27; for some sample works on the Society in addition to those listed in the bibliography, see Adrien Launay, *Histoire Générale de la Société des Missions Etrangères* (Paris, 1894), and, most recently, *La Société des Missions Etrangères de Paris: 350 siècles à la rencontre de l'Asie, 1658–2008*, ed. Catherine Marin (Paris, 2010).

20   On this see Deias, *Inventer l'Observatoire*. On the moons of Jupiter and the terrestrial longitude problem: Débarbat and Wilson, 'The Galilean satellites of Jupiter', 144–157; Jéan-Marie Homet, *Astronomie et astronomes en Provence* (Aix-en-Provence, 1982); Solange Grillot, 'Le problème des longitudes sur terre', *Vistas in Astronomy* 20 (1976), 81–84.

21   The other members of De Fontaney's group were Claude de Visdelou (1656–1737), Louis Daniel le Comte (1655–1728), Joachim Bouvet (1656–1730) and Jean-François Gerbillon (1654–1707). We should also add Fr Guy Tachard (1651–1712), on whom see Guy Tachard, *A relation of the voyage to Siam performed by six jesuits sent by the french King to the Indies and Chine in the year 1685* (London, 1688); Joachim Bouvet, *Portrait Historique de l'Empererur de Chine presenté au Roy par le père P.J. Bouvet* (Paris, 1693); Isabelle Landry-Deron, 'Les leçons de sciences occidentales de l'empereur de Chine Kangxi (1662–1722): textes des journaux des Pères Bouvet et Gerbillon' (Diplôme de l'EHESS, Paris, 1995).

22   For the appointing as Mathematiciens, see: MS B 4/10, item no. 40, Observatory Archives (Arch. Obs.); Paris, letter from De Fontaney to Cassini dated 6 May 1686, n.p.. For the obligation to correspondence with Academy, see: AAdS, PV, november 1681, vol. 9bis: 127r.

Observatory to be called the *Académie de la Chine* and the *Observatoire de Pékin*,[23] both of equal importance.

A great deal has been written about the missions of the six Jesuits sent to Asia by the Académie des Sciences (only five of whom left Siam and arrived in China in 1687).[24] In particular, the mission's chronology starting in 1685 has been reconstructed in detail in Isabelle Landry Deron's 2001 article, which focuses on the Jesuit mathematician De Fontaney and looks in depth at the instruments which were exchanged and passed around. Some works by Catherine Jami also tackle the subject, concentrating mainly on the period spent in China from 1687 onwards, and bring admirably into focus the active part played by the Royal Mathematicians of France in adapting themselves to and mingling with Chinese circles such as the Chinese Imperial court, and the way this formed part of the Academy's project. Both these authors trace an implicit but by no means negligible connection in the part played by the Paris Observatory in making these travels a success, and in particular the strategic decision-making and communication role of Giovanni Domenico Cassini.

How, then, was the mission to be organized? For its scientific project the Academy made full use of the internal functioning of the religious missions and was totally reliant on it. In a relationship of complete mutual confidence with the Academy, the group of missionaries and Academicians exploited their information networks within the Order for the Academy's benefit; being Jesuits, they already knew which Order members to ask for useful or supplementary

---

23   Ibid, n.p.
24   As far as the Chinese stage of the mission is concerned (1687 onwards) we should note especially Isabelle Landry-Deron, 'Les Mathématiciens envoyés en Chine par Louis XIV en 1685', *Archive for History of Exact Science* 55 (2001), 423–463 ; Catherine Jami, *The emperor's new mathematics: Western learning and imperial authority during the Kangxi Reign (1662–1722)* (Oxford, 2012); Jami, 'Pékin au début de la dynastie Qing: capitale des savoirs impériaux et relais de l'Académie royale des sciences de Paris', *Revue d'histoire moderne et contemporaine* 55 (2008), 43–69; Jami, 'From Louis XIV's Court to Kangxi's court: an institutional analysis of the French Jesuit missions to Chine (1648–1722)' in *East Asian Science: tradition and beyond*, eds. K. Hashimoto and Catherine Jami (Osaka, 1995), 493–499; Jami, 'The French mission and Ferdinand Verbiest's scientific legacy', in *Ferdinand Verbiest (1623–1688): Jesuit missionary, scientist, engineer and diplomat*, ed. John W. Witek (Nettetal, 1994), 531–542; Jami, 'L'histoire des mathématiques vue par les lettres chinoises (XVIIe et XVIIe siècles): tradition chinoise et contribution européenne', in *L'Europe en Chine, Mémoires de l'Institut des Hautes Etudes Chinois*, eds. Catherine Jami and Delaye Hubert (Paris, 1993), 147–167; *East Asian Science: tradition and beyond*, eds Catherine Jami, K. Hashimoto, L. Skar eds, (Osaka, 1995); Ines Županov, 'La science et la démonologie: les missions des jésuites français en Inde (XVIIIe siècle)', in *Circulation des savoirs et missions d'évangélisation (XVIe–XVIIIe siècle)*, eds Ch. de Castelnau, Aliocha Maldavsky and Marie-Lucie Copete, (Madrid, 2011), 379–400.

information, the transmission of which had to be kept as discreet as possible.[25] Following a principle for the gathering and use of information which Jacob Soll attributes to Jean-Baptiste Colbert himself (1619–1683), but which could have applied to many institutions he founded,[26] the Academy obtained the information it needed when it needed it thanks to its reliance on an organized system of information and to the efficacy and rapidity of those networks, making use of a close-knit underlying system already in existence, as can clearly be seen from its members' letters.[27] The institution made full use of those high connections and other advantages which Antonella Romano and Paula Findlen have identified as deriving from the Jesuit Order's participation in science in the modern age: members of the Order were present in many centres of power, and generated, circulated and implemented scientific ideas with the help of the Order's international networks and of the organized circulation of information.[28]

Despite the very close connection, nominally with the Academy, of the six mathematicians who left in 1685, little material is available to reconstruct the guidelines given to them on that occasion. The general rules provided them with instructions on the longitude observations to be made and the bare bones of communications with the Academy, but nothing else. Among these instructions we find various memoranda drawn up by the Observatory's savants, especially Cassini, from 1681 onwards, including one entitled 'Project for Geographical Observations' (*'Projet pour les observations géographiques'*)[29] and the 'General instruction for Geographical Observations to make along the way' (*'Instruction générale pour les observations géographiques à faire dans les voyages'*).[30] According to these memoranda, the Academy's six correspondents were to make observations whenever possible (in particular those needed for determining longitude, as described in fine detail in the latter text), and to send them to Paris by sea whenever a ship was available. De Fontaney's group

---

25 We read in a letter dated 2 November 1687 from de Fontaney to Fr Mare SJ at Siam de Ning Po, MEP, vol. 479, 23, 'If there are fathers at Louvau, you have to ask them about the observations we made here, without, however, communicating them to anyone, so that M. of the Academie will receive the news first'('s'il y a des Pères à Louvau, adressez-vous à eux pour savoir les observations que nous avons faites ici, sans neanmoins les communiquer à personne, afin que M.rs de l'Académie en reçoivent la nouvelle les premiers'); Paris.

26 Jacob Soll, *The Information Master: Jean-Baptiste Colbert's Secret State Intelligence System* (Ann Arbor, MI, 2009), 8.

27 See for instance: Vol. 479, 23, MEP; Paris, same letter of November 1687.

28 Paula Findlen, 'Athanasius Kircher and the Roman College Museum', in *Jesuit Science and the Republic of Letters*, 225–284; Romano 'Les Collèges Jésuites'.

29 PV, AAdS, vol. 9bis, year 1681; Paris, 124^v–127^r.

30 PV, AAdS, vol. 9bis; Paris, 141^r–147^v.

was also instructed to tell the Assembly what they needed in terms of books or instruments.

The details, then, were organized by degrees; the travellers' duties were organized and given explicit expression as and when they made themselves felt, as we shall see shortly; in the meantime they had to rely entirely on the organization as it stood. The expedition was also charged with observing and collecting scientific novelties of all kinds during its immensely long journey, and with making notes on every aspect of human life and anthropology of the exotic countries it would be visiting.

When the group left in 1685, de Fontaney seems to have had the essentials he needed to start his observations to verify the means of determining longitude:[31] Cassini had already given him all the necessary tables, and the savant had practised observations with him. Once en route the group had active dealings with the Academy, as clearly shown by the many requests sent from Asia: see, for instance, the '*Mémoire des instruments et livres que les Jesuites mathematiciens du Roy envoyez à la Chine supplient monseign.r le Marquis de Louvois de leur faire donner*'[32] addressed to the Academy, which lists the mathematicians' requirements in 1687 when the group had already arrived in China. Here we learn just what each of the five savants needed for his own particular work, and why.[33] Nevertheless the Academy did not always bear the cost of the

---

31 For instance: vol. 479, MEP; Paris, letter from De Fontaney to Fr Verjus, 12 August 1687, 1–14(9). Fr Antoine Verjus SJ (1632–1706) often appears in Jean de Fontaney's correspondence. He was appointed by King Louis XIV to lead the Missions to the *Levant*, and was also the right-hand man of François d'Aix de la Chaise (1624–1709), the King's confessor.

32 Vol. 479, MEP; Paris, 'Memoir of the devices and books that the Jesuit mathematicians of the King sent to China imploring the marquis de Louvois to present them, 1687', 39–40 ('Mémoire des instruments et livres que les Jesuites mathematicians du Roy envoyez a la China, supplient Mons le Marquis de Louvoy de leur faire donner, 1687'). This text is a detailed list of the needs of each correspondent, written by Fontaney himself. It is mentioned in Jami, *The Emperor's new mathematics*, 111, with a letter from De Fontaney to Cassini, dated the 8 November 1687 (MEP, vol, 479, 34, quoted without comment in Maitre, 'Le voyage du père de Fontaney', 233). François Michel Le Tellier, Marquis of Louvois (1641–1691) was the successor of the founder and first protector of the Academy, Jean-Baptiste Colbert.

33 Jean de Fontaney asked for various mathematical and astronomical instruments, including a large sextant, which, he explains, will need to be adjusted by the Observatory astronomers themselves before it is dispatched, since it will need to be used for the same observations as those made in Paris. Various books, including a copy of the herbal *Hortus Malabaricus* 'to see what is missing' ('*pour voir ce qu'il y manque*'), were requested by the other Fathers. On this topic, see Raj, 'Go-Betweens', 39–57. The gifts requested may have included 'some highly curious object' to give to the mandarins of the Chinese Court. Fr Gerbillon, in his section, explains that the books to be sent from France should be bound

Fathers' needs – not even, in some cases, for scientific instruments;[34] and the Fathers often had to decide on the routing of the Academy's letters, the instruments, and the books.[35] In their turn the Fathers had, of course, to send the Academy curiosities and books on every topic thought necessary: the group sent exotic astronomy books to France, for instance, and once in Paris these things were used not only as prized objects or collectibles but also as real sources of scientific data for comparative purposes.

As we have already mentioned, the Academy's implicit directives on the organization of correspondence were extremely general. An analysis of the way in which correspondence between Asia and Paris was organized during these early years shows that the Jesuit group was indeed supposed to write to the Paris Academy – this had been established before they left, and various letters bear it out, including some of which only fragments seem to have survived.[36] But, although the letters addressed to the Academy appear to have had a more representative role, it is in the more personal correspondence with individual members of the institution, as we shall see shortly, that we find more details about the way in which the practical work of the missions was organized: data comparisons and their results, for instance, or requests for a particular instrument or personal introduction.[37] It took a great deal of ink to make the missions function. These other, personal exchanges of correspondence worked alongside that of the Academy itself, and apparently they were quicker: during the period December 1685–June 1686 de Fontaney did indeed write to the Academy and to Louvois from Siam; but he wrote more particularly to many other savants,[38] including Cassini, whom he often asked to contact colleagues

---

and put with their outer covers in securely closed chests to be opened only on their arrival at their destination – as the instruments, too.

34 MS B 4/10 item no. 40, Arch. Obs.,; Paris, letter from De Fontaney to Cassini dated 6 May 1686, as above, n.p.

35 Other than the previous letter (in particular the letter from De Fontaney to Cassini dated 6 May 1686), see also: vol. 427, MEP; Paris, letter from De Fontaney to Charmot dated 1691, 504–506; vol. 427, MEP; Paris, letter from De Fontaney to Margiot, 1692, 875–877; vol. 429, MEP; Paris, letter from De Fontaney to Margiot dated 1695, 63–65; vol. 479, MEP; Paris, B.

36 For instance: Vol. 479, B; MEP, Letter to the Paris Royal Academy by De Fontaney dated July 1686, in 'List of letters which I have written from Siam, in particular to Europe' ('Liste des lettres que j'ay écrites de Siam, particulierement en Europe'). Another fragment in the letter from De Fontaney to Cassini dated 6 May 1686 and in MS 423, Biblioteca universitaria, fasc. 20, item no. 6; Pisa, letter from De Fontaney to Cassini, 20 October 1693. This letter is mentioned in Ancelin, 'Science, académisme',108–109, and in Cassini, *Gio. Domenico Cassini*, 275 as above.

37 See, for instance the letter from De Fontaney to Cassini, 20 October 1693.

38 For the same period, for instance to Melchisédech Thevenot (1620–1692), Philippe de la Hire (1640–1718), Jacques Borelli (1623–1689), Thomas Gouyé (1650–1725), Michael

on his behalf.[39] The Italian astronomer in particular seems to have been the contact person for the Jesuit Father in Asia for every scientific need or practical problem – a contact person who had audience everywhere and could reach people who could help, as well as procuring certain books, or the latest instrument:

> We would like to have two really talented young men here: a good clockmaker, one who can adjust any kind of watch or clock, set and install the pendulum clocks we use in our observations, and even manufacture them; he would need to have worked five or six years for M Thuret or M Massinot.[40] And another craftsman that can make mathematical instruments: compasses, quarter-circle protractors [...] We also need a good painter.[41]

---

[39] Butterfield (1634–1724). Vol. 479, B; MEP, 'Liste des lettres que j'ay écrites de Siam, particulierement en Europe'.
MS B 4/10, item no.40, Arch. Obs.; Paris, letter from De Fontaney to Cassini dated 6 May 1686 as above, n.p. 'I beg you will persuade M. Borelly [to let me have] some good glass [i.e. telescope] 36 or 40 feet long and properly tested, for the Pekin observatory or for the one we shall take to China; for I do not have any longer than 25ft long except one of 55ft, on which [...] marked, and another of 8oft. It will not be easy to pack those two for the voyage, but it would be very useful to have a couple of 30ft or 40ft. You would oblige me greatly if, after speaking with P. Verius, you would add a number of good eye-pieces which he begs you will take care of; he will pay for them'. ['Je vous prie de persuader a Mr Borelly quelque bonne verre de 36 ou 40 pieds, bien eprouvé, pour l'observatoire de Pékin, ou pour celuy que nous ferons a la Chine: car je n'en point passé 25 pieds, excepté un de 55 pieds, sur le quel il y [...] marqué, et un autre de 80 pieds. Il sera difficile de mettre ces deux en voyage mais un ou deux bons de 30 a 40 pieds seront tres utiles. Vous m'obligerez de me les accompagner de plusieurs bons oculaires dont il vous prie d'avoir soin, après avoir parlé au P. Verius, qui en fera les frais'] Here De Fontaney asks Cassini to contact Jacques Borelli (or Borelly) the Academician, chemist, physician and specialist lens-maker, as well as the Fr Antoine Verjus SJ mentioned above.

[40] The two Thurets, Isaac Thuret (c. 1630–1706) and his son Jacques (1669–1738), were two clockmakers who worked for the King and for the Academy. Massinot's line of work may well have been similar.

[41] Letter from De Fontaney to Cassini, 20 October 1693, n.p.: 'We would like to have here two young and wise men. One of whom should be a good watchmaker, with the ability to handle all kind of clocks as well as ours clocks of observation. In addition we expect him to gain the ability to build them. He should have gained five or six years of experience either with N.r Thuret or wirth M.r Massinot. The other guy should be able to build mathematical tools such as compasses, quarters of circles [...] We would need a good painter too' ['Nous voudrions avoir ici deux jeunes hommes fort sages dont l'un soit bon horloger, capable de bien accomoder toutes sortes de montres, et nos pendules d'observations , et mesme d'en faire des unes et des d'autres: il faudrait pour cela qu'il eust travaillé cinq ou

Giovanni Domenico Cassini in fact played an important part in keeping the expeditions in touch with the Academy and in dealing with practical problems and requests during the years before 1699.[42] As the mission was primarily organized around the longitude project, everything to do with it will have needed to go through him and the Observatory.

Moreover Cassini (who had always had close relationships with Jesuits, both in Bologna and in Paris), besides having written parts of the memoranda containing instructions for the voyages, and having conducted observations with de Fontaney himself, is also certainly behind the appointment of de Fontaney as expedition leader, given that they already well knew each other.[43]

Cassini was a man of deep faith and was educated in one of the Order's colleges. He had always collaborated with Jesuit scientists, cultivating fruitful working relations strengthened by shared values and mutual trust. He was the longitude project's principal contact person at the Observatory; but what made him even more the main channel of communication with the Academy's mission to Asia was precisely this close personal relationship with the leader of the Royal Mathematicians. De Fontaney's choice of the Italian astronomer in 1685 – a gesture which the latter, writing to the former years later, referred to as a grand gesture of 'friendship' – marked the beginning of a fruitful exchange between the two savants, as evidenced not only by the thread of the Academy's Minutes of Proceedings,[44] especially before 1699, but also by the prolific correspondence over the years. In it, the project concerning the Observatory and

---

six ans chez M.r Thuret ou M.r Massinot. L'autre est pour faire des instrum. De mathematiques, compas, quarts de cercles [...] Il nous faudrait aussi un bon peintre'.]

42 On another occasion Fontaney asks Cassini to send him a present for the Chinese emperor: MS B 4/10, item no.40; Paris, Arch. Obs., letter from Fontaney to Cassini, 6 May 1686: 'If Mme le Bas has sent the good 14ft telescope which I saw you had at the observatory, that would make a good present for the Emperor of China along with some fine [...], because you must not forget to send something for him' ['Si Madame le Bas a envoyé cette bonne lunette de 14 pieds, que j'ay vu chez vous a l'observatoire, ce serait un bon present à faire à l'Empereur de la Chine avec quelque beau [...] car il ne faut pas oublier d'envoyer quelque chose pour luy'], n.p.

43 See, for instance, Marta Cavazza, 'La scienza, lo Studio, i Gesuiti a Bologna nella metà del Seicento', *Giornale di Astronomia*, 32 (2006), 11–19. Giovanni Domenico Cassini was educated at the Jesuit College in Genova. Even after moving to Bologna he continued to work with Jesuit astronomers such as Giovanni Battista Riccioli (1598–1671), and he kept in touch with other members of the Order such as Athanasius Kircher (1602–1680). In Paris, the devout Catholic astronomer established contacts with various Jesuits working in southern France, such as Jean Bonfa (1638–1724), and helped in the founding of the Royal Academy of Montpellier (1706). Traces of exchanges between Cassini and members of the Jesuit Order can also be found in Spain.

44 See for instance PV, AAdS, vol. 16; Paris, 75^r.

the Academy was accompanied and supported by the two scientists' mutual confidence, friendship, and shared faith, a feature which recurs more than once in their letters written between the departure of the mission and the granting of the Rules. Friendship, religious devotion[45] and scientific collaboration blended and reinforced each other. This special relationship is shown not just in the Academy's Records of Proceedings – where it is almost always Cassini who presents novelties from Asia before 1699, even when De Fontaney had already written to the Academy – but even more clearly in the number and content of these letters.[46]

---

45 'I turn to you for everything, and I confess it is no small consolation to me that I have found such a knowledgeable and gentlemanly person as you, and such a good friend, whom I can consult at need. I hope therefore that you will remain in France throughout my time in China so that we may [...] do something in this great empire for the glory of God and the furtherance of science'. ['Vous estes mon recours pour toutes choses, et je vous avoue que ce n'est pas une petite consolation pour moy d'avoir trouvé un aussi honeste homme, aussi savant, et aussi bon ami que vous pour le consulter dans les occasions. Je souhaite pour cette raison que vous soyez aussi longtemps en France que moy a la Chine [...] nous puissions faire quelque chose dans ce grand empire pour la gloire de Dieu, et pour la perfections des sciences'], MS B 4/10, item no.40; Arch. Obs.; Paris, letter from De Fontaney to Cassini, dated 6 May 1686, n.p.

46 'Six weeks ago I wrote to the gentlemen of the Royal Academy of the Sciences. Though you have your share in that letter because you are one of the foremost among those gentlemen, nevertheless the friendship that you have done me the honour of showing to me in the past deserves my particular remembrance of you. We have at last achieved what you so often wished for, which is to meet all together in Peking to do here all that we can for the glory of God and at the same time to correspond with you on science and the making of observations. The Emperor gives us full permission for the former and wishes us to perform the latter, being himself highly curious about our science; indeed he has shown himself so in recent years, as P. Bouvet will tell you. You, Monsieur, and all the gentlemen of the Academy have therefore only to let us know what you desire; for you may suppose that we need instruction, as we are gradually becoming creatures of another world who no longer know what you would like nor what new discoveries you are making for [...] our work'. ['J'ai ecrit il y a prés de six semaines a M° de l'Academie Royale des sciences. Quoy que vous ayez bonne part a cette lettre, parce que vous y tenez un des 1er rang, neanmoins l'amitié, que vous m'avez fait l'honneur de me temoigner autrefois, merite que je me souvienne de vous en particulier. Nous voilà enfin parvenus a ce que vous desiriez si souvent, qui estoit de nous voir reunis a Pekin, pour y faire tous les biens que nous pouvons a la gloire de Dieu, et en mesme temps pour estre vos correpondants en matiere d'observations et des sciences. L'Empereur nous permet entierem.t le 1er et desire que nous fassions le 2', essant luy mesme fort curieux de nos sciences, comme il a paru ces derniers années particulierem.t , ainsi que la P. Bouvet vous dira. Il ne tiendra donc qu'a vous, Monsieur, et a tous les mons. eur de l'academie de nous marquer ce qu'il desirent: car il faut supposer que nous avons besoin d'instructions car peu a peu nous devenons des gens d'un autre monde, qui ne savent plus ce qui est de vostre goust , ni les nouvelles decouvertes que

The appointment of official correspondents who would send and receive letters to and from the Academicians was formally adopted in 1699, though the Jesuits overseas had in fact requested it long before that. Indeed, in one of his letters to the Academy in 1687, De Fontaney points out that it would save the Academy and its correspondents time and money[47] if each of the Fathers could have one particular correspondent who would act as his spokesman: this would make communication simpler and clearer, and organize the correspondence in a less piecemeal way. The suggestion was made more than ten years before the Academy's formal rule about the appointment of correspondents was introduced in 1699; and it would take twelve years before de Fontaney and his colleagues in Asia could have their own official correspondent, in the person of Fr Gouyé SJ,[48] the only Jesuit Academician.

The need for secrecy in sending information to Paris tallied well with the active control exercised by the Fathers over all the correspondence with Europe: the necessity of tracking letters sent during their missions meant that detailed lists of correspondence were often maintained in certain periods, as we have seen. Those lists, which also state by which route and which vessel a given letter had been dispatched, seem to have been made so that lost letters could be identified more readily. According to the sample that I have studied of De Fontaney's letters, he sometimes made duplicates. To prevent the loss of material received from the Academy, De Fontaney very often suggested what marks should be put on the books or other materials dispatched.[49]

Cassini, for his part, passed on the raw data from China to those who were just as interested but not so easily reachable by the Jesuits networks: the *Observationes Sinenses* (Chinese Observations) sent to the Royal Society (the English scientific academy, whose records make Cassini's paternity as clear as any signature could do) contain observations carried out in China and already compared with those made in the Paris Observatory during the period 1696–1694.[50] The Observatory also passed on to the Royal Society some letters it had itself

---

vous faites pour [...] nos travaux']. MS 423, Biblioteca universitaria, fasc. 20, item no. 6; Pisa, letter from De Fontaney to Cassini, 20 October 1693, n.p.

47   Vol. 479, MEP; Paris, letter from De Fontaney to the Paris Academy, 8 November 1687, 32–33.
48   *Index biographique des Membres et correspondants de l'Académie des Sciences*. See also: PV, vol. 18, 148ᵛ.
49   MS B 4/10, Arch. Obs., item no. 40; Paris, letter from De Fontaney to Cassini, 6 May 1686; letter from De Fontaney in Peking to Cassini in Paris dated 20 October 1693.
50   The writing of this report of celestial observations is certainly by Giovanni Domenico Cassini. MS CL. P. VIII (1) 52, 112–113; London, Royal Society Library.

received from China, extracts of which were sometimes published in the record of the English body's proceedings, the *Philosophical Transactions*.[51]

For its longitude research in Asia, in the absence of what could strictly be called standing orders, the Academy relied on the support of the ready-organized Jesuit networks and on the implicit rules mainly grounded in the social relationships amongst learned men. This collaboration among people with shared social connections, which for many years provided the basis of institutional co-operation between scientific institutions, will emerge again in the next two sections.

2 The Paris Observatory and the College of Louis le Grand

Before he left for Asia, Jean de Fontaney – missionary, colleague of the Observatory's astronomers, and one of the Royal Mathematicians since 1685 – had been a *lector* in mathematics at the Parisian college known as *Louis le Grand*, as was the Academician Father Gouyé.[52]

The college of Louis le Grand, founded in 1563 under the name *Collège de Clermont*, changed its name following a royal visit by Louis XIV, probably in 1674: the literature cited below gives various possible dates for the college's change of name. A letter from one of its fellows dated in early September 1682,[53] in which the College is already referred to by its new name, suggests that the visit had actually taken place some years earlier.

Various fellows of the college were involved in projects outside its walls, as we learn from one of the most important social histories of the establishment,[54] which links all six Royal Mathematicians who left for Asia in 1685 with the activities of Louis le Grand. The Jesuit centre gave considerable support to many of the projects of the Royal Observatory and the Academy.

---

51 MS LBC. 12, 78–81; London, Royal Society Library. Some extracts in 'Excerpta ex Litteris D. Cassini ad P. Fontenay Mathematicum Regium apud Sinas', *Philosophical Transactions* 20 (1698), 371–373.

52 Gustave Emond, *Histoire du collège de Louis-le-Grand, ancien collège des jésuites à Paris, depuis sa fondation jusqu'en 1830* (Paris, 1845), 123–124.

53 MS Astron. 578, 44, Sächsische Landesbibliothek – Staats-und Universitätsbibliothek (SLUB); Dresden, letter to Antoine Verjus dated 5 September 1682, n.p. . On this document and its content, see Deias, *Inventer l'Observatoire*.

54 Gustave Dupont-Ferrier, *La vie quotidienne d'un collège parisien pendant plus de trois cent cinquante ans. Du Collège de Clermont au Lycée Louis-le-Grand (1563–1920)* (Paris, 1921), 1:150–151.

We shall see in this section that the College was not only one of the institutions engaged in education, training and observation before the Royal Observatory was founded, but also that, in a sort of natural transition, it acted as a co-ordinating centre in view of its potent educational and social role prior to the creation of the Academy and Observatory. This was the case especially before 1685 in connection with certain astronomical observations conducted at the same time as those of the Observatory. We shall see once again how, in the absence of formal rules, institutions collaborated primarily through the collaboration of individuals.

Bigourdan describes the College as one of the foremost meeting places where the ideas for the Académie des Sciences and the Observatory itself had been formed before 1666,[55] as well as an important educational establishment for young French noblemen thanks to its teaching methods, which were indeed ahead of those of the University itself.[56]

Attention to science and the scientific education of the young formed one of the cardinal points of all the Jesuit Order's educational activity; this college in particular had engaged in astronomical observations ever since its beginnings, but increasingly so under Louis XIV.[57] The College had its own tower for observing the sky: Emond gives us a description of it in his book,[58] and it was also used in astronomy lessons for the students;[59] from that tower Ismael Boulliau (1605–1694), an astronomer, cleric and savant (though when the Académie des Sciences was founded he did not become a member), observed the lunar

---

55   Guillaume Bigourdan, 'La station astronomique du Collège de Clermont (première période) et la mission astronomique de Siam', *Comptes rendus hebdomadaires des séances de l'Académie des Sciences* 166 (January-June 1918), 833–840 (834).
56   Ibid.
57   Dupont-Ferrier, *Du Collège de Clermont au Lycée Louis le Grand*, 189.
58   Emond, *Histoire du collège de Louis-le-Grand*, 362. See also Guillaume Bigourdan, 'L'observatoire du Collège Louis-le-Grand (dernière période) et les travaux astronomiques de la mission française de Pékin', *Comptes rendus hebdomadaires des séances de l'Académie des Sciences* 166 (January-June 1918), 871–877.
59   For a better understanding of how the College and its intellectual life were organized the reader may consult Dupont-Ferrier's account of its everyday life from its foundation until the eighteenth century. Besides explaining all its teaching with a wealth of references, Dupont-Ferrier describes how it was organized for the exact sciences and mathematics and astronomy in particular. On page 184 the author shows, with many facts and references, that the College was ahead of its time in educating the young in mathematics, and that it was astronomy, taught and practised at this institution for many years, which was the main 'glory of this house' in the century of Louis XIV.

eclipse of May 1653.[60] The College devised its own suggestions on the longitude problem.[61]

The College was an important participant in scientific conversations with the royal institutions, such as the Academy or the Observatory, especially during the period before 1685. A number of observations of the heavens were carried out jointly by the Academy (i.e. the Observatory) and the College of Louis le Grand. One example was the 1682 eclipse, which, as the Academy's records of proceedings tell us, was the subject of discussions between the college and the royal astronomers; the two sites' observations of this eclipse were often co-ordinated.[62]

The College also features in the Academy's publications, which during the initial years of the assembly's activities consisted mainly of collections made by one or more Academician authors,[63] though later they took on a different form.[64] In a 1681 piece by Cassini himself summarizing observations of the Great Comet seen in the winter of 1680–1681 and all that was known about it,[65] the author writes that as he himself, de Fontaney and probably a few other savants of the College of Louis le Grand were observing the spectacular object they had to decamp to the Observatory after a while, because its location gave a better view of the sky near the horizon.

---

60 See Henricus J.M. Nellen, *Ismaël Boulliau, 1605–1694, astronome, épistolier, nouvelliste et intermédiaire scientifique: ses rapports avec les milieux du 'libertinage érudit'* (Amsterdam-Maarssen, 1994).

61 In 1663 the *Gazette de France* published a proposal by the College for discovering the 'Secret des Longitudes', as we can see in Dupont-Ferrier, *Du Collège de Clermont au Lycée Louis le Grand*, 189.

62 PV, AAdS, vol. 9bis; Paris, 157^v, on the moon eclipse observed in February 1682. *Mémoire de l'Académie des Sciences*, (Paris, 1730), 10, 612–613, on the moon eclipse observed in October 1678.

63 For one example, see Jean Picard, 'Voyage d'Uranibourg, ou observations astronomiques faites en Dannemarck', in *Recueil d'observations faites en plusieurs voyages par ordre de sa Majesté pour perfectionner l'astronomie et la géographie* (Paris, 1680).

64 For the nature of the Academy's official publications after 1699, see Mazauric, *Fontenelle et l'invention de l'histoire des sciences*.

65 Cassini, *Observations sur la comète qui a paru au mois de décembre 1680. et en janvier 1681. Présentées au Roy* (Paris,1681). On this comet, which appeared in winter 1680, and made famous by Pierre Bayle's nbook on the nature of such objects, see Marta Cavazza, 'La cometa del 1680–1681: astrologi e astronomi a confronto', *Studi e memorie per la storia dell'Università di Bologna*, nuova serie, 3 (1983), 409–66. It offers a good summary of the state of observation deployed on this comet throughout Europe – as well as on the reactions to it. On the observations of this comet at the Paris Observatory, see the chapter 'Utiliser et visiter l'instrument-monument: production du savoir et representation du pouvoir du roi', in Deias, *Inventer l'Observatoire*.

The Jesuit mission which we described in the previous section was actually hatched and developed in this observational and educational institution which predated the Observatory; once again, this was the fruits of the social intercourse shared by the College and – in this case – the Observatory and Cassini as an individual. In November 1682, at the start of formal discussions between Versailles and Paris about the Observatory project and the missions to Asia, the College received Letters Patent from the king conferring the status of Royal College and granting it a number of privileges.[66] We do not know whether its collaboration with the Royal Observatory was one of the reasons for this, nor whether it resulted among other things from pressure from the College fellows on the king's confessor, François d'Aix de la Chaise (1624–1709), which has already been remarked by the historians cited here.

The college's correspondence shows that during those months the institution's fellows were looking for a firmer constitution and a fuller recognition of the valuable contribution to science being made by the college's Jesuits.[67]

As Emond explains,[68] however, despite the official protection which the College enjoyed after Louis XIV renamed it and granted its Letters Patent, no astronomical observations seem to have been reported from within its walls between 1684 and the middle of the next century, though its teaching activities did not cease.[69] Moreover the Academy's resources were redirected elsewhere in that period. Bigourdan seems to suggest that although the institution had been brought formally under the royal wing, the continual demands for astronomical instruments at the time were costing too much even for a royal college, and in the end choked off the practice of astronomical observation there, at least until the next century.[70]

3 The Royal Observatory: A Place to Visit

An interesting case for the study of what could be considered an alliance of astronomical observation, court activities, religious interests and diplomacy, is

---

66 Emond, *Histoire du collège de Louis-le-Grand*, 135.
67 'Letter to Antoine Verjus' dated 5 September 1682.
68 'Les Jesuites avaient-ils trop presumé des intentions du monarque?', Emond, *Histoire du collège de Louis-le-Grand*, 134–135.
69 Bigourdan, 'L'observatoire du Collège Louis le Grand', 871.
70 Dupont-Ferrier's book deals with some astronomical instruments (clocks, sundials, mirrors of various geometries for optical studies, telescopes and microscopes) used in the College's classrooms during the seventeenth and eighteenth centuries.

the visit which the Siamese ambassadors paid to the Paris Observatory in September 1686.[71]

It was a very common practice among savants during the *Grand Siècle*, and one they themselves did much to publicize, to invite people from outside the Academy to visit the Observatory, try out its instruments and admire its collections.[72] Though we cannot be certain whether the Observatory made formal provision for this activity, it is one of the embodiments of the original project: the Observatory was a royal building; one of its functions as a physical representation of Louis XIV himself was to arouse the admiration of foreigners. Open day and night for its work, the Observatory was keen to welcome visitors and explain its activities to them. It was important for the Observatory to be known beyond the Academy, to be part of a network of public contacts, admired by the French court and by foreigners, and to be well promoted externally. Foreigners, indeed, would often be invited and entertained at the establishment, and real working observations were organized to charm their gaze and arouse their curiosity.

These visits were of various kinds.[73] As well as accommodating Academicians who went to conduct observations or other experiments, and sometimes spent the night there, the Observatory received passing visits during which its guests would probably take part in the routine observations already scheduled,[74] as well as planned visits duly organized as part of its day-to-day activities.

---

71 MS 423; Pisa, Biblioteca universitaria, fasc. 21, item no. 3. This manuscript's date and signature are also given in Ancelin, 'Science, académisme', 249, though according to Ancelin the visit took place in September 1687. We find a trace of this event in Van Der Cruysse, *Louis XIV et le Siam* (395), which mentions 'Cassini's Observatory' as one of the places which the ambassadors seem to have been very keen to visit. On this embassy, see, for instance, the print *La solennelle ambassade du Roy de Siam au Roy, pour l'establissement du commerce avec ces peuples d'Orient, les cérémonies de la lettre et des audiences* (Paris, 1687).

72 See in particular '*Utiliser et visiter l'instrument-monument*' in Deias, *Inventer l'Observatoire*. The Siamese ambassadors' visit is one of the examples of entertaining foreigners discussed in that paper.

73 The subject of visits to the Observatory during the Grand Siècle was first explored by Wolf (chapter on 'Les séances de l'Académie et les visites princières à l'Observatoire', 113–134), which brought very many primary sources to light. One of the more recent studies that could be mentioned on the same point is Ancelin's 2011 paper (170–199). In the section in Deias, *Inventer l'Observatoire* entitled '*Utiliser et visiter l'instrument-monument*' I have returned to the topic, using the visits to the building in another way, as pointers to the original plans for the Observatory's work, and to detect unwritten rules for its functioning.

74 An instance of this type of visit has already been described by Picolet: Guy Picolet, 'Une visite du jeune Saint-Simon à l'Observatoire de Paris', in *Cahiers Saint-Simon* 26 (1998), 58–68.

In this section we shall see one of the more fully described instances of the latter kind, which had probably been well prepared and organized in advance.

The Siamese king and Louis XIV had by then been watching and studying each other for some years. France and Siam alike were brimming with curiosity about every aspect of the other country's inhabitants, their customs and other aspects.[75] On the French side there were hopes of a religious conversion, which would among other things hold out the prospect of regular trade between the two countries. After setting up the Seminary for Missions Abroad in or around 1662, Louis XIV had succeeded, partly due to the missions carried out under the aegis of this new religious and political institution, in establishing direct and continuous contact with Siam.[76] A French embassy had already reached Siamese territory;[77] and in 1685 the Jesuits of the Royal Mathematicians expedition disembarked in Siam on their way to China.

The Siamese embassy arrived at Vincennes at the end of July 1686 and was received by Louis XIV at Versailles on Sunday 1 September of that year.[78] The mission's official object was for the Siamese to collect information on the court of Louis XIV, the only one in the world, according to Phra-Narai, king of Siam (1632–1688), which could rival his own in beauty.[79] There was much correspondence among the French in 1686, as the time approached for the Siamese to arrive, discussing how French projects in Siam would be facilitated by this embassy to France: mutual assistance between science and religion was expected

---

75 See 'Rivières du Royaume du Siam', *Journal des Savants* (1687), 381; the extract 'Siamois, leurs comèdies, funérailles, leurs lois & leurs coutumes, leur religion', *Journal des Savants* (1687), 183–187. Secondary sources include: Alain Forest, *Falcon, l'imposteur de Siam, commerce, politique et religion dans la Thaïlande au XVIIe siècle* (Paris, 2010); Lanni, *Le rêve Siamois du Roi Soleil*; Van der Cruysse, *Louis XIV et le Siam*. For the long term relations between France and Siam, see David Aubin, 'Eclipse Politics in France and Thailand, 1868', in *The Heavens on Earth: Observatories and Astronomy in Nineteenth-Century Science and Culture*, eds David Aubin, Charlotte Bigg, and H. Otto Sibum, (Durham and London, 2010), 86–117.

76 On this aspect, see in particular Ronald S. Love, 'The Missions Étrangères in Siam',1–27.

77 François Timoléon de Choisy (1644–1724), *Journal du voyage du Siam fait en 1685 et 1686*, ed. Dirk van Der Crysse (Paris, 1995); François Timoléon de Choisy, *Mémoires pour servir à l'Histoire de Louis XIV* (Clermont-Ferrand, 2008). See also vol. 879, MEP; Paris, 'Journal de Voyage au Siam de l'abbé de Lionne', 629–705. In 2001 this manuscript was published in *Etudes et documents* 13 (2001).

78 Vol. 10, MEP; Paris, 'Première audience royale des ambassadeurs siamois en France' [First royal audience of Siamese ambassadors in France], le 1 septembre 1686', 349–365 or *Abrége des Mémoires du Marquis du Dangeau*, 1, 165–167.

79 Vol. 879, MEP; Paris, 'Instructions du Roi de Siam aux ambassadeurs en France'[Instructions of the King of Siam to ambassadors in France], 163–201.

here, it seems, since the Siamese sovereign had promised the Jesuit Fathers that churches and observatories would be built so that the French could carry out observations in Siam.[80] Louis XIV gave very clear orders that the Seminary was not to interfere in matters concerning the Siamese embassy of 1686 because to do so 'could badly blight the work of missions abroad';[81] but the greater familiarity with Siamese language and culture acquired by the members of those missions meant that the Seminary's missionaries were nevertheless very important as go-betweens on this occasion in 1686 as well as on others. The missionary Abbé Artus De Lionne (1655–1713), a member of the Seminary (and the son of Hugues de Lionne, Louis XIV's foreign secretary) had earlier travelled to Thailand on Seminary business and was an expert in the language and customs of that realm. He was made lead interpreter for the Siamese during Their Excellencies' stay,[82] as we read in the memoirs of Philippe de Courcillon, Marquess of Dangeau (1638–1720). During this embassy, De Lionne – who both then and subsequently acted as the primary channel of communication on Siamese matters[83] – seems never to have left the Siamese visitors' side. According to Dangeau's court memoirs the French group which attended the three ambassadors (one of them undoubtedly Kosa Pan, dates unknown), four other gentlemen and two secretaries were never separated from them, not even for meals.[84] In this version of the memoirs we read that, after they were received by the king of France, the ambassadors began their sight-seeing tours with great liveliness and curiosity about everything.[85] The king spent a considerable amount of time with his visitors while they were at court, and many gifts were exchanged on the occasion of the numerous festivities at Versailles and visits to Paris.[86]

---

80   Vol. 10, MEP; Paris, letter dated 20 June 1686, 76.
81   'Peut être très funeste à l'oeuvre des missions étrangères'. Extract Vol. 203, MEP; Paris, 367–373, letter from Fermanel to De Lionne, 13 September 1686.
82   *Abrégé des Mémoires*, 166.
83   For instance: vol. 859, MEP; Paris, letter from de Lionne to Louis XIV, 1687, *Sur les Jésuites Français qui sont en Siam* [On the French Jesuits who are in Siam], 487.
84   *Abrégé des Mémoires*, 166.
85   *Abrégé des Mémoires*, 167–170.
86   *Abrégé des Mémoires*, 170. Vol. 10, MEP; Paris, letter from Brisacier to Fermanel, 16 December 1686, 311–314; Vol. 10, MEP; Paris, 'Traduction du compliment fait par Mr l'abbe de Lionne aux ambassadeurs du Roy de Siam dans le séminaire des Missions Etrangères de Paris en langage siamois' [Translation of the compliment made by the abbot of Lion, in Siamese language; to the ambassadors of the King of Siam in the seminary of the French foreign mission], 341–344.

There is nothing in the Academy's records or Giovanni Domenico Cassini's *Journal d'Observations*[87] to mark 27 September 1686 as the date of any particularly interesting event; and this is surely not because it fell during the Academy's vacation.[88] Nonetheless, a manuscript now conserved in Pisa, probably in Cassini's own hand but quite separate from his *Journal d'Observations*, gives a detailed account of a visit to the Royal Observatory on that date by the ambassadors of Phra-Narai.

At the end of September 1686 – on the 27th, to be precise – the ambassadors and their entourage went to the Observatory; the account in the Pisa manuscript corroborates the impression of a friendly, talkative set of people, highly curious about the work being done in that scientific establishment. Despite some language difficulties the group seems to have asked plenty of questions about what they saw and how things worked. Other observatories like that of Paris were, we know, to be built in a number of locations in Siam; and this will probably have given an additional motive to the group's curiosity. From the manuscript's account, then, it would appear that the secretaries of the Siamese and even more essentially their interpreter, the Abbé De Lionne, were present at this visit.

Now it is possible that the suggestion of going to admire the Observatory came from the ambassadors; but it is equally possible that Cassini met these curious foreigners at Versailles and invited them, as he met others including the physician, naturalist and member of the Royal Society Martin Lister (1639–1712) when the latter travelled to Paris in 1698.[89] The manuscript gives no details of any such invitation, and indeed we do not know which of the people who lived and worked at the Observatory, apart from Cassini, were in attendance that day, though we do know that customarily more than one of the astronomers would entertain visitors, especially important ones.[90] The manuscript account is written in the third person in the style of those draft reports on visits that would sometimes be later transcribed into the official records.[91]

---

87 MS D 3/1–30 [for the years 1683–1798], Arch.Obs.; Paris, Cassini I, 'Journal d'Observations faites à l'Observatoire de Paris'.

88 Long before the practice became official under the Rules, in fact, the Minutes reveal that from September until November the Academy held its vacation. Nevertheless, it is not hard to find evidence that Cassini continued to work during those months, and it often happens that some Mémoires dated September or October in the Minutes have been entered afterwards, once the Assembly's normal activities have been resumed.

89 Martin Lister, *Voyage de Lister à Paris en 1698. Traduit pour la première fois, publié et annoté par la Société des bibliophiles françois. On y a joint des extraits des ouvrages d'Evelyn relatifs à ses voyages en France de 1648 à 1661* (Paris, 1873).

90 See: Deias, *Inventer l'Observatoire*.

91 See: Deias, *Inventer l'Observatoire*.

The ambassadors were greeted 'at the door' by Cassini, we can read in the manuscript kept in Pisa, and taken to admire the building probably from the outside, as was the custom. It would appear that the visit began in the morning from the East tower, and that the visitors were encouraged to use the long telescopes which had been made ready and trained on two distant objects, as well as a *lunette equatoriale* (equatorial refractor telescope) and some *lunettes sans tuyaux*, the latter consisting of two big lenses positioned so as to form a tubeless telescope. The Siamese were invited to try these in front of the northern window, just as Cassini himself would normally use them. According to the manuscript, Cassini's explained much of the technology that had gone into the *lunettes*, the lenses themselves, and the discoveries they had enabled the Observatory to make. As was customary during visits, this one also included a demonstration of a spectacular burning glass, and a chart of the stars visible at those latitudes. The ambassadors seem to have asked for a copy of this stars chart, and Cassini undertook to have one made for them, as we learn from December entries in his faithful *Journal d'Observations*.[92]

Another map was shown to the Siamese ambassadors during this visit, as it was to all foreigners who visited the Observatory after 1683 when its first version was completed: this was a world map, complete with longitudes, drawn in ink on the floor of the West tower and continuously revised, which served as a model for mapmakers as it was updated with the very latest data on longitudes which the Academy received from more or less every part of the world, and whose projection made it a useful map for teaching and display.[93]

As in the case of other visits to the Observatory, the official records made by the savants themselves emphasize the backdrop against which the visitors, especially foreign ones, were called on to play their part.[94] The world map served to remind the Siamese in the most direct and spectacular way of the Academy's

---

92   MS D 3/5, Arch. Obs.; Paris, 17 December 1686, 126r.

93   On this map see 'Amener le monde à L'Observatoire: le parterre géographique de la salle ouest du premier étage', in Deias, *Inventer l'Observatoire*. For a shorter version, see Deias, 'A vanished curiosity from the Observatory of Louis XIV: the Parterre Géographique, a tool both of precision and of representation', forthcoming.

94   Another instance is the visit in May 1681 by the Russian ambassadors Pyotr Potemkin and Stefan Volkov, sent to France by Tsar Feodor III (1676–1682) to ask for Louis XIV's mediation to end his war with the Turks and Tatars. The visit is noted in a single line in the Academy's Records of Proceedings (PV, AAdS, vol. 9, may 1681, Paris, 99v;), to the effect that the Observatory's visitors 'observed the crescent of Venus' [translated from the French]; this shows that the savants probably wanted to amaze the foreigners with an observation which furnished implicit proof of the Copernican system, thanks to the technology of the Royal Observatory. See Deias, *Inventer l'Observatoire*.

wide-ranging research into the problem of longitudes:[95] this map, at once exotic and familiar, showed the Siamese their own country from another viewpoint, as well as giving them a vision of a world unified through science despite its wide diversity of countries and cultures.

4   Bianchini, the Sun, the Moon, and Calendar Reforms

As already mentioned, Article 27 of the Rules granted to the Academy on 4 February 1699 envisaged that each Academician should choose one or more official correspondents who would become correspondents of the Academy itself through that member. In his point-by-point commentary on the text, Fontenelle adds that after the official reading of the Rules 'All the Academicians also nominated the various persons with whom they would correspond on scientific matters, both in the [French] provinces and in foreign countries [...]';[96] they would be asked to conduct such correspondence regularly.

The criteria by which the Academicians chose their individual correspondents would surely have varied; but it is well worth taking a moment to consider, especially in some cases, the context of those decisions which will have led some Academicians to choose certain correspondents rather than others, to examine the criteria and the situations in which certain mathematicians became Academy correspondents as well as personal ones, and to see what particular advantage this had for the Academy itself.

In February 1699 Cassini chose many Italians as correspondents, undoubtedly in part for language reasons.[97] The Academy did certainly need correspondents in Italy; but while it had had ample exchanges well before 1699 with some of the correspondents chosen by Cassini and the situation was merely confirmed and put on a formal basis in 1699 – as in the case of Vincenzo Viviani (1622–1703), or the Studio of Bologna – [98] Cassini's choice, that same year, of

---

95   Another example of the way in which this map was used: the Bishop of Mesopotamia, sent to Versailles and Paris on behalf of the King of Persia, visited the Royal Observatory on 22 November 1685: 'The bishop of Mesopotamia... recognized [the location of] his see on the map and marked its position'. The account of this visit is to be found in MS D 3/3, Arch. Obs; Paris, 121r.
96   Fontenelle, *Histoire du Renouvellement*, 67.
97   *Index biographiques des Membres et correspondants de l'Académie des Sciences*. See also: PV, AAdS, vol. 18; Paris, 148ᵛ.
98   In 1699 Cassini wrote to Eustachio Manfredi (1674–1739) who had just been appointed to the chair that had been previously occupied by Domenico Guglielmini (1655–1710). Cassini, who had been in touch with Guglielmini since well before 1699, told Manfredi that the Academy would be grateful if he would correspond with him on astronomical matters

the Italian astronomer Francesco Bianchini (1662–1729)[99] as Academy correspondent was a very different story.

Rome, where the cleric and scholar Bianchini worked and prayed, must indeed have been a very interesting place from which Paris might expect to receive observational data, books and other things.[100] But that was not all: Cassini's decision was made at the very moment when various circles and institutions within the Vatican, including the Vatican Library and its Head Keeper, the chronologist, scholar and historian Enrico Noris (1631–1704),[101] were actively engaged in a major project to reform the Gregorian calendar, a project that had been a talking-point in many European countries since the late sixteenth century, and which Cassini and a few colleagues had brought to the Academy from Italy long before its official announcement in 1700. We shall now see how this came about.

The first meeting between Cassini and Bianchini was very probably, as Maria Pia Donato suspected,[102] during a journey to Italy by Cassini and his son Jacques (1677–1756) from late in 1694 until early 1696, about which we know little. Even before coming to Paris the elder Cassini had been involved in discussions of the ephemerides of Clavius (1538–1612), one of the linchpins of the Gregorian calendar reform of 1582, and the errors that could now easily be detected in it;[103] after his arrival at the Academy in 1669 he continued to argue for the need for new methods.[104]

(MS 4705, Biblioteca de l'Archiginnasio; Bologna, autograph collection, XVI, Letter from Cassini to Manfredi in 1699).

99   On this savant see John L. Heilbron, *The sun in the Church. Cathedrals as solar observatories* (Cambridge, 1999) and Id., 'la Meridiana di Bianchini e la politica estera di Clemente XI', *Giornale di Astronomia. Atti del Convegno Il Sole nella Chiesa. Cassini e le grandi meridiane come strumenti di indagine astronomica*, 32 (2006), 46–53.

100 On Rome during the seventeenth century, see the works of Antonella Romano and Maria Pia Donato.

101 For full details of Enrico Noris, see 'Noris Enrico', in *Dizionario Biografico degli Italiani,*.

102 Maria Pia Donato, 'La Vaticana e le Scienze Naturali nella Roma del Seicento' in *La Vaticana nel Seicento (1590–1700). Una Biblioteca di Biblioteche* (Vatican City, 2014), 799–818.

103 MS Latini CL. 14 no. 243, Biblioteca Marciana; Venice, 'Astronomical letter from Domenico Cassini concerning the adjustment of the Gregorian calendar', [lettera astronomica circa la regolazione del Calendario Gregoriano di Domenico Cassini], dated 20 March 1666, from Bologna. My thanks to Anna Cassini for bringing this letter to my attention.

104 'Réglement des temps par une méthode facile et nouvelle par laquelle on fixe pour toujours les équinoxes au même jour de l'année & on rétablit l'usage du Nombre d'Or, pour régler toujours les Epactes d'une mème façon' (1679) in *Mémoire de l'Académie des Sciences* (Paris, 1730), 10, 615–620.

During this trip to Italy, which Cassini made primarily to check the status of his *Meridiana* in Bologna,[105] he and his son stayed at least once in Rome. In her Life of the astronomer Anna Cassini documents his audience with Pope Innocent XII (1691–1700) in 1695, at which they discussed questions of hydraulics in the Papal dominions.[106]

Donato[107] suggests that during this stay in Rome Cassini will surely have made contact with various mathematicians and experts in chronology who were starting to discuss not only the necessity of reforming the calendar but also the production of a common version that could be adopted by the Protestant countries, which had not accepted the Gregorian reform at the end of the previous century. Such a change would considerably ease relations with many foreign countries.

Cassini made strong connections with two new contacts in 1695, probably in Rome: the astronomer Francesco Bianchini, and Enrico Noris, who had been made a Cardinal in that same year.

There were many astronomers in Rome who argued that the overhauled Gregorian calendar had to be based on sound mathematics and accurate observation; two of these were the Italian astronomer Francesco Bianchini and Gottfried Wilhelm von Leibniz (1646–1716).

Why did the call for reform occur just at this juncture? Why, in particular, did it bring about this championing of chronology by mathematicians and astronomers? Since the mid-seventeenth century[108] astronomical observation had achieved such a degree of accuracy, especially concerning eclipses of all types, that not only were the previous ephemerides in need of replacement, but it was possible to make a new and more accurate determination of the solar and lunar cycles from which the dates of Easter Day and the whole of Easter week – the very basis of every Christian calendar – were calculated.

---

105 In 1655 Cassini had seen to the restoration of the heliometer constructed by Ignazio Danti (1536–1586) in the *Basilica* of San Petronio, Bologna; he also constructed a similar device at the Paris Observatory. He restored the San Petronio meridian line to check the calendar (*Giornale de'Letterati d'Italia* (Venice, 1717); see also Cassini, *Gio. Domenico Cassini*, 65), and he and his colleagues used it mainly for studying the sun's motion; in fact it provided the first observational proof of Kepler's second law. On the 'Meridiana' of Bologna see in particular Heilbron, *The sun in the Church*.

106 Cassini, *Gio. Domenico Cassini*, 344.

107 Donato, 'La Vaticana e le Scienze Naturali', 817.

108 On this subject: Homet, *Astronomie et astronomes en Provence*, as before; Guy Picolet, eds. *Jean Picard et les débuts de l'astronomie de précision au XVIIe siècle* (Paris, 1987).

The contribution being made by the Paris Academy at that time to the observation of these phenomena was fundamental, and was being disseminated throughout Europe. The observational missions carried out all over the world in concert with the Paris Observatory were the cornerstone of European astronomy. In particular the Observatory's work on lunar eclipses furnished an opportunity not to be missed if the Gregorian calendar was to be given this salutary revision and to be adopted at last in every European country.

The correspondence with Bianchini began towards the end of 1695,[109] when Cassini, now in Genoa on his way back to Paris, wrote to him in Rome. Cassini's first known letter to Noris is the one written in October 1699, the year of the reform.[110] Surviving excerpts from a book by Noris which Cassini had used in an earlier paper read to the Academy[111] indicate that his exchanges with Noris probably began before that.

During his journey in 1695 Cassini reasserted the Gregorian calendar's overall validity but pointed out the need to revise some aspects of it: he published this argument in the *Histoire de l'Académie Royale* in 1700,[112] though it had been written earlier. The lectures on the calendar given to the Academy on his return from Italy were structured with greater definition than those he had given before leaving. Whereas his earlier intervention on the topic had been essentially concerned with methods of calculation, after 1696 the subject of the calendar within the Academy was transformed into a scientific subject for discussion and debate, with detailed interventions explaining how the matter had been dealt with in the literature and comparing this with the new ideas published in the latest books.[113]

However, the numerous rules and calculation proposals put forward by Cassini and others in the following years would certainly not have sufficed for a full reform, not least because the calculation of the date of Easter and other festivals linked to it over the course of the year also depend on the cycles of the

---

109 MS U 16, Biblioteca Vallicelliana, Bianchini collection; Rome, letter from Cassini to Bianchini dated 31 December 1695, from Genoa, 86^r–88^v.

110 MS 910, Biblioteca Angelica; Rome, letter from Cassini to Noris, 8 October 1699, from Paris,157$^{r\text{-}v}$.

111 PV, vol. 15, 31^r–42^r (April 1696); vol. 15, 145^r-149^r (July 1696); Paris, AAdS. The book was certainly Enrico Noris, *De cyclo paschali Ravennate annorum XCV* (Florence, 1691).

112 'Sur le calendrier' in *Histoire de l'Académie royale des sciences pour l'année MDCC avec les Mémoires de Mathematique & de Physique, pour la même année* (Paris, 1703), 124–126.

113 Some examples in the PV (AAdS): for 1696, vol. 15, 31^r-42^r, 149^r; for 1700, vol. 19, 183^r; for 1697, vol. 16, 143^r-151^v; Paris, AAdS. Francesco Bianchini, 'Réflexions sur des mémoires touchant la correction grégorienne, communiquées par M. Bianchini à M. Cassini', in *Histoire de l'Académie Royale des Sciences pour l'année MDCCIV avec les Mémoires de Mathematique & de Physique, pour la même année* (Paris, 1706), 142–145.

moon – specifically, the first full moon after the sun has moved through the equinox. Lunar observations and the technology that made them possible were making huge strides almost daily, but were still the subject of ongoing research and verification. The observation of lunar eclipses and lunar phases, also more and more precise since the middle of the seventeenth century, was accordingly crucial in developing greater knowledge of the lunar cycle.

Observations of such phenomena at the Observatory were increasingly frequent after 1697; Bianchini and others in Rome were kept informed by letter;[114] and the published descriptions of those observations often mentioned their use in tracking the lunar and solar cycles for the purpose of calendar research.[115]

In 1697 the Academy received a suggestion for 'calendar alignment' from Erhard Wegelius (1625–1699), professor of mathematics in the city of Jena; this seems to have been the first such proposal from Protestant Europe, and Cassini undertook to study and reply to it.[116] His correspondence with Francesco Bianchini also continued during those years, until his choice of Bianchini as correspondent at the start of 1699.[117]

It is clear from the Academy's publications that Cassini's choice of Bianchini as correspondent did not result from this project, which had begun well before the following announcement in a publication of 1700:

> This year a proposal from Germany that to some extent concerns the Académie des Sciences well illustrates the importance that Astronomy may have on some occasions in matters Ecclesiastical & Political. (...) M. le Comte de Pontchartain considered the said proposal important enough for it to be mentioned to the King. That importance was only enhanced by the fact that, upon the change being made in Germany, the authorities in Rome began seeking ways to bring about a full alignment on the Calendar (...) The King ordered letters to be sent to M. le Prince de

---

114 For co-ordinated eclipse observations in Paris and in Rome see for instance: in 1696: PV, AAdS, vol. 15; Paris, 91^r–95^v. In 1703, vol. 22, AAdS; Paris, 29^v.

115 'Sur les deux éclipses de cette année, et principalement sur celle de Lune, employée à l'examen du Calendrier', (1697) [On the two eclipses of this year, especially on the moon one, used for the exam of the Calendar], in *Histoire de l'Académie royale des sciences, depuis 1686. Jusqu'à son Renouvellement en 1699* (Paris, 1733), 2, 322–331.

116 PV, AAdS, vol. 16; Paris, 'Ad propositionem conformandi Calendaria' [On the proposal to reform the calendar], followed by Cassini's answer 'Medium Expeditissimum Conformandi Calendaria Christianorum in perpetuum utriusque partis bene placito' [The swiftest means of bringing the Christians' calendar into conformity for ever with the agreement of both sides], 56^v-59^v.

117 PV, AAdS, vol. 18; Paris, 148^v.

Monaco,[118] being then his Ambassador in Rome, informing him of what had been done in France in the matter of the Calendar, & on 3 August 1700 M. le Prince de Monaco wrote back to M. le Comte de Pontchartain that he had discussed the matter with M. le Cardinal Spada, who had been full of praise for the King's kind attention to the Papal Court, saying that the Congregation of Rites would decide nothing without consulting the Académie des Sciences since that body had a far better grasp of these matters than anyone in Italy.[119]

According to its official publications the Paris Academy became involved in the affair of chronology reform because it had considerably greater scientific expertise than was available in Rome, and therefore provided an indispensable hub for such reform. The same role of expert consultant is referred to in Leibniz's letter to the Academy, a foreign associate since 1699, which was read to its Assembly on 24 February 1700. The German mathematician urged the Academy to collaborate on this matter so that the adjusting of the calendar might 'profit from so favourable a conjuncture',[120] by which he probably meant the advances in scientific research which Louis XIV had made possible by setting up the Academy and its Observatory and funding their studies, but also the new correspondence rules with foreign countries.

Evidently the Academy became an important centre for international coordination on this subject; in great measure this must be due to the fact that it provided a more neutral meeting-ground than Rome, but it was also largely due to the web of relationships built by Cassini in Rome itself before 1700. Here the Academy's publications show us only the tip of the iceberg: as we shall see, the calendar issue was also managed by the Observatory's astronomers, and in particular by the Cassini family, once the Academy had made its official entry into the business.

---

118   The AAdS still preserves part of this exchange, see: 'pochette des séances' (dossier) for the year 1700; Paris, AAdS. See for instance: lettre par le prince de Monaco à Jérome de Pontchartrain, 3 août 1700 [letter from the prince of Monaco to Jérome de Pontchartrain, 3 august 1700]. In this letter, which also mentions Cassini, the prince replies to a letter from France written by Pontchartrain on the calendar issue. The prince of Monaco expresses the approval of the Academy 'which is far more enlightened than we are on these matters'. [translated from the French].

119   *Histoire de l'Académie Royale des Sciences pour l'année* MDCC *avec les Mémoires de Mathematique & de Physique, pour la même année* (Paris, 1703), 124.

120   AAdS, dossier '1700'; Paris, letter from Leibniz to the Paris Académy dated 8 February 1700, no. 46.

The news that Bianchini had been chosen as a foreign member by the Royal Academy of Paris reached him while he was away from Rome for some months on account of his father's death.[121] He decided to wait until he had returned to Rome and a trusted colleague was leaving for Paris before sending his thanks and asking in the same letter (in June) to 'beg that I might be sent some information [on the position of Venus in the Zodiac] which I urgently need before I can go on with my Chronology work'.[122]

The Academy was rapidly becoming a centre for the gathering, sorting and forwarding of suggestions from various Protestant countries. The famous extract from one of Leibniz's letters to the Academy, read out on 24 February 1700, explaining his wishes for a project 'on a matter of public interest', sc. to spread one single calendar to the whole of Christendom 'so that in future we can all agree on the truths of astronomy',[123] was followed by various other proposals from the Protestant side.[124] It cannot therefore have been hard for the entire Academy to be persuaded that this opportunity to collaborate officially with Rome's project was not to be missed. Great Britain and the Royal Society were also highly interested in the question, as shown by many like-minded articles on the topic, which appeared in the *Philosophical Transactions*,[125] as well as by English requests for calendar-related curiosities.[126]

The year 1700, as well as seeing a voluminous correspondence between Noris and Bianchini in Rome and Cassini in Paris, was a turning point.[127] After

---

121 MS B 4/9, Arch. Obs, item no. 54bis; Paris, letter from Bianchini to Cassini, 29 June 1699, 1–3.
122 Ibid, 1.
123 Extracts from the letter: PV, AAdS, vol. 19, february 1700; Paris, 78^v-80^r. The whole letter can be found in the dossier '1700'; AAdS, February 1700, letter from Leibniz dated 8 February 1700, no. 46.
124 Dossier '1700', as above.
125 Some examples: John Wallis, 'A Letter [...] to Sir John Blencowe (one of his Majesty's Justices of the Court of Common-Pleas) Concerning the Observation of Easter for this Present Year, on April 24, 1698', *Philosophical Transactions* vol. 20, no. 240, (1698) 185–189; Houghton, 'The Conclusion of the Protestant States of the Empire, of the 23d of Sept. 1699, Concerning the Calendar', *Philosophical Transactions*, vol. 22, no. 260 (1700), 459–463; Ralph Thoresby, 'An Extract of a Letter [...] to Dr Hans Sloane, S.R.S. concerning some Swedish Coyns; and a Calculation for the Finding of Easter', *Philosophical Transactions* vol. 24, no. 297, (1705), 1901–1902; George Earl of Macclesfeld, 'Remarks upon the Solar and the Lunar Years, the Cycle of 19 Years, commonly called the Golden Number, the Epact, and a Method of finding the Time of Easter, as it is now observed in most Parts of Europe', *Philosophical Transaction* vol. 46, no. 495 (1750), 417–434.
126 PV, AAdS, vol. 15bis; Paris, 171^r, Paris.
127 See also on this Commission: Heilbron, *The sun in the Church* and Donato, 'La Vaticana e le scienze naturali'.

the death of Innocent XII and the election of the Francophile Pope Clement XI (1700-1721), a Holy Commission was finally established in Rome to sift proposals for calendar reform. The idea of setting up such a body had been Innocent's; and one of the practical arguments in its favour had been that the centenary year 1700 should be the one to start the revised calculations for the new chronological structure.

Clement appointed Enrico Noris, who had been First Keeper of the Vatican Library since 1692, to head the Commission; Bianchini was made its secretary.[128] Cassini was invited to sit on the Commission, which included mathematicians and clerics from all over Europe, but his place in Rome was in fact taken by his nephew Giacomo Maraldi (1665-1729),[129] probably because he himself was by now too elderly for the task. Maraldi was an astronomer at the Observatory and the Academy's representative there. He continued to write to Paris, and throughout the period of the commission's labours conducted observations in Rome with colleagues including Bianchini.

The Academy had multiple representations in this international Roman body, not only through Maraldi, but indirectly through its correspondent Bianchini too. Cassini, for his part, though he seems no longer to have held any official positions, made no secret in his correspondence with Noris of the fact that the Academy was using him as a spokesperson with a commission to engage with the calendar issue.[130]

In Rome the Parisian institution certainly played a leading role in the calendar affair; and we see from the letters that the Academy remained an essential intermediary for the traffic of ideas and information on this subject between Rome and many of the Protestant countries. Louis XIV seems to have kept himself personally updated on progress, and Cassini was charged with seeing to this:

> The Royal Academy of Science having been consulted by means of other letters about the determination of the movable feasts, I was commissioned to handle the matter [...]. After that paper had been examined by the Academy's appointees it was presented to the King by the kind offices

---

128 'Eloge de Francesco Bianchini', in *Histoire de l'Académie Royale des Sciences pour l'année* MDCCXXIX *avec les Mémoires de Mathematique & de Physique, pour la même année* (Paris, 1731), 102-115. The appointment is mentioned as well as in PV, AAdS, vol. 22; Paris, 21^{r-v}.

129 For instance, see: PV, AAdS, vol. 22. Paris, 21^{r-v} and MS U 16, Biblioteca Vallicelliana; Rome, letter from Cassini to Bianchini, from Paris, 4 august 1704, 121r-122r.

130 MS 635, Biblioteca Angelica; Rome, letter from Cassini to Noris, 22 March 1700, from Paris, 99^r-100^r.

of its President M. l'Abbé Bignon[131] and its Protector M. the Comte de Pontchartain,[132] Minister and Secretary of State. They were ordered to send it to Your Eminence, it being his Majesty's will that a reply to it should be awaited before it was sent to Germany, so that the Holy See should not be forestalled in the correction of an error which the merest idiot might see was necessary in view of our observation here of the lunar eclipse on the night before this fifth of March.[133]

We should not be entirely surprised at this fast-track channel of communication in the persons of the Italian astronomer himself within the Academy and his family in Catholic Rome. Cassini had had very close relations with the Holy See from the beginning of his career, with a great deal of collaboration and high mutual esteem.[134] Rome itself and various circles within the Vatican had always welcomed and favoured this most religious and devoted astronomer, who had until 1669 been the finest jewel of the conservative university of Bologna (then within the Papal dominions). Cassini had always been supported in his astronomical activities in and with various churches. This relationship, which remained so sound as pope succeeded pope from the 1650s until 1700, developed over the years, in his travels from Bologna to the Papal Court, his dealings with Kristina of Sweden (1626–1689), and the confidence placed in him when he was commissioned to manage some tricky hydraulic engineering in the Papal dominions. Cassini had always been supremely popular among the religious authorities who heavily relied on his knowledge and inventiveness, and among people in general for his social connections as a Catholic.

---

131 Jean Paul Bignon (1662–1743), Secretary of the Academy.
132 Jerome de Pontchartain (1674–1747).
133 'L'Accademia Regia delle Scienze essendo stata consultata per altre lettere sopra la determinazione delle feste mobili, mi deputò a scrivere sopra questo soggetto (...). Doppo che questa scrittura è stata esaminata dai deputati dell'Academia e stata presentata al Re per mezzo del Sig. r Abbate Bignon presidente e dal Sig. re Conte de Pontchartain ministro e segretario di stato e protettore della medesima Academia. Sono stato incaricato d'inviarla a V Em. za, volendo sua Maestà che se n'attenda la risposta prima d'inviarla in Alemagna, a fine che la Sta. Sede non sia prevenuta nella correzione necessaria dell'errore, che l'eclisse della luna che habbiamo qui osservato la notte precedente il quinto di questo mese di marzo rende visibile anco agli idioti'. MS 635, Biblioteca Angelica; Rome, letter from Cassini to Noris, 22 March 1700, from Paris, 99^r-100^r (extraits from 99^r and 100^r).
134 See for instance: MS 423, Biblioteca universitaria, fasc. 20, item no.10; Pisa, letter from Giacomo Maraldi to Cassini, from Rome, 19 july 1701, n.p. Cited in Ancelin, 'Science, académisme', 82.

Jean Souchay, in his chapter on the Observatory's astronomer and geometrician Philippe de la Hire,[135] briefly mentions the contribution made by De la Hire's 1700 planetary ephemerides to the calendar project. Specifically, Souchay describes these tables, which were published soon after the appeal by Leibniz to the Academy in 1700, as the Academy's astronomical response to the German mathematician. But although we know that more than one Observatory astronomer made important contributions by way of calculations and observations, there is no doubt that for the Academy and the Observatory the question of the calendar had been raised well before 1700, that it had been the Cassini family which had introduced the Academy to it, and that the Academicians most involved in the real discussions of the matter were those savants with Catholic, Italian social connections, who knew and trusted the gilded environment of the Vatican..., in short, so far as the Academy of that time was concerned, the Cassini family. In particular, the correspondence between that family and Bianchini clearly shows that it was Cassini and Maraldi, and they alone, who sent to Rome the observations made by the Academy and its Observatory.[136]

An event contemporary with the work of the Commission in Rome and connected with it was the construction in 1702 of the meridian line of the church *Santa Maria degli Angeli e dei Martiri* which Clement XI commissioned from Francesco Bianchini.[137] This monumental instrument took its place as a rival to the other celebrated meridian lines of Italy, foremost among them Cassini's meridian line in Bologna, and was used in the Commission's chronology work as a resource for studying the motion of the sun.[138] The Pope inaugurated it in person.

The death of Noris in 1704, however, and the Wars of the Spanish Succession (1700–1713)[139] obliged Clement XI to abandon this reform project despite the immense amount of work done up to that point.

---

135 Jean Souchay, 'La Hire à l'Obsrevatoire de Paris', in *Philippe de La Hire (1640–1718). Entre science et architecture*, eds. Hélène Rousteau-Chambon, Joël Sakarovitch (Paris, 2013), 93–106 (97).

136 This topic is dealt with in greater depth in Deias, *Inventer l'Observatoire*.

137 Beside the 'Éloge' of Francesco Bianchini, on this occasion Bianchini published *De Nummo et Gnomone Clementino* (Rome, 1703). On the correspondence between Cassini and Bianchini during the construction of the meridian Line see Deias, *Inventer l'Observatoire*.

138 Cornelio Desimoni's contribution on 'Notizie di Paris Maria Salvago e del suo Osservatorio astronomico in Carbonara', (*Giornale Linguistico di Archeologia*, 1875 and 1876) suggests that Giacomo Maraldi helped Bianchini in the construction of this Meridian.

139 Donato, 'La Vaticana e le scienze naturali', 818. Ancelin seems to argue that the work of the Papal Commission had to be abandoned because people in France lost interest. Ancelin, 'Science, académisme', 83.

The Cassini-Bianchini correspondence, which is now kept mainly in Paris and Rome, went on until 1708.[140] Though both continued to work on chronology, to discuss it and to write about it until that date, Bianchini's name appears very seldom in the Academy's Minute of Proceedings after the Papal Commission had abandoned its work.[141] Their personal relations continued, and so did the Rome astronomer's collaboration with the Observatory: they exchanged observations and compared notes by letter – the Cassinis sent the latest news and books to Rome to aid Bianchini's research, as well as De la Hire's tables of planetary movements, of course, and the Ephemerides contained in the *Connaissance des Temps*;[142] and the two astronomers did meet again, in late August 1712 when Bianchini arrived from Rome charged with duties primarily as the religious representative of those around the Pope. It was the last time he met Cassini, who died a few days afterwards.

5   Conclusion

In this chapter I have sought to outline some of the activities of the Académie Royale des Sciences and the way they were organized during its first three decades (from its founding until the adoption of its formal Rules in 1699). In doing so I have used an approach informed by the social history of science.

The rules by which the institution functioned in that period were not made explicit, but customary working patterns – effective, though fairly informal and more or less unmentioned – can be found by looking at the institutional premises and social milieus where science was carried out in connection with Academy projects, and seeing the Academy's output through sources other than its official publications, such as letters and other documents of more restricted circulation. Academicians' letters and observation journals often afford us a more rounded view of a scientific institution than one restricted to its publications; and they are the sources we have to consult when the latter are silent.

Thus we can uncover new details enabling us to find traces of certain practices, which sometimes later crystallize into rules. They show how scientific achievements were also fostered by personal relationships between individuals,

---

140 MS U 16, Biblioteca Vallicelliana, Bianchini collection; Rome, letter from Cassini to Bianchini, 10 December 1708, 129r–130r.
141 PV, AAdS, vol. 25, 316r, 318r, 346v; Paris.
142 MS B 4/9, Arch. Obs., item no. 57; Paris, letter from Bianchini to Maraldi, 26 April 1707, 15.

and by shared values and habits. We can likewise reassess the contribution made by scientific establishments such as the Royal Observatory, built for the Academy in 1667, about which little is known at present.

The Royal Observatory assisted the Academy in various major projects, not only by making an important contribution in terms of strictly scientific results, but also through a whole range of activities connecting the Academy with the outside world and in particular with other countries, such as visits to the Observatory by ambassadors, courtiers, and princes.

Specifically, Giovanni Domenico Cassini's letters admirably illustrate the way in which the Observatory often performed a crucial role in transmitting and circulating information between the Academy and foreign lands in the age of Louis XIV. Accordingly this can be seen as a very important nexus for a number of mutually dependent projects of international collaboration in which France and Louis were involved. As an essential intermediary between the French Crown and various Asian countries, or between the papal entourage, Protestant governments and the Academy on matters concerning calendar reform, the Observatory played its part in a Europe-wide ecosystem of governments, institutions and projects during the seventeenth century, regardless of whether there were any written rules.

CHAPTER 7

The Early History of the Paris and London Academies: Two Paths Towards the Institutionalization of Science

Aurélien Ruellet and François Mallet

> This assembly [the Montmor Academy] is the Mother of all those which have been formed since its foundation in this Kingdom, in England, and in the Netherlands.[1]

In this often-quoted speech, the French physician and philosopher Samuel Sorbière traced back the early Royal Society to the Parisian meetings of the Montmor Academy. Unsurprisingly, this was a line consistently adhered to by the proponents of the *Académie des Sciences* throughout its early decades. The episodic presence of many Englishmen in France and their attendance to Parisian learned meetings at the time of the Civil war and the Interregnum could indeed account for this circulation of models from the continent to England. Back in the 1930s already, Harcourt Brown had gathered such statements in his invaluable study *Scientific Organizations in Seventeenth century France*, which went some way towards challenging this long-dominant narrative.[2] By unearthing various letters and speeches, he proved that French travellers witnessed early meetings of the London Royal Society and that this greatly helped shape the institutional framework of the French meetings.

This paper aims to revisit this long-standing question with the benefit of fresh evidence. The underlying goal here is to understand how the emerging scientific institutions in France and England brought radically different answers to the problem of the relationship between scientific knowledge and aristocratic civility. In France and England alike, aristocratic civility long

---

[1] Guillaume Bigourdan, 'Les premières réunions savantes de Paris au XVIIe siècle', Comptes-rendus hebdomadaires des séances de l'Académie des sciences (1917), 129–134, 159–162, 216–220.
[2] Harcourt Brown, *Scientific Organizations in Seventeenth Century France (1620–1680)* (New York, 1967), 91–94.

provided a supportive framework for scientific endeavours. Aristocrats, among other members of the ruling class, were approached for their ability to bestow positions in households or to support careers through their influence in various administrations. This accounts for the ubiquity of dedications in early-modern printed books, even if, as is common knowledge, most of those dedications were ultimately ignored. Support from the elites was at a premium, as far as they provided funds for experiment devices or the required facilities for these pursuits.

But their role was not strictly confined to money-lending. Aristocrats' involvement was also instrumental in buttressing the knowledge-claims of various categories of practitioners and in investing those claims with the prestige of the *sanior pars* of society. This is a well-documented feature, already discussed from a variety of perspectives. Christian Licoppe thus spoke of occasional 'nominal transactions' between scientists and aristocrats, the former gaining credit and money while the latter fashioned an image of learned aristocrats for themselves.[3] Steven Shapin and Simon Schaffer famously argued that Boyle and Hooke devised a 'social technology' relying on quality witnesses to validate their experimental accounts.[4] Building on this thesis, Shapin further proposed that the epistemology of early modern science ultimately depended on a broader feature of the early modern mindset: the social construction of trust and trustworthiness, whereby individuals' presumed trustworthiness mirrored their social rank.[5] These critics thus developed a potent conceptual framework to study the social context of scientific practices at the dawn of the age of experimental science. Unfortunately, it is proving difficult to test.

In the first part of this article, astronomical observations are used as a way of gauging the significance of aristocratic patronage in the process of knowledge-making. The second part examines the attempts at organizing scientific sociability under the aegis of aristocrats, both in France and in England,[6] something which has often proved disappointing, as the case of the Parisian

---

3 Christian Licoppe, *La formation de la pratique scientifique. Le discours de l'expérience en France et en Angleterre (1630–1820)* (Paris, 1996), 84–87.
4 Simon Schaffer, Steven Shapin, *Leviathan and the Air-Pump. Hobbes, Boyle and the Experimental Life* (Princeton, 1985), 25–26.
5 Steven Shapin, *A Social History of Truth. Civility and Science in Seventeenth-Century England* (Chicago, 1994).
6 This paper makes extensive use of the concept of sociability, not so much in the original meaning which Simmel ascribed to it i.e., briefly put, a form of social interaction devoid of practical concerns or instrumental goals, 'the playful form of socialisation' – but rather as

Montmor Academy shows. The third part argues that the Parisian exile that many English virtuosi experienced was a counter-model from which they tried to depart at the time of the Restoration, as they could then build upon the kind of experimental community that Boyle had devised in Oxford at the same time. The last part shows that this path also proved very influential in France, even if the French themselves unsurprisingly downplayed it.

1   A Case of Elusive Support? Astronomical Observations

In the first half of the seventeenth century, aristocratic support is almost nowhere to be found. This is best illustrated through the example of astronomical observations, as attested by a crucial publication. In his 1901 *Annales Célestes*, the French astronomer Guillaume Bigourdan expanded on a sweeping survey started by Alexandre Pingré in the eighteenth century and drew a list of all the astronomical observations that had been printed so far, thus providing a valuable source index.[7] Studies of lunar and solar eclipses reveal that in the first decades of the seventeenth century most of the recorded observations were performed by lone individuals or by small groups which seem to have very rarely included aristocrats. Even where they were in attendance, noblemen and persons 'of condition' did not lend money nor credit to the astronomers. John Palmer, rector of Ecton parish in Northamptonshire, wrote in his *Catholique planisphaer* that 'At Ecton Anno Dom. 1652 on Munday March 20 before Noon, [he] observed the great Eclipse of the Sun by a Telescop [...] in the company of halfe a score Gentlemen and ministers [his] Neighbours'.[8]

---

    developed by French historiography since the 1970s. To name just a few, Maurice Agulhon, Emmanuel Leroy-Ladurie and, not least, Daniel Roche expanded on the notion and contributed to lending it a much broader scope. Yet even in their work, it retains strong implications of informality, casualness or playfulness, the coffeehouse or the theatre being for example described as hotspots of sociability. Used by sociologists, the word came to refer to 'the whole spectrum of relationships that an individual builds with others, considering the form of these relationships' (Michel Forsé, 'Les réseaux de sociabilité : un état des lieux', *L'Année sociologique*, 41, 1991, 246), and this is the definition we propose to adopt throughout this paper. On these questions of historiographical uses, see Carole Anne Rivière, 'La spécificité française de la construction sociologique du concept de sociabilité', *Réseaux* 1 (2004), 207–231. For an English use of the notion, see Gregory S. Brown, *Literary Sociability and Literary Property in France, 1775–1793. Beaumarchais, the Société des auteurs dramatiques and the Comédie Française* (Aldershot, 2006), especially the introduction.

7 Alexandre Guy Pingré, *Annales célestes du dix-septième siècle*, ed. G. Bigourdan (Paris, 1901).
8 John Palmer, *The Catholique Planisphaer* (London, 1658), 210.

Observers of the 1652 solar eclipse	Place of observation	Witnesses
Jean Béchet, Jean Picard	Collège de Navarre	
Gilles Personne de Roberval, Claude Mylon	Garden of Pierre Brûlart, abbé de Saint-Martin	Pierre Brûlart, abbot of Saint-Martin
Ismaël Boulliau	Hôtel de Thou	Jacques-Auguste II de Thou
Pierre Bourdin, François Gaynot	Collège de Clermont	Henri II de Savoie, archbishop of Reims
Pierre Petit, Jacques-Alexandre le Tenneur, Adrien Auzout, Jacques Buot	Hôtel de Pierre Petit, rue sainte-Nicaise[9]	Cardinal de Retz
Nicolas de Bourdin (?), Jean-Baptiste Morin, Antoine Agarrat	Palais du duc d'Orléans [Luxembourg Palace]	Gaston d'Orléans

In France, the situation was slightly different and the observational accounts made over the period devoted a growing importance to the mention of witnesses. While barely present in the 1620s and 1630s, they became quite common in later observations. Pierre Gassendi himself saw fit to record the presence of 'great people' in his astronomical diary when he observed the solar eclipse of June 1639. In fact those spectators acted as an impediment to carrying out precise measurements and 'prevented the height of the eclipse from being observed'.[10]

For all this corpus of evidence, we should be wary not to overstate the role of 'social technology'. In their observational accounts, some of the most serious observers show a deliberate insistence on the experimental apparatus and their own expertise rather than on the illustrious crowd that witnessed the proceedings. Pierre Petit thus introduced his account by a detailed presentation of his instruments: a quadrant, two clocks and a large sundial to measure time; two four-feet-long telescopes to observe occultation via projection. A 15 inch-wide parabolic mirror was also used to gauge the weakening of sun rays:

9 Le Roux de Lincy, *Notice sur le plan de Paris de Jacques Gomboust* (Paris, 1858), 78.
10 Pierre Gassendi, *Opera Omnia*, 6 vols (Lyon, 1658), 4:433.

before the eclipse, they could melt a lead ball but could not set fire to a piece of dry wood at the climax point.[11] However, some observers clearly placed wilful emphasis on the genteel settings in which their observations unfolded. This includes the astrologer Jean-Baptiste Morin or the mathematics teacher Antoine Agarrat, who both performed observations for Gaston d'Orléans, King Louis XIV's uncle. The two astronomers dutifully recorded how the prince guided and assisted them over the course of their 1652 and 1654 observations.[12] Morin's depiction of the 1652 eclipse is one of masque staging:

> I warned his Serene Highness the Prince that the eclipse was about to start and that everything was ready. And so the eclipse started a short while after his Serene Highness and his Highly Esteemed Spouse had entered the room with many dukes, marshalls and other magnates.[13]

Shortly after the eclipse, the mathematician had to leave the terrace and give way to another courtier, the abbot Michel de Marolles, who wanted to present the Prince with his translation of Horace.[14] As for Agarrat, his account is one encomiastic tour de force:

> The eclipse being completely over, His Royal Highness wanted to know at which time it started & asked me to do the calculations, in front of Him and in the presence of the aforesaid gentlemen. I had not even started to draw the figure for the demonstration of the calculation that Monsieur [His Royal Highness] told me that one ought to find the arc of the equator […] His Highness even looked for the Sinus that were needed for the aforesaid calculations and thus found that the beginning was at 8 o'clock minus 30 seconds & asked me to write down everything I had noticed of this eclipse.[15]

Surrounded by the prince's retinue and by other expectant courtiers, the mathematician had to become something of an entertainer to remain the

---

11 Pierre Petit, 'Observationes aliquot eclipsium solis et lunae cum notis ad id pertinentibus', in Jean-Baptiste Duhamel, *Astronomia Physica seu de Luce, Natura et Motibus Corporum caelestium Libri Duo* (Paris, 1660).
12 Jean-Baptiste Morin, *Eclipsis solis observata parisiis in Aurelianensi palatio* [date and origin unknown], 1; Antoine Agarrat, *Eclipses du soleil observees aux annees 1652 & 1654* (Paris, 1654), 3–5.
13 Ibid, 1–2.
14 Michel de Marolles, *Mémoires* (Paris, 1656), 191–192.
15 Agarrat, *Eclipses*, 3–5.

focus of the proceedings, even if it meant that subsequent observations lacked precision. For the 1656 sun eclipse, the observer Antoine Marchais even forgot to measure the latitude of the place of observation (Blois) beforehand.[16]

In the 1650s, astronomers, whether they were *virtuosi* or actually made a living out of their pursuits, seemed to choose between two increasingly diverging lines of conduct: one implied various degrees of autonomy from the aristocratic framework; the other group craved proximity with aristocrats and the positions and honours they were able to bestow. Those diverging views are to be found in the publications that followed the eclipses and in the 'literary technologies' they used: Antoine Agarrat's observational account of the 1654 eclipse is a short, lively and didactic leaflet, providing little written description but adorned with detailed engravings of the phases of the eclipse, whereas Boulliau's books feature austere height and time charts.[17] The two types of observers did not seem to share the same set of epistemic views, nor did they target the same readership, although such divergences, of course, do not cover the whole picture, as some people, such as Auzout, self-consciously alternated between the two methods: he cast horoscopes for a well-off clientele but was at the same time a pioneer of observational astronomy.[18] Be that as it may, would-be professional astronomers certainly tried to distance themselves from the figure of the court entertainer: the engineer and mathematician Pierre Petit, who enjoyed a good reputation among the astronomical community, harshly disparaged Jean-Baptiste Morin's findings, deeming his measurement of the 1652 sun eclipse baffling and unreliable.[19]

This distrust was to continue unabated and astrologers were gradually excluded from observational astronomy: the two communities were drifting apart, as astronomers sought to enhance their status.[20] The 1666 sun eclipse was a harbinger of the new trends to come. Several groups carried out a raft of observations. One of those groups was lodged by the *contrôleur général des finances* Jean-Baptiste Colbert in his *hôtel particulier*, but whether he himself

---

16 Observatoire de Paris, Boulliau manuscripts, B5, 12, unpaged: Antoine Marchais, *Serenissimo augustimoque principi Gastoni Franciae... eclipseos solaris quae contigit vii. Kal. Febr. MDCLVI.* [date and origin unknown]; letter from 'Henry' to Boulliau.

17 Gassendi's diary was not meant to be published. For Boulliau: Ismaël Boulliau, *Astronomia Philolaica* (Paris, 1645); Id., *Observatio secundi deliquii lunaris* (Paris, 1653); Id., Pierre Bourdin, *Observatio eclipsis lunari quae contigit anno D. 1653 Martii 13. P.M.* [date and origin unknown].

18 Robert Mckeon, *Établissement de l'astronomie de précision et œuvre d'Adrien Auzout* (Paris, 1965).

19 Petit, *Observationes*, 13.

20 For France, see Hervé Drévillon, *Lire et écrire l'avenir: l'astrologie dans la France du Grand Siècle, 1610–1715* (Seyssel, 1996).

was attending is doubtful.[21] Thus, a small assembly of astronomers, who were to form the core of the Paris Academy, were participating in an observation in the house of the king's senior minister but in his absence. Within the space of a few decades, the terms of exchange between astronomers and powerful patrons had started to shift. The ruling class no longer expected scientists to entertain and to astonish; on the contrary, it was now providing astronomers with the requisite setting for observations to be properly performed, and without a genteel audience in attendance.

The observations of eclipses thus provide a general framework to analyse the limits of the supposedly mutually benefiting relationships between scientists and gentlemen. The former needed to be supported by the latter and accordingly craved the resources of patronage, but felt increasingly uncomfortable with the compromises that this support seemed to involve.

2   Learned Circles and Aristocratic Support: The Example of the Montmor Academy

This clearly bears upon the cognate question of the institutionalisation of learned circles, a process that could appear as a remedy to the pitfalls of genteel patronage. By participating in institutions in which expectations or proper behaviour were laid down in rules and regulations and of which science would be the self-avowed purpose, men of science and aristocrats alike could hope to benefit equally from their association. Both in England and in France, early attempts at scientific institutionalisation were yet tortuous and difficult, for a range of reasons hereafter detailed. The *Accademia dei Lincei*, born under the aegis of Prince Francesco Cesi, was as exceptional as it was short-lived and did not prove an easy model to emulate. Only the greatest aristocratic households, such as the Northumberlands, could muster the kind of resources needed to play host to the work of an academy, albeit an informal one.[22] At the beginning of the seventeenth century, not many aristocrats were ready to sponsor a circle exclusively dedicated to the advancement of natural philosophy. It would be tempting to overestimate the role of the 'Welbeck circle', sponsored by the Cavendish family, and bearing only a passing resemblance to a proper

---

21   A discussion of this observation can be found in David J. Sturdy, *Science and Social Status: The Members of the Académie des Sciences, 1666–1750* (Baltimore, 1995), 74–75.

22   Gordon R. Batho, 'Thomas Harriot and the Northumberland Household' in *Thomas Harriot: an Elizabethan Man of Science*, ed. Robert Fox (Aldershot, 2000), 28–47; Id., 'The Finances of an Elizabethan Nobleman: Henry Percy, Ninth Earl of Northumberland (1564–1632)', *The Economic History Review*, 9 (1957), 433–457.

academy.[23] The fact is, aristocratically supported circles were nowhere to be found in England or France until the 1640s. Scientific sociability flourished outside the protection of genteel patronage. It also grew in groups in which science was only one, and not the foremost, of many interests ranging from poetry to antiquarianism.[24]

The scientific scene lacked structure and support, especially in England where there was no strong academic tradition and where a budding experimental community could feel estranged from what was happening on the continent. The English men of science were at first quite in admiration of their French counterparts. The correspondence between Theodore Haak and minim friar Marin Mersenne reveals that the latter's work as a scientific intelligencer was held up as a model for all to follow.[25] Charles Webster showed how a group of scientifically-inclined men, comprising mathematicians and physicians, gathered in London from 1645 onwards to perform experiments, and sometimes replicate what was done on the continent. On occasions, they were accompanied by persons of rank, as in 1648, when the Count Palatine and Lord Herbert witnessed the Torricellian experiment.[26] After 1648, amidst the institutional turmoil of the third civil war, this 1645 group disbanded. John Wilkins, a pivotal member, moved to Oxford where he set up an 'experimental philosophy club' which gathered at Wadham College from 1649 onwards and was soon endowed with proper rules and regulations. Some of its members even planned to erect a laboratory and an observatory but asked for sponsorship.[27]

Mersenne, who acted as the driving force behind / an inspiraton for the participants of the 1645 club, is often credited with being at the origin of the Parisian academic movement.[28] Around 1636, the minim friar established his Place Royale convent, an informal gathering of mathematics-minded *virtuosi*.

---

23 Timothy Raylor, 'Newcastle's Ghosts. Robert Payne, Ben Jonson, and the "Cavendish Circle"', in *Literary Circles and Cultural Communities in Renaissance England*, eds. J. Summers, T.-L. Pebworth (Columbia, 2000), 92–114.
24 Such as *the cabinet des frères Dupuy* in Paris.
25 Brown, *Organizations*, 43–63.
26 Lettre from Haak to Mersenne, quoted in Brown, *Organizations*, 271.
27 'It is a reall designe amongst us, wanting only some assistance for execution, to erect a Magneticall, Mechanicall, and Optick Schoole, furnished with the best Instruments, and Adapted for the most usefull experiments in all those faculties': Seth Ward, *Vindiciae Academiarum* (Oxford, 1654), 36.
28 The entangled history of French circles has already been well documented. Brown, *Organizations*, is still very valuable. Most of his findings are summed up in Simone Mazauric, 'Aux origines du mouvement académique en France: protohistoire des académies et genèse de la sociabilité savante, 1617–1666' in *Académies et sociétés savantes en Europe, 1650–1800*, eds. Daniel-Odon Hurel, Gérard Laudin (Paris, 2000), 35–47.

After his death in 1648, the meetings moved through a succession of venues and were sponsored by a series of different hosts (Jacques le Pailleur, Claude Mylon), although these probably did not contribute more than basic meeting space and some participation in the discussions.

By the beginning of the 1650s, the main meeting venue was undoubtedly the house of the rich master of requests Henry Louis Habert de Montmor. A wealthy office-holder and a member of the *Académie Française*, Habert de Montmor lodged Gassendi from 1653 onwards, but he was not a dedicated atomist and held Descartes's views in high regard. His hotel in rue Sainte-Avoye, in the Marais, a fashionable and aristocratic neighbourhood, seems to have become a meeting point for the remaining participants of the earlier assemblies.

Those meetings soon attracted so many participants that some kind of organisation was needed. In 1657, rules and regulations were drafted by Samuel Sorbière and Abraham Duprat and laid down in a 1658 letter to Thomas Hobbes.[29] Among other things, this text presented the way sessions were to be conducted and how speakers were to behave. For every session, two people were to read reports without being interrupted by the audience. The questions, should there be any, were to be asked afterwards. The rules also defined conditions for admission as a member of the audience: peers were granted the right to elect new members. Applicants had to be 'curious of natural things', but a 'man of merit' could still be elected. In a letter to Huygens, the poet Jean Chapelain observed that 'the assembly was large, and numbered more than forty persons, among them were two Cordons bleus, the Marquis de Sourdis and Monsieur du Plessis Guénégaud, both secretaries of State, several Abbés of the nobility, several masters of requests... '.[30] A later remark by Sorbière seemed to confirm that the audience was indeed of a genteel make-up: 'we should rejoice that people of noble condition, as well as of great mind and superior knowledge, should share in this curiosity [...] Our physical enquiries are greatly honoured by their presence'.[31]

But in spite of the gentility of the audience, the attendants sometimes did not abide by the etiquette of court civility. This is suggested by the often-cited example of the skirmish which pitted physicist Gilles de Roberval against Montmor: Roberval told Montmor, the host of the academy, 'that if he were a

---

29   Samuel Sorbière, *Lettres et discours de M. de Sorbiere* (Paris, 1660), 631–635 (letter to Hobbes).
30   Christiaan Huygens, *Œuvres Complètes, Tome II, Correspondance, 1657–1659*, ed. D. Bierens de Haan (The Hague, 1889), 174, letter from Chapelain à Huygens, 10 may 1658, quoted and translated in Brown, *Organizations*, 84.
31   Sorbière, *Lettres*, 201 ('discours prononcé dans une assemblée de physiciens chez Monsieur de Montmor, le 14 juin 1658').

master of requests himself, he would be worth a hundred times more than him'.³² By insulting an aristocrat in his own house and by committing a 'very stupid thing' according to Boulliau, Roberval was breaking the rules of genteel behaviour and was touching Montmor's 'point d'honneur'. Fortunately, this quarrel did not end up in a duel, with Roberval simply being excluded from later meetings. But Chapelain, a regular participant in the academy, could not fail to notice that the 'assembly which met in his house has languished somewhat since the outburst which occurred between him and M. De Roberval'.³³

This was not the only instance of disturbance. Describing an unspecified gathering in a 1663 speech, Sorbière recalled that 'the concert did not last long, and soon after the first meeting, there was some dissonance'.³⁴ Two groups of people were especially to blame, according to Sorbière, for disturbing the smooth running of the meetings. First, there were those who indulged in 'endless talk' and who came to the academy only to 'pass the time and gain esteem'. Then came those who only 'preached experiments'³⁵ whereas the goal of the academy was initially to achieve a 'learned and happy combination of experiments and reasoning'. Other sources besides Sorbière's own account of the rue Saint-Avoye experiments offer an insight into the academy's undertakings. One is the probate inventory of Montmor's goods, which was established after his death in 1679. Among sundry curiosities, books and paintings, the public notaries in charge of the inventory listed an 'egg-shaped lodestone', several pieces of amber, a large ivory sundial, two microscopes, 16 ostrich eggs, a burning mirror, tortoise shells and a human skeleton.³⁶ This description bears strong echoes of Sorbière's own description of the house in his speech: 'M. De Montmor [was] so kind as to offer us the use of an infinity of machines and instruments, with which he ha[d] exercised his curiosity for thirty years'.³⁷

The learned sociability that developed in Montmor Academy was gradually parting company with potentially tedious but meaningful research work and was becoming increasingly entertainment-oriented. In his 1663 speech,

---

32   Huygens, Œuvres, II, 287, 6 december 1658. This famous quote is commented in many studies. Here are a few examples: Mario Biagioli, 'Le prince et les savants: la civilité scientifique au XVIIᵉ siècle', Annales HSS 50 (1995), 1417–1453, 1420–1422; Catherine Goldstein, 'L'honneur de l'esprit: de la République des mathématiques' in Dire et vivre l'ordre social en France sous l'Ancien Régime, ed. Fanny Cosandey (Paris, 2005), 191–230; Steven Shapin, 'The House of Experiment in Seventeenth-Century England', Isis, 79 (1988), 373–404.
33   Huygens, Œuvres, 2:468. Translated in Brown, Organizations, 108.
34   For Sorbière's speech, see: Bigourdan, 'Les premières', 160–161.
35   Ibid, 161–162.
36   Archives Nationales (Caran, Paris), MC/ET/LI/420, probate inventory, 27 February 1679.
37   Quoted in Bigourdan, 'Les premières', 216–217. Translated in Brown, Organizations, 127.

Sorbière even came to question the viability of a framework based on genteel authority: 'because there are people who only ask for wondrous things [...] it will be difficult to meet their expectations or satisfy their impatience'.[38] This evidence indicates that the works of the academy had shifted from proper investigation of natural phenomena to entertainment.

In 1663 a split occurred, with some of the usual participants leaving Montmor Academy to join other gatherings, such as the one hosted by the marquis de Sourdis.[39] The academy was undergoing a profound crisis; Sorbière had tried to head it off by making frequent appeals to Colbert for state support of their activities, as this paper discusses later.

3   Englishmen's Parisian Exile: A Founding Experience or a Counter-model?

In the 1650s, some Englishmen had been experiencing those Parisian milieus first hand. It was not genuine exile for all of them: some of the Englishmen that lived in Paris in the 1640s or 1650s had been frequent visitors earlier in the century; others were on their Grand Tour. The scientific clout of Paris in the 1640s, then home to Gassendi and Mersenne, probably even turned the exile into a welcome opportunity for some scientifically-inclined minds. John Evelyn's diary records how the young aristocrat attended chemistry lessons delivered at the *Jardin des Plantes* or visited a cabinet of wonders that adorned the pump of the Pont-Neuf.[40] Kenelm Digby lodged at the *collège de Boncourt*, just next to the *Jardin des Plantes*: in 1644–1645, Descartes paid him the courtesy of a visit and engaged with him in learned discussion, as was reported by Baillet, the latter's first biographer.[41] The English exiles were even able to contribute to the learned circles. Thus, in 1647 the Marquess of Newcastle, William Cavendish, hosted a dinner which gathered Gassendi, Descartes and Hobbes. In the mid-1640s, his brother Charles is known to have discussed mathematics with Mersenne and some members of his *academia parisiensis*, similarly to the young William Petty.[42] Later on, the Frenchman Charles du Bosc, a friend of

---

38   Quoted in Bigourdan, 'Les premières', 217, commented in Brown, *Organizations*, 124–127.
39   Bigourdan, 'Les premières', 218.
40   John Evelyn, *The Diary of John Evelyn*, ed. W. Bray (New York, London, 1901), 1:250, 255–256, 268–269.
41   Adrien Baillet, *Vie de Monsieur Descartes*, 2 vols (Amsterdam, 1691), 2:244.
42   Marin Mersenne, *Correspondance*, ed. C. de Waard, B. Rochot, A. Beaulieu, R. Lenoble, R. Pintard (Paris, 1932–1988), 13: 200, 14: 308; For a letter remark by William Petty, see Timothy Raylor, 'Exiles, Expatriates and Travellers: Towards a Cultural and Intellectual

both Thomas Hobbes and Kenelm Digby who had spent several years in England, attended several sessions of the Montmor academy.[43] Beyond limited clues offered by correspondence material or diaries, it is quite difficult to get a sense of the daily life of the English community in Paris during the civil wars and the Interregnum.

There is little doubt that this experience bolstered the cultural exchanges between the two countries, even if the overall influence of the French exile on these travellers has been recently downplayed.[44] If nothing else, this forced experience was most likely central in shaping Restoration communities of interest. Walter Charleton, one the 1650s English exiles, may have provided an account of such communities in his oft-quoted book *The Immortality of the Human Soul* published in 1657. This treatise features a conversation taking place in the Luxembourg garden between three characters, Athanasius, Isodicastes and Lucretius, each meant to be easily recognisable through a set of distinct features. 'The Parts they bear in the Discourse, sufficiently discover their Derivations' reads 'the advertisement to the reader' penned by the editor. Athanasius voices Charleton's Epicurean opinions. Lucretius stands as John Evelyn's literary persona. As for Isodicastes, he has been broadly identified by commentators as Henry Pierrepont, Marquess of Dorchester.[45] Yet there are no records of Dorchester ever travelling to France during the 1640s and 1650s. Could such dubious identification mean that there is nothing more to the personae and the imaginary Parisian setting than an elaborate literary conceit? While such a rhetorical function cannot be entirely dismissed, it hardly exhausts the full meaning of the dialogue.

It has been suggested lately that Isodicastes could be identified as Kenelm Digby and this hypothesis is supported by several facts, not least Kenelm Digby's on-and-off presence in Paris in the 1640s and 1650s.[46] The dialogue featured in the treatise, if not the exact transcript of a real conversation, could

---

History of the English Abroad, 1640–1660', in *Literatures of Exile in the English Revolution and Its Aftermath, 1640–1690*, ed. Philip Major (Burlington, 2010), 15–44 (17).

43 Bigourdan, 'Les premières', 161.
44 Raylor, 'Exiles', 15–44.
45 J.M. Armistead, 'Introduction' in Walter Charleton, *The Immortality of the Human Soul* (New York, 1985), i-xv; Sabina Fleitmann, *Walter Charleton (1620–1707), 'Virtuoso': Leben und Werk* (Frankfurt am Main and New York, 1986), 91.
46 Line Cottegnies, 'Le "renouveau" de l'épicurisme en Angleterre au milieu du dix-septième siècle de Walter Charleton à Margaret Cavendish. Une histoire franco-britannique', *Études Epistémé* 14 (2008), 123–173 (125). The main arguments for this explanation have been developed elsewhere: Aurélien Ruellet, *La Maison de Salomon. Contribution à l'histoire du patronage scientifique et technique. France, Angleterre (ca. 1600–ca. 1660)*, PhD (2014), 411–416.

nevertheless capture some aspects of Cavalier sociability at the time of the aristocrats' exile, with the Luxembourg garden, where the discussion is supposed to happen, used as a metaphorical place of exile. The first part of the book is not so much devoted to the question of the immortality of the human soul as to a survey of current affairs and to a brief sketch of academic life in Paris. Whereas Lucretius-Evelyn suggests to Athanasius-Charleton that he should indulge in learned conversation, the latter confesses that he has little taste for the tense and somewhat unruly atmosphere of the debates:

> As for that way of Divertisement, by free and unbiassed Philosophicall Conferences you speak of; I approve it as very available both to the gentle weaning of the Mind from sad apprehensions, and the exercise of its more agreeable Habits. [...] For, though among the French there be many excellent Wits, and men eminent for their abilities in all kinds of Learning; Yet I observe them generally to be of a temper more fit for hot and testy Disputes, then calm and peaceable Debates, in way of Disquisition: and commonly, they are so fierce and ardent in defence of their own preconceived opinions, that they account it a piece of disrespect and incivility in any man that seems to doubt, or call the verity of them in question. So that a Noble person of our Nation, who hath lived long in this City, and is able to give a true Character of the French Genius, as to this particular, was pleas'd to tell me within these few daies, that their humour of prejudice to all that is not their own, though really much better than their own, extends also to their Tenents in Arts and Sciences; And that it would be hard for me to find a Scholar among them, who would not rather lose the opportunity of investigating a truth, by an equitable and patient comparing of the strength of other mens reasons with his own, then not appear to have clearly understood the full nature of the thing, before it was proposed.[47]

Athanasius also laments the idle 'verbosity' of the French discussions, to which Lucretius adds that French discussions are spoiled by 'great opinionators', who, for the sake of theoretical grandstanding, prove unable to contribute to debates in a meaningful way. This, of course, is a barely disguised dig at Cartesianism and Gassendism. In contrast, Lucretius and Athanasius extoll the English way of conducting discussions. The two friends, though philosophical opponents, take pride in belonging to a civil nation. Athanasius praises the virtues

---

47   Charleton, *Immortality*, 15–16.

of the Royal College of Physicians, whose organisation is explicitly paralleled with Solomon's house:

> In the Colledge of Physicians in London, (which without offence to any thing, but their own Modesty, I may pronounce to be the most eminent Society of men, for Learning, Judgement and Industry, that is now, or at any time hath been, in the whole World) you may behold Solomons House in reality.[48]

According to Charleton, the College of physicians succeeded in implementing a collaborative work ethics, thus contributing to a common goal:

> that though the Fellows of this Colledge apply themselves severally to this or that particular Province, each one according to the inclination & delight of his own private Genius; Yet, when they meet together in Consultations, they are so candid and liberal in the communication of their single observations and discoveries, that no one of them can long be ignorant of the notions of all the rest: And the noble Emulation that hath equally enflamed their ingenious breasts, makes them unanimous in co-operating toward the Common design, the erecting an intire and durable Fabrick of solid Science; such as posterity may not only admire, but set up their rest in.[49]

Athanasius-Charleton finally develops the idea of a *translatio studii* that paradoxically would see the centre of enlightenment move to a war-stricken England:

> You will think it lesse strange, that Britain, which was but yesterday the Theatre of War and desolation, should to day be the School of Arts, and Court of all the Muses. Omnia secula suum habent Genium, qui mortalium animos in certa studia solet inflectere.[50]

The praise of pacified sociability and collaborative work is further enacted in the dialogue between the two friends. Lucretius-Evelyn and Athanasius-Charleton might disagree on the question at stake, i.e. the immortality of the

---

48 Ibid, p. 34; on this parallel, see Charles Webster, 'The College of Physicians: "Solomon's House" in Commonwealth England', *Bulletin of the History of Medicine* 41 (1967), 393–412.
49 Charleton, *Immortality*, 43.
50 Ibid, 50.

human soul, but they nonetheless never depart from courteous delivery. This successful outcome owes a lot to the contributions of aristocrats: it falls to Isodicastes (literally 'the fair judge') to act as a referee, as Athanasius-Charleton clearly points out:

> And now, though you have brought, I confess, most excellent Arguments to prove it, and both satisfied all my Doubts, and solved all my Objections: yet whether you have so Demonstrated it, as to exclude all Dubiosity, and compell assent (which is the propriety of perfect Demonstration) in a pure Natural Philosopher, who refuseth to admit any other conviction, but from the Light of Nature; I must leave to the judgement of our Arbiter, the noble Isodicastes, who will not, I am well assured, deliver any but an equitable Censure in the Cause.[51]

The two debaters, albeit on opposing sides, manage to reach some kind of common ground by calling on the judgement of persons of quality. Isodicastes, who is described by Lucretius-Evelyn as 'a perfect virtuoso', is a perfect fit.[52] A new layer of meaning is thereby added to the game of aliases and identification. Isodicastes might be a literary persona for Kenelm Digby, a genuine natural philosopher involved in various forms of scientific circles, whether it be at Gresham College or in Paris, but also a rich nobleman described as an avid book collector and a great patron of learning. He is known to have been performing alchemical experiments at Gresham College in the 1630s, and may have invited Descartes to visit him in England in the early 1640s. He was also the recipient of many dedications.[53] This could suggest that Athanasius-Charleton actually called for the support and fair judgement of aristocrats in the organisation of scientific gatherings. That such arbiters were already to be found in England, for example in the guise of Kenelm Digby, is of course a fact not to be overlooked.

4 The Invention of the English Experimental Sociability

Highly praised by Theodore Haak at the beginning of the 1640s, the French scientific scene came under harsh criticism during the Interregnum. As the

---

51 Ibid, 186–187.
52 Ibid, 19.
53 Franklin B. Williams, *Index of Dedications and Commendatory Verses in English Books before 1641* (London, 1962), 53.

exiled Englishmen exposed themselves to the French way of doing science, the experience certainly yielded some disappointment. Breaking free from this continental mould was all the easier as, at the same time in Oxford, Englishmen were inventing a new form of collaborative etiquette.

After John Wilkins left Oxford for Cambridge in 1658, the 'Experimental philosophy Club', or what remained of it, moved to Robert Boyle's house on High Street. The son of a wealthy officer who made a fortune out of Irish plantations, the young Robert Boyle could enjoy comfortable land revenues.[54] He was thus able to act as a patron of science. The experimental community gradually built around Boyle a 'paradigm' of the new experimental sociability to come.[55] The young aristocrat was appropriating the norms of genteel sociability in order to enforce a new kind of scientific inquiry. Through his aristocratic breeding, he was inclined, and indeed expected, to display qualities of hospitality and munificence. His laboratory was said to be open to every man of honour who wanted to visit it or to attend an experiment. Deliberately breaking away from alchemists' deeply-rooted emphasis on secrecy, Boyle promoted a new kind of collaborative work, one that was nevertheless strictly defined and limited by the rules of genteel civility. Entering the laboratory was like stepping into a noble house, and demanded that a number of unspoken conditions be met, i.e. that the host be favourably acquainted with the visitor, either personally or by hearsay, or recommendation. The visitor was expected to abide by two sets of values, or rules of etiquette: an aristocratic code whereby one was supposed to behave courteously in a noble house; and an experimental code according to which one had to fully appreciate and respect what was being done in a laboratory. In the case of Boyle, this experimental etiquette involved giving pride of place to the collection of empirical evidence, the famous 'matters of facts', and undue emphasis on theoretical investigation of causes would have been frowned upon.

As early as the 1650s, Boyle rejected the dogmatism and the acrimonious mood of philosophers and valued the courtesy and probabilism of experimenters. Relying on his experimental successes and on his genteel identity, he became 'master in credibility', as Shapin put it.[56]

The ensuing events have become common knowledge. From 1658, learned gatherings resumed in London at Gresham College. In November 1660, the assembly in question decided to gain formal status. In July 1662, a royal charter granted by King Charles II gave birth to the Royal Society. Those members of

---
54   Michael Hunter, *Boyle, Between God and Science* (New Haven, 2009), 39–40.
55   Shapin, *Social History of Truth*.
56   Ibid, 291.

the 1645 group who were still alive took part in its creation but were outnumbered by newcomers, many of whom were of genteel extraction. Boyle, an assiduous member of the early years, was one of them but he was joined by other noblemen: Robert Moray, viscount William Brouncker, John Evelyn, Kenelm Digby, Paul Neile, not to mention a host of other figures, less prominent or active in the first years of the Royal Society. Boyle was pivotal to the workings of the new academy, to which he lent his own assistant, Robert Hooke, defended it through multiple controversies, and helped shape the Baconian ideology of the institution. The Royal Society adopted Boyle's epistemic views and its motto, *Nullius in Verba*, suggested by Evelyn, epitomised the prevalence of experimentation and the distrust of theoretical constructs.[57]

The early years of the Royal Society owe a lot to the model crafted by Boyle but may also reflect the fact that the company deliberately departed from the French modes of sociability observed at the time of the exile. It is no mere coincidence that the active members of the years 1660–1663 include Charleton, Evelyn, Moray, and, to a lesser extent, Digby, who all lived in France for some time during the Interregnum and some of whom (Moray being probably an exception) took part in learned gatherings.[58] The members of the Royal Society agreed on a model of sound policy in order to ward off tensions. According to Shapin and Schaffer, the implicit Baconian ideology of the early Royal Society was as much political as methodological. By focusing on 'matters of fact' and by avoiding lengthy discussions on principles and theoretical systems, the founders of the Royal Society also confined themselves to the realm of the natural word and deliberately excluded political or religious debates. They were thus elaborating a model of concord in keeping with the widespread thirst for appeasement and reconciliation following the turmoil of the Interregnum. After the Great Fire of London, the gatherings were relocated for a few years to Arundel House, the Duke of Norfolk's London residence: the Royal Society was becoming an aristocratic-dominated company operating along the lines of genteel civility and located in a noble house. With Boyle, scientific sociability seems to have found an equilibrium point: the genteel setting and scientific practices were mutually benefiting from this association.

While there is no question that the members of the Royal society thus coined a new model of collaborative work and blazed a path of their own,

---

[57] Hunter, *Boyle*, 131–132, 144–145; Peter Dear, 'Totius in Verba: Rhetoric and Authority in the Early Royal Society', *Isis* 16 (1985), 144–161.

[58] Charles Webster, *The Great Instauration. Science, Medicine and Reform (1626–1660)* (London, 1975), 92 for a list of the 'active' members.

quite different from the continental experience, it did not prevent Montmorians from laying claim to the new venture. Sorbière, in his May 1663 speech at Montmor Academy boldly and proudly asserted:

> This assembly is the Mother of all those which have been formed since its foundation in this Kingdom, in England, and in the Netherlands, and which have the same desire as we to advance the science of natural things and to improve the liberal arts and Mechanics. It is on the plan that drawn up here in 1657, or on a part of it, that work is done today elsewhere.[59]

Fontenelle, Cassini, Chapelain or Melchisedech Thevenot held similar opinions, which all reflect blatant chauvinism,[60] though Sorbière's views are not entirely unsubstantiated. Henry Oldenburg, who was to become secretary of the Royal Society, and the astronomer Christiaan Huygens both spent some time in France before moving to London and took part in the meetings of the Montmor Academy, in 1659–1660 and 1660–1661 respectively. But these, according to Harcourt Brown, are the only two known instances of men who attended the works of the Parisian company before joining the Royal Society.[61] And what they reported from those meetings bore little comparison to the Royal Society. In his letters to Saporta, Oldenburg described sessions dominated by theoretical problems and philosophical systems. 'The Opinions of Descartes' were put up for discussion, as were 'the influence of the Stars' or 'the Insufficiency of movement and figure to explain the phenomena of Nature', this latter attack on Descartes being led by an Aristotelian.[62] As for Huygens, he attended several disputes, among which those opposing Rohault to Auzout and Pequet to Bourdelot. Therefore it is unlikely that the Royal Society would have been trying to espouse the Montmor Academy's template. Sorbière might be right on one point, though: the sense of discipline he called for in his 1657 rules seems to have been properly adhered to in London. Attending a session of the Royal Society in 1663, Sorbière could not fail to admire the orderly progress of debates:

> Nobody rushes to talk nor takes pride in talking lengthily or saying everything he knows. Speakers are never interrupted and disagreements

---

59   Bigourdan, 'Les premières', 160, discours du 3 avril 1663. Quoted and translated in Brown, *Organizations*, 124.
60   Ibid, 93–115. See also Simone Mazauric, *Fontenelle et l'invention de l'histoire des sciences à l'aube des Lumières* (Paris, 2007).
61   Brown, *Organizations*, 95–96.
62   Quoted and translated in Ibid, 99–102.

remain contained and are never voiced in a disrespectful tone. Nowhere will you find anything more civil, courteous, and better conducted than this assembly, such as I was given to observe.[63]

Sorbière also wonders at the pivotal position of experiments, which clearly prevailed over lengthy discussions: 'participants present in a few words what they think is suitable to say about the experiment that the secretary proposed'. In the hotel of rue Sainte-Avoye, demonstrations and experiments were mainly a spectacle whose function was to entertain a genteel audience, whereas in England, they were at the core of an inductive knowledge-building process.

In the end, it is unclear who exactly should receive credit for these differences. The diverging influences of Descartes in France and of Bacon in England have been pointed out. As was previously mentioned in this paper, culturalist explanations have also been put forward, with Charleton deriding French 'opinionators' and their complex discussion style, and Thomas Sprat, the first historian of the Royal Society, vaunting plain-dealing and forthright approach of the English to debates, which stood in sharp contrast to the affectation exhibited by Frenchmen.[64]

If there was indeed a transfer of models between France and England, it most likely occurred from England to France, not the other way around. During the summer of 1663, three Montmorians – Sorbière, Monconys and Huygens – were allowed to attend the meetings of the Royal Society, and Sorbière's *Relation d'un voyage en Angleterre* was the direct result of this trip.[65] But as early as May 1663, with Sorbière's speech in front of the Montmor Academy, English influence on the French's endeavours seems blatant:

> And thus I think that we should make room for experiments and remain silent whenever someone wants to conduct one. [...] However there would be nothing fairer than to allow anyone to indulge his curiosity and to put to the test anything of which he is uncertain. For all the experiments that have been debated in this assembly, and put up in our records, are thereby authenticated for the purposes of posterity.[66]

---

63 Samuel Sorbière, *Relation d'un voyage en Angleterre* (Paris, 1664), 90.
64 Shapin, *Social*, 97–98.
65 On the complicated reception of this book in England or Denmark, see Louis Roux, 'Introduction', in Samuel Sorbière, *Relation d'un voyage en Angleterre*, (Saint-Etienne, 1980), 7–28.
66 Bigourdan, 'Les premières', 216–217.

Through these lines, Sorbière, though a rather lukewarm advocate of experimentalism himself, sketched a Baconian program and paid tribute to English science. In his 1664 *Relation*, a book that he dedicated to Louis XIV, he was confident that the Royal Society would 'extend a trove of useful inventions from England to foreign nations' and celebrated 'English nobility, [...] almost uniformly learned and thoroughly enlightened'. He reserved special praise for 'Mylords Dibgy, Boyle, Brouncker, Moray, Devonshire, Worcester [who] erected laboratories, built machines, opened mines and hired hundreds of different types of craftsmen to try and design new inventions'.[67] Robert Moray, although 'engaged in the running of the State and a man of such rare merit, who all his life had occupied high offices in the army or cabinets', could nonetheless be seen 'setting up machines in St James's Park and adjust[ing] telescopes himself', 'creating bewilderment among most courtiers, who never look at the stars, and would see it as a blot on their reputation if only they were interested in anything else than devising new ways to dress'.[68] Admiring the English accomplishments, Sorbière also asked the king to lay the groundwork for a similar institution in France, more or less reprising arguments already laid out in his 1663 speech:

> If chance and the work of a few individuals have advanced our arts and sciences to the point where they currently stand, just imagine how much could be accomplished with clear leadership given to so many able men, the support of several distinguished noblemen, public authorities and the magnificence of a mighty monarch?[69]

What followed is an often-told narrative in the history of science. Colbert, the powerful finance minister, acceded to Sorbière's suggestions. By 1663, Chapelain was trying to convince several foreign learned men to come to France on behalf of the minister. Around 1664, Auzout, Petit and Thevenot designed the blueprint for a 'company of science and arts' designed to avoid the mistakes which had caused the failure of the Montmor Academy. Colbert was to select the members: Cartesians and Jesuits were initially excluded, as were the noblemen who did not display a genuine interest in science.[70] But the company was nevertheless a genteel one: no craftsmen were to be admitted. Harcourt Brown

---

67 Sorbière, *Relation*, 80.
68 Ibid, 74.
69 Ibid, 115.
70 On the first months of the academy, see Sturdy, *Science*, 64; Roger Hahn, *Anatomie d'une institution scientifique, L'Académie des Sciences de Paris, 1666–1803* (Paris, 1993), 1–22; Brown, *Organizations*, 145–149.

carefully traced the debates and hesitations that finally led to the creation of the Academy in 1666, which he describes as a compromise between the Colbertian desire to control the cultural production of the kingdom and the prospect of a likely opposition from other cultural groups or institutions, such as the Sorbonne or even *Académie française*. Although Colbert and his entourage took their cue from a variety of sources – the main ones being the Royal society and the Florentine *Accademia del Cimento*– , the result, according to Harcourt Brown, 'bears but slight resemblance to foreign models, either Italian or English'. From February 1666, a growing group started gathering in Colbert's library in Rue Vivienne. France finally had its own academy. Not until 1699 was this academy to be endowed with rules and regulations. In his *Histoire de l'Académie Royale des Sciences*, Fontenelle neverthess recorded a few guidelines which, on paper at least, were to frame the work of the new company: the members were to receive pensions from the king; they were expected to keep up relationships with organisations of a similar nature; their proceedings were to be kept secret unless otherwise decided. Indeed the first few weeks of the *Académie* saw the gradual establishment of an institutional routine. Sessions were to be held twice a week, with all members expected to attend, a precautionary measure designed to avoid division into groups of interests. Future organisational issues were to be put to the vote and proper minutes of debates and meetings to be drawn.[71] Such informal rules alone were not expected to prevent all skirmishes, the ultimate authority for maintaining order being vested in Colbert and the king. French scientists found their own route towards autonomy, and ultimately, professionalization – one which involved subjection to the crown – a path already taken by the Belles-Lettres when the *Académie française* was founded.[72]

From the 1620s to the 1660s, scientific sociability underwent major transformations that were ultimately enshrined in new institutions. This process was far from linear and involved a great deal of international transfers. The main incentive for institutionalisation was to place those gatherings on a firm footing and prevent the skirmishes that occurred in some groups and were somewhat amplified by the genteel context. The support offered by noblemen was unreliable and unsystematic, and tended to shift scientific practices towards entertainment, at the expense of lengthy and sometimes thankless enquiries. State support, in the case of the *Académie des sciences*, or royal incorporation in the case of the Royal Society, show that the State indisputably became a

---

71   Sturdy, *Science*, 145–147.
72   This is the main argument of Christian Jouhaud, *Les pouvoirs de la littérature: histoire d'un paradoxe* (Paris, 2000).

major source of sponsorship for scientific communities of interest. Crucially, this institutionalisation occurred in bottom-up fashion, as an answer to the expectations of men of science and to their explicit demands much more than a trigger for the latter. The Leviathan was indeed made of men and built upon their conflicts.

PART 3

Making and Reporting Experiments: Scientific Styles and Publishing Policies

CHAPTER 8

Professionalizing Doubt: Johann Daniel Major's Observation 'On the Horn of the Bezoardic Goat', Curiosity Collecting, and Periodical Publication

Vera Keller

A casual glance through the many monstrous births, strange facts and dubious reports of the *Miscellanea Curiosa*, the journal of the *Academia Naturae Curiosorum*, would appear to consign its authors at worst to an unskeptical credulity and at best to an older culture of unfiltered commonplacing.[1] The title of the journal itself suggests a disordered compilation of curiosities. Such a cursory view would be misleading, however. The accounts of fantastic events, depictions of curious creatures, and dubious identifications in the journal can be read as part of a strategy for flushing out all possible reportage on nature, only to hold it up to communal criticism. They offer evidence of skepticism, rather than credulity, concerning contemporary abilities to distinguish truth from falsehood. The strange facts filling the journal's pages corresponded to an intentional and explicit editorial policy of publishing provisional knowledge that, in the serial format of the journal, could be further questioned and corrected over time.

On the basis primarily of the English *Philosophical Transactions,* Alex Csiszar has recently argued that 'the early modern origin of the scientific journal is something of a mythology'.[2] Other, more institutionalized journals, such as the *Miscellanea Curiosa*, however, challenge Csiszar's claim. Early modern journal publication fundamentally transformed scholarly practices, changing not only the time-frame of scholarship, but expectations around critical review and professionalization. The journal recruited forms of enclosed or repositorial

---

1 Special thanks to Ann Blair for her extremely helpful comments on a draft of this piece. All translations are my own. On strange facts, Lorraine Daston and Katharine Park, *Wonders and the Order of Nature 1150–1750* (New York, 1998), 248–251. On the circulation of 'factoids' within natural history, see Fabian Krämer, 'Why There was no Centaur in Eighteenth-Century London. The Vulgar as a Cognitive Category in Enlightenment Europe', *Wissenschaftsgeschichte und Geschichte des Wissens im Dialog: Connecting Science and Knowledge*, eds. K. von Greyerz, S. Flubacher and P. Senn (Göttingen, 2013), 317–345.
2 Alex Csiszar, *The Scientific Journal: Authorship and the Politics of Knowledge in the Nineteenth Century* (Chicago, 2018), 18.

knowledge, including both collections of objects and of natural historical observations, and published them within an institutional and programmatic framework designed for on-going, collaborative review. This entailed subjecting the named individuals who submitted questionable accounts to doubt. The editorial stance adopted by the editors of the journal suggested that an ability to doubt and to be doubted served in itself as a measure of authority, identifying the cutting-edge explorer of provisional knowledge in contrast to previous models of commonplacing and curiosity collection. These changing expectations, I argue, supported the shift noted by Peter Burke around 1700 from a culture of curiosity to one of research.[3]

This essay focuses on a single, short observation, 'On the horn of the bezoardic goat', published by Johann Daniel Major (1634–1693), chair of medicine at the University of Kiel and member of the *Academia*, in the *Miscellanea Curiosa* in 1677.[4] It described a horn given by the Hamburg curiosity collector and future city librarian, David Schellhammer (1627 or 1629–1693) to Major for his collections. In a printed critical commentary, the editors of the journal called the indentification of the horn into doubt, blaming Schellhammer rather than Major for the error.

This caught Schelhammer completely by surprise. Many forms of critique, particularly in print, were to be expected between members of the Republic of Letters.[5] Nested within a densely related local and vernacular collecting scene in Hamburg, however, Schellhammer participated in a culture that regularly traded access to curiosities for credit and reputation. His relationship to more agonistic learned conventions and expectations was marginal, and he did not expect his gift to be repaid with public criticism. Within the rapidly evolving platform the early modern journal offered for authorship and doubt, Schellhammer's culture of vernacular curiosity came into conflict with professionalizing scholarly practices.

Major, who relied on Schellhammer and his networks for a continual supply of global *naturalia*, attempted to placate the furious Schellhammer in a lengthy letter offering ten reasons why this public critique should be considered acceptable behavior. Among members of the *Academia*, Major proved particularly innovative in developing new literary technologies for collecting and critiquing prior knowledge. Like Descartes before him, Major solicited doubts

---

3   Peter Burke, *A Social History of Knowledge: From Gutenberg to Diderot* (Cambridge, 2000), 46.
4   Johann D. Major, 'De Cornu capri bezoardici', *Miscellanea curiosa*, 8 (1677), 1–4.
5   Ann Blair, 'Scholarly Critique in early modern Europe', *H-France Salon*, 7 (2015), Issue 20, #2.

on his own work in a form of author-initiated peer review.[6] He is currently best known for his comparative publications on global museology, which he considered the foundation of an entirely new science of *Kunstkammer* organization, curation and cataloguing. His museology, including his techniques for managing doubt within the collection, developed from the interaction between vernacular collecting and the *Academia*'s formalization of critical review. The incident of the bezoardic goat thus illuminates broader changing mores concerning authorship and doubt at the moment of the early modern journal's genesis.

The publishing strategies of the *Academia* illustrate particularly dramatically what was at stake in shifting from monographic to periodic publication. The correspondence-based *Academia Naturae Curiosorum* was founded in 1652 and renamed the *Leopoldina* in 1687 after gaining recognition from Leopold I of the Holy Roman Empire.[7] Responding to criticism that its previous monographic publication program merely collected old knowledge out of books without encouraging future discoveries, Philipp Jakob Sachs von Lewenheimb (1627–1672), the municipal physician of Wrocław (Breslau) and the president of the academy, founded its journal in 1670.

This was an abrupt change. The *Academia* previously hoped to produce monographs comprehensively collecting everything known about an individual medical simple. The monograph aimed to offer the definitive last word on a particular subject and was perforce based upon compilation. The journal, by contrast, was designed to be open-ended and unfiltered. It offered the immediate, varied communications of a multiplicity of observers. The journal editors purposefully steered the journal toward the publication of provisional material. They also supplied a critical apparatus, in the form of *scholia* and editorial

---

6   On Descartes, ibid, 10. Major did this regarding a priority dispute he had with the Royal Society for blood infusion in Johann Daniel Major, *Chirurgia infusoria, placidis Cl. Virorum dubiis impugnata, cum modesta, ad eadem, responsione* (Kiel, 1667).

7   On the *Academia,* Uwe Müller. ed. *Salve Academicum II. Beiträge zur Geschichte der Deutschen Akademie der Naturforscher Leopoldina* (Schweinfurt, 1991). Mason Barnett, 'Medical Authority and Princely Patronage: The *Academia Naturae Curiosorum*, 1652–1693' (Ph.D. thesis, University of North Carolina, Chapel Hill, 1995). Wieland Berg and Benno Parthier, 'Die kaiserliche Leopoldina im Heiligen Römischen Reich Deutscher Nation', in *Gelehrte Gesellschaften im mitteldeutschen Raum (1650–1820)*, eds. D. Döring and K. Nowak (Leipzig, 2000), 39–52. Richard Toellner et. al, eds. *Die Gründung der Leopoldina – Academia Naturae Curiosorum – im historischn Kontext, Johann Laurentius Bausch zum 400. Geburtstag* (Stuttgart, 2008). Margret Garber, 'Chymical Curiosities and Trusted Testimonials in the Journal of the Leopoldina Academy of Curiosi', *Bridging Traditions: Alchemy, Chemistry, and Paracelsian Practices in the early modern Era,* eds. K.H. Parshall, M.T. Walton, and B.T. Moran (Kirksville, Mo., 2015), 79–100.

commentary. The observations published in the journal, they stressed, were not to appear as authorized matters of fact, but more as the opinions of individual authors within an on-going conversation.

In both monographic and periodical publication, the authors of the *Academia* aimed to note the names of their sources very carefully, yet the motivation for such citation practices shifted along with the change in format. In the monographs, citing authors illustrated due diligence, that is, that compilers of the monographs indeed brought a large body of work to bear on their topic. By ascribing views to others, citation also functioned to shift responsibility away from authors themselves. Additionally, according to the explicit rules of the *Academia*, citing authors afforded a means of offering credit. Offering credit continued to function as a method of enticing contributors to the new journal in its early days.[8] Increasingly, however, named authors could expect not only to receive credit, but also to be called on to respond to doubts. This had the effect of shaping the nature of authorial citation into a means of holding authors to account, documenting the moment that a particular authorial opinion reached print within the new temporality of periodical publication.

Practices of citation in the early modern scholarly journal therefore had a role to play in the development of critical footnoting. Something 'like the modern system of documentation' gradually emerged over 'the course of the later seventeenth and eighteenth centuries'.[9] As Anthony Grafton notes, only 'the use of footnotes enables historians to make their texts not monologues but conversations, in which modern scholars, their predecessors, and their subjects all take part'.[10] Facilitating such conversations between past and future scholars, placed in relation to the objects of natural history, motivated the shift in the *Academia*'s publishing platform.

1   Between Worlds: *Academia,* University, Court, City and Market

A professional identity helped consolidate the *Academia* despite its wide extent and paper existence. In contrast to the English Royal Society that prided itself on the gentlemanly and thus amateur and heterogeneous quality of its naturalists, the *Academia* was built around a single professional identity – the

---

[8]   Credit could also serve as a means for encouraging contributions to solo-authored monographic work, as in Conrad Gessner's strategy discussed in Ann Blair, 'The 2016 Josephine Waters Bennett Lecture: Humanism and Printing in the Work of Conrad Gessner', *Renaissance Quarterly,* 70 (2017), 1–43.
[9]   Anthony Grafton, *The Footnote: A Curious History* (Cambridge MA, 1997), 220.
[10] Ibid, 234.

physician. The interests of members of the *Academia* and thus articles in the journal in fact extended far beyond medicine (and anyone was invited to submit). Nevertheless, the professional identity of the *Academia* offered shared empirical tools, such as the medical genre of the *observatio*.[11] The professional identity of the members of the *Academia* also meant that, despite their far-flung locations, members negotiated similar interactions between the publication standards of the *Academia* and their other roles, such as those of city, court or academic physician, and their other networks which often included collectors, apothecaries and *Materialisten* (dealers in crude *materia medica*). The professionalization of doubt in the journal illuminated the tensions between the role of physicians qua members of the Academy versus as participants within locally embedded and less institutional networks.

Major was ideally situated to navigate and interrogate the conflicting cultures of collecting and observation to be found in several audiences – Hamburg merchant circles, the princely *Kunstkammer*, the university, and the *Academia* with its new journal. Originally from Breslau, Major studied in Wittenberg and Padua. He practiced medicine in Wittenberg as a newly minted physician between 1661 and 1663 and then was hired by the city of Hamburg to serve as a plague doctor from 1663. At Sachs' urging, the young Major was elected to the *Academia* in 1664, under the *cognomen* Hesperus to match Sachs' Phosphorus (evening and morning stars). In a meteoric rise for his career, Major was one of the first faculty, as chair of medicine, invited to join the new university founded in Kiel in 1665 by the twenty-four year old Duke Christian Albrecht of Schleswig-Holstein (1641–1695) and his all powerful and bibliophiliac chancellor, Johann Adolph Kielmann von Kielmansegg (1612–1676). In this setting, Major enjoyed access not only to the curiosity markets of Hamburg and the spectacular Gottorf court collections (which had purchased a collection from Bernhard Paludanus), but to extraordinarily well stocked libraries. Although large libraries have previously been considered a 'rarity' in this area, Kielmansegg's library alone held 42,000 titles, in addition to the Gottorf court library, the new university library, and the city libraries of nearby Lübeck and Hamburg.[12]

---

11 On the *observatio*, Gianna Pomata, 'Sharing Cases: The *Observationes* in early modern Medicine', *Early Science and Medicine*, 15 (2010), 193–236. Gianna Pomata, 'Observation Rising: Birth of an Epistemic Genre, 1500–1650', in *Histories of Scientific Observation*, eds. L. Daston and E. Lunbeck (Chicago, 2011), 45–80. And Dirk van Miert. ed. *Communicating Observations in Early Modern Letters (1500–1675), Epistolography and Epistemology in the Age of the Scientific Revolution* (London, 2013).

12 Peter Burke mentions just Wolfenbüttel as a rare example of a large library in seventeenth-century Northern and Eastern Europe. Peter Burke, *A Social History of Knowledge: From*

To such resources, Major added various forms of pedagogical collections. With the support of the chancellor, Major built an academic medical garden on the grounds of the Duke's summer palace.[13] He also offered both his students and the public lessons in experimental natural philosophy, during which he encouraged them to manually investigate the objects in his own collections.[14] An eclectic corpuscularian who drew on a wide European tradition, Major would issue translations and editions of such authors as Descartes and Fabio Colonna among the more than 100 titles he published.[15] Yet, he was sensitive to the contemporary criticism that German scholars in particular suffered from the itch to write. According to Daniel Georg Morhof, Major's colleague at Kiel, Germans 'don't write books, they vomit them'.[16] Major himself criticized Conrad Gessner, known as the Pliny of Germany, for compiling such huge works of natural history that he appeared to suffer from 'diarrhea of the

---

Gutenberg to Diderot (Cambridge, 2000), 69. On Kielmansegg's library, Jonathan I. Israel, *Radical Enlightenment: Philosophy and the Making of Modernity 1650–1750* (Oxford, 2001), 139.

13   Johannes Reinke, *Der älteste Botanische Garten Kiels: Urkundlich Darstellung der Begründung eines Universitäts-Instituts im siebzehnten Jahrhundert* (Kiel, 1912), 24–30.

14   Johann D. Major, *Collegium medico-curiosorum hebdomatim intra aedes privatas habendum intimat aequis Aestimatoribus studii experimentalis* (Kiel, 1670).

15   For Major's bibliography, Johannes Moller, *Cimbria Literata* (Copenhagen, 1744). For his biography, W. Rudolph Reinbacher, *Leben, Arbeit und Umwelt des Arztes: Johann Daniel Major (1634–1693), Eine Biographie aus dem 17. Jahrhundert, mit neuen Erkenntnissen* (Linsengericht, 1998). On his polymathic ambitions in Kiel, Georg Braungart and Wolfgang Braungart, 'Mißlingende Utopie – Die Neuen Wisseschaften auf der Suche nach fürstlicher Patronage. Zu Johann Daniel Majors See-Farth nach der Neuen Welt (1670), in *Res publica litteraria. Die Institutionen der Gelehrsamkeit in der frühen Neuzeit*, eds. S. Neumeister and C. Wiedemann (Wiesbaden 1987), 367–387. Cornelius Steckner, 'Medico erudito aut necessarium. A Cartesian Utopia Erudita of 100 sciences, published by J.D. Major (1634–1693) in 1670, and its institutional background', *Actes du XXXIIe Congrès International d'Histoire de la Médicine*, ed. Eric Fierens (Brussels, 1991), 723–733. Hole Rößler, 'Utopie der Bildung. Der Entwurf einer "Polymathia experimentalis" in *Johann Daniel Majors See-Farth nach der Neuen Welt/ ohne Schiff und Segel* (1670)', in *Polyhistorismus und Buntschriftstellerei: populäre Wissensformen und Wissenskultur in der Frühen Neuzeit*, ed. F. Schock (Berlin, 2012), 191–220. On the shared interests of Morhof and Maior in investigating the deep past, Dieter Lohmeier, 'Das gotische Evangelium und die cimbrischen Heiden. Daniel Georg Morhof, Johann Daniel Major und der Gotizismus', *Lychnos* (1977–78), 54–70.

16   Daniel G. Morhof, *Polyhistor literarius, philosophicus et practicus*, II (Lübeck, 1732), 225. 'Scribunt enim multi, imò vomunt libros'. Many similar criticisms are collected and refuted in Bernhard P. Karl (praeses), *Meditationes crudiores de Germania artibus literisque nulli secunda* (Rostock, 1698).

pen'.[17] Both Major and Morhof worked to develop supple new forms of arranging collections and excerpting and retrieving information from the massive collections in their orbit, without being overwhelmed by them.

They did so in the context of an area rich in innovative methods for arranging and accessing information in slimmed-down collections. Faculty at the Hamburg gymnasium such as Joachim Jungius, Vincent Placcius, and Martin Fogel, for instance, pioneered the use of 'excerpt cabinets' as a means of arranging, accessing and recombining their notes.[18] Their colleague, Peter Lauremberg, recommended cases (*thecas*) containing specimens of the 'natural forms of metals, earths, stones, and other minerals' similar to herbaria. With 'minimal expense and without great pomp', such cases offered 'indescribable utility'.[19]

For Major, such a critical review, selection, and re-organization of collections took the form of what he considered a new discipline of 'Tactica conclavium', or the proper setting up of collections, based upon serial studies of collecting practices around the world.[20] This entailed the transformation of the *Kunst-und Wunderkammer* into a targeted, research collection.

Major rejected the insatiable build-up of gargantuan hoards in favor of a select, well-ordered collection that could be continually accessed and deployed in experimentation and pedagogy. He overhauled the arrangement of objects within space inside boxes and cabinets, custom-designed for the easy retrieval of objects for use. He linked objects to an ambitious cross-referenced cataloging technique associating each object to the on-going learned debates about it. Major would open his own public museum in Kiel in 1688, the *Museum*

---

17 Kiel University Library S.H. 21, Major, *Adversaria Cimbrica*, note 67. Digitized at urn:nbn: de:gbv:8:2-1808502urn:nbn:de:gbv:8:2-1808502.

18 On Placcius, inter alia, Ann Blair, *Too Much To Know: Managing Scholarly Information Before the Modern Age* (New Haven, 2010), ch. 2, Blair, 'The Rise of Note-Taking in Early Modern Europe', *Intellectual History Review* 20, 3 (2010), 303–316 and Martin Mulsow, 'Vincent Placcius. Freundschaftsethik, gemeinsame Forschung und moralphilosophische Lehre am Akademischen Gymnasium in Hamburg', in *Das Akademische Gymnasium zu Hamburg (gegr. 1613) im Kontext frühneuzeitlicher Wissenschafts- und Bildungsgeschichte*, ed. Johann A. Steiger with Martin Mulsow and Axel E. Walter (Berlin, 2017), 87–102. On Fogel, see Carola Pipenbring-Thomas and Maria Marten, eds. *Fogels Ordnungen: aus der Werkstatt des Hamburger Mediziners Martin Fogel (1634–1675)* (Frankfurt a.M., 2015).

19 Peter Lauremberg, *Laurus Delphica, seu consilium, quo describitur methodus perfacilis ad medicinam* (Leiden, 1621), 35.

20 Johann D. Major, *Unvorgreiffliches Bedencken von Kunst- und Naturalien-Kammern ins gemein* (Kiel, 1674). Johann D. Major, *Vorstellung etlicher Kunst- und Naturalien-Kammern/ in Africa/ und an Gräntzen Europae* (Kiel, [ca. 1675]). *Vorstellung etlicher Kunst- und Naturalien-Kammern/ in America und Asia* (Kiel, 1674).

Cimbricum, a purposefully small installation that could at most fit six people at a time.[21] Major could afford to be discriminate in his collection not only due to the massive resources to which he had access in the region, but to the way that learned correspondence and periodical publication networked his museum to a wide array of other collections.

As a transitional figure, Major has too often been read on one side of the divide between the playfully disordered and semiotic Renaissance and Baroque *Kunstkammer* on the one hand and the orderly and divided Enlightenment museum on the other. For the former, Horst Bredekamp has influentially and misleadingly selectively quoted Major on his desire for his *artificialia* to appear on the walls of his public museum in 'a scattered, deliberate disorder'.[22] At the other extreme, Cornelius Steckner has described Major's *Museum Cimbricum* as plunging us 'suddenly in the Information technology of the eighteenth century'.[23]

Such polar views of Major's museology have their roots in Major's own new contrast between the uninformed, public audience of a collection and a professionalized curator. Rather than seeing the curator and the guests of a collection as more or less equals (or, in the case of the princely collection, of the curator as a distant social inferior to many guests), Major desiderated an expert curator separated by a vast gulf from the common expectations of a public, to whom he nevertheless attempted to address his collections. Major complained that 'the keys of many collections were given not to the learned, but to clockmakers and ivory turners, which was why so many beautiful naturalia were lying in such strange confusion among so many different cabinets and chests, and often out of indifference lost, broken, and destroyed, since their keepers understood their art and craft very well, but of the basic sciences, however, little or nothing'. Only someone experienced in experimental sciences would be qualified to order and keep a collection. The greatest rarity in the world was

---

21 On Major's museology, Cornelius Steckner, 'Das Museum Cimbricum von 1688 und die cartesianische "Perfection des Gemüthes": Zur Museumswissenschaft des Kieler Universitätsprofessors Johann Daniel Major (1634–1693)', *Macrocosmos in Microcosmo: Die Welt in der Stube: zur Geschichte des Sammelns, 1450 bis 1800,* ed A. Grote (Opladen, 1994), 603–628. Jan Drees, 'Das Kieler "Museum Cimbricum" (1688) des Johann Daniel Major (1634–1693) und seine Beziehungen zum Gottorfer Hof', *Jahrbuch des Schleswig-Holsteinische Landesmuseums Schloss Gottorf* (1994/5), 38–53. And Stefan Kirschner, 'Vom privaten Naturalienkabinett zur öffentlichen Schausammlung: Johann Daniel Majors "Museum Cimbricum" (1689)', in *Popularisierung der Naturwissenschaften,* ed. Gudrun Wolfschmidt (Berlin, 2002), 64–77.

22 Horst Bredekamp, *The Lure of Antiquity and the Cult of the Machine: The Kunstkammer and the Evolution of Nature, Art and Technology* (Princeton, 1995), 73.

23 Steckner, 'Das Museum', 615.

a well-ordered collection, and thus one should not 'put a priceless pearl next to a bezoar simply because both of them are expensive; rather, the former belongs among the shells and snails, and the latter among the different parts and excrements of four-footed animals'.[24]

The intentional disorder cited by Bredekamp, as Major repeatedly clarified, was not part of his ideal prescription for a collection, but rather a concession to the expectations of the museum's public audience. Major had indeed hung on the walls of his museum some objects 'here and there, without order', but only, he claimed, so that 'something Kunstkammerish' would immediately greet the eyes of the inexperienced visitor, who would expect such playful disarray. This first, disordered impression could be excused as a means of engaging the spectator and making him or her more likely to continue to explore the strictly ordered collection arranged in Major's cabinets lining the rest of the space.[25] For the same reason, one cabinet devoted to *naturalia* selected only for their worth (rather than their role in illustrating nature) served to charm the ignorant portion of the museum's audience, who, not knowing how precious the proper order in disciplines was, desired to see only rare things.[26]

Despite Major's instrumentalist explanation for including a touch of the usual 'Kunstkammerishness', Major's brief mention of disorder has been understood to stand for his museological project, and the episteme underlying it, as a whole. Jan Westerhoff has extended Bredekamp's citation of Major's purposeful disorder to symbolize what Westerhoff calls a 'Baroque semiotics' of disorder and pansemioticism, to which he has also linked polyhistoric culture, of which the *Polyhistor* of Major's colleague Morhof is the best known example.[27] Alessandro Ottaviani, who notes Major's comment about the disordered *artificialia* but also the extreme order in Major's other prescriptions, sees an 'asymmetry' in the 'peremptory order' imposed on *naturalia* and the 'curious nonchalance regarding the presentation of *artificialia*', an asymmetry in which 'one might detect signs of the lack of equilibrium that was to lead to the decline of the *Wunderkammer*'.[28]

Major was caught, it is true, between two worlds. As a member of two young and ambitious institutions, the *Academia naturae curiosorum*, founded in 1652,

---

24   Major, *Unvorgreiffliches Bedencken*, sig. C3ʳ.
25   Johann D. Major, *Museum Cimbricum, oder insgemein so-genennte Kunst-Kammer* (Plön, 1688), 8. See also Major, *Musei Cimbrici*, sig. A3ᵛ.
26   Ibid.
27   Jan C. Westerhoff, 'A World of Signs: Baroque Pansemioticism, the Polyhistor and the Early Modern Wunderkammer', *Journal of the History of Ideas*, 62 (2001), 633–650.
28   Alessandro Ottaviani, 'The Coral of Death: *Kunst-und Wunderkammern* between Temporality and Allegory', *Nuncius*, 30 (2015), 281–319 (308).

and the new Kiel university, or *Academia Christiana Albertina*, founded in 1665, Major's penchant for sweeping reform could be well supported. Yet, a collection is not a clean slate, as Major's concession to some expected disorder indicates. By its very nature, the collection demands engagement both with an inherited reservoir of objects, audience expectations, and cataloging practices, as well as with the marketplace and its vocabularies of expertise and information management. The incident of the bezoardic goat, whose name, according to a popular but false etymology, derived from the bazaar, allows us to explore shifting collecting credentials between the marketplace, the court, the university, and new, extramural learned societies.

2   Doubt and Critique in the *Miscellanea Curiosa*

The case of the *Miscellanea Curiosa* sharpens the potential for conflict between these differing realms since the *Academia* and its journal were far more professionalized than, for instance, the Royal Society and its initially privately published *Philosophical Transactions*. In contrast to the work of members of the *Academia*, the note-taking techniques of seventeenth-century English naturalists have received extensive attention, and the *Philosophical Transactions* has often been heralded as an ancestor of the modern scientific journal.[29] Yet, on the issue of citation, so central to modern research publication, English naturalists were notably weak, whereas German scholars were notoriously robust.[30]

---

29   Maurizio Gotti, 'The Experimental Essay in Early Modern English', *European Journal of English Studies*, 5 (2001), 221–239 and Maurizio Gotti, 'The Origins of the Experimental Essay', in *Investigating Specialized Discourse* (Bern, 2008), 171–188. Scott Black, 'Boyle's Essay: Genre and the Making of Early Modern Knowledge', in *Making Knowledge in Early Modern Europe: Practices, Objects, and Texts, 1400–1800*, eds. Pamela Smith and Benjamin Schmidt (Chicago, 2008), 178–198. James Paradis, 'Montaigne, Boyle, and the Essay of Experience', in *One Culture: Essays in Science and Literature,* ed. George Levine (Madison, 1987), 59–91.

30   Bryce Allen, Jian Qin and F.W. Lancaster, 'Persuasive Communities: A Longitudinal Analysis of References in the Philosophical Transactions of the Royal Society, 1665–1990', *Social Studies of Science*, 24:2 (1994), 279–310. For instance, the *Philosophical Transactions*' summary of 24 of the 160 observations that appeared in the first issue of the *Miscellanea curiosa* mentioned just two names (both of other accounts already mentioned in the *Miscellanea* themselves). 'Review of *Miscellanea Curiosa*'. The references are to Lusitanus and Olearius. The second review of the *Miscellanea Curiosa* in the *Philosophical Transactions* briefly enumerated 26 of the 260 observations in the volume, mentioning no names. 'Review of *Miscellanea Curiosa*', *Philosophical Transactions*, 7, (1672), 5024–5026.

The publications of the members of the *Academia* are a case in point. Their numerous references were not only a symptom of a different scholarly style, but a matter of institutional policy. From its founding in 1652, the *Academia* projected an ambitious monographic publication program that would offer authoritative accounts of medical simples. The statutes of the *Academia* stipulated that credit was to be offered generously. According to the first draft of the laws of the *Academia Naturae Curiosorum* in 1651/2, members of the Academy were to draw upon respectable authors, their own observations, and credible accounts, without however, remaining silent concerning the names of these authors; honorable mention about each person who had contributed should be made. A later draft further explained that this was 'so that it should stimulate them to support our work. It is generous, says Pliny, and a sign of decency of mind to fully point out those through whom we have advanced'.[31]

In the very first work published under the aegis of the *Academia*, Sachs' 1661 work on grapes, the *Ampelographia*, Sachs alluded to this policy. Since 'it is honest to declare through whom you have made progress [a reference to the Plinian commonplace mentioned in the *Academia*'s statutes]', Sachs noted that 'the reader would find authors cited in good faith and correctly disposed in honeycombs [*alveolos*], lest anybody seem to be defrauded from their deserved credit'.[32] Sachs referred to the notion, drawn from Seneca and Horace and so central to practices of compilation, of the author as a bee. Flitting from book to book, the author/bee takes varied material from others, makes it into honey, and re-arranges it in the honeycombs of his own writing, under his own name.[33] Sachs differentiated himself from this practice. Rather than viewing others as his own raw material, Sachs promised to give them credit as producers themselves; his textual infrastructure, his honeycombs, would include references to those makers. Such citation was not primarily intended to cast doubt or make statements appear to be the provisional claims of a single author. It was meant to offer credit through publication and therefore promote participation in a paper-based association.

In the first two decades of the *Academia*'s existence, very few monographs appeared, and three out of the first four published under the rubric of the *Academia* were the work of Sachs. Perhaps because they were so good at crediting

---

31   Müller, 'Die Leges', 249. See also 28.
32   Philipp J. Sachs von Lewenheimb, *Ampelographia sive Vitis Viniferae Eiusque Partium Consideratio Physico-Philologico-Historico-Medico-Chymica* (Wroclaw, 1661), sig.)(7ʳ On this work as the first to appear in the *Academia*'s program, see Müller, 'Johan Laurentius Bausch und Philipp Jacob Sachs von Lewenhaimb. Von der Gründung der *Academia Naturae Curiosorum* zur Reichsakademie', in *Die Gründung der Leopoldina*, 13–41 (29).
33   eg., Blair, *Too Much*, 128.

others, these far-ranging monographs faced extensive criticism for uncritically compiling previous work. In 1671, Leibniz, for instance, complained that the members of the *Academia* did not publish what they had 'discovered through their own experience', but they merely 'scribbled together already known things out of other books'.[34] Leibniz complained that their method 'was better suited to establishing a repository than to providing openings'. As Neil Kenny explains, Leibniz rejected the *Academia's* approach because 'it was stuck in a collecting tendency ('repository') rather than a narrating one (creating 'openings' leading to future new knowledge)'.[35] Yet, as Leibniz himself went on to acknowledge, the *Academia* had veered in a new direction, following the trend of periodicity, 'so that they will publish from time to time new medical observations' according to the example of the journals of the English, French, and Italians.[36]

In 1670, the *Academia* issued an open call for submission to a new journal. It asked authors to contribute their 'flowers' to be disposed within the 'honeycombs' of the *Academia*; in return it promised the honorable mention of their names, 'not upon some quickly withering summer flowers, but on long-lasting paper'.[37] The *Academia* printed its revised laws in the second issue of the journal, which repeated the promise of honorable citation. All 'Observations, Experiments, Inventions, Problems, and anything of this sort' communicated to the journal should be published in the order in which it was received by the editors, with 'the honorable title of he who communicated it and to whom it was communicated'. Members communicating observations from non-members to the journal were to refrain from editorializing; they were welcome to offer polite criticisms or to point out literature on similar topics in *scholia* appended to individual observations. They should not do so too vituperatively, however, lest potential authors be scared away.[38]

In compliance with this policy, many seemingly doubtful reports appeared in the pages of the journal, only gently excoriated in attached *scholia* by the editors of the journal or other members of the *Academia*. As a result, critics found the early journal still unsatisfying. In a 1679 plan on how to form a society for the collaborative writing of natural history, Leibniz thought it would be

---

[34] Gottfried W. Leibniz, 'N. 44, Bedencken von Aufrichtung einer Academie oder Societät in Teutschland, zu Aufnehmen der Künste und Wissenshafften', *Politische Schriften*, IV, 1 *1667–1676*, ed. Paul Ritter (Berlin, 1983), 548.

[35] Neil Kenny, *The Uses of Curiosity in early modern France and Germany* (Oxford, 2004), 192.

[36] Leibniz, 'Bedencken von Aufrichtung', 548. For Leibniz's criticisms see also Mücke and Schnalke, *Briefnetz Leopoldina*, 24–25.

[37] *Academia naturae curiosorum*, 'Epistola invitatoria', *Miscellanea Curiosa*, 1 (1670) 1–8.

[38] 'Sacri Romani Imperii', sig. h2^v. See also 'Epistola invitatoria', 6.

better if the *Academia* targeted their efforts and winnowed contributions more rigorously. 'What is certain should be separated from what is not, and the probable from the improbable; a catalog of desiderata should be made, query lists should be circulated, and decisive experiments should be prescribed'.[39] Likewise, Morhof suggested, in the private *collegia* he offered in Kiel on natural history in the 1670s (later published as part of his famous *Polyhistor*), that it would be better if the Academy's journal published already tested experiments. He discussed the various ways different learned societies wrote natural history in his chapter, '*Quomodo Historia Naturalis sit instituenda*'; the Academy's current method of reporting observations secondhand, he complained, would not achieve their goal of an 'accurate natural history'.[40] Following the death of Sachs, the secretary of the Royal Society, Henry Oldenburg, urged the new editors, Heinrich Volgnad and Johannes Jänisch, to further vet the submissions to the journal.[41]

Such advice and criticisms were taken to heart. Johann Michael Fehr (1610–1688), the President of the *Academia* himself, urged Volgnad and Jänisch to verify the veracity of submissions.[42] Volgnad and Jänisch, however, stood their ground. Despite the desires of critics for the publication of fully vetted and tested material, the editors of the journal, in a number of editorial interjections through the 1670s, instead adjusted the reader's expectations.

The *Academia* had repeatedly charged authors to communicate observations and the findings of their experiments to the new journal in such a way that they appeared to readers 'as though depicted in a painting'.[43] This standard for the language employed in the observations might set the expectation of an entirely clear, perfect description of an established fact, that is of knowledge captured and immobilized for the reader. It might remind us of the Robert Boyle's technology of virtual witnessing, that is, 'the production in a reader's mind of such an image of an experimental scene as obviates the necessity of either direct witness or replication', achieved through factual description and

---

39   Gottfried W. Leibniz, 'Consilium de scribenda historia naturali indagandis causis aptissima ineundaque in eam rem societate (1679)' in *Politische Schriften, 1677–1689*, IV (Berlin, 1986), 858.

40   Danish Royal Library, Thott 178 folio. D.G. Morhof. *Historia naturalis dictata in Collegio a D.G. Morhofio. 1676*, 144–145.

41   Henry Oldenburg, *Correspondence, 1672–1673*, 9, ed Alfred R. Hall and Marie Boas Hall (Madison, 1973), 171.

42   Krämer, *Ein Zentaur in London*, 273.

43   'Epistola invitatoria', 6. 'quasi in Tabulâ delineatum'. *Academia naturae curiosorum*, 'Historia succinta & brevis ortus & progressus S.R. Imp. Academiae Naturae Curiosorum', *Miscellanea Curiosa* 2 (1671), 2, sig. e2^r, 'quasi in una Tabula delineatum' and 'Leges', in Ibid, sig h2v, 'quasi in una Tabula delineatum'.

highly finished engraving.[44] This style allowed the subjective positions of authors and the artifactual nature of their writing to fall from view, making the matter of fact appear to crystallize, seemingly objectively and uncontentiously, before the readers' eyes.

Yet, Volgnad and Jänisch made clear that this was not their intent by later qualifying this aesthetic demand. In a 1676 epilogue, they emphasized the provisional nature of published articles, saying 'We do not only admire the paintings that an Apelles, a Titian or a Dürer finished, but also the first lines they sketched'. The image of natural history offered to the gaze of the viewer in the journal, they claimed, served not as a metonym for the natural object himself, but as the incipient attempts of a particular author, awaiting future work by others.

> The work that we are undertaking certainly can't be considered that of a single or a few years, but one that the many centuries that preceded us have not been able to complete. Let it be enough if we attempt to explore every day a small part of that which our predecessors have left us in rude form, and do not let anyone think poorly of our century if it should offer our grandchildren material with which they might sharpen their intellect.[45]

In a postscript to an appendix, the editors of the journal in 1680, Johann Burg and Gottfried Schultz of Breslau, again defended themselves against publishing doubtful material, saying 'it never entered the mind of the praiseworthy Sachs, the creator of this journal, nor that of his colleagues and successors, that everything that is collected in the journal should be received as though it constituted the indubitable and infallible truth'.[46] Each reader should determine the truth themselves from the various opinions gathered together; expecting a rigorous examination of all the observations and experiments by the editors would be 'absurd and impossible'. Rather than initially vetting all material in order to publish only what was absolutely certain, the editors encouraged the long-term questioning of the publication, inviting readers to submit their criticism 'without any ad hominem attacks, but only inspired by love of the common good'.[47] This was perhaps in contrast to the situation that obtained in

---

44   Steven Shapin and Simon Schaffer, *Leviathan and the Air-pump: Hobbes, Boyle, and the Experimental Life* (Princeton, 1985), 60.
45   Heinrich Volgnad and Johannes Jänisch, 'Epilogus', *Miscellanea Curiosa* 5 (1676), 332.
46   Johann Burg and Gotffried Schultz, 'Postloquium', *Appendix anni noni et decimi ephemeridum medico-physicarum naturae-curiosorum*, 9 and 10 (1680), 327–330.
47   Ibid.

PROFESSIONALIZING DOUBT 213

Restoration England where 'flickers of doubt' concerning named witnesses were 'few and far between until the early decades of the eighteenth century' due to codes of purposefully unprofessional, gentlemanly conduct.[48]

The institutional need to encourage support for the *Academia* by offering credit came into tension with the scholarly need to doubt submissions for the sake of a more assured natural history. The path forward taken by the editors of the journal was the professionalization of doubt. Rather than serving as gatekeepers, preventing doubtful material from reaching print and focusing the publication upon a coherent research agenda, they continued to welcome, as the journal title suggested, miscellaneous observations. They countered this somewhat indiscriminate publication, however, by repositioning the references and critical apparatus of the journal. All the honorifics of and citations to authors did not entail uncritical acceptance of their authority; rather, authors should expect and welcome future questioning. As its editorial interventions illustrate, the platform that the journal offered for assigning credit could equally be made to serve as a means of raising doubts by identifying individual, sometimes dissenting, voices within a scholarly chorus.[49]

3   Major's Observation and the Editorial Critique

This was the delicate position Volgnad and Jänisch were developing when Major submitted his 'On the horn of the Bezoardic Goat' in 1676. Given Major's stature in the *Academia*, questioning his observation was a sensitive matter. Besides for being a frequent contributor to the journal, Major also composed the *Memoria Sachsiana* on Sachs' death in 1672 (reprinted in the *Miscellanea Curiosa* in 1676 and 1688).[50] In Volgnad and Jänisch's editorial commentary on Major's observation and Major's response to it in his private letter to Schellhammer, we can see what was at stake in publicly critiquing named individuals in journal publication in the period.

'On the horn of the Bezoardic Goat' is the very first observation in the eighth year of the *Miscellanea curiosa*.[51] A tipped-in engraving illustrated the 22.5-inch horn in life size [Fig. 8.1]. Major reported how his dear friend and great expert in exotic things, the honored Schellhammer, sent the horn to him from

---

48   Daston and Park, *Wonders*, 249.
49   Leibniz would come to change his view of the journal by the 1690s. Marion Mücke and Thomas Schnalke, *Briefnetz Leopoldina: Die Korrespondenz der Deutschen Akademie der Naturforscher um 1750* (Berlin, 2009), 25.
50   Johann D. Major, *Memoria Sachsiana* (Leipzig, 1675).
51   Major, 'de Cornu', 1–4.

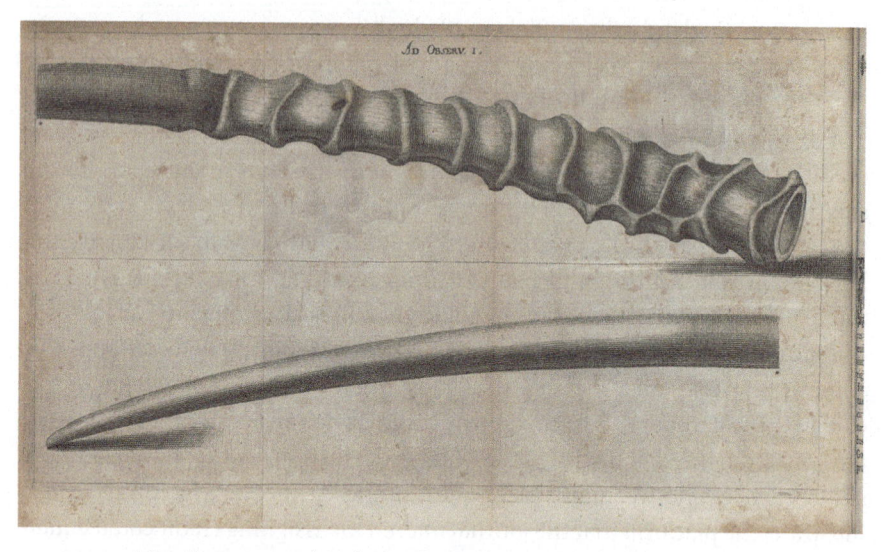

FIGURE 8.1 *Miscellanea curiosa* (1677), Houghton Library. GEN LSoc 1711.5*

Hamburg. Major compared the gently curving horn to an Italian cornetto and pointed out that it differed strikingly from the intensively spiral horns found in the nearby princely *Kunstkammer* of the Gottorf court, described by the court savant and collection cataloger, Adam Olearius (1599–1671), also as that of a 'Bezoar goat'.[52]

Major hypothesized that reasons for the difference between the two should be sought in a difference of species, or age, or sex. He pointed out that a variety of different horns could be found in various works. For example, the horn of the Pazam, a 'species of bezoardic animal' described by Lodovico Moscardo, seemed to coincide with Olearius' goat. Meanwhile, the figure of the horn of the bezoardic animal found in Jacob Bontius' commentary on Garcia d'Horta seemed closer to Major's, since Bontius described those goats as 'not very dissimilar from European goats, except that they have erect [rather than spiral] and longer horns'. Major professed himself astounded that neither Ferrante Imperato, nor Manfredo Septala, nor Ole Worm seemed to have this horn in their extensive collections.[53]

According to Major, a great friend of Schellhammer's, who was a most experienced chymist and a wealthy possessor of the choicest rarities, often

---

52 Adam Olearius, *Gottorffische Kunst-Cammer: Worinnen Allerhand ungemeine Sachen/ So theils die Natur/ theils künstliche Hände hervor gebracht und bereitet* (Schleßwig, 1666), Table 9, Fig. 7.

53 Perhaps because they identified it as that of a gazelle. Terzago, for instance, lists both straight and curved horns of gazelles in Septala's collection. Terzago, *Musaeum Septalianum*, 79.

PROFESSIONALIZING DOUBT

demanded that Schellhammer give the horn to him instead of to Major. The chymist argued that it might be possible to extract a volatile salt from the horn far superior to that from rhinceros horn or any other animal. Major, however, believed this medical need for a horn of a bezoardic goat to be just a pretext; clearly this man merely wanted to add the horn to his already impressive collections. Major did not deny that bound within the horny texture lay viscous-earthy particles and a not ignoble mixture of certain balsamic salts. It was much easier to extract these, however, through scraping rather than subjecting it to the fire, as the chymist wished to do, since the salubrious salts might easily disappear as soot. Also, Major contended, there shouldn't be any more of such particles in the horns than in the skull of the animal, so the chymist didn't really need the horn in particular for medical purposes. Furthermore, Major cited Bontius' doubts about the efficacy of bezoar stones in general; after all these stones troubled the miserable goats as much as kidney stones did humans. Major was truly grateful that Schellhammer had chosen to give the horn to him, and he wished to offer him public thanks.

The editors' critique of this observation does not appear immediately in a *scholion* following the observation, but in an appendix toward the end of the volume. They encouraged their audience to read between the lines of Major's observation.

> Do not think, dear reader, that our most honored colleague Dr. Major was really persuaded that the image he showed was a horn of a bezoardic goat. Rather, you may much more certainly believe that he preferred to publish the horn under that title in order to offer thanks to that great friend, who gave him that horn as a precious gift and endowed with that distinguished name, even though he himself tacitly realized how truly different it was.... Here and there horns are depicted among authors and exhibited in museums under the famous name of the bezoardic, however, they are too different from each other, even when you give them a superficial, desultory once-over, so that, without a more thorough investigation, it is impossible that some slight doubt not arise about the true appearance of these horns. But if we consider the subject a little more attentively, it easily appears that that distinction, if not from the carelessness or inexperience of the painter or engraver, has its origin for the most part from difference in sex, or perhaps even of age.[54]

---

54 Heinrich Volgnad and Johannes Jänisch, 'Addenda ad observationem I', *Miscellanea Curiosa* 8 (1677), 188–190 (188).

In this passage, the editors' criticisms ranged widely. They raised suspicions concerning the taxonomic motives and qualifications of the Hamburg collector who supplied Major with the horn. They questioned the identification of this particular horn and of horns throughout European collections. They doubted the utility of horns as a taxonomic indicator in general, given the possibility of variety through age, sex, and the violence incurred through the behavior of head-butting animals. Finally, they further extended their doubt to practices of image production and replication in natural history more generally, due to the carelessness of artists.[55] The image of the horn in Caspar Bauhin's *On the Bezoar stone*, the editors complained, was imitated from Clusius' commentary on Garcia d'Orta very carelessly by the engraver. Meanwhile, when Aldrovandi cited Clusius' account, he offered an image of an animal that had nothing at all in common with Clusius' description. Aldrovandi's image was clearly related to the horns at Gottorf described by Olearius, the editors contended, and both differed from Clusius'.

The greatly varying contorsions of domestic goat horns 'that we have seen curve entirely in a circle', as well as the two bezoardic horns that Dr. Volgnad had among his rarities, and a third which his brother, Philip Volgnad, a Breslau apothecary, possessed, indicated that age could perhaps make a difference. On the other hand, Lodovico Moscardo contrasted four images as those of distinct animals: the horn of a gazelle, very similar to Major's image, the horn of a *Pazam*, not dissimilar to Olearius', the horn of an ibex, and the horn of a rhinoceros.[56]

Given such variety of specimens, and the doubtful previous scholarship on the subject, the editors of the journal left two possibilities open. Maybe the horn was indeed from a bezoardic goat, but entirely different from the normal horn of this animal either as a sport of nature or through some kind of external cause, such as violence inflicted upon it, as one might expect to find in a 'head-butting kind of animal'. Alternatively, which 'seems to us and to the most praiseworthy Major to be more likely, it is that of the gazelle'. They were persuaded of this by the image show by Moscardo, the description from Pierre Belon, and the recent account of a gazelle which had appeared in Oldenburg's *Philosophical Transactions*. The gazelle appeared as a deus ex machina, leaping out of an authoritative journal and offering an entirely new solution.

The editors were wrestling with a truly difficult problem. As Daniel Margòcsy has pointed out, trust in the veracity of description and identification

---

55   Volgnad and Jänisch, 'Addenda', 188–190.
56   Lodovico Moscardo, *Note overo memorie del Museo di Lodovico Moscardo* (Verona, 1672), 241.

'was such an important issue in the study of quadrupeds because other naturalists could not verify the author's account by consulting their own collection, a somewhat less pressing problem in botany, conchology and entomology'.[57] While still large, the horns stood in for circulating the quadruped itself in collections. However, the separation of the horns from the body of the original specimen offered some matter for doubt. Furthermore, the size and curvature of horns certainly varied according to age. In today's terms, we might classify the animal whose horns were illustrated by Major as the scimitar-horned oryx (*Oryx dammah*) of North Africa.[58] The animal we now would call the bezoar goat, the *Capra aegagrus aegagrus* (native to the Middle East) has the backwards-curving horn that was depicted by Clusius and poorly copied by Bauhin. We would call the animal depicted by Aldrovandi and whose horns were in the Gottorf collections a blackbuck antelope, or *Antilope cervicapra* (native to India), with spiral horns and no beard. Bezoars do occur both in *Capra aegagrus aegagrus* as well as in *Antilope cervicapra*.[59] Thus, 'bezoardic' is an unhelpful species categorization as it might truthfully refer to a number of animals. Even defining a goat versus an antelope appears to remain a difficult task today, with the entire bovine family re-organized genetically in 2011 and still under debate.[60]

The editors sought a solution with reference to the seemingly less problematic category of the gazelle. They concluded their discussion by referring to Oldenburg's translation from Claude Perrault's dissections of animals from the royal menagerie at the brand-new Parisian Royal Academy of Sciences. Perrault described a gazelle 'or wild African Shee-goat' who has 'horns black also, streak't cross-ways, 15. inches long, very sharpe, pretty streight, but a little turned outwards about the middle; in part hollow'.[61] Within a few years, however, Perrault himself would come to doubt even the conceptual category of

---

57 Dániel Margócsy, *Commercial Visions: Science, Trade, and Visual Culture in the Dutch Golden Age* (Chicago, 2014), 66.
58 Special thanks to wildlife biologists Edward Davis (UO) and Katherine Brakora (UCSF) for correspondence concerning the possible identification of this animal.
59 W.D. Ian Rolfe, 'Materia medica in the seventeenth-century Paper Museum of Cassiano dal Pozzo', *A History of Geology and Medicine*, eds. C.J. Duffin, R.T.J. Moody and C. Gardner-Thorpe (London, 2013), 137–156.
60 José R. Castelló, *Bovids of the World: Antelopes, Gazelles, Cattle, Goats, Sheep, and Relatives* (Princeton, 2016).
61 Henry Oldenburg, ed. 'Description Anatomique d'un Cameleon, d'un Castor, d'un Dromedaire, d'un Ours, et d'une Gazelle (Paris 1669)', *Philosophical Transactions* 4 (1669), 991—96, (995).

'gazelle' and his ability to extrapolate from the details of this animal's anatomy to the wider category.[62]

4 Collecting Expertise of Hamburg and the Authority of the *Academia*

The editorial criticism of Major's collector friend from Hamburg called into doubt the collecting expertise of an individual upon whom Major relied. David Schellhammer, the friend whom Major thanked so effusively for the horn, regularly supplied Major with curiosities for Major's teaching collection in Kiel. Major lost no opportunity to offer not just him, but his entire family credit.

Schellhammer stemmed from a family of Lutheran pastors who were also collectors.[63] Of the four Schellhammer brothers, Johann, Sigismund, David, and Dietrich, the first three were all pastors noted for their curiosity cabinets in, respectively, the Hague, Bevensen (in the duchy of Braunschweig-Lüneburg), and Hamburg.[64] In print, Major celebrated all three Schellhammer collections in his 1674 catalog of the world's collections, part of a work dedicated to David Schellhammer's in-law, Johann Krahmer, also a collector in Hamburg.[65] Major's catalog of collections informed many other accounts and itineraries. Major's work as a whole was republished (without crediting him) within fellow *Academia* member Michael Bernhard Valentini's 1704 *Museum museorum*, including the catalog of collections.[66] That same year, another *Academia* member, Daniel Wilhelm Moller in a work on collections drawing heavily on Major, included Schellhammer's among the distinguished collections of Hamburg (also noting Major's in Kiel, and the collections of Sachs and of the Volgnad

---

62 Anita Guerrini, *The Courtier's Anatomists: Animals and Humans in Louis XIV's Paris* (Chicago, 2015), 136–155.
63 On Schellhammer, Moller, *Cimbria Literata*, 590–591. Christian Petersen, *Geschichte der Hamburgischen Stadtbibliothek* (Hamburg, 1838), 49–52. A. Wetzel, 'Drei Briefe des Hamburger Bibliothekars David Schellhammer', *Mitteilungen des Vereins für Hamburgische Geschichte*, 13–15 (1893), 278–283.
64 Ole Borch, for example, visited Johann's collection in the Hague in 1663. H.D. Schepelern, ed. *Olai Borrichii itinerarium 1660–1665* (Brill, 1983), 296.
65 Major, 'Catalogus', sig. D4^v.
66 Michael Bernhard Valentini, *Museum Museorum, oder vollständige Schau-Bühne aller Materialien und Specereyen, nebst deren natürlichen Beschreibung... Aus andern Material- Kunst- und Naturalien-Kammern, Oost- und West-Indischen Reiss-Beschreibungen* (Frankfurt, 1704), 19–21.

brothers in Breslau, among others).[67] The Hamburg merchant Kaspar Friedrich Jenquel, in his 1727 *Museographia* (with notes by *Academia* member Johann Kanold), drew a list of former collections almost entirely from Major's 1674 account, including the Schellhammer collections.[68] Long after the Schellhammer brothers' deaths, therefore, their collections haunted catalogs and itineraries, a palimpsest remaining from Major's celebration of them in print.

Major also celebrated another Schellhammer collection of which only ghostly traces remain. The three brothers were collaboratively writing a now lost two-volume manuscript on collecting. Major attempted to rope their manuscript into his own project on reforming collecting practices. In a battery of frequent letters in the fall of 1676, Major begged an unwilling Schellhammer for a look at the brothers' collaborative work. On 23 September 1676, for instance, he asked for a large Armadillo as well as just the chapter titles of the Schellhammers' work for use in his own museological work.[69] This was the same month that Major sent his group of observations, including on the horn of the bezoardic goat, to Volgnad and Jänisch.

On 21 October 1676, Major again wrote to Schellhammer, suggesting that David's brother in the duchy of Braunschweig-Lüneburg might encourage the Duke there to support his museological project.[70] He had grand plans for its continuation. As he pointed out in another letter, of 31 October 1676, he had made a start two years ago, in the series of pamphlets he had published then, in establishing a heretofore untouched independent science ('Wissenschaft') called 'Tactica Conclavium'. Nobody could be as much help to him in its continuation as the three Schellhammer collectors, whom he calls the 'German Plinys'. He praised their amateur and middling status as collectors, commending them for beginning to collect, not to showcase their pride or money, but only for their own pleasure and the honor of God. He admired how they utilized the opportunities of so many merchant ships returning out of the East and West Indies as well as their widespread correspondence, so that they ended up with such complete chambers of naturalia and choice treasures of nature, that they won positions serving lords and princes. Seeing the constant success and careful reports of the Schellhammers, he claimed, he would rather

---

67   Daniel Wilhelm Moller, *Dissertatio de Technophysiotameis, von Kunst-und Naturalien-Kammern* (Altdorf, 1704), 43–44.

68   Kaspar Friedrich Jenquel, *Museographia* (Leipzig, 1727), 187 and 198; for Major's in Kiel, 201. On Jenquel, see Anja Silvia Goeing, 'Mapping Curiosity: Kaspar Friedrich Jenquel's Recommendations for visits of Cabinets in Europe', https://curiositas.org/mapping-curiosity-kaspar-friedrich-jencquels-recommendations-for-visits-of-cabinets-in-europe-1727 [November 17, 2014].

69   Staats-und Universitätsbibliothek Hamburg, Sup. ep. (95, 30) d.

70   Staats-und Universitätsbibliothek Hamburg, Sup. ep. (95, 31) d.

have a small section of their manuscript than whole pages compiled by hacks that were available in the bookshops.[71]

If Major wished to further enhance David Schellhammer's reputation by mentioning his name in his observation on the bezoardic goat horn, he must have failed. The journal's editorial appendix, insinuating that Schellhammer was at fault for a misidentification to which Major would never fall prey, clearly distinguished between learned colleagues such as Major and collectors such as Schellhammer who endeavoured to endow their objects with greater value by bestowing prestigious titles upon them. Schellhammer expressed his concerns to Major about the incident and a lengthy response in a letter of 6 July 1678 from Major survives.

Major offered ten reasons why he was not bothered at all by what the editors added without any offense ('wolmeinendlich citra ullius offensione addiderunt'): (1) The note ('annotatio') was very polite, without insulting anyone. (2) Everyone is free to dissent from one another concerning worldly affairs. (3) When they disagreed with Major as soon as they received his observation, and they compared the very accurate image sent by Major with authors as well as with their own examples drawn from originals, Major himself began to doubt whether it really was a bezoardic horn. Since there wasn't enough time to examine the matter more thoroughly and revise his views before publication, via correspondence Major had permitted the editors to add their own opinion. (4) Isn't it enough that it should be considered the horn of a gazelle? Truly, that is just as rare in our land as the bezoardic horn. (5) It is possible that these things are depicted variously on account of sex, age, variety, size, etc., and there may yet be some considered to be the horn of the gazelle, which might still be identified within the genus of bezoardic horns, but this is merely a conjecture and is not at all certain. (6) Schellhammer confessed himself amazed that the editors did not look at the original horn themselves before passing judgment upon it. Major countered that it would not be practical to travel with it to Breslau, and the image corresponded sufficiently with the original. Moreover, everyone is aware that one cannot rely equally well on all figures in books. There are still some things in the world that can be copied without too much effort, and there are also hands in the world that, using a poor drawing, can represent it well enough so that a reader of a book in which the image appears does not need to consult the original. By the by, Major said, he planned shortly to edit a short discourse on errors in natural philosophy due to images drawn from Thomas Browne's *Vulgar errors*. Often, these errors were not the fault of the image makers, since they frequently had to make images without any sketches

---

71   Staats-und Universitätsbibliothek Hamburg, Sup. ep. (95, 34) d.

or originals at all, and except for regular geometric bodies, it is impossible exactly to produce an image purely out of verbal description. Often authors portentously described a thing that did not exist in order to amaze readers. This kind of error is truly not at all rare, among which the vegetable Tartarian sheep, which is painted far too neatly as a sheep, the crown of serpents, the wings of flying dragons, and more than a hundred images out of the *Cosmographia* of Muster and the *History of the Northern Peoples* by Olaus Magnus could be counted. Returning to the matter of the comments on the bezoardic horn, (6) The editors showed themselves willing to consider Major's specimen under the title of bezoardic horn, in that they compared it to the three preserved by the Volgnads in Breslau as 'bezoardic horns'.

For his seventh point, Major, always handy with his scissors, cut out a section from Schelhammer's original letter to him and pasted it into his response with red sealing wax (as he also did in other letters to Schellhammer). Schellhammer claimed that a 'Mr. Longon' from Harburg had seen the object and considered it to be an actual horn of a bezoar goat. This was no doubt the 'Bartold de Longon' of Harburg whom Major listed in his global catalog of notable collections.[72] Major professed to be confused by this claim, since to his knowledge that gentleman had never visited him.

Continuing on to his eighth point, Major wrote that if you compare our horn with that very different one with the same name described by Olearius, we shouldn't presume that the former possessor, Bernhard Paludanus, that adept ('*mysta*') and keenest of judges, should have given a wrong name to the exemplar, which is still in Gottorf. (9) If Schellhammer read what Moscardo had to say about the horn of the gazelle, including its image and its description taken out of Belon and the Calceolarian Museum, he would swiftly change his mind. Or maybe one could say that in its own way the gazelle belongs to the genus of bezoar goats. That would be an easy way to for Major to quit the dispute, with both of them being right. (10) In the meantime, the editors had called even the English journal of Oldenburg as a witness. Major could write no more, but he hoped that considering these things, Schellhammer would see that he (Major) incessantly ('etiam atque etiam') testified to Schellhammer's honesty and worth ('candorem'), signing his letter reassuringly as, 'the one most addicted to you, with all honesty and attentive service, as long as I live'.[73]

Major's stance accords well with the attitudes repeatedly expressed by the editors of the *Miscellanea curiosa*. Given that the skepticism regarding the

---

72 Major, *Unvorgreiffliches Bedencken*, sig. D5^r.
73 Johann D. Major to David Schellhammer, Staats- und Universitätsbibliothek Hamburg, Sup. ep. (95, 37) d.

bezoardic horn came from within his own institution and gave him the benefit of the doubt, Major was able to strike the pose of the professional scholar who could take such critical review in stride and question his own assumptions. He viewed the inherited body of natural historical wisdom, including the existence of such doubtful objects as the Tartarian sheep or the crown of serpents, with a skeptical eye. The journal existed in order to collect and question precisely that material.

5   Schellhammer's Farrago

The intersection of a vibrant culture of collecting in Hamburg with new literary technologies made the region of a hotbed of techniques for sifting through the corpus of inherited books and objects and for interfacing between them. Major's colleague at Kiel, Daniel Georg Morhof, well known for inaugurating a new era of critical bibliography in his *Polyhistor*, paid particularly close attention to the literary technologies of natural history. As student notes indicate, Morhof was lecturing on the art of excerpting and criticizing authors from 1672 and on natural history from at least 1676. These lecture notes made their way into his famous *Polyhistor* little changed, including a critique of current collecting practices.[74]

In the *Polyhistor*, Morhof praised the account of collections across Europe that Major had included within a little 1670 utopian work, *Journey to a New World without a Ship or a Sail*. He noted that Major was still at work on the topic. However, Morhof desiderated something more, that is, a single study of museums gathered out of all the already published descriptions of museums, noting their differences and various advantages. It would be best if such a work were to observe an 'exquisite order', if for example, it discussed those species conserved in museums according to their various classes in the mineral

---

[74]   Copenhagen. Danish Royal Library. Fabr. 135. kvart. D.G. Morhof, *Polyhistor sive de eligendis cumque fructu legendis auctoribus commentatio lectionis privatis anno 1672*. For the context of the University of Kiel and local library collections, see Paul Nelles, 'Historia Litteraria and Morhof: Private Teaching and Professorial Libraries at the University of Kiel', *Mapping the World of Learning: The Polyhistor of Daniel Georg Morhof*. ed. Françoise Waquet (Wiesbaden, 2000), 31–56. Nelles writes, 46, 'Moller refered to Morhof's private teaching as an "academy" and, if we are to believe Morhof, the *Polyhistor* was first printed in order to head off rogue publication of the work from student notes'. Comparing Morhof's *Polyhistor* to the student notes of private *collegia* extant in Copenhagen shows that Morhof's claim was likely true; doing so also raises the profile of natural history in the genesis of Morhof's *Polyhistor*.

kingdom. This would be of great use but would certainly not be the work of one man.[75]

Surely, Morhof was aware that this was precisely what his colleague Major intended to accomplish in his new discipline of the *Tactica conclavium*. To Morhof's desire for a complete study of museums, his editor, the former Kiel student Johannes Moller (1661–1725), added a note drawing attention to Major's 1674 works on the topic as well as to the manuscript on collecting natural history by David Schellhammer highly praised by Major. According to Moller, Major anonymously published a 1679 Latin pamphlet on collections, entitled *A Library without books (Bibliotheca sine libris)*, now lost. At the same time, he published a German poetic version of the pamphlet in folio entitled *A Great Treasure, brought together out of Most parts of the World, or a Poetic Interim-Discourse on Chambers of Art and Nature (Grosses Reichthum, zusammengebracht aus den meisten Schätzen der Welt: oder Interims Discurs von Kunst- und Naturalien Kammern)*, which he dedicated to Schellhammer. This publication took the awkward form of a heavily footnoted poem. The first footnote, referred to Major's previous four folio pamphlets on collecting. It announced that, should further warfare not intervene, Major planned on publishing at least twelve more issues. Major conceptualized this poem as a place-holder meant to show that he planned to continue, although he never did.

In his dedication of the poem, Major thanked Schellhammer for enriching his collections with more than a hundred objects, among which he noted 'a strange and valuable horn, considered to be the horn of a bezoar-animal brought from the Indies'.[76] Major explicitly characterized his dedication of the poem to Schelhammer as payment for these gifts, as a sort of 'poetic bill of exchange' imitating the style of merchants.[77] In a letter dated 20 January 1679 to Schellhammer, Major reiterated that he was pleased to find a way to show his thanks to Schellhammer by dedicating his little poem to him, due his owed gratitude ('ex gratitudine debita').[78]

Apparently, Schellhammer had finally relented and allowed Major to peruse the brothers' manuscript. In his dedication, Major also praised Schellhammer's manuscript extensively, listing a few of its subjects and describing the work as having the potential (should its author complete it) to serve as a 'general

---

75 Morhof, *Polyhistor literarius*, 133–134.
76 This is extant as a unique, partial exemplar in the Leibniz Bibliothek, Hannover, G-A 8053. *Grosses Reichthum*, sig. A2ʳ.
77 Ibid.
78 Major to Schellhammer, 20 Jan. 1679, Staats- und Universitätsbibliothek Hamburg, Sup. ep. (95, 40) d.

inventory of the rarest things of nature'.[79] If he returned to life, Pliny would envy it, and a whole chorus of authorities (Democritus, Theophrastus, Galen, Solomon, Cardanus, Albertus Magnus, Olaus Magnus, Agricola, Gesner, Aldrovandi, Bauhin, Oviedo, Jonston, Welsch, Cesi, Bacon, Scaliger, Marggraf, Piso, Olearius, Monconnys, Peiresc, Septala, Moscardo, Bellon, Bontius, da Orta, Clusius, Calceolari, Imperato, Hernández, Kircher and Worm) would heartily approve of it.

According to Moller, Major's praised proved to be pure hyperbole. The manuscript was not at all what Morhof desiderated, that is, a physico-historical work on the rarities of nature, gathered together out of various museum descriptions and travel narratives. Schellhammer's friend, Rudolf Capell, professor of rhetoric at the Hamburg gymnasium, also recommended Schellhammer's two-volume quarto manuscript, Moller noted.[80] Moller had seen it, however, he added, and he found it very lacking.[81]

In his *Cimbria Literata*, a study of the scholarship of the region, Moller criticized Schellhammer's manuscript further. There he described Major's hyperbolic praise for the manuscript in greater detail. According to Major, the Schellhammer manuscript was collected out of ancient and modern authors in diverse languages, as well as from Schellhammer's own careful, daily *experientia*. Yet, Moller suggested, Major praised Schellhammer excessively in gratitude for the objects Schellhammer and given to his own collection. Moller had read the manuscript himself, invited by the author, and found it to be, 'just a farrago of stories about exotic *naturalia*, drawn from various authors (many of whose names the author himself admitted that he neglected to add out of a certain carelessness [*incuria*]), rude and indigested, and not at all satisfying the desideratum of Georg Hieronymus Welsch ... for a model physical-medical collection (*Idea Pinacothecae Physico-Medicae*)'.[82] Moller refered to the *desiderata* list for medicine published by the esteemed *Academia* member Georg Hieronymus Welsch in 1676. Welsch's list, illustrative of inventive new literary technologies for collective research, became a touchstone among *Academia* members seeking to yoke their collections of singular observations to larger

---

79   Johann D. Major, *Grosser Reichthum, zusammen gebracht aus dem meisten Theilen der Welt* (Kiel, 1679), sig. A2^r.
80   Rudolf Capell, *Nummophylacium Luederianum* (Hamburg, 1679), sig. Mm^r.
81   Morhof, *Polyhistor*, 133–134.
82   Moller, *Cimbria literata* I, 590–591.

collaborative goals.[83] Major too advertised that he was aware of Welsch's planned '*Pinacotheca Universalis*' and had corresponded with Welsch about it.[84]

In contrast to the members of the *Academia Naturae Curiosorum* such as Welsch, with their rapidly proliferating scholarly apparatus, Schellhammer exhibited '*incuria*' in his lack of citation. He did not participate in the forms of diligent curiosity, involving careful inspection and pain-staking labor, upon which those 'curious about nature' prided themselves.[85] Schellhammer's manuscript is now lost, but a surviving excerpt on locusts, copied by the Gotha court savant Hiob Ludolf in his *Ethiopian History*, justifies Moller's criticism.

> In America, locusts are eaten and taste like crabs. In *Terra firma* they have great barrels full, dried and salted. According to someone else: in the Arabian desert they are cooked and ground. And another: In Guinea the locusts fly in thick swarms, like a thick cloud, and darken the sky. And they are killed and dried by the sun and eaten by them. They supposedly taste good, having flesh white like a crayfish, etc.[86]

One can easily see why Moller found this so disappointing. The manuscript appears to have been precisely the kind of commonplace compilation that the *Academia*'s strictures regarding careful citation to particular authors sought to avoid. Without any references to particular sources, any discussion of the possible categorical confusion between grasshoppers, locusts and cicadas (à la Thomas Browne's discussion of this subject in the *Pseudodoxia*), and with very vague allusions to geographic locations, Schellhammer offered little indication concerning what might be doubtful in these accounts and how one would go about further researching them. It was hopelessly out of date.

Compare, for example, the standards for commonplacing of David Schellhammer's first cousin once removed, Günther Christoph Schelhammer (1649–1716). G.C. Schelhammer moved in a very different stratum of collecting, whether of text or of objects. His father had taught in Jena, and he himself was

---

83　Georg H. Welsch, *Somnium vindiciani sive Desiderata medicinae* (Augsburg, 1676). See, for instance, Johann Conrad Peyer's 'Ceratographia desiderata Merycologiae sciagraphiae, Rupicaprarum cornua perennia', *Miscellanea curiosa*, 11 (1682), 207–211, which points out that Welsch desiderated a systematic study of the form and use of horns and which also doubted Welsch's account of chamois' seasonal loss of horns.

84　Major, *Unvorgreiffliches Bedencken*, sig. B2ʳ. The *Pinacotheca* only reached the stage of manuscript notes. Augsburg, SuStB 8° Cod. Aug. 26 and 27.

85　Kenny, *The Uses of Curiosity*, 188.

86　Hiob Ludolf, *Historia Aethiopica* (Frankfurt, 1681), 30.

elected to the *Academia* in 1679 and would succeed Major as professor of medicine at Kiel. He had his own curiosity cabinet, which his close friend, Leibniz (who also saw Major's collections in Kiel) visited.[87] G.C. Schelhammer published an edition of his father-in-law Herman Conring's *Introduction to the Art of Medicine*, to which he appended a guide to medical literature by Johann Rhode (1587–1659), the Danish professor of medicine at Padua and a mentor of Sachs von Lewenheimb there.[88] The text by Rhode that G.C. Schelhammer edited included a commonplacing technique recommending ten categories. Category 7, 'Electa', corresponds perhaps best to 'strange facts'. Many others, however, are aimed at identifying error, doubts, differing opinions and points of contradiction (such as 'Critica'; 'Vindiciae'; 'Variae Lectiones'; 'Dubia & contradictiones', etc). Only a single category, *axiomata medica*, collected knowledge deemed utterly certain.[89] Rhode's classificatory system illustrates how contemporaries constantly tweaked commonplacing practices in a search for methods of managing dubious material. G.C. Schelhammer, however, declared himself unsatisfied with any commonplacing technique identified as yet, including Rhode's.[90]

Perhaps in part because his natural historical commonplace collection never became public, Schellhammer's reputation as a collector survived the editorial doubting of the *Academia* intact. In 1679, Schellhammer parlayed his reputation as a collector into the coveted position of librarian of the eminent Hamburg city library.[91] Rudolf Capell praised the Hamburg city library, noting its collections of 'rarities of antiquity, of nature, and art, both domestic and exotic', and commending its keeper, Schellhammer.[92] Capell made a donation to the library in 1681, as had many scholars from the Hamburg Gymnasium

---

[87] Horst Bredekamp, *Die Fenster der Monade: Gottfried Wilhelm Leibniz' Theater der Natur und Kunst* (Berlin, 2004), 31–33.

[88] Günther C. Schelhammer, ed. *Hermanni Conringii in universam artem medicam singulasque ejus partes introductio... accesserunt Johannis Rhodii aliorumque in arte principum virorum consimilis argumenti commentationes* (Speyer, 1688). Major, *Memoria Sachsiana*, 20.

[89] Schelhammer, ed., *in universam artem medicam*, 133–134.

[90] Ibid, 152.

[91] Schellhammer describes in a 1679 letter to Major the many political machinations he faced in vying for the position. Kiel, Cod. Ms SH406, F, published in Wetzel, 'Drei Briefe', 280–281. His brother Dieterich Schellhammer was a member of the city council. Werner Kayser, Hellmut Braun and Erich Zimmermann, eds. *500 Jahre wissenschaftliche Bibliothek Hamburg 1479–1979. Von der Ratsbücherei zur Staats-und Universitätsbibliothek* (Hamburg, 1979).

[92] Rudolf Capell, *Lectionum Bibliothecariarum Memorabilium Syntagma* (Hamburg, 1682), sig.)(vii^v)-)(viii^r.

before him, such as Johann Adolph Tassius, Joachim Jungius, and Vincent Placcius.[93] In addition to books and manuscripts, the library held a collection of surgical instruments, anatomical preparations and works of art and nature, based on the original donation of city physician Paul Marquard Schlegel. Schellhammer characterized its several thousand natural rarities as 'of so great a number that one would hardly find as many in Holland'.[94] Schellhammer's own collection of mineral specimens would be added to the collection in 1693. The library's collection of *naturalia* would form the basis of the Hamburg Natural History Museum founded in 1843.[95]

6   Comparing and Cataloging in Early Modern Collections: Major's Philosophical Book-keeping

The culture of collecting textual commonplaces and objects, the library and the museum, were never too distant in this period, and they were particularly intertwined in the Hamburg city library, as Flemming Schock has pointed out.[96] Morhof argued that museums offered natural history, as it were, 'the common places of nature', if they were well organized and distinguished according to categories; the published books pertaining to collections, such as the *Museum Calceolarianum* or the *Museum Wormianum*, served as the indices to these common places.[97] Major proposed that collections be ever more densely networked to an array of publications in a practice he would term 'philosophical book-keeping'.[98] The ways he sought to categorize objects in a collection and link them to ongoing scholarship differs greatly from Schellhammer's commonplacing technique, especially in the ways it highlighted doubt. Developing a tool-kit for handling doubt and responding to recent discoveries distinguished

---

93   Johann A.R. Janssen, *Ausführliche Nachrichten über die sämmtlichen evagelisch-protestanischen Kirchen... sowie über deren Johanneum, Gymnasium, Bibliothek und die dabey angestellten Männer* (Hamburg, 1826), 38.
94   Petersen, *Geschichte*, 50. The Schellhammer family had long been supporters of the library. David's brothers, Sigismund, Dietrich and Johann, and cousin Günther Christoph all made donations to the library in 1649, 1660, 1681, and 1684, respectively. Petersen, *Geschichte*, 37–38.
95   Michael Bergeest, *Bildung zwischen Commerz und Emanzipation: Erwachsenenbildung in der Hamburger Region des 18. und 19. Jahrhunderts* (Münster, 1995), 168–169.
96   Flemming Schock, *Die Text-Kunstkammer. Populäre Wissenssammlungen des Barock am Beispiel der 'Relationes Curiosae' von E.W. Happel* (Köln, 2011), 199.
97   Morhof, *Polyhistor*, 133.
98   Major, *Museum Cimbricum*, 25.

the professional curator in Major's museology just as it was coming to signify the professional scholar in the *Academia*'s new journal.

The collection catalog offered the curator his professional tools, for it provided the interface between the objects and the world of on-going learned publication about them. Each object, including works of art, should be cataloged according to the 'purely natural bodies' out of which they were made, 'reduced to their physical order, as so many objects of a well-founded, curious technico-mathematic experimental-physics'.[99] In other words, the collections' objects became experimental subjects, and needed to be cataloged 'according to the Spirit of today's Experimental Century'.[100] The catalog could also refer to live specimens found in other parts of the property in gardens and menageries, as well as to paper collections, such as the rarities of the world 'in life size and color, or, where the body is too large, according to the right proportion in a large Folio'. Such a paper museum 'should include not only what everything is called, and where it is found, but also its inner qualities and the chiefest trustworthy experiments that have ever been made on it in this century in Germany, Italy, France, Denmark, Holland and in England'.

Major announced in 1674 that his *magnum opus* would be entitled the *Leopoldine Theatre of Nature, or the Eminent Natural Philosophy to be accommodated especially for this Experimental Century*, a work he never finished.[101] He continually kept David Schellhammer updated on it. In a letter of 2 March 1680, he reported slow progress, having collected a 'sciagraphia' or outline of the main sections of the great work.[102] In 1688, G.C. Schellhammer praised Major and the idea of the *Leopoldine Theatre of Nature*, which would serve 'as an index to all collections', but he noted that it was still not completed.[103]

That year, Major further developed the categories of his catalogs in a short work advertising the opening of his own new public collection, the *Museum Cimbricum*. All things that can be collected, he wrote, can be divided either into 'true, essential things deriving from God and nature, or false, imposed, and simply supposed out of idolatry or poetic liberty'. The latter he later gave the name '*non-entibus physicis*'.[104] Yet, between the category of the extant and the

---

99 Major, *Unvorgreiffliches Bedencken*, sig. C4^v.
100 Ibid., sig. D2^r.
101 Major, *Unvorgreiffliches Bedencken*, sig. A2^r. In a dedication to August Friedrich of Holstein-Gottorf, Major identified his edition of Fabio Colonna's study of the *purpura* as preliminary to this work. J.D. Major, ed. *Fabii Columnae... de purpura* (Kiel, 1675), sig. *3^r.
102 Staats-und Universitätsbibliothek Hamburg, Sup. ep. (95, 43) d.
103 Schelhammer, ed., *in universam artem medicam*, 294.
104 Major, *Museum Cimbricum*, 37, also refers to the 'Non-Entia, oder Rerum Fictarum Simulacra'.

fictional, lay that of the doubtful. The catalog of *naturalia* was to include a category of 'Incerta, Dubia, aut penitus Ignota'. for example, to a red stone that cannot be determined to be a work of art or of nature, or to 2 or 3 white round pieces, that could be petrified things, exotic fruits, incomplete formations of strange shells and mother of pearl, or something else.[105]

While idealized and prescriptive accounts of collections ignored the doubtful, that category must have been as prominent in contemporary collections as Anonymous was in libraries.[106] In collection inventories, we find many unidentified objects. For example, Paludanus' head of the bezoar goat, cataloged by Olearius in Gottorf, can also be found in the 1710 and 1743 inventories of the Gottorf collections. In 1710, it was inventoried next to several other identified animals as well as 'twelve horns from unknown animals'. The function of such inventories was as an entirely practical enumeration of resources. It was thus desirable that everything be identified; categorizing an object as unknown was a last resort. Little doubt was cast upon items to which an identity had already been assigned. Thus, although in the seventeenth century doubts were already raised concerning the Gottorf horns as being those of a 'bezoar goat', since blackbuck antelopes are not goats, the horns were still cataloged as those of a 'bezoar goat' in 1743, with a reference back to Olearius' catalogue.[107]

By showcasing the doubtful, Major brought it into the orbit of learned research, making it an active category to be applied to the collection in a sifting process networking the objects in a collection to ongoing scholarship. The term Major used was *conferre* (to compare). *Conferre* might refer to an accumulatory practice of 'bringing together' or collecting, or to a more antagonistic sifting that pitted one piece of evidence against another, so that one might triumph and exclude the other. Comparison, of course, was not at all a new scholarly technique, since comparing variant readings to arrive at an authoritative text is the foundational practice of philology, and scholars had long been exporting this practice to other realms.[108] Major continued to bring critical comparison to new arenas, for instance, in his surveys of global practices of collecting and display. He also described in 1670 how, in a medical course

---

105   Major, *Museum Cimbricum*, 32.
106   eg. Georg Seger, *Synopsis methodica rariorum tam naturalium quam artificialium quae Hafniae servantur* (Copenhagen, 1653).
107   Mogens Bencard, Jørgen Hein, Bente Gundestrup and Jan Drees, *Die Gottorfer Kunstkammer* (Schleswig, 1997), 234. 'ein Horn von einem Bezoar Kopff... Zwölff stück Hörner von unbekandten Thieren'. p. 359. 'Die 2 Hörner von einem Bezoar-Bock... . Tab. 9. No. 7. pag. 13'.
108   eg. Constance Smith, 'Jean Bodin and Comparative Law', *Journal of the History of Ideas* 25 (1964), 417–422.

taught from museum objects in his own collection, students would not only have the opportunity to subject objects to a wide range of experiments, but also to compare them with printed descriptions and images.[109] His response to Schelhammer showed himself and the journal's editors arriving at doubts about the identity of the horn by comparing a wide range of objects, drawings, and texts. He also noted there his plans to compose a future work on the errors of natural philosophy following a large-scale comparison of images, texts, and objects. By extending comparison to collecting practices, Major sharpened the differences between *conferre* as a form of additive collecting, as in a physical collection where doubtful objects were allowed to remain or as in a commonplace collection where contradictions co-existed, and *conferre* as a practice training laser-like attention upon doubtful objects as a way means of rendering them ever more certain.

Major made identifying doubt the hallmark of his experimental practice. He even elicited doubts about his own scholarship. Immediately following his observation on the bezoardic goat in the 1677 issue of the *Miscellanea Curiosa*, Major published an observation on the anatomy of a dolphin, which he described as a corrective to what he had published before on the topic in the 1673 issue of the journal.[110] In a work on his claimed invention of blood infusion (about which he was engaging with the Royal Society in a priority dispute), Major published correspondence from across Europe that he had invited to raise doubts about his invention, alongside a catalog of the doubts, and a point-by-point response.[111] As he explained in a letter to his colleagues at Jena, requesting their doubts, he was asking for them 'not so that I might seek out material for contention, according to the cursed manner of the present century, but rather so that I might try to proceed cautiously, ... and that I might attempt slowly to bring into credit an invention believed by some to be impossible'.[112]

Major also raised doubts about the contents of his collection. His 1688 vernacular guide to his newly opened public museum included a list of his natural objects, where we meet again 'a black Horn, like a musical cornetto, of a Bezoar-animal (or more likely, in a related way, from an Indian Gazelle, or billygoat)'.[113] In thus highlighting the doubt raised by his journal editors, Major

---

109   J.D. Major, *Collegium medico-curiosum* (1670), unpaginated. '... cum Autoribus in super, qui Exotica, selectioraque alía scripserunt, ac nitidissimas addunt Imagines, conferent'.
110   Major, 'De respiratione', 2–3.
111   Major, *Chirurgia infusoria*.
112   Staats-und Universitätsbibliothek Hamburg, Sup. ep. 44, 115, fol. 111r.
113   Major, *Museum Cimbricum*, 9.

differentiated himself from the unphilosophical collector. His collections participated in new forms of scholarly critique supported by the journal.

7   Conclusion: Culture of Facts and Culture of Citation

Martin Mulsow has characterized Hamburg as participating in a 'culture of fact', and in particular, of those facts Lorraine Daston has called 'strange'.[114] Strange facts were singular phenomena deployed to challenge prior systems in early modernity. Thus, while individual strange facts were used in order to cast entire systems into doubt, strange facts themselves were not often questioned, particularly when reported as the observation of a named individual. Yet, in the late seventeenth century, Hamburg was also developing a new culture of citation.

The culture of facts efficiently assimilated many accounts under conveniently shared rubrics, such as 'locust' or 'bezoar goat'. In that culture, *conferre* was compilatory. In contrast, the culture of citation developed by scholars of Major's generation brought particular views together in a more agonistic, critical forum. It included apparatus for questioning its own categories and for assigning dubious claims to particular authors. In a culture of citation, name-dropping served to identify a provisional opinion with an author in order to engage that author in a debate, rather than to offer that author tribute in an exchange of material for credit (as Major himself was suspected of doing in the case of his praise for Schellhammer).

The differences between a culture of fact and a culture of citation can be seen through a comparison of two collections of curiosities: the *Academia*'s journal, the *Miscellanea curiosa*, and the 'half-learned' journal, the *Grössester Denkwürdigkeiten der Welt oder so genandte Relationes curiosae* (1682–1691) of Eberhard Werner Happel (1647–1690).[115] While Happel in fact attuned his journal to a public that could not read Latin, he claimed that it was aimed at the

---

[114]   Martin Mulsow, 'Entwicklung einer Tatsachenkultur: Die Hamburger Gelehrten und ihre Praktiken 1650–1750', *Hamburg: Eine Metropolregion zwischen Früher Neuzeit und Aufklärung*, eds. J.A. Steiger and S. Richter (Berlin, 2012), 45–64.

[115]   Karin Unsicker, *Weltliche Barockprosa in Schleswig-Holstein* (Neumünster, 1974), 150–156 and Thomas Habel, 'Wilhelm Ernst Tentzel as Precursor of Learned Journalism in Germany: *Monatliche Unterredungen* and *Curieuse Bibliothec*', in *Scholars in Action: The Practice of Knowledge and the Figure of the Savant in the 18th Century*, André Holenstein, Hubert Steinke, and Martin Stuber, eds., I (Leiden, 2013), 289–318.

learned.[116] He even issued an open call to scholars to send him material for publication. Only Major, his former professor, briefly responded.[117] Other scholars largely ignored him. Happel instead preyed upon their work, scanning new learned journals for the curious, the sensational, the controversial and the exotic. He mined the *Miscellanea curiosa* for strange facts, shorn of their critical apparatus and skeptical framework. Scholars proved snide about the result, even while using him as a shortcut; Jena professor Georg Wolfgang Wedel wrote in a 1686 letter to fellow *Academia* member, Günther Christoph Schellhammer, 'I haven't yet seen the Hamburg *Ephemerides* except for those patchworks of Happel in the vernacular'.[118]

Sometimes Happel credited the *Miscellanea curiosa*. For instance, in his very first issue, he cited the journal for the article, 'The unusual radish', published by Wedel, and Volgnad's observation on a 'naturally figured tree', one of a collection of observations by Volgnad on nature at play.[119] Happel also noted how Johann Daniel Major wrote 'to a good friend' that when cutting open a lemon, he found inside another small lemon, just as if the fruit had been found in an animal'.[120] Major had published an observation on this 'pregant' lemon in the *Miscellanea curiosa*, to which Heinrich Volgnad appended a *scholion* that Happel did not include.[121] In this case, rather than Happel preying upon the *Miscellanea curiosa*, it is possible that Happel received Major's report through

---

116 Thomas Habel, 'Wilhelm Ernst Tentzel as Precursor of Learned Journalism in Germany: *Monatliche Underredungen* and *Curieuse Bibliothec*', *Scholars in Action: The Practice of Knowledge and the Figure of the Savant in the 18th Century*, A. Holenstein, H. Steinke, and M. Stuber, eds. (Leiden, 2013), 292.

117 Flemming Schock, 'Enzyklopädie, Kalendar, Wochenblatt. Wissenspopularisierung und Medienwandel im 17. Jahrhundert', *Wissenschaftsgeschichte und Geschichte des Wissens im Dialog: Connecting Science and Knowledge*, eds K. Greyers, S. Flubacher and P. Senn (Göttingen, 2013), 155–185, (180). This was a two-way street. Even academics such as Major sometimes drew on such compiled shortcuts, with varying degrees of compunction. Major draws on a similar author, Erasmus Francisci, *passim* in *Vorstellung etlicher Kunst- und Naturalien-Kammern/ in America und Asia*. In his observation the crowns of serpents, Johann L. Hannemann drew both on Francisci and on Happel, whom he called an excellent polyhistor. Hannemann, 'De corona serpentum', 130.

118 Christian S. Scheffel, ed. *Guntherum Christophorum Schelhammerum epistolae selectiores* (Wismar, 1727), 157.

119 E.W. Happel, *Grössester Denkwürdigkeiten der Welt oder so genandte Relationes curiosae* (Hamburg, 1682–1691), 339. '"Der natürlich-gebildete Baum" Doctor Volgnad, Collector Ephemer. germ. Curios. führt ad Ann. 6 & 7. Observ. 239 pag. 349'. Heinrich Volgnad, 'Rariora quaedam naturae sive luxuriantis sive ludentis exempla', *Miscellanea curiosa*, 6 and 7 (1675 and 1676), 345–353.

120 Happel, *Grössester Denkwürdigkeiten der Welt*, 488.

121 Johann D. Major, Observatio CCXLI, 'De citro in Citro', *Miscellanea Curiosa* (1672), 371. Volgnad included a scholion, 371–372. Happel later cited Major's observations on palingenesis. Happel, *Relationes Curiosae*, 32.

another source-their mutual friend, David Schellhammer. In the second issue of the *Relationes curiosae*, Happel described the collections of 'Exotica and beautiful Orginalia from all the parts of the world' that his 'good friend' Schellhammer oversaw in the Hamburg library, where he devoted great efforts to making 'all sorts of rarities' available. Both the book and rarity collections were open to any *'Liebhaber'* (amateur) four hours a day.[122]

Happel's journal has been called a virtual, or textual *Kunstkammer* since Happel mined both actual collections and textual collections.[123] He utilized longstanding practices of commonplacing and re-use common to his era, yet in his uncritical compilation of wonders, Happel's journal could not stand up to the evolving scholarly standards of the time. Nevertheless, Happel's essay, 'The wonderful *Kunst-Kammer*' in the 1687 *Relationes curiosae* has been seen as emblematic of Baroque collecting practices in general, including those of Major in particular.[124] Scholars today often do not distinguish between the culture of strange facts, exemplified by Schellhammer and further developed by Happel, and the newly professionalized techniques for citing references and doubting authority being developed in the same region.[125]

The ability to name names and raise doubts about them distinguished the avant-garde collector belonging to 'the present Experimental century', to use Major's frequent phrase. Major's attempts to praise Schellhammer's works and gifts in his publications only served to highlight the differences between Schellhammer's culture of fact and the newly professionalized culture of citation. Schellhammer saw the doubt attached to his name as a betrayal of the gift he had given Major; Major argued that such editorializing was a part of publishing provisional knowledge. In his observation on the bezoar goat, Major not only received doubts phlegmatically, but raised several himself, such as whether species, sex, or age were responsible for the differences in horns, whether Schellhammer's chymical friend was honest about his motivations for wishing to acquire the horn, and whether bezoars were really efficacious. For professionals and academics like Major, establishing standards for giving and receiving doubt was crucial to the disciplinary formation of experimental studies.

---

122 Eberhard W. Happel, 'Die Holsteinischen Bibliotheken', *Relationes curiosae* (1685), 332.
123 Schock, *Die Text-Kunstkammer*.
124 Steffen Siegel, 'Die 'gantz accurate' Kunstkammer. Visuelle Konstruktion und Normierung eines Repräsentationsraum in der Frühen Neuzeit', *Visuelle Argumentation: Die Mysterien der Repräsentation und die Rechenbarkeit der Welt*, eds. H. Bredekamp and P. Schneider (Munich, 2006), 159–160 and 172–30. Schock, *Text-Kunstkammer*.
125 Williams usefully distinguishes between the 'gatherer' Johannes Praetorius, a writer akin to Happel, and the model of the organizing *polyhistor* of Morhof. Gerhard S. Williams, *Ways of Knowing in early modern Germany: Johannes Praetorius as a Witness to his Time* (Aldershot, 2006), 13.

What was at stake, then, for Major to publish an observation whose very identity he doubted and to allow the journal editors to attach such skepticism to his friend's name? Given that Major questioned the medical efficacy of bezoars and told Schellhammer that he was equally happy to possess the horn of a gazelle as that of a bezoar goat, we further have to ask what the significance of this object was for him at all. For Major, exploring doubt was part of linking the collection to experimental questions more broadly. The doubtful horn of the bezoar goat in his collection and the discussion it began to generate in the pages of the *Miscellanea curiosa* served as valuable material for the collaborative rewriting of natural history. Major's 'philosophical book-keeping' would have required a constant movement between the collections (Morhof's 'common places of nature'), learned publications across Europe, and the catalog, as the latest experiments were brought into relation with the collection's objects. New experimental findings would mean shifting the categories of the collection and moving objects in and out of the grey zone of doubt. Likewise, objects from the collection would be recruited for on-going discussion in learned periodicals.

Such movements would integrate the practices of collecting, cataloguing, and writing natural history over time. From the start, Major envisioned his slim studies of collections as a serial publication. He originally envisioned publishing at least thirty issues, to appear monthly, beginning with those collections as far away as possible in America and Asia, and culminating in a study of his hometown, Breslau.[126] He hoped this format would encourage much correspondence bringing new material to his attention. In a letter of September 19 and 20, 1674 to Schellhammer, Major sketched out the first ten issues he had planned, reporting that the first would appear in October. He was hoping he could read the Schellhammer brothers' manuscript before he got to issues number nine and ten on Holland later that year.[127]

Major normally published in quarto, but the five issues of his global series that did appear (each between 12 and 16 pages long), did so in folio, beginning with *Unvorgreiffliches Bedencken von Kunst- und Naturalien-Kammern ins gemein* of 1674 to the poetic place-holder, the *Great Treasure* of 1679 that Major dedicated to Schellhammer and which proved to be the last in the series. Given the slim volume and vernacular nature of these works, the folio format seems like a poor choice. Each considered separately, they appear to be folio

---

126   Johann Daniel Major, *Vorstellung etlicher Kunst- und Naturalien-Kammern/ in America und Asia* (Kiel, 1674), sig. A4ʳ.
127   Staats-und Universitätsbibliothek Hamburg, Sup. ep. (95, 19) d.

PROFESSIONALIZING DOUBT   235

pamphlets, the characteristic format of continental news gazettes evolved from the ephemeral single *Flugblatt* or broadsheet. This wasn't the format for learned periodicals like the *Miscellanea Curiosa*, which appeared in annual or biennial, stout, quarto editions. The vernacular language, folio format and serial publication of Major's texts situated them oddly between an on-going and thus provisional publication and a more magisterial folio volume, into which Major's texts could be collected and bound, as did happen.[128] Once accumulated into a more robust volume, they might enjoy a prominent position on a shelf alongside the lavishly illustrated folio catalogs of collections of individuals and later of institutions, such as the *Museum Calceolarianum* (1622), the *Museum Wormianum* (1655), the *Note over memorie del Museo di Lud. Moscardo* (1656 and 1672), or, later the *Museum Romani Collegi Societatis Jesu* (1678) and the *Museum Regalis Societatis* (1681). These were the works that Morhof had envisioned as a majestic index to the commonplaces of nature held in the museum, as the visitor moved back and forth between book and the disposition of objects around the museum. Through his serial surveys of global collections, Major further mobilized this alternation between objects and the scholarly literature about them.

Major entitled his planned *magnum opus*, of which these slim, serial folios were the start, the *Leopoldine Theatre of Nature, or the Eminent Natural Philosophy (Physicae) to be accommodated especially for this Experimental Century*.[129] The title of Major's imagined *magnum opus* appears to represent collecting on behalf of the *Academia*, since Leopold I, to whom the early issues of the *Miscellanea curiosa* were dedicated, was already being courted as a patron of the society which would be renamed the Leopoldina. Both Major's folio monthlies and the annual quartos of the *Miscellanea Curiosa* illustrate how contemporaries envisioned periodical publication as integral to transforming learned practices. The serial, unfinished form that Major's museological work took beginning in 1674 corresponds to the purposefully provisional and doubtful stance that the editors of the *Miscellanea curiosa* adopted over the course of the 1670s. Instead of offering the reader a picture of natural history already delineated, demanding our assent, it offers us a sketch, that is, a view of knowledge on the move, asking for our questions and contributions.

---

128   Volume G-A 8053 in the Leibniz Bibliothek, Hannover, compiles fourteen of Major's publications. The Göttingen copy has four of Major's 1674 and 1675 folio pamphlets bound together. Niedersächsische Staats- und Universitätsbibliothek Göttingen, 4 PHYS MATH I, 305. Likewise, see Rudolf Capell's advice to include five of Major's publications within a collection library, Capell, *Nummophylacium Luederianum,* sig. Kk^v-Kk1^r.
129   Major, *Unvorgreiffliches Bedencken,* sig. A2^r.

CHAPTER 9

Experiments on Collections at the Royal Society of London and the Paris Academy of Sciences, 1660–1740

Michael Bycroft

1   Introduction

The early histories of the Royal Society of London and the Paris Academy of Sciences provide us with something like a natural experiment in the role of institutions in early modern science. Both institutions were founded in the same decade, the 1660s. They both included all of nature, and only nature, in their purview: although they studied the human body and human industries they steered clear of topics that were overtly moral or political or theological. As a rule, when studying nature their members preferred experiment and observation over *a priori* principles; and when explaining nature they tended to appeal to the shape and size and motion of pieces of matter rather than appealing to Aristotelian forms or Neoplatonic sympathies. Their members included most of the leading practitioners of this approach to nature who were then active in their respective nations. In both institutions, at least some of the members met weekly to discuss books, articles, theories, inventions and experiments. They kept minutes of these meetings, and they arranged for the publication, in books or periodicals, of the findings they considered most useful or interesting. The two institutions were not identical, but they were so alike that their differences, and the causes of those differences, should not be too hard to identify. In particular, it should not be too hard to identify the differences in the kind of science they pursued – differences in their preferred methods, topics, or forms of communication – and to trace those differences to institutional factors – such as their size, wealth and composition.[1]

---

[1] This summary is drawn from standard histories of the two institutions such as Michael Hunter, *Establishing the New Science: The Experience of the Early Royal Society* (Woodbridge, 1989); Marie Boas Hall, *Promoting Experimental Learning: Experiment and the Royal Society 1660–1727* (Cambridge, 1991); David Sturdy, *Science and Social Status: The Members of the Académie des Sciences, 1666–1750* (Woodbridge, 1995); and Roger Hahn, *The Anatomy of a Scientific Institution: the Paris Academy of Sciences, 1666–1803* (Berkeley, 1971).

Insofar as there is a consensus about these differences, it concerns the way French and English inquirers conceived of scientific experience, and especially the way their conception of experience was reflected in the way they wrote about experiments. Elements of this consensus can be found in an influential paper by Thomas Kuhn and a provocative book by Simon Schaffer and Steven Shapin, works that were published in 1976 and 1985 respectively.[2] The consensus took on its present form in the 1990s, in a flurry of papers and chapters written by Peter Dear, Lawrence Holmes, Christian Licoppe, and Lorraine Daston.[3] These papers developed a contrast between English and continental science that was quickly incorporated into textbooks on the Scientific Revolution, textbooks that are still widely used today.[4] Each of these secondary texts emphasises some elements of the question and ignores others, but together they suggest a clear and plausible thesis.

The thesis is this. The English reported their experiments in a detailed, discursive, chronological and circumstantial manner, whereas the French were terse, selective, logical, and prone to generalisation. To use Holme's words, the English wrote *narratives* whereas the French developed *arguments*. The institutional reasons for this preference were that the Academy had more material resources than the Society, was more visibly endorsed by its patron, and was more collaborative in its activities. Material wealth meant that the academicians received generous pensions and had access to a well-equipped laboratory, which meant in turn that they did too many experiments to report them all. The close collaboration between academicians – the fact that the empirical scientists among them met once a week and worked together on collective

---

2   Thomas Kuhn, 'Mathematical Versus Experimental Traditions in the Development of Physical Science', *Journal of Interdisciplinary History*, 7:1 (1976), 1–31; Steven Shapin and Simon Schaffer, *Leviathan and the Air-Pump: Hobbes, Boyle, and the Experimental Life* (Princeton, 1985).
3   Peter Dear, 'Totius in Verba: Rhetoric and Authority in the Early Royal Society', *Isis*, 76 (1985), 145–61; Peter Dear, 'Miracles, Experiments, and the Ordinary Course of Nature', *Isis 81* (1990), 663–83; Frederic L. Holmes, 'Argument and Narrative in Scientific Writing', in *The Literary Structure of Scientific Argument: Historical Studies*, ed. Peter Dear (Philadelphia, 1991), 164–81; Christian Licoppe, *La formation de la pratique scientifique: le discours de l'expérience en France et en Angleterre (1630–1820)* (Paris, 1996); Christian Licoppe, 'The Crystallization of a New Narrative Form in Experimental Reports (1660–1690)', *Science in Context*, 7 (1994), 205–44; Lorraine Daston, 'Strange Facts, Plain Facts, and the Texture of Scientific Experience in the Enlightenment', in *Proof and Persuasion: Essays on Authority, Objectivity, and Evidence*, eds. Suzanne Marchand and Josine H. Blok (Turnhout, 1996), 45–50, 56–9.
4   Steven Shapin, *The Scientific Revolution*, 2nd edition (Chicago, 1998 [1996]), 83–85. John Henry, *The Scientific Revolution and the Origins of Modern Science*, 3rd edition (New York, 2008 [1997]), 52–55. Peter Dear, *Revolutionizing the Sciences: European Knowledge and its Ambitions, 1500–1700*, 2nd edition (Basingstoke, 2009 [2001]), 12–13, 130–134, 137–139.

projects – meant that there was a large body of knowledge that they held in common and that they could therefore omit in the papers they read at their weekly meetings.[5] Close collaboration meant that the academicians took eachother at their word, and the visible endorsement of Louis XIV meant that the French public took them at their word. These bonds of trust help to explain the French preference for argument over narrative because – as Shapin and Schaffer proposed and as most subsequent authors have supposed – a narrative has an air of verisimilitude that an argument does not.

This thesis has a lot going for it. It has stood the test of time, it is based on a great deal of solid research, and it neatly integrates the intellectual and institutional aspects of a wide swathe of seventeenth-century science. However the thesis is in need of revision, extension and renovation. An obvious defect is that much of the early empirical support for the thesis – especially in the work of Kuhn and Dear – was concerned with Frenchman who died before the Academy was formed, such as Marine Mersenne and Blaise Pascal. More recent studies of experimental research at the Academy have made the obvious point that much of this research contained very little mathematics and therefore does not fit into the 'mathematical tradition' that Kuhn identified on the continent. Some of these newer studies, notably Holmes' on chemistry, have preserved Kuhn's basic idea that the French preferred argument over narrative. But others take a different view: in her book on dissection at the Academy, Anita Guerrini argues that the leading anatomist at the institution up to the 1680s, Claude Perrault, had 'faith in the unique fact' and made little attempt to generalise beyond individual specimens.[6] Similar points hold for the early Royal Society of London, where there were nearly as many variants of Baconianism as there were Baconians, and where mathematicians and naturalists had persistent and sometimes heated disagreements about the correct form of natural inquiry.[7] Any attempt to contrast the Academy and the Society on methodological grounds must take these internal variations into account.

---

5 'Empirical scientists' translates the French term *'physiciens'*, practitioners of *'la physique'*. From 1699 the Academy's members were formally divided into six disciplines, three under the heading *physique* (chemistry, botany and anatomy) and three under the heading *mathématique* (geometry, mechanics, astronomy). Since 1666 the *physiciens* and *mathématiciens* had met on different days of the week (Bernard le Bovier de Fontenelle, 'Preface', *Histoire de l'Académie Royale des Sciences, 1666–1669*, 1 (1733), 1–16, on 15).

6 Anita Guerrini, *The Courtiers' Anatomists: Animals and Humans in Louis XIV's Paris* (Chicago, 2015), 152, cf. 153–155, 243.

7 Mordechai Feingold, 'Mathematicians and Naturalists: Sir Isaac Newton and the Royal Society', in *Isaac Newton's Natural Philosophy*, eds. Jed Z. Buchwald and I. Bernard Cohen

These are reasons for caution in drawing such contrasts, but there are also grounds for expansion. So far there has been remarkably little attempt to *systematically* compare the methodology of experimenters at the Academy and the Society. Most authors focus on one institution and make occasional references to the other, often drawing heavily on existing studies when they cross the Channel. There is also a need for *close* comparisons, where the French and the English are compared in their treatment of the same topic. Perhaps the most compelling piece of evidence in Kuhn's 1972 paper, as far as the England/continent contrast is concerned, is his comparison between Pascal's writings on hydrostatics and Boyle's on the same topic.[8] Historians inspired by Kuhn's paper have often returned to this example, but they have not often provided other examples of the same kind. Kuhn's paper stands out for another reason: among the studies cited so far, it is the only one that pushes the comparison between the Academy and Society into the eighteenth century.[9] No doubt the two institutions changed significantly around 1700 – consider the Academy's first formal constitution of 1699 and the appointment of Isaac Newton as President of the Society in 1703 – but this should not discourage us from seeking methodological continuity across the turn of the century. Finally, the 1990s studies cited above tended to see experimentation through the lens of literature, with the result that methodological contrasts between the Society and Academy were couched in terms of the structure of experimental reports, the kinds of pronouns they deployed, the length and complexity of their sentences, and so on. The underlying insight was that the same experiment – the same set of objects, instruments and gestures – can be written up in radically different ways depending on the epistemological and metaphysical commitments of the writer. This is no doubt true, but it is equally obvious that experiments are not wholly defined by what people write about them – objects, instruments and gestures can differ in their own right.

This chapter argues for a new contrast between the Academy and the Society, one that is both cautious and expansive. I shall argue that the academicians did something that the Fellows did rarely: they took a *large* collection of natural objects and then performed the *same* operation on *all* the items in that collection. The inferences they drew from these trials were comparisons between the properties of the different materials in the collection. The

---

(Cambridge MA, 2000), 77–102. William Lynch, *Solomon's Child: Method in the Early Royal Society of London* (Stanford CA, 2001), esp. 21–33.

8   Kuhn, 'Mathematical versus Experimental Traditions', 13.
9   Daston and Holmes cover some French science after 1700 but do not compare it to any contemporaneous English science. Licoppe covers both French and English science after 1700, but does not say whether the pre-1700 contrast that he identifies persisted after 1700.

academicians made extensive use of this procedure, and since they had no name for it the historian is obliged to invent one. I propose 'material-driven experimentation'. Section 1 illustrates this procedure by comparing the Academy's study of the chemistry of plants (which was driven by materials) with Robert Boyle's study of the spring of the air (which was not). These two projects will be familiar to readers of Shapin, Schaffer, Dear and Holmes. Section 2 introduces a new pair of examples, one that is particularly telling because the two investigations in question – by Boyle and the French chemists Samuel Duclos and Claude Bourdelin – had a great deal in common, starting with their shared interest in the chemical analysis of mineral waters. Section 3 extends the contrast into the eighteenth century by examining experiments on minerals on either side of the Channel. I argue that there was no English equivalent to the systematic experiments on minerals carried out by the academicians René Réaumur and Charles Dufay between 1710 and 1740.

My claim about this contrast is a modest one: it applies to the cases that I consider here. But these cases are sufficiently varied and important to call for an explanation. Section 4 offers four institutional explanations for the French penchant for material-driven experimentation. Two of these explanations, namely material resources and close collaboration, are already part of the received view about the contrasting experimental styles of the Academy and Society. The third factor, the bias towards useful research at the Academy and entertaining research at the Society, is known to historians of the two institutions but not usually invoked to account for differences in their scientific output. The fourth factor, which I shall call 'institutional inertia', accommodates an individual (Charles Dufay) who defies the three other explanations. If my contrast and my explanation for it are correct, several theses about the comparative development of the Society and Academy must be reconsidered. These theses are that the 'English' and 'Continental' approaches to experimental science converged in Isaac Newton's studies of light and colour; that natural philosophy and natural history were combined more intimately at the Society than at the Academy; and indeed, the fundamental thesis that the academicians favoured arguments in their experimental reports whereas the Fellows favoured narratives.

2   A New Contrast: The Chemistry of Plants and the Spring of the Air

Holmes illustrates the distinction between narrative and argument by comparing Robert Boyle's *New Experiments Physico-Mechanical, Touching the Spring of the Air and its Effects* (1660) to the Academy's *Mémoires pour servir a l'histoire des plantes* (1676). Since I wish to contrast my own distinction with Holmes', it makes sense to introduce my distinction with the same two examples. Consider, firstly, the Academy's project on the chemistry of plants. This project began in 1667 and ended some time around 1700, and in the intervening period it was arguably the most substantial programme of experimental research carried out at the Academy.[10]

The material basis of this project was a collection of plants. These were grown at the King's Garden (Jardin du Roi) in Paris, in a plot created for the purpose early in the 1670s and managed by two members of the Academy, Nicolas Marchant and his son Jean Marchant.[11] The size of the collection may be inferred from a set of engravings that were made in the seventeenth century with the intention of publishing them alongside the Academy's written descriptions of the plants at the Garden. Each of the 319 engravings represented a different species, and almost all were drawn from life, suggesting that the Marchants cultivated, or at any rate had access to, at least 319 different species.[12]

The second part of the project was executed by the chemist Claude Bourdelin and took place at the Academy's laboratory at the King's Library (Bibliothèque du Roi). Bourdelin distilled over 500 plants between 1670 and his death in 1699, a feat that has caught the eye of several historians.[13] The uniformity of these trials has received less attention than, but was just as important as, their quantity. The aim of the project was to compare the components of different plants, and to this end Bourdelin made every effort to carry out the same set of operations on each species. Denis Dodart made this clear in his *Mémoires pour servir à l'histoire des plantes* (1676), the most detailed account of the plant project published in the seventeenth century.[14] 'As a *basis for comparisons* between plants and between their parts', Dodart wrote, 'we thought it necessary to have a *universal and principal method* that was capable of drawing from the plants

---

10 Holmes, 'Argument and Narrative', 167–171. See also Yves Laissus, 'Les Plantes du Roi: note sur un grand ouvrage de botanique préparé au XVIIe siècle par l'Académie Royale des Sciences', *Revue de l'histoire des sciences* 22 (1969), 193–236; Alice Stroup, *A Company of Scientists: Botany, Patronage, and Community at the Seventeeth-Century Parisian Royal Academy of Sciences* (Berkeley, 1990), chaps. 6–7; Frederic L. Holmes, 'Analysis by Fire and Solvent Extractions: The Metamorphosis of a Tradition', *Isis* 62 (1971), 129–48, on 133–136.
11 Stroup, *Company of Scientists*, 79–80.
12 Laissus, 'Plantes du roi', 211–220, annexe.
13 Eg. Laissus, 'Plantes du roi', 212–20; Holmes, 'Fire Analysis', 133–6.
14 Denis Dodart, *Mémoires pour servir à l'histoire des plantes*, in *Mémoires de l'Académie Royale des Sciences* (1731 [1676]), 427–536.

the most distinct, the least altered, and the greatest number of substances possible'.[15]

The third part of the project was made up of the 'comparisons' to which Dodart referred. Dodart hoped that Bourdelin's trials would lend themselves to a particular kind of comparison, namely contrasts between the behaviour of different groups of plants. For example, Dodart reported that 'almost all the aromatic plants gave an essential oil, and almost none of the other plants gave one'.[16] This statement groups all species according to some property (whether or not they are aromatic) and links that property to another one (whether the plant gives an essential oil). At the end of the *Histoire des plantes*, Dodart implied that this kind of contrast was one of the most promising routes to new knowledge of the medical virtues of plants. He proposed to group plants according to their response to distillation, and then to look for medical virtues common to the species in each group. He hoped that, in the long run, these correlations would reveal the causes of the virtues of plants and thereby enable physicians to enhance those virtues.[17] In the meantime, Dodart settled for a series of more modest comparisons between the substances Bourdelin extracted from different plants. He drew attention to extracts that were previously unknown to physicians, to those that were known to physicians but only in a small number of plants, and to those that were present in *all* the plants that Bourdelin examined.[18]

The plant project may seem like an unexceptional piece of seventeenth-century Baconian experimentation. Dodart's book certainly has a Baconian flavour, with its sharp distinction between facts and conjectures, its tendency to accumulate the former and sideline the latter, and its embrace of experimentation as opposed to passive observation.[19] The plant project may even have been Baconian in inspiration, a conscious effort to realise what Bacon had called a 'chemical history of vegetables'.[20] But there was more than one

---

15 'Nous avons crû devoir prendre *pour fondement des comparaisons des Plantes*, & de leurs parties entre elles, *une maniere universelle & principale*, qui soit capable de tirer des Plantes, & de leurs parties le plus de substances qu'il se pourra, les plus distinctes & les moins alterées' (ibid., 463–4, emphasis added).

16 'Presque toutes les Aromatiques ont donné de l'huile essentielle, & presque aucune des autres n'en a donné' (Ibid, 465).

17 Ibid, 520.

18 Ibid, 463, 465–466, 507, 532, 533.

19 Ibid, 443–444, 447, 461–462, 531–532.

20 Francis Bacon, 'Preparative Toward Natural and Experimental History', in *Works of Francis Bacon*, eds. James Spedding, Robert L. Ellis, and Douglas D. Heath, 8 (London, 1857), 351–384, on 376. Cf. Christian Huygens' opinion that 'The principal work and most useful occupation of this Assembly should be, in my opinion, to work on the Natural History,

way to be a Baconian in the seventeenth century, and the way of Dodart and Bourdelin was quite different from the way of the English chemist Robert Boyle. Consider Boyle's *New Experiments Physico-Mechanical, Touching the Spring of the Air*.[21] Few would deny that this was a Baconian report of a Baconian investigation. Yet there was little room in Boyle's project for the three components that made up the French study of plants.

Most obviously, there was nothing in Boyle's investigation that corresponded to the common and exotic plants amassed by Nicolas and Jean Marchant at the King's Garden. Boyle did refer to various materials in *Spring of the Air*, but this set of objects was small and motley compared to the large and ordered collection at the Jardin. In one passage, on the production of bubbles in liquids placed in an air pump, Boyle reported trials on ten different liquids. Yet even this modest set of materials was unusually large in Boyle's experiments on the spring of the air. His study of respiration, which included trials on a lark, a sparrow, and a mouse, were more typical of this investigation.[22]

Secondly, Boyle did not perform the *same* operation in each of the 43 experiments that he listed in *Spring of the Air*. It is true that these experiments had an operation in common, namely the placement of bodies in the receiver of an air pump and the subsequent removal of the air from the pump. But there were many other operations in Boyle's investigation that were *not* common to all 43 experiments, or even to two or more of them. Consider experiments fourteen and sixteen. In the former, Boyle installed a gun in the receiver in such a way that he could pull the gun's trigger from outside the receiver. In the sixteenth experiment he held a lodestone outside the receiver and observed its effect on a magnetised steel needle placed inside the receiver. The principal difference between these experiments was not the materials involved, since in both cases the key component was made of steel (the cock of the gun in the former experiment, and the needle in the latter). The difference was instead the shape of the steel object and the way it interacted with other parts of the apparatus.[23]

Finally, when it came to comparing the results of his trials, Boyle showed little interest in comparing different kinds of material. The contrast that

---

somewhat according to the plan of Verulam [ie. Francis Bacon]'. Quoted in Peter Anstey, 'The Methodological Origins of Newton's Queries', *Studies In History and Philosophy of Science Part A*, 35 (2004), 247–269, on 249–250.

21 Robert Boyle, *Works*, eds. M. Hunter and E. Davis, 14 vols (London, 1999), 1:141–306.
22 Bubbles at Boyle, *Spring of the Air*, 222–225, respiration on 274–275. Cf. the small number of materials that Boyle used in his experiments on corrosive liquors (pp. 296–297) and on spontaneous ebullition (pp. 297–298).
23 Ibid, 189–92.

dominated his 43 experiments was not a contrast between materials but between the outcome of a trial in air and the outcome of the same trial in the absence of air. Boyle found such contrasts in his experiments on the survival of candle flames, the descent of columns of mercury, and the respiration of animals, to mention only the most famous examples.[24] These examples supported Boyle's chief conclusion, namely that 'the pressure of the Air might have an interest in more Phænomena then men have hitherto thought'.[25] As this quote suggests, the generality of Boyle's conclusion lay in the wide range of phenomena he covered – from the bursting of bladders to the ebullition of liquids – and not in the variety of materials he employed. In the plant project, plants were the main material resource, the main source of variety between trials, and the main basis for comparisons between those trials. In Boyle's project these functions were performed by instruments and phenomena rather than materials.

To be sure, the academicians were not wholly uninterested in varying the state of their apparatus. For them this meant comparing the properties of plant products that had been distilled over a vigorous heat to those that had been distilled in a slower and milder manner. But these were preliminary trials that Dodart used to defend the procedure (distillation) that he and Bourdelin applied in the main part of the investigation. By contrast, Boyle's investigation consisted almost entirely in comparisons between trials carried out in air and the same trials carried out in a vacuum.[26] Conversely, Boyle was not wholly uninterested in comparing the behaviour of different materials in his air pump. He did so in his trials on the operation of corrosive liquids, the spontaneous boiling of warm liquids, the respiration of animals, and the production of bubbles in liquids.[27] However these trials were branches of Boyle's investigation rather than the main trunk. Even when he inquired how a phenomenon varied according to the materials involved, he did so only after demonstrating that the phenomenon in question depended upon on the air's 'Power or Principle of self-Dilatation'.[28] And, as noted above, only in the case of bubble-production did he test more than a haphazard handful of objects. Even in that case, indeed *especially* in that case, the contrast between Boyle and Dodart is clear. Dodart compared the behaviour of different bubble-producing liquids in a vacuum; unlike Boyle, he showed no interest in comparing the behaviour of a given

---

24   Ibid, 184, 192–201, 274–276.
25   Ibid, 192, cf. 166.
26   Dodart, *Histoire des plantes*, 468–482, esp. 472.
27   Boyle, *Spring of the Air*, 222–25, 274–75, 295–96, 297–98.
28   Ibid, 165.

liquid in ordinary air with the behaviour of the same liquid in a vacuum.[29] Whereas Boyle compared different states of the air-pump, Dodart compared different kinds of substance. Boyle's investigation and the Academy's were both Baconian, but only the latter was organised around a collection of materials.

3   A Closer Comparison: Mineral Waters

Although there is a clear contrast between the plant project and Boyle's hydrostatics, the causes of this contrast are not easy to identify. Perhaps the contrast in approach is due, not to institutional differences, but to the fact that the two projects dealt with different topics (the spring of the air versus the chemistry of plants), or the fact that one employed a traditional operation (distillation) whereas the other employed a novel one (evacuating an air pump). To rule out these explanations we need to consider two investigations that are as alike as possible in their subject and methods. The chemical analysis of mineral waters provides one such comparison. Bourdelin, aided by the chemist Samuel Cottereau Duclos, analysed a large number of French mineral waters between 1667 and 1671; their results were published in Duclos' 1675 book *Observations sur les eaux minerales de plusieurs provinces de France*.[30] An English edition appeared soon afterwards, but it did not reach Boyle before he saw through the press, in 1685, his *Short Memoirs for the Natural Experimental History of Mineral Waters*.[31]

These texts shared not only their principal subject-matter (chemical tests of the contents of mineral waters) but also their commitment to reporting the results of particular trials (something that distinguishes Duclos' book from Dodart's on plants) and their efforts to grapple with a common set of practical and methodological difficulties (leaky bottles, variations in waters taken from the same source, waters that contained a confusing multitude of different substances, and so on).[32] These similarities make the differences between the two texts all the more striking. Simply put, Duclos' book was about mineral waters whereas Boyle's was about tests of mineral waters. Duclos and Bourdelin

---

29   Dodart, *Histoire des plantes*, 506.
30   Samuel C. Duclos, *Observations sur les eaux minerales de plusieurs provinces de France, faites en l'Academie Royale des Sciences en l'année 1670 & 1671*, Mémoires de l'Académie Royale des Sciences, 4 (1731 [1675]), 31–90. Cf. Fontenelle, 'Analise de plusieurs eaux minerales', *Histoire de l'Académie Royale des Sciences, 1666–1669*, 1 (1733), 27–36.
31   Boyle, *Works*, 10: 205–49, on 206.
32   Duclos, *Eaux minerales*, 33–4, 37, 80, 83–4, 88; Boyle, *Mineral Waters*, 216, 238–39, 250.

collected a large number of mineral waters and carried out a few standard tests on each of them. By contrast, Boyle gave a long list of tests that he examined in a thorough manner but only on a small and erratic inventory of mineral waters.

The difference is apparent in the structure and rhetoric of the two books. Roughly speaking, Boyle organised his results into sections that each correspond to a different test, whereas Duclos' sections correspond to different kinds of mineral water.[33] Accordingly, Duclos played up the 'large number of waters from different sources' that he and Bourdelin had examined.[34] By contrast, Boyle prided himself on the number and variety of tests he had considered – or, as he put it, on the 'the many wayes I propose, of discovering the natures or Qualities of Mineral Waters'.[35] Granted, Boyle also wrote in his introduction that he had tested 'all sorts of Mineral Waters'.[36] But most of his prefatory rhetoric, like the structure of his book, was geared towards the multiplication of tests rather than the accumulation of waters.

What about his actual practice? Did Boyle investigate mineral waters in a different way to Dodart and Bourdelin, or did he simply clothe his results in different attire? Some simple accounting suggests that the difference was not merely cosmetic. Duclos recorded tests on water from 89 separate springs; the corresponding figure for Boyle was 13.[37] By contrast, Boyle described 48 tests carried out at the spring and in the laboratory, whereas Duclos mentioned only 24 of the same two kinds of test.[38] The differences do not end there. It is clear from Duclos' text that Bourdelin performed more or less the same tests on *each* of the 89 mineral waters that he examined. This may be inferred from the fact that Duclos reported the same kind of *results* for each of the mineral waters, and because it is not plausible that Duclos simply invented these results. The question, then, is whether Boyle followed the same procedure as Duclos – whether he performed his tests on *each* of the mineral waters at his disposal.

---

33 In Duclos' case, this applies only to one section of the text (47–81). But this is the longest part of the text by a considerable margin, and much longer than the section devoted to the tests themselves (37–39).
34 '...un grand nombre d'eaux de différentes sources' (Ibid, 39, cf. 46).
35 Boyle, *Mineral Waters*, 216–17.
36 Cf. ibid, 236.
37 Duclos, *Eaux minerales*, 47–81; Boyle, *Mineral Waters*, 236, 240, 243. Many sites in England and France had several springs that derived from the same source. The above figures refer to springs rather than sources. The equivalent figures for sources are 64 examined by the French and 11 by Boyle.
38 Boyle, *Mineral Waters*, 215–224; Duclos, *Eaux minérales*, 37–39.

The answer is that he did not, though the evidence for this answer is not straightforward. The problem is that Boyle is usually vague about which mineral waters he tested. Often he names one or two springs and adds that he tested 'some others', or 'many others'; sometimes he simply writes that he has tested 'more than one'; on some occasions he refers enigmatically to 'those Mineral Waters, I have had occasion to examine'; on one occasion he boldly declares that he has found common salt in 'all the English Mineral Waters'.[39] Only for one procedure (measuring specific gravity) does he give a complete enumeration of the eleven waters he subjected to that procedure; for no other procedure does he name more than four waters.[40] Still, there are two conclusions we may legitimately draw from this vagueness. One is that Boyle was not especially concerned about performing his tests on every possible mineral water. If he had prided himself on that form of thoroughness, it is unlikely that he would have been so careless with his records – note that he reports *other* circumstances of his experiments on mineral waters in great detail. The other conclusion is that, when Boyle makes no reference (not even a vague reference) to trials on extra waters, we can suppose that he did not perform such trials.

The second of these conclusions applies to several of Boyle's tests, including some important ones. The test that he discusses in greatest detail is the use of oak galls (and various substitute substances) to test for the presence of iron, copper and vitriol in mineral waters. In this long discussion he names only two springs, Spa in Germany and Tunbridge in England. He covers several different topics in this discussion, and reports several trials on each. Only for some of these topics does he say or imply that he has tested more than the two waters he names.[41] Elsewhere, discussing tests for vitriol, he says simply that he has not found vitriol in springs 'about London', implying that he did not try any remoter waters.[42] Another kind of incompleteness in Boyle's trials is that he, unlike Dodart, was willing to report the results of trials carried out by remote correspondents and short-term visitors to London, and to experiment upon the salts that others had extracted from mineral waters.[43] Boyle also reported experiments that, as far as this reader can tell, he only performed on one water.[44] In short, Boyle did a considerable number of experiments on mineral

---

39   Eg. respectively, Boyle, *Mineral Waters*, 237, 238; 238, 240; 242; 243.
40   Ibid, 236.
41   Ibid, 224–233.
42   Ibid, 243.
43   Ibid, 243, 244, 248.
44   Ibid, 239, 141.

waters that he did not personally extend to all, or even to most, of the 13 waters that he examined over the whole course of his investigation.

This is not to say that Boyle was less thorough than Duclos and Bourdelin. Rather, he was thorough in a different way. He was thorough about his tests, not about the waters he tested them on. His treatment of acidity was characteristic: after listing the traditional tests of this property, he pointed out that these tests gave conflicting results when applied to certain substances, and he recommended a new test of his own devising.[45] Even when Boyle tested several mineral waters in the same way, his main aim was not *compare* those particular waters. For example, when he compared the acidity of German and English waters, his aim was not to show that the former were the more acidic but to show that his test of acidity was better than the traditional ones. Elsewhere he showed that three different waters gave very different amounts of *caput mortuum*. But what excited him was not the inequality *per se* but the fact that tiny concentrations of salt or metal could confer great powers on a liquid – a fact that suggested to him that the salt or metal had entered mineral waters as 'fumes or exhalations' rather than as solids. Boyle did not roam as widely as the academicians, but he probed more deeply.[46]

4   An Eighteenth-century Comparison: Minerals and Electricity

The Academy's chemical studies of plants and mineral waters lost much of their distinctive character after 1700. In both cases, a comprehensive survey of many different materials gave way to a series of probing, piece-meal studies of particular kinds of material. One might say that the French became more English.[47] However plants and mineral waters are not the only candidates for material-driven experimentation. Minerals were also well-suited to this kind of investigation, and they underlay some key experimental projects at the Academy in the first three decades of the eighteenth century. The authors of these projects were René Réaumur and Charles Dufay. Both possessed large collections of minerals, and both carried out systematic experiments on their collections. They led the way as collectors *and* as experimenters. There was no such overlap at the Royal Society of London in the same period. In England,

---

45   Ibid, 240. Cf. Boyle's long discussion of the oak galls test (224–233) and Duclos' brief invocation of the same test (*Eaux minerales*, 38).
46   Ibid., 242, 245–247.
47   On plants, see Holmes, 'Fire Analysis', 136–141. On mineral waters, see Michael Bycroft, 'Iatrochemistry and the Evaluation of Mineral Waters in France, 1600–1750', *Bulletin of the History of Medicine* 91 (2017), 303–330.

the most prolific collectors of minerals and the most prominent experimenters were not the same people. This was a difference that made a difference, as we shall see by comparing experiments on electricity carried out on either side of the Channel.

Let me begin with Réaumur. Historians agree, and several contemporary sources confirm, that the distinguished naturalist possessed a large collection of minerals in the 1720s.[48] A study of his published and unpublished work shows that between 1716 and 1730 he used items from the collection to study the composition of metal ores, the conversion of iron into steel, the production of porcelain, and the expansion of wet earths, roughly in that order. In each of these cases he performed the same operation on a large number of minerals and compared the outcomes of these numerous trials.

Briefly, Réaumur's operations and his conclusions were as follows. In the earliest project, carried out between 1716 and 1719, Réaumur oversaw assays of 104 metallic ores.[49] His aim was to identify unexploited or under-exploited mines in France.[50] In his work on steel, published in 1722, he sought not only to identify useful substances but also to establish rules concerning the contrasting properties of different kinds of material – in particular, rules about the quality of steel produced by different kinds of iron.[51] Réaumur's aim in his research on porcelain was to find French substitutes for the two substances that he knew to be the main ingredients of this sought-after Eastern commodity. His method was to heat as many French minerals as he could get his hands on: 'earths of every kind, chalk, boles, marls, clays, common earths, sands of every kind, gravels, every species of stone, marbles, agates, flints, crystals, sandstones,

---

[48] René Réaumur, 'Reflexions sur l'utilité dont l'Académie des sciences pourroit être au royaume, si le royaume luy donnoit les secours dont elle a besoin', transcribed in Ernest Maindron, *L'Académie des sciences: histoire de l'Académie, fondation de l'Institut national*, (Paris, 1888), 103–10, on 108–109; René Réaumur, 'Remarques sur les coquilles fossiles de quelques cantons de la Touraine, et sur les utilités qu'on en tire', *Mémoires de l'Académie Royale des Sciences*, 1720, 400–416, on 401; René Réaumur, 'Idée générale des differentes manières de faire la porcelaine', *Mémoires de l'Académie Royale des Sciences* (1727), 185–203, on 199; Edme-François Gersaint, *Catalogue raisonné de coquilles et autres curiosités naturelles* (Paris, 1736), 31. Cf. M. Terrall, *Catching Nature in the Act: Réaumur and the Practice of Natural History in the Eighteenth Century* (Chicago, 2014), 134–136, 141.

[49] Christiane Demeulenaere-Douyère and David Sturdy, *L'Enquête du régent, 1716–1718: sciences, techniques, et politique dans la France pré-industrielle*, (Turnhout, 2008), 37–39, 795–865.

[50] Réaumur, 'Reflexions sur l'utilité', 108–109.

[51] René Réaumur, *L'Art de convertir le fer forgé en acier, et l'art d'adoucir le fer fondu* (Paris, 1722), 154–171.

granites, talcs, plasters, slate, etc'.[52] Earths were the subject of Réaumur's last major project that drew on his mineral collection. There he considered the practical problem of determining the required thickness of walls built against banks of earth. His solution to this problem was to establish 'rules' concerning 'the dilation of different earths', and he carried out 'a great number of experiments' in search of these rules.[53]

Réaumur's mineral project was less unified than its prototype, the plant project I described above. The four strands of Réaumur's project were each based on a different group of minerals, and the results of each were published in different volumes of the Academy's *Mémoires*. Moreover, the papers in question included much that cannot be described as material-driven experimentation. Nevertheless, each of those papers included much that *does* resemble the systematic experimental studies of plants (and mineral waters) that we find in the seventeenth-century Academy.

We find the same pattern of research in several papers by Réaumur's protégé, Charles Dufay. This may come as a surprise. Whereas Réaumur is equally famous for his collections and his experiments – as recognisable for his minerals and insects as for the thermometer that bears his name – Dufay is known primarily for his methodical investigations of electricity and luminescence. Yet Dufay's collecting was not confined to the official business of the King's Garden, where he served as Intendant in the 1730s.[54] Dufay was also a prominent

---

[52] 'Tout ce qui est compris dans le genre des matiéres terreuses, s'offroit à ces essais; les terres de toutes especes, les crayes, les bols, les marnes, les glaises, les terres ordinaires, les sables de toutes qualités, les graviers, les pierres de tous les genres, les marbres, les agathes, les cailloux, les cristaux, les grès, les granits, les talcs, les plâtres, les ardoises, &c' (Réaumur, 'Idée générale', 190, cf. 193–201). See also René Réaumur, 'Second mémoire sur la porcelaine', *Mémoires de l'Académie Royale des Sciences* (1729), 325–346, on 330–31. The earliest dated manuscripts concerning Réaumur's porcelain trials are from November 1718: Archives de l'Académie des Sciences, Réaumur archive, dossier 55 ('Porcelain'), ff. 56–59. Later porcelain trials appear in Réaumur archive, dossier 55, dossier 52 ('Physique: terres, sables, pierres'), dossier 54 ('Mines'), dossier 59 ('Brouillons sur les minéraux, les metaux'), and in Archives de la Manufacture nationale de Sèvres, Y39. I am grateful to Grace Chuang for sending me electronic copies of the Sèvres manuscripts.

[53] René Réaumur, 'De la nature de la terre en générale, et du charactere des differentes especes de terre', *Mémoires de l'Académie Royale des Sciences* (1730), 243–83, on 277.

[54] Dufay's life and work are summarised in Bernard le Bovier de Fontenelle, 'Eloge de M. Dufay', *Histoire de l'Académie Royale des Sciences* (1739), 73–83; Pierre Brunet, 'L'Oeuvre scientifique de Charles François du Fay', *Petrus Nonius* 3 (1940), 77–95; John L. Heilbron, 'Dufay, Charles-François de Cisternai', *Dictionary of Scientific Biography*, ed. Charles C. Gillispie (Detroit, 2008), 4 :214–17, on 214. More detail on Dufay can be found in Michael

collector in his own right, one with a special interest in precious and semi-precious stones. Fontenelle tells us as much in his obituary, but says nothing about the contents of Dufay's collection or how he used it in his experimental research.[55] The answers to both questions can be found in eight experimental reports that appeared in the Academy's *Mémoires* and *Histoire* between 1724 and 1739.[56]

These papers show, firstly, that Dufay had access to most of the minerals that were recognised as gems in early eighteenth-century France. 27 minerals are listed as semi-precious stones (*pierres fines*), and 10 as precious ones (*pierres précieuses*), in the authoritative *Oryctologie* published by Antoine-Joseph Dezallier d'Argenville in 1755.[57] Of these minerals, Dufay's did experiments on 17 of the semi-precious ones and all 10 of the precious ones. It is significant that Dufay examined almost all of these 27 gems in research he had completed by 1725 or 1728. This suggests that he already possessed a substantial collection of gems early in his career. Equally important is the fact that each of the stones mentioned in the 1725 and 1728 papers was roasted, dissolved in acid, or impregnated with acid-based dyes, and that in later papers Dufay roasted both sardonyx and diamond. Dufay clearly had gems to spare. In a 1735 paper he gave us an all-too-brief glimpse of the physical state of his collection: 'I have been working for several years to form a cabinet of fine stones, of jaspers,

---

Bycroft, 'Physics and Natural History in the Eighteenth Century: the Case of Charles Dufay', unpublished PhD dissertation, University of Cambridge, 2013.

55   Fontenelle, 'Eloge de Dufay', 81–82. Dufay bequeathed his collection to the King's Garden; short descriptions of the gems there appear in Antoine-Joseph Dezallier d'Argenville, *L'Histoire naturelle éclaircie dans deux de ses parties principales: la lithologie et la conchyliologie* (Paris, 1742), 199; Louis-Jean-Marie Daubenton, 'De la connoisssance des pierres précieuses', *Mémoires de l'Académie Royale des Sciences*, 1750, 28–38, esp. 30.

56   'Sur une pierre de Berne qui est une espece de phosphore', *Histoire de l'Académie Royale des Sciences*, 1724, 58–61; 'Mémoire sur la teinture et la dissolution de plusieurs especes de pierres', *Mémoires de l'Académie Royale des Sciences* (1728), 50–67; 'Mémoire sur un grand nombre de phosphores nouveaux', *Mémoires de l'Académie Royale des Sciences* (1730), 524–35; 'Second mémoire sur la teinture des pierres', *Mémoires de l'Académie Royale des Sciences* (1732), 169–81; 'Second mémoire sur l'électricité: quels sont les corps qui sont susceptibles d'électricité', *Mémoires de l'Académie Royale des Sciences* (1732), 73–84; 'Sixième mémoire sur l'électricité: quel rapport il y a entre l'électricité et la faculté de rendre de la lumière', *Mémoires de l'Académie Royale des Sciences* (1734), 503–26; 'Recherches sur la lumière des diamants et de plusieurs autres matières', *Mémoires de l'Académie Royale des Sciences* (1735), 347–72; 'Sur le cristal d'Islande', unpublished paper summarised in Fontenelle, 'Eloge de Dufay', 81.

57   Antoine-Joseph Dezallier d'Argenville, *L'Histoire naturelle éclaircie dans une de ses parties principales, l'oryctologie* (Paris, 1755), 152–245. Dufay's gems and d'Argenville's are tabulated and compared at Bycroft, 'Physics and Natural History', table 4, 182.

agates, prisms, and singular crystallisations [which are] arrayed in drawers divided into compartments'.[58]

The same eight papers show that Dufay used his gems in just the way that Réaumur had used his minerals. In each of those papers, Dufay described how he had applied the *same* operation to *each* of a *large* number of gems, and usually to several other minerals as well. He heated gems, rubbed them, mixed them with acid, exposed them to sunlight, and refracted rays of light through them. He did so to find out about electricity, luminescence, double refraction and the artificial coloration of hard stones. Dufay's research on these topics appeared in separate papers that were published over the course of fourteen years. He nevertheless conceived of these papers as contributions to a single overarching project. As he wrote in 1730: 'Some years ago I formed the intention of examining, by every means I could think of, the nature of all fine stones'.[59]

So much for the French. What about their English counterparts? Was there a Réaumur or a Dufay at the Royal Society of London in the early decades of the eighteenth century? A review of the main experimenters and mineral collectors who were active at the Royal Society in this period suggests that the answer is 'no'. The principal mineral collections in London at the time belonged to John Woodward and Hans Sloane. Woodward gathered his first mineral in 1688, became a Fellow of the Royal Society of London in 1693, and by 1724 had acquired over 6,800 English minerals and some 2,500 foreign ones, an impressive hoard that he kept at his lodgings at Gresham College, where he served as Professor of Physic from 1692.[60] Hans Sloane became a Fellow in 1685, acquired major mineral collections from his friends William Courten and James Petiver, displayed these and other minerals at his home in Bloomsbury and (from 1742) Chelsea, and died in 1753 in the possession of nearly 11,000 mineral specimens.[61] Sloane and Woodward were both, in their own ways, distinguished scientists, but neither was a notable experimenter. Granted,

---

58   Dufay, 'Lumiere des diamants', 357.
59   Dufay, 'Phosphores nouveaux', 526.
60   V.A. Eyles, 'Woodward, John', in *Dictionary of Scientific Biography*, ed. C. Gillispie, 14:500–503, on 501; Hugh Torrens, 'Early Collections in the Field of Geology', in *The Origins of Museums: the Cabinet of Curiosities in Sixteenth and Seventeenth Century Europe*, eds. Oliver Imey and Andrew MacGregor (Oxford, 1985), 211–12; Wendell Wilson, *The History of Mineral Collecting* (Tucson, 1994), 67–68.
61   Gavin de Beer, *Sir Hans Sloane and the British Museum* (London, 1953), 132; John Thackray, 'Mineral and Fossil Collections', in *Sir Hans Sloane: Collector, Scientist, Antiquary, Founding Father of the British Museum*, ed. Andrew MacGregor (London, 1994), 123, 160. Wilson, *Mineral Collecting*, 65–67.

Woodward famously based his theory of the earth's history on his measurements of the specific gravity of a range of minerals; and Sloane subjected some of his minerals to chemical analyses and to the intense heat at the focus of a concave mirror.[62] But these studies cannot be compared with the sustained programmes of experimentation pursued by Dufay and Réaumur.

When we turn to those who *did* distinguish themselves as experimenters in England, we find that they had little to do with mineral collecting. Francis Hauksbee, Stephen Gray and Stephen Hales all fall into this category. Hauksbee, the Society's Curator of Experiments from 1703 to 1713, is highly regarded for his experiments on electricity, electroluminescence, and capillary action.[63] Gray announced and explored the phenomenon of electrical conduction in a series of letters sent to the Royal Society between 1708 and 1735.[64] And Hales' experimental studies of plant chemistry and animal physiology made him 'the leading English scientist during the second third of the eighteenth century'.[65] Yet none of these names appear in the most comprehensive modern survey of early modern mineral collecting.[66] Hales did use a collection, namely the plants and trees at the royal garden of Hampton Court, but this was evidently not a collection of minerals.[67] Gray also had a collection of sorts, namely the various objects that he identified as electrical – that is, objects that attract light objects when rubbed. However this 'collection' was small, homely and haphazard compared to the systematic catalogue of minerals (including many from his gemmological cabinet) that Dufay referred to in his own survey of electrical bodies.

Hauksbee deserves special attention because his position as Curator made him central to the Society's experimental programme and because his experiments ranged more widely and were more consequential than Gray's. Now, Hauksbee was not averse to applying his experimental talents to materials of different kinds. His experiments on the specific gravities of metals and other minerals, and on the refractive indices of fluids, are two notable examples. Interestingly, Hauksbee obtained the metals in these experiments from Hans

---

62   Martin Rudwick, *The Meaning of Fossils: Episodes in the History of Palaeontology*, 2nd ed. (Chicago, 1985), 82; Thackray, 'Mineral and Fossil Collections', 131–132.
63   John L. Heilbron, *Electricity in the 17th and 18th Centuries: A Study of Early Modern Physics* (Berkeley, 1979), 229–49. John L. Heilbron, *Physics at the Royal Society During Newton's Presidency* (Los Angeles CA, 1983), passim.
64   Heilbron, *Electricity*, 229–249.
65   Henry Guerlac, 'Hales, Stephen', in *Dictionary of Scientific Biography*, ed. Gillispie, 6:35.
66   The 1,200 names in 'Census of Mineral Collectors, 1530–1799', in Wilson, *Mineral Collecting*, 157–199.
67   Guerlac, 'Hales, Stephen', 38, 38 n. 35.

Sloane, perhaps from the physician's private collection; the other minerals were gathered from a coal-pit by a certain Fettiplace Bellers, FRS, and Hauksbee concluded from his measurements that Woodward had been wrong to maintain that denser minerals occur in deeper strata.[68] These intersections between collecting and experimenting were nevertheless atypical in Hauksbee's oeuvre. His most productive line of research, on luminescence and electricity, was driven by instruments rather than materials. He made progress in these areas not by trying new materials but by changing his apparatus, as when he used the pressure of the atmosphere (rather than his own hand) to agitate the mercury in a glass vessel, when he rubbed the vessel directly (rather than rubbing its contents), and when he rubbed the vessel by setting it (rather than his hand) in motion. Hauksbee did make one very significant choice of material, namely the use of glass rather than amber as a generator of electricity.[69] But this choice was a natural extension of his earlier experiments on glass vessels, not the result of an exhaustive search of candidate materials.[70]

The contrast between Dufay and his English contemporaries is particularly clear in the case of electricity. Dufay took experiments from Hauksbee and Gray and subtly altered them to fit his material-oriented view of experimentation. Consider his treatment of Hauksbee's experiments on filled glass tubes. In his *Physico-Mechanical Experiments* (1709), Hauksbee compared the electricity of an air-filled tube with that of a sand-filled tube. He observed that the former was more electrical (that is, it drew brass leaf more strongly when rubbed) than the latter. Dufay read about these experiments in the Italian edition of Hauksbee's book, and reported his own version of them in a paper published in the 1733 edition of Academy's *Mémoires*. Dufay compared the electricity of tubes filled respectively with sand, bran and water; he observed that the former tube was the easiest to electrify and the latter the hardest to electrify.[71]

---

68 Francis Hauksbee, 'A Description of the Apparatus for Making Experiments on the Refractions of Fluids: With a Table of the Specifick Gravities, Angles of Observations, and Ratio of Refractions of Several Fluids', *Philosophical Transactions* 27 (1710), 204–7; Francis Hauksbee, 'A Description of the Several Strata of Earth, Stone, Coal, Etc. Found in a Coal-Pit at the West End of Dudley in Straffordshire: By Mr. Fettiplace Bellers, F.R.S. To Which Is Added, a Table of the Specifick Gravity of Each Stratum', *Philosophical Transactions* 27 (1710), 541–44; Francis Hauskbee, 'The Specifick Gravities of Several Metalline Cubes, in Comparison with Their Like Bulks of Water', *Philosophical Transactions* 27 (1710), 511–12.

69 Rubbed glass generated more electricity than rubbed amber; the former revealed new properties of electricity and made known properties easier to study.

70 On Hauksbee's experiments on electricity and luminescence, see Heilbron, *Electricity*, 229–249.

71 Francis Hauksbee, *Physico-Mechanical Experiments on Various Subjects* (London, 1709), 113; Charles Dufay, 'Troisième mémoire sur l'électricité: des corps qui sont les plus

The difference between the two experiments may seem slight: Dufay tried only one more material than Hauksbee, and he did not try air. The two experimenters differed greatly, however, in their interpretation of their results. Hauksbee noted that the sand had expelled the air from the tube, and concluded that air is essential for the production of electricity. Dufay noticed something quite different about the contents of the tube, and drew a different conclusion. He noticed that sand is a crystalline material (and therefore easy to electrify), that bran is a form of dried vegetable matter (and therefore hard to electrify), and that water spoils electrical experiments (and therefore very hard to electrify). Dufay concluded that materials that are easy to electrify confer the same property on the glass tube that contains them. For Hauksbee, the sand was significant because of what it *did* – it removed the air from the tube. For Dufay, the sand was significant because of what it *was* – a crystalline material, and therefore an electrical one. Hauksbee saw the tube in the way Boyle saw the receiver of the air pump: as a space that allowed him to compare the behaviour of things in air with their behaviour in a vacuum. Dufay saw the tube in the way *Dodart* saw the air pump: as a space that happened to be devoid of air and that was useful because it allowed him to compare different materials.

Gray may be contrasted with Dufay in a similar way to Hauksbee. As noted above, Dufay's list of electrics was longer than Gray's, and included more minerals. But the two men also differed in the way they used their respective materials. The Frenchman listed all of the electrics he knew in a single paper, and asked the same question of each – do they attract light objects when rubbed? By contrast, Gray never gave a single list of all the electrics he had discovered. To construct such a list the historian must rummage through the Englishman's various papers and lift the items out of the relevant passages. The explanation for this is not that Gray's investigation was disorganised but that it was not organised around materials. Each time Gray studied a new set of electrics, he did so with a particular purpose in mind, and he used the materials that suited his purpose. On the first occasion that he mentioned new electrics his aim was simply to give a list or 'Enumeration' of the new ones. On the second occasion he gave a similar enumeration, but this time he electrified the objects 'by communication' (that is, by contact with a rubbed tube) rather than by rubbing

---

vivement attirés par les matières électriques, et de ceux qui sont les plus propres à transmettre l'électricité', *Mémoires de l'Académie Royale des Sciences* (1733), 233–254, on 242-44. Dufay's identification of sand with mineral crystals may have been inspired by Réaumur, who made this identification in a paper published in 1730: Réaumur, 'Nature de la terre', 249.

them directly. Later in the same paper he electrified a map of the world, a table cloth and umbrella – objects he chose not because of their composition but because they all had large surface areas. Finally, in another set of experiments Gray electrified 20 kinds of sulphur, pitch and resin – not to show that they were electric but to see how they retained their 'electrick virtue'. Gray listed electrics in the same haphazard way that Boyle listed mineral waters. Unlike Dufay and Réaumur, and like Hauksbee and Boyle, Gray was not a proponent of material-driven experimentation.[72]

5   Four Institutional Explanations

On the received view, the French preference for argument over narrative was due to the ample material resources of the Academy, the close collaboration between its members, and the visible endorsement it received from the king. The first and second of these factors go a long way towards explaining the French penchant for material-driven experimentation. This was certainly a resource-intensive form of inquiry, requiring a large collection, a chemical laboratory, and at least one dedicated chemist. Nor is there any doubt that material-driven experimentation benefited from close collaboration between naturalists and experimenters. There was also a third factor, to do with the interests of scientific patrons on either side of the Channel. The experiments of Bourdelin and Réaumur were useful but dull, and as a result they appealed more to the kings and ministers who sponsored the Academy than to the virtuosi who sustained the Society. Each of these three factors are important, but none is clear-cut and they all admit of counter-examples. Indeed, one of the counter-examples (Dufay) is so glaring that it calls for a fourth kind of explanation, namely that institutions can perpetuate practices even when the original causes of those practices are no longer present.

The material resources that mattered most for material-driven experimentation were laboratories and collections. Bourdelin analysed plants and mineral waters in a laboratory that was installed in the King's Library (Bibliothèque du Roi) in the first years of the Academy's existence. This laboratory was not only well-equipped and generously maintained, but also conveniently located

---

[72]   Stephen Gray, 'An Account of Some New Electrical Experiments', *Philosophical Transactions* 31 (1720–1721), 104–7, on 106–7; Stephen Gray, 'A Letter Containing Several Experiments Concerning Electricity', *Philosophical Transactions* 37 (1731–1732), 18–44, on 19–20, 21–23 (metals and stones), and 31–33; Stephen Gray, 'A Letter Containing a Farther Account of his Experiments Concerning Electricity', *Philosophical Transactions* 37 (1731–1732), 285–91, on 291 (resins and bitumens).

in the very building where the Academy's empirical scientists held their weekly meetings. These factors ensured that chymistry, and along with it the examination of *materia medica* such as plants and mineral waters, was a central part of the Academy's early experimental programme. The absence of an equivalent facility at the Royal Society helps to explain why most of its Curators of Experiments, and notably Hauksbee and Robert Hooke, showed little interest in the differences between species of plants, animals and minerals.[73]

This explanation only goes so far, however. Many Fellows, not least Robert Boyle, undertook chymical research at make-shift laboratories installed in their homes; and others did so at universities, including the University of Oxford, where Robert Plot presided over a purpose-built laboratory from 1683. In addition, the French chemists ceased to have access to a single, centralised laboratory after 1699, when the Academy moved from the King's Library to the Louvre, where there was no room for a new laboratory. Even for the period before 1699, the presence of the laboratory does not explain the peculiar character of the Academy's chemical investigations. Why did the academicians analyse such a large number of plants and minerals and mineral waters, as opposed to developing more powerful techniques of analysis? The explanation lies partly in the state of chemical knowledge – it was only *after* the projects on plants and mineral waters, and to some extent *because* of them, that the academicians discovered the need to drastically alter their analyses. But there is an institutional explanation as well, to do with the kind of administrative resource that the French crown placed at the disposal of the academicians.

The point is easiest to make in the case of Réaumur's experiments on minerals. Réaumur acquired these minerals by way of a survey of French mineral resources that he carried out on behalf of the Regent, Philippe II, between 1716 and 1718. The Regent aimed to produce a comprehensive appraisal of the mineral wealth of his kingdom, and to this end Réaumur drafted a questionnaire – including a request for mineral samples – that was sent to each of France's 38 Intendants. The latter was a network of regional officials who answered directly to the king. Their loyalty to the crown, the resources they commanded in their own regions, their wide geographical coverage, and their past experience with centralised surveys such as this one, all meant that the Intendants were ideal partners in Réaumur's quest for 'a complete set of all the different earths

---

[73] Except when those differences served as evidence for a hypothesis couched in mechanical terms, as in Hooke's use of fossils to support his theory that geological change is driven by earthquakes. See Rudwick, *Meaning of Fossils*, 53–56, 61–65, 73–76; Torrens, 'Early Collections', 210–211.

and metals... in France'.[74] Similar points hold for the plants and mineral waters that Bourdelin examined in the King's Library. The plants came from the King's Garden, an institution that was, like the Academy, part of the royal household and therefore administered by one and the same individual, the Surintendant des Bâtiments du Roi. The mineral waters that Bourdelin analysed in Paris may have been sent there by the *corps* of medically-trained officials who since 1605 had been appointed by the king's physician to run the growing number of spas around France.[75] It is worth recalling also that the Academy's anatomists had much more success than their English counterparts in acquiring animals for dissection from royal menageries.[76] Royal patronage opened doors to royal institutions, and these institutions allowed the Academy to acquire large and varied collections of natural objects with relative ease.

Having acquired such collections, why lug them into the laboratory? Why not simply put them on display, as Sloane did with his minerals, or press them into the service of classification and conjecture, as Woodward did with his own collection? The Academy's laboratory is part of the answer, as is the fact that the academicians had the luxury of building collections with the laboratory in mind. But there is another answer: the close collaboration between academicians meant that the collectors among them were constantly rubbing shoulders with the experimenters. This applies most clearly to the plant project, which depended on a long-term collaboration between gardeners (Jean and Nicolas Marchant) and experimenters (Duclos, Bourdelin and Dodart). No such interaction took place between, for example, Nehemiah Grew and John Ray. In the last quarter of the seventeenth century, these two Fellows had overlapping interests in plants, and complementary talents for classifying plants and experimenting upon them.[77] They surely would have worked together if, like Bourdelin and the Marchants, they were obliged to meet weekly, over a

---

74   Gersaint, *Catalogue raisonné*, 31.
75   Laurence W. Brockliss, 'The Development of the Spa in Seventeenth-Century France', *Medical History Supplement* 10 (1990), 23–47, on 34.
76   Guerrini, *Courtier's Anatomists*, 112–117; Noah Moxham, 'Edward Tyson's *Phocaena*: A Case Study in the Institutional Context of Scientific Publishing', *Notes and Records*, 66 (2012), 235–252, on 241.
77   On Grew's anatomical studies see Alan G. Morton, *History of Botanical Science: An Account of the Development of Botany from Ancient Times to the Present Day* (London, 1981), 178–95; and on Grew's chemical experiments on plants see Anna Marie Roos, 'Nehemiah Grew (1641–1712) and the Saline Chymistry of Plants', *Ambix* 54 (2007), 51–68; cf. C.R. Metcalfe, 'Grew, Nehemiah', in *Dictionary of Scientific Biography*, ed. Gillispie, 5:532–536. Ray's work on plant classification, along with his experiments on germination and the motion of sap, are summarised in Morton, *Botanical Science*, 195–213; cf. C. Webster, 'Ray, John', in *Dictionary of Scientific Biography*, ed. Gillispie, 12: 313–318.

long period of time, to discuss their research. But Ray had neither the inclination nor the obligation to abandon the bucolic country estates where he pursued his ground-breaking work on botanical classification; and Grew's contributions to the Society depended on a series of endowments that were as fickle as they were short-lived.[78] Collectors and experimenters worked together at the Academy because *all* the empirical scientists at the Academy worked together – at least, they did so to a greater degree than their English counterparts.

Grew's experience with scientific fundraising suggests another reason for the distinctive character of the Academy's experimental programme. When John Wilkins created a paid research post for Grew in 1672, he did so in the hope that Grew's dissections of plants would provide 'entertainment' for Fellows at the Society's weekly meetings.[79] Wilkins was all too aware that most of the Society's income derived from the membership fee and annual subscription that it imposed on Fellows; that the Society's survival therefore depended on attracting new Fellows and retaining existing ones; and that dull and repetitive meetings were unlikely to achieve either of these ends. The point generalises: throughout the period under consideration, the individuals who selected experiments for performance or discussion at the Society's meetings had the dual aim of investigating nature and entertaining subscribers.[80]

The situation in France was quite different. The Academy depended on the continued support of the king and his immediate representatives, especially the ministers Jean-Baptiste Colbert, Michel François Le Tellier (marquis de Louvois), Louis Phélypeaux de Pontchartrain, and the Regent, Philippe II. These men were not concerned to amuse themselves at the Academy's meetings (which they rarely attended) but to enhance the glory of their king and increase the health, wealth and power of his kingdom.[81] As a result, the

---

78 Metcalfe, 'Grew, Nehemiah', 313; Michael Hunter, 'Early Problems in Professionalizing Scientific Research: Nehemiah Grew (1641–1712) and the Royal Academy, with an Unpublished Letter to Henry Oldenburg', in *Establishing the New Science: The Experience of the Early Royal Society* (Woodbridge, 1989), 261–78.

79 Hunter, *Establishing the New Science*, 265, cf. 34, 39.

80 Ibid, 34; Michael Hunter, *The Royal Society and Its Fellows, 1660–1700: The Morphology of an Early Scientific Institution*, (2nd edn, Stanford in the Vale, 1994), 82–83; Boas Hall, *Promoting Experimental Learning*, 15, 28.

81 Stroup, *Company of Scientists*, Chapter 5 (on Colbert, Louvois, and Pontchartrain), 107–111 (Louvois); Sturdy, *Science and Social Status*, 58–59 (Louis XIV), 63–68 (Colbert); Sturdy and Demeulenaere-Douyère, *Enquête du Régent*, 17–18 (Philippe II). Robin Briggs has urged us to 'jettison...any notion that the Académie was seriously intended [by French ministers, before 1699 and perhaps afterwards] to play an active technological role': Robin Briggs, 'The Académie Royale des Sciences and the Pursuit of Utility', *Past and Present* 131

Academy was perfectly capable of research that was dull and repetitive on the scale of weeks and months, as long as it produced glorious or useful outcomes on the scale of years and decades. Colbert approved of the plant project because it mixed medicine and natural philosophy; the Marquis de Louvois, Colbert's narrowly utilitarian successor, singled out Bourdelin's study of mineral waters as an exemplary piece of royal science; and the Regent expressed his satisfaction with Réaumur's study of steel and iron by granting him an annual pension of 12,000 livres.[82] It is hard to imagine these projects flourishing at the Society, for the simple reason that Fellows would not have been amused by the endless distillations and calcinations that made up a large portion of the research of Bourdelin and Réaumur. Material-driven experimentation, which was repetitive by definition and dull by implication, was much more attractive to the Academy's patrons than it was to the Society's.

Boyle's study of mineral waters may seem an exception to this rule, for two reasons. Firstly, Boyle was under no pressure to please the Society's patrons, since he was independently wealthy and he published his book on mineral waters in his own name and not the Society's. Secondly, Boyle claimed that his main purpose in studying mineral waters was the eminently practical one of helping physicians 'to find the vertues and effects of Mineral Waters'.[83] Appearances are deceiving, however. It is true that Boyle did not write *Mineral Waters* on behalf of the Society. But his readership included the kind of 'virtuosi' whom the Society tried to attract to its meetings – men who read Boyle for his 'unusual Experiments' and not just for his 'useful Observations', to borrow two phrases from the publisher's preface to *Mineral Waters*. This audience, no less than Hauksbee's, would have been disappointed by a straightforward survey of the contents of all of England's mineral waters, which is what Duclos offered in his *Eaux minérales*. The 'unusual Experiments' that the publisher had in mind probably included such things as Boyle's discovery of miscroscopic living beings in one mineral water, and his demonstration (mentioned above) that the medical virtues of some mineral can be traced to extremely small amounts of earthy matter. There was no place for such digressions in Duclos' book, an omission that is plausibly explained by the fact that the books' aims were useful rather than curious.

(1991), 38–88, on 55. However Briggs implies that the real role of the Academy was basic research, not entertainment, so the contrast with the Society survives his analysis. At any rate, Briggs agrees that the chemical studies of plants and mineral waters, and Réaumur's studies of steel and iron, were among the few projects geared towards utility before 1699.

82   Stroup, *Company of Scientists*, 48, 51 (plant project), 108–109 (mineral waters); Sturdy and Demeulenaere-Douyère, *Enquête du Régent*, 51.
83   Boyle, *Mineral Waters*, 217.

The same fact also explains the emphasis that Duclos placed on describing the contents of mineral waters, as opposed to perfecting general tests of their contents. From the utilitarian perspective, the Academy's project was preferable to Boyle's because it had the advantage of the latter (it covered nearly all the springs that mattered to French physicians) without the drawback (it did not require physicians to do any tests themselves). From the point of view of a chymist, however, Boyle's project was surely the more attractive one. For a chymist the more interesting question is not whether this or that mineral water contains iron (for example), but whether oak galls or some other substance is the best test for the presence of iron, in any liquid. Boyle's mixed audience of physicians and virtuosi, and his own chymical interests, meant that he had much to gain from developing tests of mineral waters and little to gain from applying them equally to every mineral water in England. Duclos and Bourdelin, working with Louis XIV and Colbert in mind, had the opposite pattern of interests.[84]

Charles Dufay is a more stubborn anomaly than Boyle. None of the explanations I have considered so far appear to apply to his mineral-driven studies of electricity, luminescence, and double refraction. Dufay's minerals did not derive from a state-sponsored programme of collecting but from a loose network of friends and acquaintances; most of the experiments he performed on them had no useful purpose beyond the investigation of nature; and Dufay did these experiments himself, without any sustained help from other members of the Academy. Apparently, Dufay's version of material-driven experimentation did not depend upon generous state support, close collaboration between scientists, or the pressures of utilitarian patrons. The solution to this conundrum is to observe that Dufay's research on gems was modelled on earlier investigations that had one or more of those three properties.

The models were Réaumur, who was Dufay's mentor and collaborator in the 1720s; and Dufay's own earlier experiments on varnish and glass-making. It was Réaumur who drew Dufay into the Academy in 1723. He did so partly on the basis of Dufay's study of Chinese varnish, a project that involved trying many different recipes for varnish in the hope of identifying European substitutes for the ingredients in the Oriental original. At the time, Réaumur was in the midst of his own quest for a European recipe for an Eastern commodity, namely

---

84 The explanation given in this paragraph and the previous one do not require the existence of the Royal Society of London. Boyle would have had a mixed audience of virtuosi and physicians even if the Society had not existed. But the explanations do require the existence of the Paris Academy. In general, I do not claim that institutional factors completely explain differences in experimental style, only that they help to do so.

porcelain. Réaumur was attracted to Dufay because the younger man reminded him of himself. Naturally enough, the newly elected chemist continued the tradition of material-driven experimentation of which Réaumur was then the stand-out practitioner. Dufay's study of glass, published in the Academy's *Mémoires* for 1727, bore the stamp of his mentor and collaborator. It was an exhaustive, unglamorous, utilitarian search for substances that produce acid-resistant glass. Dufay's studies of artificial stones, published in 1728 and 1732, were in the same style. It is no surprise that Dufay took the same systematic approach when he investigated electricity, luminescence and double refraction between 1724 and 1738. In sum, Dufay shows both the limits and the strength of institutional forces at the Academy. There were (obviously) many experimental projects in the Academy that did not have utility as their goal, collaboration as their social form, and a royal collection as its material basis. Nevertheless, some of these projects were shaped by projects that *did* have that goal, that social form, and that material basis. In some cases at least, the contrast between the Academy and the Society persisted in the absence of its original causes.

6   Conclusion

I have tried to establish a new contrast between French and English experimenters, and to identify some institutional causes of that contrast. The contrast is not meant to apply to every piece of empirical work carried out by all members of the Royal Society and the Paris Academy in the first eighty years of their existence. My aim has instead been to consider a sufficient number of important cases in sufficient detail to support claims about the institutional forces that were at work in those cases.

Needless to say, it is desirable to test these claims against other cases and to search for other causes. It would be especially useful to consider pre-1700 cases that do not involve Robert Boyle, such as Nehemiah Grew's study of the chemistry of plants, Edward Tyson's animal dissections, and Martin Lister's natural history of mineral waters, all of which had parallels in Paris.[85] We are also in need of more post-1700 comparisons. A good place to start would be Stephen Hale's studies of the physiology of animals and the 'staticks' of vegetable matter, projects that had contemporaneous analogues in Réaumur's studies of the

---

85   On these projects see Roos, 'Saline Chymistry of Plants'; Anna Marie Roos, *The Salt of the Earth: Natural Philosophy, Medicine, and Chymistry in England, 1650–1750* (Leiden and Boston, 2007), appendix; and Moxham, 'Edward Tyson's *Phocaena*'.

digestive mechanisms of birds and George Buffon's research on the mechanics of wood.[86] Concerning causes, the Academy's chemical studies of plants and mineral waters, with their distinctive systematic structure, may have had precedents at the King's Garden, which since the 1648 had combined a large collection of plants with regular chemical teaching.[87] One wonders also whether the French integration of collecting and experimenting had anything to do with the sharp division that existed at the Academy between 'physical' sciences and 'mathematical' ones, a division which meant that botanists and mineralogists occupied the same disciplinary category, and met on the same day of the week, as chemists and anatomists. Certainly there is more to be said about the similarities and differences between this division and the corresponding split in England between mathematicians and naturalists.[88]

Enough has been said, however, to suggest some revisions to existing views about the comparative history of the early Society and Academy. The first view concerns Isaac Newton. Kuhn and Dear see Newton as the great integrator of the English and Continental styles of experimentation, and they may well be right that Newton combined an English attention to experimental detail with a Continental fondness for mathematical arguments.[89] But Newton arguably played the opposite role if we set aside the distinction between argument and narrative and contrast the French and the English in terms of the relationship between experimenters and collectors. Newton was not himself a noted collector of plants, animals or minerals, though he did possess a small collection of the latter.[90] And according to the standard history of early modern experimental physics, Newton was one of the main agents of the bifurcation that occurred in the eighteenth century between natural history on the one hand and experimental natural philosophy on the other.[91] If there was a convergence in the French and English approach to collections it was not effected by Newton but by Dufay, who used his mineral-driven trials to bring order to the instrument-driven spectacles of Hauksbee and Gray.

---

86 Frederic L. Holmes, 'Scientific Writing and Scientific Discovery', *Isis* 78 (1987), 220–35, on 230–231; Lesley Hanks, *Buffon avant l'Histoire naturelle* (Paris, 1966), 151–68.
87 I am grateful to an anonymous reviewer for suggesting this explanation. See Yves Laissus, 'Le Jardin du Roi', in *Le Jardin du Roi et le Collége Royal dans l'enseignement des sciences au XVIII siécle*, ed. Yves Laissus and Jean Torlais (Paris, 1986), 287–341, on 336, note 1; and Allen G. Debus, *The French Paracelsians: The Chemical Challenge to Medical and Scientific Tradition in Early Modern France* (Cambridge, 2002), 80–84.
88 Feingold, 'Mathematicians and Naturalists'.
89 Kuhn, 'Mathematical versus Experimental Traditions', 18; Peter Dear, *Discipline and Experience: The Mathematical Way in the Scientific Revolution* (Chicago, 1995), chap. 8.
90 Wilson, *Mineral Collecting*, 185.
91 John Heilbron, *Elements of Early Modern Physics* (Berkeley, 1982), 5.

The relationship between natural history and experimental philosophy is another topic that takes on a new complexion when we pay attention to the relationship between collectors and experimenters. The phrase 'experimental philosophy' first became widely used in England in the 1650s and 1660s, and in this context the phrase was associated with the view that natural philosophy should begin with the compilation of a particular kind of natural history. These natural histories were made up of lists of topics or questions, each of which served as a prompt for the collection of relevant experiments and observations. Since this form of experimental philosophy did not spread to France until the 1730s, it is tempting to conclude that natural history and natural philosophy remained separate in France until that period.[92] Yet the examples of Duclos, Bourdelin, Réaumur and Dufay show that there was a rich tradition of combining natural history and experimentation at the Paris Academy from the 1660s onwards. The compilation of Baconian natural histories was only one way of merging natural history and natural philosophy; experimenting on natural history collections was another, equally pervasive procedure. This is not to say the two procedures were distinct. It would be difficult to re-cast Bourdelin's analyses of mineral waters and plants as replies to a set of questions, except in a way that would make a mockery of the Baconian procedure, that is by asking hundreds of questions of the form 'what are the contents of plant X?' The fact that Boyle framed his study of mineral waters as a Baconian natural history may help to explain why he did not systematically test a large number of different waters.[93]

Finally, the contrast I have been developing here has implications for the consensus view that the French differed from the English in preferring argument over narrative. Were the French more selective than the English when they reported experiments, and were their reports more structured and less chronological? Is the *amount* of selection and structure the key factor? Or is it the *kind* of selection, and the *kind* of structure, that truly separates the French

---

92 Peter Anstey and Alberto Vanzo, 'The Origins of Early Modern Experimental Philosophy', *Intellectual History Review* 22 (2012), 499–518, esp. 516–518. Peter Anstey, 'Philosophy of Experiment in Early Modern England: The Case of Bacon, Boyle and Hooke', *Early Science and Medicine* 19 (2014), 103–32. Peter Anstey, 'Bacon, Experimental Philosophy and French Enlightenment Natural History', in *Natural History in Early Modern France: The Poetics of an Epistemic Genre*, eds. R. Garrod, K. Murphy and Smith (Leiden, 2018), 205–240. I am grateful to Professor Anstey for sharing with me a draft of the latter paper.

93 On Boyle's use of natural histories, see Michael Hunter, 'Robert Boyle and the Early Royal Society: A Reciprocal Exchange in the Making of Baconian Science', *British Journal of the History of Science*, 40 (2007), 1–23; and Peter Anstey and Michael Hunter, 'Robert Boyle's "Designe about Natural History"', *Early Science and Medicine* 13 (2008), 83–126.

from the English? The case of mineral waters favours the latter view. Boyle's *Mineral Waters* and Duclos' *Eaux minérales* were both selective and structured; the difference is that Boyle put the accent on the tests he carried out whereas Duclos emphasised the mineral waters he tested. Time will tell whether this new view can be extended to other cases.

CHAPTER 10

The Uses of Licensing: Publishing Strategy and the Imprimatur at the Early Royal Society

Noah Moxham

The importance of early scientific institutions to the production and dissemination of natural knowledge has been the subject of intensive scholarly scrutiny. Those analyses have frequently focussed on the varying degrees to which the new institutions of the late seventeenth century – notably the Royal Society of London and the Académie Royale des Sciences in Paris – succeeded in realising their own early ambitions and in answering the expectations of their founders and patrons. It is also frequently taken for granted that the new institutions were significant innovators in the realm of scientific publishing. While there have been valuable and detailed accounts of the geneses and production histories of particular works, attempts to situate these projects more broadly and to understand how they fit into the publishing strategies of early scientific institutions, and how and why those strategies emerged in the first place, have only recently begun to emerge. Anita Guerrini's recent study of the Paris Académie's anatomical projects, which she uses to situate the Académie's activity for the first thirty years of its existence, is an excellent recent example. Further back, Mario Biagioli's important essay on the Florentine Accademia del Cimento constructs the core of its argument around the presentation of the Cimento's one key publication, the *Saggi di Naturali Esperienze* (1667).[1] This essay is an attempt to provide a similar overview for institutional natural philosophical publishing at the Royal Society during the seventeenth century. The Royal Society's publishing practices are a great deal more varied than those of either the Parisian or Florentine Academies, partly because it simply published a

---

1 See for example Sachiko Kusukawa, 'The *Historia Piscium* (1686)', *Notes and Records: The Royal Society Journal of the History of Science* 54 (2000), 179–197; Anita Guerrini, 'The King's Animals and the King's Books: The illustrations for the Paris Academy's *Histoire des Animaux*', *Annals of Science* 67 (2010), 383–-04, and *The Courtier's Anatomists: Animals and Humans in Louis XIV's Paris* (Chicago, 2016); Adrian Johns, 'Miscellaneous Methods: Authors, Societies and journals in Early Modern England', *British Journal for the History of Science* 33 (2000), 159–186; Jean-Pierre Vittu 'La formation d'une institution scientifique: le Journal des Savants de 1664 à 1714', *Journal des Savants* (2002), 179–203; Mario Biagioli, 'Scientific Revolution, Social Bricolage, and Etiquette', in Roy Porter and Mikuláš Teich, eds., *The Scientific Revolution in National Context* (Cambridge, 1996), 11–54.

great deal more and partly because its relations with its founding patron were not as narrowly determining. However, an examination of the first books published under its aegis show that those relations were decidedly influential in setting the Society's early agenda and its practices of communication, and careful attention to those and subsequent shifts allow us to track developments in the Society's understanding of itself as well as its favoured modes of self-projection.

The foundation of the Royal Society envisaged the publishing and dissemination of natural knowledge as part of its purpose, not in the sense of making publishing part of its official remit but by giving it the power to license works for the press on its own authority. The grant of an imprimatur through the Society's Charter of 1662 (renewed in 1663) was a rare and important attribute of the new foundation. Following a long period of relative freedom of the press during the Wars of the Three Kingdoms and the Interregnum, the Restoration was a time of intense retrenchment, codified by the Licensing Act of 1662 and enforced by Charles II's enthusiastic Overseer of the Imprimery, Roger L'Estrange.[2] The licensing privilege set the new Society apart from the usual mechanisms of censorship and oversight vested in the civil and ecclesiastical authorities. This study focuses on the period from 1663, when the Society issued its first license, to 1695, when the lapse of the 1662 Act made the privilege legally irrelevant.[3]

The terms of the license were interpreted as allowing the Society to appoint typographers, rather than to set up as a printer on its own account (as was the case at, for example, the University of Oxford, and as might otherwise have been contemplated if the intention expressed at the first informal meeting of the Society, of establishing a 'college for the promoting of physico-mathematical experimental learning', had been carried out).[4] This limitation, without which

---

[2] On L'Estrange's career, and power over the London print trades, see Peter Hinds, *'The Horrid Popish Plot': Roger L'Estrange and the circulation of political discourse in late seventeenth-century London* (Oxford, 2010).

[3] Adrian Johns, in his seminal study of the relationship between early modern natural knowledge-making and the London print trades, has given a valuable overview of the licence and how it notionally governed the interactions between the Society and its appointed printers – see *The Nature of the Book: Print and Knowledge in the Making* (Chicago, 1998), 492–497. Johns is mainly concerned with those interactions, however, rather than in the evolving (and plural) ways in which the Society understood the utility of its privilege, and what that privilege implied about the institution's relationship to particular works or authors, which are the concern of the present essay.

[4] Thomas Birch, *History of the Royal Society of London*, 4 vols (London, 1756–1757), 1:3 On the development of the University Press at Oxford see Jason Peacey, 'Printers to the University: 1584–1658' and Vivienne Larminie, 'The Fell Era: 1658–1686', in Ian Gadd (ed.), *The History of Oxford University Press Volume I: Beginnings to 1780* (Oxford, 2013), 50–77 and 78–106.

the subsequent history of the Society's publishing endeavours might have been somewhat simpler, probably arose from the fact that the Stationers' Company, the professional guild regulating the London print trades, already existed. It would have been impossible for the Society's Charter to establish the new body as a printer and publisher in its own right without impinging upon the privileges awarded to the Stationers by their own Charter of 1558.

1 Contrasting Uses of the Imprimatur: *Sylva* (1664) and *Micrographia* (1665)

The right to license books for publishing under an institutional imprint does not, however, afford us a simple definition of what constituted 'Royal Society publications'. The precise outlines and degree of closeness implied in the association varied in particular instances.[5] For example, the first of the books published under the Society's imprimatur, John Evelyn's *Sylva*, was produced in response to queries from the Commissioners of the Navy originally addressed to the Royal Society in 1662.[6] *Sylva* was printed and published along with two shorter treatises, one by Evelyn himself and the other by his friend and correspondent John Beale. Their typographical presentation clearly shows that they were meant to be understood as Royal Society works. *Sylva* was equipped with an elaborate, rubricated title-page which mentions the Society four times, as the original commissioner of the work, as its licenser, and with

---

5 *Sylva* certainly received the first license issued by the Royal Society, but was not the first publication whose author sought to associate it with the Royal Society. That honour belongs to John Graunt's *Natural and Political Observations on the Bills of Mortality* (1662), the third, expanded edition of which was later licensed by the Society in 1665. The 1662 edition was dedicated to the Society's pre-Charter president, Robert Moray, and Graunt had presented the Society with 50 copies and successfully leveraged the gift to obtain election (Birch, *History*, 1:75–77). I am grateful to Michael Hunter for drawing my attention to this peculiarity; for his discussion of it, and the precise sequence of the Society's involvement, see Hunter, 'John Webster, the Royal Society and *The Displaying of Supposed Witchcraft* (1677)', *Notes and Records* 71 (2017), 7–19.

6 For a brief but useful discussion of *Sylva*'s reception, see Gillian Darley, *John Evelyn: Living for Ingenuity* (New Haven, CT, 2003), 180–181; and for the broader context of 17th century arboriculture, L. Sharp, 'Timber, Science and Economic Reform in the Seventeenth Century', *Forestry* 48 (1975), 51–86; on its framing within the context of the Society's commitment to useful knowledge and the History of Trades project, see Michael Hunter, *Science and Society in Restoration England* (Cambridge, 1981), 93–94, 98–101; on its early production history see V.P.J. Arponen, 'The Cultural Causes of Environmental Problems: A Wittgensteinian Approach to Social Action' (PhD Diss., University of Edinburgh, 2012), esp. 50–66. I am grateful to Caroline Spearing for drawing my attention to this work.

the arms of the Society (designed by Evelyn himself) firmly on display; Evelyn's own account confirms much of this, and also appears to record his pride at *Sylva*'s distinction as the first printed work to emerge from the Society:

> Oct: 15 1662 I this day delivered my Discourse concerning *Forest-trees* to our *Society* upon occasion of certaine *Queries* sent us by the Commissioners of his Majesties Navie: being the first Booke that was Printed by Order of the Society, & their Printer, since it was a Corporation.[7]

Evelyn's stateliness of phrase conveys his sense of the symbolic importance of the event, and the editor of his diary suggests that this passage was added after the fact. This would explain the long delay between the apparent award of the imprimatur and *Sylva*'s eventual appearance in print, almost eighteen months later. There is no contemporary record of a meeting of the Society's Council to specify the award of the imprimatur: the minutes of October 15 indicate only that 'he was desired to print the paper read by him'. Evelyn's paper in fact pulled together 'the several suggestions offered by others in distinct papers, by way of answer to the queries of the commissioners of the navy'. Jonathan Goddard, Christopher Merret and John Wilkins were appointed along with Evelyn to make a suitable extract from the papers to answer the Commissioners – indicating that the Society did not anticipate that the printed version of Evelyn's paper, or even the manuscript itself, would give the naval commissioners what they wanted. The following week Evelyn – this time just Evelyn – was reminded of his promise, and two weeks later, on November 5, he consulted with Peter Pett, a naval Commissioner who had been elected a Fellow at the same meeting, about what to prioritise in his account. (Pett suggested the preparation of acorns for planting).[8] The draft work was serially augmented over the ensuing months: five short treatises on cider were added, and it was anticipated that a piece by Jean de la Quintinye on the cultivation of melons would be included (it was eventually published in the *Philosophical Transactions* in 1669).[9] In December 1663 the third part of the work, Evelyn's *Kalendarium Hortense*, was added; and on the same date a resolution was passed in the Society's Council, confirming the appointment of John Martyn and James Allestry as the Society's designated printers, and establishing a form of words for the imprimatur. At the same time it was stipulated that two members of Council would be required to peruse any work proposed for licensing by the Society,

---

7 *The Diary of John Evelyn*, ed. E.S. de Beer, 6 vols, (Oxford, 1955), 3:340.
8 Birch, *History*, 1:117, 118, 120.
9 Birch, *History*, 1:213, 215, 347–348.

though the minutes record no such report nor the award of an imprimatur on the date given in the published volume.[10]

There were some delays involved, concerned with the eventual scope of the published volume and the Society's temporary uncertainty on the question of whether its Charter did in fact give it the power to license books, but there can be no question that *Sylva* and its associated treatises – particularly *Pomona* – were collaborative productions in which the Society had been closely involved at every stage.[11] *Sylva* incorporated contributions from Jonathan Goddard, Christopher Merrett, and John Winthrop. Goddard's and Winthrop's were both read to the Society during the summer and autumn of 1662. Winthrop – the colonial governor of Connecticut, in London temporarily to negotiate a Charter formally establishing the colony and an active participant in the affairs of the Royal Society during his sojourn – communicated his paper on the manufacture of pitch and tar before the paper from the naval Commissioners had even been received.[12]

The *Sylva* volume arose out of a specific request for advice from the government, yet its scope almost certainly exceeded that of the advice originally called for.[13] While on the face of it all that was called for was a set of written responses, for which manuscript would presumably have sufficed, there was a broader logic to the Society's decision to publish the result. The original queries have been reprinted in a recent essay by Beryl Hartley; lacking Evelyn's manuscript digest, however, we cannot precisely frame the relationship of the Society's actual response to the queries themselves.[14] Yet the practical recommendations laid out in *Sylva* would clearly be of greater use the more widely they were disseminated. There is no indication that this wider publication was specifically requested by the Commissioners, and the Society undertook not only to supply practical advice on improving the supply of timber in the British Isles but to broadcast the techniques for doing so. It is equally evident from the presentation of the volume and its title-page that the Society was anxious to

---

10   The imprimatur in *Sylva* is dated 3 February 1663/4; though there was a Council meeting that day, there is no record of the award of the imprimatur, nor of any report from the assigned referees, Jonathan Goddard and Christopher Merrett. Birch, *History*, 1:377–380.

11   On the ambiguity of the licensing power in the Society's charter, see Birch, *History*, 1:344 and 346–347, 14 and 21 December 1663.

12   Birch, *History*, 1:87–88, 2 July 1662; 'The manner of making Tarr and Pitch in New-England. &c. by Mr Winthrop', RS Register-Book Original (RBO) 1:179–184.

13   Birch, *History*, 1:111, 17 September 1662.

14   Beryl Hartley, 'Exploring and communicating knowledge of trees in the early Royal Society', *Notes and Records* (2010) 64, 229–250, Appendix 1.

secure the public credit for its practical contribution to the welfare of the nation, and the prestige of being consulted by the crown.

The proximity of these several events – the initial grant of the Society's Charter, the communication of official requests for advice, and the Society's prompt mobilisation of its resources in response – suggest that close relations and cooperation were anticipated between the Society and government. The Society's official incorporation appears to have underlined its availability for this kind of advisory role, and the Fellows' swift response their eagerness to develop the relationship. The resulting collaborative book was designed to advertise the Society's capacities in this regard. *Sylva* was also a reasonable commercial success, running to five editions by 1729. The attribution of the treatise to Evelyn plays down the appearance of collaborative production to modern eyes, but there were precedents for the attribution to a single author of works of natural philosophy associated with a group of writers and researchers in mid-seventeenth century England. The *Reformed Common-Wealth of Bees* (1655), for example, was the product of collaboration and joint information-gathering by members of the circle around Samuel Hartlib, but Hartlib's name alone appeared on the title-page.[15]

The Society's possible reasons for not claiming authorship of *Sylva*, when it clearly wanted the credit of having ushered it into the world, are worth exploring here. One might be a wish not to defraud Evelyn and his collaborators of the credit due to them in selecting and arranging the material, or indeed of the profit of the book's eventual sale. Relatedly, the Society, whose resources were very limited, may not have wished to assume the risk of publication – no publication issued under the Society's imprimatur received more than notional support prior to 1685, when the institution decided to publish the *Historia Piscium* of Francis Willughby and John Ray. Even that was published under the deceased Willughby's name, despite the fact that the Society funded the publication and Ray was responsible for most of the text and for sourcing the illustrations. Although the Society's Charter envisaged all sorts of ways in which the institution could act as a corporate body, it appears that the Society was either unable or unwilling to understand scientific authorship in those terms.

The third book to appear under the Society's imprimatur also had its origins in a collaboration. This was *Micrographia*, published early in 1665. Recent scholarship has debated the extent to which this volume should be considered

---

15 Mark Greengrass, 'Hartlib, Samuel (c.1600–1662)', *Oxford Dictionary of National Biography*, (Oxford, 2004; online edn, Oct 2007) [http://www.oxforddnb.com/view/article/12500, accessed 24 February 2016].

the work of Robert Hooke or Christopher Wren or both.[16] Internal evidence – notably the high degree of organisation in the sequencing of observations and illustrations, coupled with Hooke's strenuous use of the first person throughout – indicates that the volume as published is largely Hooke's work. (The attribution of some of the insect illustrations to Wren has been weakened by the discovery of microscopical drawings of insects by Hooke from 1660 and 1661 that closely resemble several of the published illustrations).[17] The sequence can be summarised roughly as follows. Wren had been producing microscopical drawings of insects as far back as the 1650s; in April 1661 he was informed of the King's wish that he continue to prosecute these investigations, but in the event little further work appears to have been done and Wren asked to be excused from the task by August.[18] At that time the work was reassigned, with the King's permission, to Hooke (and to one Vander Diver, about whom nothing else is known); Hooke was reminded to proceed with his microscopical observations with a view to their publication in March 1663/4, and in July to mount them in a handsome book suitable for showing to the King, from whom the Society anticipated a visit that never materialised.[19]

By June 1664 the Society was treating the publication of Hooke's observations as a strong but as yet uncertain possibility, passing a resolution to the effect that 'in case Mr Hooke's microscopical observations should be published by order of the Society, they might be perused by some members of the Society'. The President, the mathematician and courtier William, Visount Brouncker, was nominated for this task in the first instance, and asked to select a suitable second referee when he had finished.[20] The language is once again ambiguous, and it is not clear whether this order establishes a protocol for what might happen when the book was finished, or whether it represents a

---

16   See in particular Lisa Jardine, *On a Grander Scale: The Outstanding Career of Christopher Wren* (London, 2002), 97–100, 276–278, who plays up Wren's involvement; and, by contrast, Mark Jervis, who deploys recent archival finds by Janice Neri to argue that Hooke's insect drawings, in particular, draw upon his own previous work and not upon Wren's. Jervis, 'Robert Hooke's *Micrographia*: an Entomologist's Perspective', *Journal of Natural History* 47 (2013), 2531–2573.

17   Janice Neri, 'Some early drawings by Robert Hooke', *Archives of Natural History* 32 (2005), 41–47.

18   Birch, *History*, 1:21, 8 May 1661; J. A. Bennett, *The Mathematical Science of Christopher Wren* (Cambridge, 1983), p. 77.

19   Birch, *History*, 1:213, 25 March 1663; 1:272, 6 July 1663. The development of Hooke's microscopical observations and the sequence of events leading up to publication are well summarised in Steven Inwood, *The Man Who Knew Too Much: The Strange and Inventive Life of Robert Hooke* (London, 2002), 61–63.

20   Birch, *History*, 1:442.

THE USES OF LICENSING 273

decision to press ahead with perusal of the manuscript prior to licensing and publication. Two months later (24 August) Hooke delivered a paper on petrifactions, described in the minutes of the Society as being 'designed by him as a part of his microscopical book, then in the press'. Almost uniquely in the annals of the early Royal Society, this is followed up with a specific editorial judgement: 'The Society approved of the modesty used in his assertions, but advised him to omit what he had delivered concerning the ends of petrifaction'.[21]

Lacking the manuscript, we cannot establish whether Hooke obeyed this instruction or not. The printed text of Observation XVII, 'Of Petrify'd Wood, and other Petrify'd bodys', does in fact contain speculations about the ultimate ends of the petrifaction of wood and shells – and a contention that this property has some larger and more intelligible purpose than a mere 'plastick virtue'.[22] It is not possible to determine, however, whether what we have represents a text edited in conformity with the Society's wishes or one that ignored them. The Society was evidently concerned in either case that the speculative assertion of a higher purpose in nature in a book published under the institution's imprimatur would be understood as enjoying official endorsement. It is also striking that the Society felt free to intervene at this level of detail.

The negotiations over the book rumbled on. Though the Society knew it to be in the press in late August, and had appointed readers to approve it for licensing as long ago as June, it was not until 23 November 1664 that the imprimatur was finally awarded, and then with the strict proviso that Hooke's preface should clarify the limits of the Society's endorsement:

> [It was ordered] that Mr Hooke give notice in the dedication of that work to the Society, that though they have licensed it, yet they own no theory, nor will be thought to do so; and that the several hypotheses laid down by him therein, are not delivered as certainties, but as conjectures; and that he intends not at all to obtrude or expose them to the world as the opinion of the Society.[23]

Hooke observed to Boyle, in a letter dated the following day, that the Society's deliberations had already delayed *Micrographia*'s publication, the sheets of which had been ready from the press for over a month:

---

21   Birch, *History* 1:463.
22   Robert Hooke, *Micrographia, or some physiological descriptions of minute bodies* (London, 1665), 103–112, particularly 111–112.
23   Birch, *History* 1:491.

> [...] the stay that has retarded the publishing of them, has been the examination of them by several members of the society; and the preface, which will be large, and has been stayed very long in the hands of some, who were to read it. I am very much troubled that there is so great an expectation raised of that pamphlet, being very conscious, that there is nothing in it, that can answer that expectation; but such as it is, I hope I shall prevail with the printer to dispatch it some time this or the next week.[24]

The prefatory materials as eventually published feature precisely such a disclaimer as the Society asked for, in which Hooke, in even more extravagantly self-deprecating terms than he used in the letter to Boyle, absolved the Society of any responsibility for the speculative parts of the book. (The characterisation of *Micrographia*, a large and expensively produced folio volume, as a 'pamphlet' is a fairly theatrical example).[25]

The broader point here is simple but significant. The Royal Society was not yet sure how to use its imprimatur, or what it was seen to represent in the wider world. The institution's careful distancing of itself from Hooke's speculative sallies in *Micrographia* implied that it understood itself as closely implicated in what was published with its license – an understandable preoccupation, given that in the case of *Sylva* the Society had been concerned precisely to emphasise its involvement in the book's genesis and production. This uncertainty about how the work would be attributed in the minds of the public can only have been increased by the fact that it began life as a royal commission. *Micrographia* was similar to *Sylva* in that respect, but its ambitions were more nebulous and less practical. In each case the Society left the writing and the organisation of material to the respective authors, but was markedly more willing to be identified with *Sylva*'s practice than *Micrographia*'s speculation.

Micrographia also raises questions about the Society's oversight procedures. As we have seen, the institution took an apparently careful editorial interest in the contents of *Micrographia*, yet did not actually assign the book for perusal until it was already printing. This made the preface and dedication correspondingly important, since they represented opportunities to address issues raised by the Society in response to the main text. In addition to Hooke's own evidence

---

24 Hooke to Boyle, 24 November 1664. Michael Hunter, Lawrence M. Principe, and Antonio Clericuzio, eds, *The Correspondence of Robert Boyle*, 6 vols. (London, 2001), 2:412–413.

25 For Hooke's sensitivity on the application of the word 'pamphlet' to his work, and the negotiation of genre, format and prestige in scientific publishing in the seventeenth-century, see Moxham, 'Edward Tyson's *Phocaena*: A case study in the institutional context of scientific publishing', *Notes and Records* 66 (2012), 235–252, at 238.

for the delays to the preface in particular, we can see from the fact that the sequence of page signatures in the preface is separate from the main sequence that it was probably a late addition. The gatherings of the preface are signed a1 to g2 and interpolated between gathering A (the dedications to the King and the Royal Society) and gathering B (the beginning of the main text).[26] Gathering A, since it features a disclaimer of the kind requested by the Society on 23 November, was presumably held back and printed after that date. The peculiarity of the sequence of signatures and the delay in approving the Preface suggests that the Society was anxious that it too should be covered by the dedicatory disclaimer. It also indicates, however, that the Society wished to benefit by association with an impressive work of natural philosophy.

There is, in short, internal and external evidence to demonstrate the complexity of the composition, printing, and institutional oversight of *Micrographia*. This is enough to indicate both the Society's anxious involvement, its epistemological concerns about what it lent its name to, and its understanding that the imprimatur could be read as an endorsement of a work's contents. At the same time we can see that the Society's oversight came into play *after* the book had gone to press, suggesting that it was not in the first instance being deployed as an editorial mechanism, although the Society turned out to have strong editorial concerns which it tried – perhaps not entirely successfully – to see addressed in the finished work.

The status of both *Sylva* and *Micrographia* as Royal Society publications is complicated by their origins in courses of inquiry that amounted to royal commissions – from the Navy in the case of *Sylva*, and directly from the Crown in the case of *Micrographia*. That status conferred a degree of external obligation upon the Society to carry out, if not necessarily to publish, the commissioned research. The decision to publish can, to varying degrees in each case, be read as a wish to draw public attention to the link between the Society's work and the government. Most subsequent work published under the Society's imprimatur, however, did not originate in requests from the crown but in the research priorities of individuals or those the Society devised for itself. What, therefore, conditioned the Society's use of its imprimatur, and what did it signify in cases where the work to which it was awarded reflected the Society's own priorities rather than those of the government, or the whims of the monarch?

---

26 Hooke, *Micrographia*, 'The Preface', sigs. a1^r-g2^v. The disclaimer, part of the dedication to the Royal Society, appears on A2^v.

2 Keeping Their Distance: Sprat's *History* and the *Philosophical Transactions*

The next two well-known works to be published under the Society's aegis also enjoyed complex relationships with the imprimatur. These were the *Philosophical Transactions* of Henry Oldenburg, and Thomas Sprat's apologetic *History of the Royal Society*. *Philosophical Transactions* is well-known as the earliest example of a scientific periodical – it followed narrowly on the heels of the Parisian *Journal des Sçavans*, whose first issue appeared some ten weeks earlier but which was more a review of books than a site of research communication and whose remit included legal, literary, historical, and above all theological, in addition to scientific and medical works.[27] The first issue of *Transactions* was licensed by the Society's Council on 1 March 1665 (OS), and dated 6 March (Oldenburg had apparently produced a draft version before the Society a few weeks earlier, by 3 February).[28] As some historians have been careful to emphasise, *Transactions* was not an official publication of the Society, in the sense that its contents bore no very strict relationship to what went on in the Society's meetings and the Society accepted no responsibility for it, the imprimatur notwithstanding. Sprat's *History*, by contrast, which *was* intended to be narrowly reflective of the Society's activity, and in whose compilation and composition the Society took an active and detailed interest, did not appear under the institutional imprimatur but through the normal licensing channels of the book trade.[29]

Why were the two works treated differently? After all, with a stronger degree of institutional editorial input into *Transactions* both might have had similar representative functions, with the *History* supplying a backlog of experimental performances from the early period of the Society's activity by a number of different authors which *Transactions* brought up to date. Yet no such continuity of function emerged, and in fact the two appear to have been kept intentionally separate. The *History* was a long time in development, partly because of the closeness of the Society's scrutiny of it and partly because of the disruptions to the print trade in London occasioned by the plague epidemic of summer 1665 and the Great Fire of September 1666. It eventually appeared in 1667,

---

27   Jean-Pierre Vittu, 'Formation d'une institution scientifique', *Journal des Savants* (2002), 179–203 and 349–377; David A Kronick, *A History of Scientific and Technical Periodicals* (Metuchen, NJ, 1962).

28   Birch, *History*, 2:18; Robert Moray to Christiaan Huygens, 13 February 1665 (NS). See *Oeuvres Complètes de Christiaan Huygens*, 22 vols (The Hague, 1888–1950), 5:234–235.

29   The licenser in this instance being William Morrice, Secretary of State since the Restoration and never a Fellow of the Royal Society. See Sprat, *History*, title-page.

having first been mooted as early as 1663.[30] Yet despite the fact that by the time *History* appeared in print there had been over two years' worth of issues of *Transactions* there was no overlap between their contents. The *History*, which was intended partly as a justification of the Royal Society's existence through a demonstration of its experimental performances to date, the selection of which was in the hands of the Society's council, rigorously excluded the contents of the *Transactions* from this justification of the new institution. This was, no doubt, partly to avoid simple duplication. But it also reflects the status and function of the early *Transactions*, and there is very little evidence that the early periodical was viewed as a suitable outlet for the Society's research ambitions.

Why was this so? The answer lies partly in the origins of *Transactions*, which are first hinted at in the summer of 1664 when Oldenburg wrote to his patron-cum-employer, Robert Boyle, asking him to think of possible clients for a 'weekly letter [...] both of state and literary news' that Oldenburg proposed to supply.[31] Oldenburg provided just such a service to Boyle, and evidently hoped to extend it to find a way of converting his considerable labour on behalf of the early Royal Society to some sort of financial advantage. The proposal never got off the ground, apparently for want of subscribers. Shortly after Oldenburg learned of the proposals for what became the *Journal des Sçavans*, whose editors sought to recruit him as their English agent and correspondent, however, he first mooted the idea of a printed periodical of philosophical news.

The early *Transactions* consisted overwhelmingly of scraps of news, fugitive pieces, extracts of letters, and translations from foreign printed sources, often cut and pasted together if they were on related subjects, sometimes separated out into distinct items. The notion of the paper or research article as the natural unit of scientific communication in print was much slower to take hold than historians of science have tended to realise, and the earliest scientific periodicals correspondingly much less like modern research journals. A great deal of what the early *Transactions* contained was reported at second or even third hand; for instance, most of its Italian content was filtered through French correspondents or the *Journal des Sçavans*. Oldenburg used the *Transactions* to

---

30 See Michael Hunter's important essay on Sprat's *History*, 'Latitudinarianism and the "Ideology" of the early Royal Society: Thomas Sprat's *History of the Royal Society* (1667) reconsidered', in *Establishing the New Science: The Experience of the Early Royal Society* (Woodbridge, 1989), 45–81, 49–52. Hunter emphasises the extent to which Sprat's own intellectual preoccupations and style shaped the work as published, perhaps provoking some of the hostile responses the *History* received.

31 Oldenburg to Boyle, 24 August 1664. See A.R. Hall and M.B. Hall, eds, *The Correspondence of Henry Oldenburg*, 13 vols. (Madison, WI, 1965–1986), 2:210.

advertise the experimental capacities of the Royal Society, to preview and promote the works of his patron, Boyle, to encourage replication or continuation of courses of experiments, as a tool for systematic data-gathering, and to appeal for confirmation of scientific news and rumours.

Oldenburg's general practice depended on making available what was obscure. The emphasis of his 'accounts of books', for instance, which rapidly became an important part of *Transactions*, and a statistically significant part of the total page count in any given year, was invariably upon summary rather than criticism or evaluation. More broadly, a considerable proportion of what appeared in the pages of the periodical originated outside the Society's meetings and has left no trace in the record of the minutes. This is not an absolutely reliable guide – after all, we have seen evidence above that not every decision of the Council or piece of activity at a Society meeting was systematically recorded, as in the case of the *Sylva* imprimatur. Nevertheless, it remains the case that between forty and sixty percent of the items published in *Transactions* made no appearance in the Society's minutes, while a similar proportion of material was of foreign origin.[32]

The reliance on foreign and external material was reinforced by the prolonged interruption of the Society's meetings early on in the periodical's career. Only four issues of *Transactions* had appeared before the Society broke up for the summer of 1665, as many of the members retreated from London while the plague epidemic was at its height. Although there were informal meetings and experimental demonstrations in Oxford, and attempts by small groups within the membership to further its experimental programme, the Society was not officially constituted between July 1665 and February 1666.[33] This meant that issues of the periodical could not be licensed by the Society – the core of the membership at Oxford obtained licenses for its publication from the University Vice-Chancellor – and simultaneously interrupted the flow of material from the Society itself. Oldenburg was threatened with a critical shortage of material, and the proportion of overseas material he published in *Transactions* correspondingly increased, setting a pattern that would remain fairly durable even after the Society's return to London. It is worth enquiring

---

[32] For a tabulation of this data from the early *Philosophical Transactions* see Moxham, 'Authors, Editors and Newsmongers: Form and Genre in the *Philosophical Transactions* under Henry Oldenburg', in Joad Raymond and Noah Moxham, eds, *News Networks in Early Modern Europe* (Leiden, 2016), Table 20.1, 480.

[33] For the Oxford group's meeting, and the conviction that this could not legally constitute the Royal Society, see Boyle to Oldenburg, 30 September 1665, *Oldenburg Correspondence*, 2:535–537.

why Oldenburg did not seek to draw upon the accumulated stock of unpublished material in the Royal Society's archives and register-books, as well as the letters that continued to come in from the Continent. There are several possible reasons. One was the sense that it was the Society's prerogative to dispose of this material, and with the Society disbanded for the time being there was no legitimate way for Oldenburg to seek permission to include it in *Transactions*; another, that this stock was intended to form the basis of future publications, Sprat's projected *History* among them, and that it should consequently be left intact.

Certainly, it does not appear to have occurred to the Society to give Oldenburg permission to draw upon its accumulated reserves to make up the possible shortfall of publishable material while the interruption of the meetings continued. Yet the Society evidently encouraged the continuation of *Transactions*, and agreed to help him by negotiating on his behalf with Oxford printers and by supervising the presswork and proof correction.[34] Oldenburg had already begun, on his own initiative as far as we can tell from surviving documents, to take steps to have *Transactions* continued at London. The evidence suggests that the Royal Society's printers, John Martyn and James Allestree, did not wish to undertake them on the terms originally agreed, particularly amid the disruptions to the trade and the book-buying public caused by the plague, but that they were also unwilling to permit Oldenburg to take his business elsewhere.[35] The Society's printers apparently believed that the grant of a Royal Society imprimatur, and their own appointment as printers to the Society, effectively gave them an exclusive license to publish the books it authorised. The Society disagreed, and a letter from Robert Moray to Oldenburg appears to express the belief that Martyn and Allestry could be legally compelled to publish the *Transactions* according to the terms Oldenburg had originally agreed.[36] In the end the point was never tested as a question of law because Allestry, who

---

34 Moray to Oldenburg, 11 October 1665; Boyle to Oldenburg 22 October 1665; Boyle to Oldenburg, 28 October 1665, all in *Oldenburg Correspondence*, 2:563–564, 576–577, 580–581.

35 The issues of how far Allestry and Martyn could be constrained by the Society, and whether their status as sworn printers to the Society amounted to a monopoly, is discussed in Johns, *Nature of the Book*, 495–496.

36 Moray to Oldenburg, 23 July 1665, *Oldenburg Correspondence*, 2:446–447. Though Moray and Oldenburg evidently exchanged many letters during the summer and autumn of 1665 it is for the most part only Moray's half of the correspondence that survives. The letter of 23 July is plainly a reply to a letter in which Oldenburg had informed Moray of a discussion he had had with Martyn and Allestry about the continuing publication of *Transactions*.

was either in Oxford himself by late summer or in direct contact with Moray through other channels, gave permission for subsequent issues to be printed there.[37]

Though the senior Fellows of the Society were eager to have Oldenburg continue the *Transactions* even while the institution was on hiatus, and clearly thought of the periodical as a valuable addition to the enterprise of promoting natural knowledge, it is equally plain that they did not view it as a suitable site for the systematic publication of the research directly sponsored by the Society. In autumn 1665 this may have been because they felt constitutionally debarred from doing so, but matters did not notably change once the Society formally reconvened in London in early 1666. Oldenburg's assiduous activity as Secretary, as a philosophical correspondent and translator, and later as editor of *Transactions*, supplied the Society with an extra strand of activity, one that increased in importance as time went on, but which was distinct from the Society's early ambitions actually to produce as well as to promote new natural knowledge. The Society was quick to see the potential utility of the periodical, especially as an instrument for expanding the natural-philosophical community and for gathering information (though they did not routinely order papers for publication in its pages until 1686, and the devolution of responsibility for the *Transactions* to the Society's salaried Clerk, Edmond Halley).[38] But for as long as *Transactions* continued to feature letters, translations, and fragments of uncorroborated news from the European learned world, which the Society could have no opportunity to authenticate, there remained a significant distinction between knowledge-claims that were communicated from outside the Society, without verification, and those that the Society could claim to have directly witnessed and which, in an important number of cases, it had spent its own limited resources to produce.[39] The fact that *Transactions* consistently contained communications of the former kind may have contributed to the Society's reluctance to use the periodical as its venue of choice for publishing the latter.

---

[37] Moray to Oldenburg, 10 October 1665, *Oldenburg Correspondence*, 2:559–562.

[38] Halley was forced to resign his fellowship before taking up the clerkship precisely so that he would be compelled to obey the instructions of Council on a range of matters, in a way that could not be required of full Fellows. See Birch, *History* 4:453.

[39] This argument is more fully articulated in Moxham, 'Fit for print: developing an institutional model of scientific periodical publishing in England, 1665–ca. 1714', *Notes and Records* (2015), 241–260.

3 Experiment and Print, 1674–1682

This argument gains force from an examination of the various publishing schemes essayed in the Royal Society in the 1670s and 80s. In October 1674, for example, a new project was devised, intended to spread the burden of the Society's experimental research among the senior Fellowship, in order to help 'put life' back into the Society's meetings. The intention was to designate 'eminent members' to supply 'experimental exercises' for all meetings, a fact that was announced in the summonses sent out to the Fellowship as the Society's meetings resumed following the summer recess. In December this was more carefully specified: every member of the Council was to supply at least one substantial discourse a year, or be mulcted forty shillings.[40] Oldenburg gave an account of the immediate results in a letter to Martin Lister dated 19 December:

> The persons, yt have, since our new regulations, entertain'd ye Society wth their Experimental Exercises, are, Mr Boyle, Dr Wallis, Sr Wm Petty, Mr Hook, Dr Grew, Mr Ray; ye first treated of the *Mechanical Origine or Production of Fixtnes;* ye second, of ye *Gravitations of Fluids;* ye 3d, of *the Usefulness of ye Consideration of Duplicat and Subduplicate Proportions to Human Life;* ye 4th, Of a *New Astronomical Quadrant;* ye 5th, *Of Mixture;* ye 6th,, of ye *Seeds, and Specifique Difference of Plants.* As these pieces will, doubtlesse, all be printed in due time, and those yt shall follow ym; so it was thought good, forthwith to print yt of Sir Wm Petty's; ye reason whereof will appear in his Dedication.[41]

Many of those pieces were indeed printed in due time. Apart from Petty's, which Oldenburg mentioned, John Wallis's *Discourse on Gravity and Gravitation* and Nehemiah Grew's *Discourse of Mixture* were each printed as freestanding treatises, while Hooke's quadrant design was published as part of his *Animadversions upon the Machina Coelestis* of the Danzig astronomer Johannes Hevelius.[42] All of these works were licensed by the Society, and all were fairly short – Wallis's is a 36-page quarto, while Grew and Petty printed their

---

40   Birch, *History* 3:139, 20 October 1674.
41   *Oldenburg Correspondence* 2:147–148.
42   Hooke, *Animadversions upon the first part of the Machina Coelestis of* [...] *Johannes Hevelius* (London, 1674), 45–75, for a description of his clock-driven equatorial quadrant.

treatises in duodecimo (166 and 138 pages respectively).[43] These lengths are comparable in view of the difference of format, and not dissimilar to an issue of *Transactions*, which by the 1670s typically consisted of between 24 and 32 quarto pages. Again, then, the Society elected not to use *Transactions* to publish discourses that were explicitly designed to revive the Society's experimental work, to enliven meetings that were perceived to be moribund, and to reverse a growing public reputation for working on abstruse and trivial questions.[44] Oldenburg gave an account of Petty's discourse in number 109 of *Transactions*, situating it as part of a deliberate programme of experimentation designed to elucidate hard problems and to show the Society in a productive and favourable light.[45] Once again, when the Society perceived a need to revive and publish its experimental activity, *Transactions* was not the vehicle of choice.

In December 1676, for example, a committee was established with a view to scouring the Society's registers for publishable material.[46] We do not know whether it actually met, but it seems improbable that this material was intended for publication in small doses in *Transactions*, since it would have called for a radical transformation of Oldenburg's usual practice in compiling the periodical and significantly curtailed his editorial independence, without any concomitant offer from the Society to take up even part of the financial burden. The plan was revived in January 1678, Oldenburg having died in the interim, alongside another scheme for reviving the Society's experimental work and publishing, 'in the name of the Society', annual compilations of systematically-prosecuted research on particular topics to be determined in advance.[47] Neither project bears much resemblance to *Transactions* as Oldenburg had managed the publication. Something like both these plans were actually put into execution in the late 1670s, however, under the aegis of the Society's two new Secretaries, Robert Hooke and Nehemiah Grew.[48]

---

43 John Wallis, *A discourse of gravity and gravitation, grounded on experimental observations, presented to the Royal Society the 12. of November 1674* (London, 1675); Nehemiah Grew, *A discourse made before the Royal Society, Decemb. 10, 1674, concerning the nature, causes, and power of mixture* (London, 1675).
44 William Petty, *The discourse made before the Royal Society the 26. of November 1674, concerning the use of subduplicate proportion* (London, 1674).
45 'An Account of Three Books', *PT* 9 (1674), 209–210, for Oldenburg's account of Petty's *Discourse*.
46 Birch, *History* 3:328, 21 December 1677.
47 Birch, *History* 3:367–368.
48 Appointed, after much manoeuvering on the part of Hooke in particular, on November 30 1677. Birch, *History* 3:353; Inwood, *The Man Who Knew Too Much*, 256–258.

Transactions underwent a hiatus of about six months before reappearing under Grew's editorship, and the six issues he produced over the next 14 months contained a high proportion of material dredged up from the Society's archives – much of it from the very earliest of the Society's register-books, some of it by Fellows now deceased (and who were therefore no longer in a position to give a more expansive or methodical treatment of their subjects).[49] Similarly, three treatises published by Robert Hooke in 1678, *Cometa*, *Microscopium*, and *De Potentia Restitutiva*, conform broadly to the scheme for publishing treatises on particular topics. (The first two were published together under the collective title of *Lectures and Collections*, and the third separately later that year).[50] All three incorporate material from other authors, including Continental correspondents, excerpts from foreign printed sources, and accounts of work by Hooke himself as well as other Fellows. All were licensed by the Society, and I contend that they are to be understood as fulfilling the brief laid out in the Council directive of January 1678.

The Council issued fresh instructions to the same effect in December 1679, specifying that 'there shall be one subject fixed upon for the Society to proceed upon for the ensuing time, as their main work, until they are satisfied with that subject', and that 'something concerning their progress' should be published within a year, 'or as soon as they are satisfied, that it is brought to perfection'. At the same time orders were issued to ensure a regular supply of experiments, to establish properly enforced protocols for the prompt recording of the experiments in the register-book, and to guarantee the presence at each meeting of a number of Fellows who had read up on the subject under examination so as to be able to offer informed comment. These strictures plainly reflect concern about the state of the Society's experimental programme, its publications, and its administrative procedure, and they envisage a collective effort to address them. These initiatives were followed up with an order 'that the Secretaries take care to have a small account of philosophical matters, such as were the *Transactions* by Mr Oldenburg, and under the same title, published once a quarter at least; and that it be recommended to them to do it monthly, but at least that it be done quarterly'.[51] (Hooke, who as Curator of Experiments and Secretary could expect the burden of these resolutions to fall disproportionately upon him, hedged on the last question. He eventually compromised by

---

49   *Philosophical Transactions* 12 (1677–8), numbers 137–142.
50   Hooke, *Lectures and Collections made by Robert Hooke* (London, 1678).
51   Birch, *History*, 3:513–514.

putting out issues of a new periodical, the *Philosophical Collections*, but with neither the regularity nor the frequency that the Society hoped for). The separate treatment of the projected experimental publishing programme and of *Transactions* implies a separate conception, resting on the distinction between what the Society commissioned or paid for, and what was merely communicated to it. This distinction effectively held until at least 1682, when Hooke's replacement as Secretary gave rise to broad organisational changes.

It is also worth remarking that the late 1670s also saw efforts by outsiders to take advantage of the Society's licensing privilege. Very few works by non-Fellows were licensed by the Society (other than in *Transactions*), and the few exceptions should probably be understood as special cases. Michael Hunter has drawn attention to John Webster's attempt to exploit the Society's privilege for his *Displaying of Supposed Witch-craft* (1677), having previously been refused a licence by the ecclesiastical authorities, and to the irregularity of its licensing by the Vice-President, Jonas Moore, while the Society was not in session; and the late 1670s also saw one of the few cases of a work meeting with outright rejection.[52]

The early 1680s also saw attempts to revive the Society's experimental work. Following Hooke's replacement as Secretary in November 1682, the anatomist Edward Tyson and the chemist Frederick Slare were appointed to supplement his work as Curator of Experiments, and instructed to arrange between them to provide at least one experiment or demonstration per meeting, in their respective areas of expertise.[53] Bounding the curators by discipline in this fashion meant that the systematic prosecution of specific areas of research was in effect built in to the Society's organisational structure.

In contrast to the Society's previous practice or intention when it came to the research it sponsored, however, the bulk of the experimental reports thereby produced appeared in *Transactions* rather than being held over for publication as separate tracts or gathered volumes.[54] This change in established

---

52   Michael Hunter, 'John Webster'; the author whose work was turned down by the Society was Moses Rusden, *A Further Discovery of Bees*, who presented his work to the Society for licensing but whose request was complicated by the fact that his royalist construction of bees was founded on errors of natural history (as the Royal Society's reader remarked). See Johns, *Nature of the Book*, 494 n. 100.
53   Birch, History, 4:187–188, 28 February 1683.
54   Several months' worth of Frederick Slare's chemical experiments were published together in *Philosophical Transactions* 13 (1683), no. 150, 289–302; Tyson's dissections, which tended to produce much longer papers, were published as he performed them (see for example *PT* 13 25–46, 'Viperi Caudi-sona [rattle-snake]'; *PT* 13, 154–161, 'Lumbricus Teres [round-

practice, if not policy, should be seen in the light of the Society's reorientation at this period, and the rise in Oxford and Dublin of analogous Philosophical Societies. *Philosophical Transactions* was revived by the London Society's secretaries, Francis Aston and Robert Plot, early in 1683, and until the beginning of 1686 was run as a joint enterprise between London and Oxford, where Plot doubled as Secretary of the Oxford Society.[55] The two institutions were in frequent communication, regularly exchanging letters and passing on papers, experimental materials, and copies of the minutes of their respective meetings. This process of active co-operation considerably reduced the dependence of the London Society on foreign communication. At the same time there was a pronounced decline in the London Society's foreign correspondence following Oldenburg's death that made such material harder to come by in any case.[56] Oxford's status as almost a partner organisation of the Royal Society did away with many of the epistemological difficulties attendant upon trusting research communicated from outside the Society, and which, because it could had not witnessed it, the London group could not credibly authenticate. The Oxford Society's membership and official leadership overlapped considerably with the London Society's, their internal organisation and procedures were very similar, and they were in constant contact, even deliberately replicating one another's research.[57] The distinction between the Society's own research and what was published in *Transactions* no longer needed to be insisted upon so strongly; particularly since the new editors, Aston and Plot, felt free to run it on their own terms rather than narrowly confining themselves to Oldenburg's model.[58]

---

worm]'; *PT* 13, 113–144, 'Lumbricus Latus [tapeworm]'; *PT* 13, 359–385, 'Tajacu sive Aper Mexicanus Moschiferus [Mexican musk-hog or collared peccary]'.)

55   Birch, *History*, 4:170–171, 13 December 1682.

56   On the decline of the Society's foreign correspondence see Hall, *Promoting Experimental Learning*, 98–103. The period of systematic co-operation between the London and Oxford Societies has received little scholarly attention, although Hall notes the steady flow of experimental communications from Oxford to London in 1683 and 1684 (Hall, *Promoting Experimental Learning*, 84), but is strongly apparent in the correspondences and papers reprinted in RT Gunther, *Early Science in Oxford*, 15 vols., (Oxford, 1923–67), 12, *passim*.

57   Birch, *History*, 4:190–191, has Plot despatching samples of earths to the Royal Society, where Slare would later replicate chemical experiments performed on them at Oxford. See M.B. Hall, 'Frederick Slare F.R.S. (1648–1727)', *Notes & Records of the Royal Society* 46 (1992), 23–41, 26.

58   For instance, in their willingness to contemplate paying authors, silent partners, and longer research articles. See Gunther, *Early Science in Oxford*, 12: 15, 17, 22.

4 Natural History and Institutional Support of Scientific Publishing, 1682–88

This period coincides with two other important trends. The first of these is the Society's greater willingness to *invest* in publishing as well as experiment, exemplified by the Council's consenting to take a large subscription (60 copies) of the revived *Transactions*, amounting to an outlay of about £25 a year. This is a small sum, but it comfortably exceeds everything the Society had spent on publishing up to that date, and this willingness to view publishing projects as a legitimate source of expenditure encouraged new ventures. The most notable, indeed notorious of these, was the posthumous compilation and publishing of Francis Willughby's icthyological work. Another joint venture between London and Oxford, the resulting *Historia Piscium* has been amply documented, and the disabling cost of its production and its contribution to souring relations between the London and Oxford Societies are well known.[59] But the *Historia* itself is part of a second trend, towards the publication under the London Society's imprimatur of catalogues of its own collections, of large works of natural history, in particular, and of works in translation from foreign institutions. Between 1681 and 1688 the Royal Society gave its imprimatur, besides the *Historia Piscium*, to the catalogue of the Royal Society's respository; (*Musaeum Regalis Societatis* by Nehemiah Grew, 1681); Grew's *Anatomy of Plants* (1682), which the Royal Society had sponsored in the form of a series of demonstrations, for which Grew was paid;[60] to Richard Waller's translation (1684) of the 1667 *Saggi di Naturali Esperienze*, by the Florentine Accademia del Cimento; to translations of the Parisian Académie's *Mémoires pour Servir à l'Histoire Naturelle des Animaux* (1676), and *Mesure de la Terre* (1671), both published in 1688 and respectively translated by Waller's brother-in-law Alexander Pitfeild, and by Waller himself; and to John Ray's two-volume *Historia Plantarum* (1688).[61] There is also a curious middle case, of Martin Lister's 1682 translation

---

59 See in particular Sachiko Kusukawa, 'The Historia Piscium (1686)', *Notes and Records*, 54 (2000), 179–197, for a thorough survey of the volume's production history.

60 For a comprehensive account of Grew's *Anatomy* and the Society's role in bringing it about, see Michael Hunter, 'Early problems in professionalizing scientific research: Nehemiah Grew (1641–1712) and the Royal Society, with an unpublished letter to Henry Oldenburg', in Hunter, *Establishing the New Science*, 261–278.

61 Richard Waller (trans.), *Essayes of Natural Experiments Made in the Academie del Cimento* (London: Benjamin Alsop, 1684); Alexander Pitfeild (trans.), *Memoir's for the Natural History of Animals, Containing the Anatomical Descriptions of Several creatures Dissected by the Royal Academy of Sciences at Paris* (London, 1688); Waller (trans.), *An Account of the Measure of a Degree of great Circle of the Earth* (London, 1688); and John Ray, *Historia Plantarum*, 2 vols (London, 1686–8). C.A. Rivington's checklist of works published under

and annotation of Jan Goedart's work on insects. The volume was printed at York, and does not bear the institution's imprimatur, yet the record of the minutes shows Lister presenting the book to a meeting of the Society, 'which he was going to print', which he desired 'might be printed with the Society's approbation'; the Society, in turn, encouraged him to 'proceed with [its] speedy publication'.[62] Presenting a work prior to print with the express aim of seeking the Society's approval for its publication would normally have been understood as a request for the grant of the imprimatur, and the fact that the Society merely gave its verbal blessing may reflect Lister's wish to print the book at York and the fact that the Society was still unsure of whether its writ, and that of its imprimatur, ran outside of London.

Between 1681 and 1688, then, the Society licensed, published, or encouraged the publication of a series of large-scale descriptive, anatomical, and taxonomic works in natural history, none of them originating in its own research, covering plants, animals, fish and insects (if we extend the period to include John Ray's posthumous edition of Willughby's *Ornithologia* birds are also included; a little further, and we can include the 1697 edition of Marcello Malpighi's posthumous works, the manuscripts of which were entrusted to the Society). This is also the period, of course, during which the Society licensed, and Edmond Halley coaxed from its author and supervised through the press, Isaac Newton's *Philosophiae Naturalis Principia Mathematica*, whose significance the Society instantly grasped to the extent of offering to pay for the printing (before realising the state in which the publication of *Historia Piscium* had left its finances, and promptly devolving the responsibility onto the impecunious Halley).[63]

Unsurprisingly, *Principia* has taken up most of the scholarly attention to scientific publishing in the Royal Society during the 1680s, which has helped to obscure the broader pattern of natural-historical publishing. Another common strand in many of these works is a concern that valuable research might be lost, either through the dispersal of a dead natural historian's papers – as in the case of Ray's editions of Willughby – or because the works themselves were

---

the Society's imprimatur prior to 1708, among other errors, omits all the translated works; see Rivington, 'Early Printers to the Royal Society', *Notes and Records of the Royal Society* 39 (1984), 1–27, 22–27. Most of these are made good in a supplement to the paper published two years later: 'Addendum: Early Printers to the Royal Society', *Notes and Records* 41 (1986), 219–220.

62 Birch, *History*, 4:94, July 13 1681.
63 See Birch, *History*, 4:480, 483–485; for an overview of *Principia*'s passage through the Society, see Richard S. Westfall, *Never at Rest: A Biography of Isaac Newton* (Cambridge, 1987), 444–447.

rare and difficult to obtain.[64] Waller's explicit rationale for the translation of the Florentine Academy's experiments was the rarity of the volume and the fact that the Cimento was defunct by this time.[65] Similarly the translation of the publications of the Paris Academy, originally published in lavish royal folio format and magnificently illustrated by Sébastien Leclerc, and whose status as offerings to Louis XIV from the academy he had founded meant that virtually none of the original print run of 200 copies found their way into general circulation.[66] (The comprehensiveness of the Paris academicians' surrender of their work to the Crown can be gauged by the fact that twenty-four copies – one for each of the pensionary academicians – were gifted back to the institution by the Sun King's chief minister, Jean-Baptiste Colbert).[67] Even with the publication of an expanded edition in 1676, it was at least a decade before the Fellows of the Royal Society could lay their hands on a copy.[68] The purpose of translating the volume – Waller also produced scaled-down versions of Leclerc's engravings – was, Pitfeild's preface made clear, to make available the fruits of the academicians' research.[69] The English volume was a moderate success, going into a second edition in 1702. As Anita Guerrini has observed, until the work of the Academy was reprinted in less luxurious editions in the 1730s, as part of the retrospective *Histoire de l'Académie Royale des Sciences* compiled by Bernard le Bovier de Fontenelle, by far the most accessible version of the *Histoire des*

---

[64] The Royal Society was not the only institution to reproduce valuable works of natural history languishing in manuscript whose authors were dead or otherwise unable to publish. On the extremely complex genesis and publishing history of Francisco Hernandez's work on Mexican plants, *Rerum Medicarum Novae Hispaniae Thesaurus*, reconstructed from a partial transcript of Hernandez's manuscripts by the Accademia dei Lincei in Rome, see Silvia da Renzi, 'Writing and Talking of Exotic Animals', in Marina Frasca-Spada and Nicholas Jardine, eds, *Books and the Science in History* (Cambridge, 2000), 151–168.

[65] Waller, [Dedication], *Essayes of Natural Experiments*, sig. π4r-v.

[66] The academicians also erased themselves as individuals from the publication, insisting on presenting it as a collaborative work, partly as a strategy for boosting the collective authority of the Academy and partly as a way of offering up the work more completely as Louis XIV's creation. See Guerrini, 'The King's Animals'.

[67] See Anita Guerrini, *The Courtiers' Anatomists*, 163.

[68] Oldenburg included an account of the 1671 edition in *Philosophical Transactions* 11 (1676), 591–596, in which he warned that readers would find the work itself almost impossible to obtain. When Edward Tyson cited the *Histoire* in his anatomy of a porpoise (*Phocaena*, 1680), the best evidence suggests he was working from Oldenburg's review and, possibly, the five anatomical descriptions published in 1669 by the Académie as a quarto pamphlet. See Moxham, 'Edward Tyson's *Phocaena*', 251–252.

[69] See Pitfeild, 'The Publisher to the Reader' in *Memoirs for a Natural History of Animals*, sig. [A]2r.

Animaux was its English translation.[70] (The problem of making the knowledge produced by the Academy's research accessible and usable was implicitly acknowledged by the lengthy summary of the *Mémoires* published in Jean-Baptiste Du Hamel's 1698 history of the Academy).[71]

5 Conclusion

The Royal Society's publishing activity in the 1680s should not by any means be viewed as a systematic natural history produced under the Society's own auspices; its involvement in bringing this material to the public was after the fact in most cases, and sometimes at second hand. Instead, I suggest, it should be read as reflecting a broader understanding of what the Society's chartered purpose of 'promoting natural knowledge' might entail, and the role of publishing in that purpose. The grant of the Society's imprimatur for the publication of research it had had no direct hand in producing or commissioning was in some sense opportunistic, insofar as it tended to co-opt other people's research into the Society's apparent output. It also reflects the role of contingency in the development of the Society's publishing practices, in that it parallels the rise to prominence within the Society of men like Richard Waller, whose particular talents lay in the direction of scientific illustration and translation, and later the botanist, collector and physician Hans Sloane. Both men's principal interests lay in natural history, and both had long and influential careers in the Society's administration (from the mid-1680s and early 1690s respectively).[72] This trend may be interpreted as an attempt to carve out a new identity for the Society, one that did not depend solely on the primary production of experimental knowledge from within the institution, as had been anticipated at its inception. (The tenacity of experiment as a component of the Society's self-understanding is evident from its periodic attempts to revive an experimental programme through the mid-1680s and again in the early eighteenth century).[73]

---

70   Guerrini, *The Courtiers' Anatomists*, 163, 247–249.
71   Jean-Baptiste Du Hamel, *Regiae Scientiarum Academiae Historia* (Paris, 1698), 115–129.
72   Waller served as Secretary from 1687 to 1709, and then again from 1710 until 1714, while Sloane became Secretary in 1692 and served until 1713.
73   1687, with the departure of Denis Papin for Germany, effectively marked the beginning of a long decline, though not a total eradication of experiment as a feature of Society meetings until the presidency of Isaac Newton in 1703 (See Hall, *Promoting Experimental Learning*, 88–97). For the promotion of experimental demonstrations under Newton, by Francis Hauksbee and later John Theophilus Desaguliers, in physics and chemistry in

What this closer examination of the Royal Society's publishing practices over a period of thirty years reveals is not a carefully-executed grand strategy, but a series of experiments – some planned, and some contingent. They reflect an initial uncertainty about the legal status, and the practical effect, of the imprimatur, and the Society's developing sense of how it might be used to secure the public credit of the Society, whether that meant flaunting the status of its research as a royal commission, as in the case of *Sylva*, or to apply the Society's stamp to a raft of work completed elsewhere but brought to the light of day, or made more widely available, by its efforts and those of its members, as in the case of the natural-historical publications of the 1680s. They also reflect the consistently secondary status of the *Philosophical Transactions* in the collective mind of the Society, though not necessarily of the wider natural-philosophical community, as a medium for publishing credible and verifiable claims to knowledge through at least the early 1680s. That status is particularly apparent where the Society announces its ambitions as a producer of natural knowledge on its own account, as in the series of discourses published in 1674, or the plans for systematic tracts of 1678–9.

This point is particularly important, since there has been a tendency even among informed historians of science and scientific publishing to identify the *Transactions* too closely with the Society, and in particular the periodical's contents with the institution's activity. This is not to say that the Society did not value the *Transactions* or the role it performed as a repository of communications from beyond the Society (and even of occasional, stand-alone performances from within it), and as a way of keeping the natural-philosophical community informed of new discoveries, developments and publications. It would be truer to say that the Society, especially early on, viewed the production and the communication of natural knowledge as distinct enterprises, and did not view the *Transactions* as more than at best a partial fulfilment of its ambitions. The Society's imprimatur, occasionally backed with its money, could be used to assert the institution's status by association; to appropriate the work of others; to put into wide circulation what was obscure and difficult to obtain; and to give an official seal of approval, akin almost to the stamp of peer review, to particular works and their contents.[74] On other occasions that approval would have to be qualified, as in the case of *Micrographia*, where

---

particular, see Hall, ibid., 116–132, and John Heilbron, *Physics at the Royal Society during Newton's Presidency* (Los Angeles, CA, 1983), *passim*.

74 Mario Biagioli has argued, in an important essay, for the imprimatur to be understood as a precursor of peer review. I would not wish to dispute this interpretation, but would argue, as above, that this function intersects, to varying degrees in particular cases, with a number of others that exercise mutual influence upon one another. Biagioli, 'From Book

Hooke's speculative and methodological flights exceeded what the Society was happy to put its name to. (Paradoxically, in the one case in which the Society bore strong collective responsibility for a work's publication it became shy of being seen to approve too conspicuously of its own products and proceedings, and refrained from licensing Sprat's *History* itself). The Society was evidently less concerned about the award of the imprimatur when what was at stake was chiefly utility – as in the case of *Sylva*, or the translations and posthumous publications of the mid-1680s – than when it implied epistemic approval (*Micrographia* or the *Philosophical Transactions*). This study also demonstrates the value of paying very careful attention to apparently small changes in the Society itself, as when the appointment of additional Curators of Experiments in 1682/3 and a new secretarial regime helped bring about a significant reorientation of the Society's efforts and a productive period of collaboration with Oxford that was largely concerned with endeavouring to integrate experiment and communication. The promotion of the link between the content of meetings and the communication of experiment gradually helped to normalise what would be the Society's practice over the next century, as the mainstream of the Society's activity became the hearing and publication of papers.

Acknowledgements

I am very grateful to the editors, to the anonymous readers for Brill, and to audiences in Berlin and London who heard and commented on versions of this essay. I am also particularly grateful to Michael Hunter, for typically generous and incisive comments on a draft, and for sharing his own work on John Webster and the Society's imprimatur ahead of publication.

Censorship to Academic Peer Review', *Emergences: Journal for the Study of Media & Composite Cultures* 12 (2002), 11–45.

Summarizing Commentaries – 'Institutions and knowledge systems: theoretical perspectives'

Jürgen Renn and Florian Schmaltz

1   What Were Academies in the Early Modern Period?

Academies are, in general, institutions concerned with the production, preservation, and circulation of knowledge, and hence part of what one may call a knowledge economy.[1] Which epistemologies and specific modes of knowledge production were characteristic of academies as scientific institutions in early modern Europe? Early modern academies were of very different types with different functions and lifetimes. They were nevertheless seen by contemporaries as belonging to comparable institutional genres.

The scientific academies under consideration were all more or less composed of a restricted group of agents, typically not many more than a hundred. These agents of knowledge production, who considered themselves members of an intellectual elite, were normally male members of the upper-classes with male-specific bonding behaviors and habitus. They acted according to rules that they mostly determined for themselves and sometimes wrote down. The members shared the conviction that they were an exclusive community producing knowledge that was not necessarily delimited by traditional systems of knowledge. Their exclusive group identity, combined with this sense of freedom, was an essential feature of academies, by way of which they sought to distinguish themselves from the existing structures of knowledge production – from institutions such as the universities and, in particular, knowledge agencies associated with the Church.

Their practices in this framework comprised rituals, discussions, readings, collecting, exploring artifacts or samples taken from nature, experimenting, corresponding with each other, and representing the academy to each other and to the outside world. Their results were articulated in written and sometimes printed reports, papers, and books. This interaction with the outside

---

1   The concept of knowledge economy was introduced in: Jürgen Renn and Malcolm D. Hyman, 'The Globalization of Knowledge in History: An Introduction', in *The Globalization of Knowledge in History*, ed. Jürgen Renn (Berlin, 2012), 15–44. See also: Jürgen Renn, *The Evolution of Knowledge: Rethinking Science in the Anthropocene* (Princeton, 2020), especially Chapters 8–10.

world, partly made possible by the printing culture of that era, is another hallmark of academies that distinguishes them from other bodies such as guilds and freemasons, which were characterized by their secrecy or the non-dissemination of their knowledge.

The academies were part of a Europe-wide network of institutions concerned with knowledge production and dissemination, such as other academies and universities. They received recognition from these mutual relations but also from local power and patronage structures, whose constituents shared their conviction of producing knowledge that was in some sense meaningful, new, and even useful.

2   How Did the Academies Emerge?

Academies are unthinkable without the transformation of the ancient model of the Platonic academy in the fifteenth century, which was carried out by humanists such as Marsilio Ficino (1433–1499).[2] In contrast to previous historiography, Ficino's 'academy' was not a firm institution but rather an informal circle of scholars, and thereby in accordance with the fifteenth-century conceptual understanding of an academy as a gathering of literary men or a private humanist school, as opposed to a medieval university.[3] It is no coincidence that some of the earliest scientific academies, such as the Accademia telesiana, were concerned with philosophy, literature, and sciences.[4] Initially, academies were weakly institutionalized and represented informal circles that often depended on patronage. They were characterized by the desire to jointly create novelties.

The further development of academies was shaped by existing models of institutionalization such as the guilds, religious orders, and the system of privileges. These models could be and were adapted in order to provide, among other things, greater longevity, a corporate identity, broader recognition of their findings, and protection for their members.

Another force driving this increasing institutionalization, developing within the space of possibilities delineated by contemporary institutional models,

---

[2] The transformation may be characterized as an "allelopoiesis." For the concept of *allelopoiesis*, see: Johannes Helmrath, Eva Marlene Hausteiner, and Ulf Jensen, (eds.), *Antike als Transformation: Konzepte zur Beschreibung kulturellen Wandels* (Berlin, 2017).

[3] James Hankins, 'The Myth of the Platonic Academy of Florence', *Renaissance Quarterly*, 44 (1991), 429–475.

[4] Pietro Daniel Omodeo (ed.), *Bernardino Telesio and the Natural Sciences in the Renaissance* (Leiden, 2019).

was competition among nascent institutions of a similar kind as well as competition engendered by the fact that knowledge production in other bodies, such as universities and religious orders, was embedded within different boundary conditions – those determined by political and religious power structures and ideologies.

A further motivation was an increasing need for the resources and collaboration necessary to produce knowledge in the fields of natural sciences and technology, sometimes spurred by specific outside challenges such as newly arising technical challenges or the demands of European colonial expansion.

Another important motivation was the existence of a market for new knowledge that could no longer be satisfied exclusively by the existing knowledge producing institutions. Think, for example, of the formative role in shaping the Lisbon Academy played by economic and military demands related to navigation, architecture, and the need for educating practitioners. Or think of the quest for cultural recognition driving the foundation of the Accademia del Cimento in the aftermath of Galileo's rise and fall. Given that the well-established producers of knowledge, such as universities, guilds, and religious orders, had a corporate structure, those agencies producing less-confined knowledge to meet newly arising demands were also pressed into taking such a corporate form. The alternative of acting as individuals within existing institutions engendered higher transaction costs.

3 How Did Academies Change?

One function of the rules set up to establish academies was to determine their mechanisms of self-reproduction, for example, by cooption or nomination. These mechanisms played a crucial role in determining their lifetimes, their dependence on local power structures or, inversely, their autonomy, and more generally their life cycles, including the variations they underwent. Variation and selection indeed played an important role in the evolution of academies, albeit in very diverse 'fitness landscapes'. These fitness landscapes were not simply given, however, by external, contextual, social, or political conditions; they were continuously transformed by the knowledge production itself, thus establishing a reciprocal causality in the sense of what evolutionary theorists have called 'niche construction'.[5] This reciprocal causality is particularly

---

[5] Manfred D. Laubichler and Jürgen Renn, 'Extended evolution: A conceptual framework for integrating regulatory networks and niche construction', *J Exp Zool B Mol Dev Evol.* 324 (7) (2015), 565–577.

evident in the realm of publishing where the increasing literary production at one location encouraged knowledge consumption and production elsewhere, thus canalizing and hence stabilizing the development of certain forms of knowledge organization as well as specific dissemination formats such the scientific journal, which remains with us today.

This is probably also true for the wider context of scientific knowledge production in absolutist and mercantilist states because these states, some on their way to becoming capitalist and industrialized societies, increasingly relied on the production of technical and specialist – if not scientific – knowledge. But clearly this process was also partly driven by the intrinsic dynamics of the Europe-wide network of academic institutions and scientists, creating a characteristic matrix connecting practical with scientific knowledge production. In the nineteenth century, academies and professional schools also spread as new institutions in countries outside Europe.[6]

This network comprised increasingly well-established mechanisms of knowledge exchange and certification, eventually transforming locally effective mechanisms for generating symbolic capital into a global recognition system. This created in turn a tension between the local dimension of academies and the universal claim of the knowledge produced by them, driving a deepening institutionalization of procedures for knowledge evaluation and control. The role of social networks in the evolution of academies is also crucial in terms of funding, connecting them with other institutions such as courts, the Church, state agencies, and so on.

The network of intellectual exchanges probably had a self-similar structure in the sense that the network of relations among intellectuals within one institution may have been similar to the network among the institutions themselves.[7] A more extensive analysis of the network topology of academies could validate this claim.

4   How Did Academies End?

In later periods, some academies became instrumental in spreading the Industrial Revolution to other countries, transferring its characteristic matrix of

---

[6] Jürgen Renn and Helge Wendt, 'Knowledge and Science in Current Discussions of Globalization', in *The Globalization of Knowledge in History*, Ed. Jürgen Renn (Berlin, 2012) 45–72, at 52.

[7] Jürgen Renn, Dirk Wintergrün, Roberto Lalli, Manfred Laubichler, and Matteo Valleriani, 'Netzwerke als Wissensspeicher', in *Die Zukunft der Wissensspeicher forschen, sammeln und vermitteln im 21. Jahrhundert*, eds, Jürgen Mittelstraß und Ulrich Rüdiger (Munich, 2016), 35–79.

practical and scientific knowledge from England, where it first emerged, to these other countries. But while the activities of the academies were thus interwoven with a growing demand for technical rationality, their origin in attempts to challenge existing boundaries and confinements of discourse also turned them into important islands of communicative rationality that produced knowledge beyond practical demands. In this way, they followed historical trajectories that they themselves had laid out – sometimes with long-term effects, if one considers, for instance, the role of the Leopoldina in the process of German unification today.[8]

Academies also had a specific impact on the development of the public sphere and civil society. They were institutions that fostered the emergence of scientific communities and a society open to their insights. Publicity through journals, books, public talks, and demonstrations presenting research results became an important precondition for scientific controversies and reliability tests, and these practices were a driving force not only for the development of scientific progress but for that of the public sphere as a whole, including the development of interfaces between the worlds of science and that of politics. On the other hand, the elitist heritage of academies has prevented them to this day from overcoming their pretense of representing exclusive sites for knowledge production rather than developing more participatory and integrative models to suit a knowledge economy befitting democratic societies facing today's challenges of the Anthropocene by providing the interdisciplinary and transdisciplinary knowledge needed to address these challenges.[9]

---

8   *Wissenschaftsakademien im Zeitalter der Ideologien: politische Umbrüche, wissenschaftliche Herausforderungen, institutionelle Anpassungen. Arbeitstagung des Projektes zur Geschichte der Leopoldina vom 22. bis 24. November 2012 in Halle (Saale)*, eds Rüdiger Vom Bruch, Sybille Gerstengarbe, Jens Thiel, and Simon Renkert (Stuttgart, 2014).

9   *Das Anthropozän: Zum Stand der Dinge,* eds Jürgen Renn and Bernd Scherer (Berlin, 2015); Helmuth Trischler, 'The Anthropocene', NTM. *Zeitschrift für Geschichte der Wissenschaften, Technik und Medizin*, 24 (2016), 309–335; Renn, *The Evolution of Knowledge*.

Index

Academia Christiana Albertina 208
Academia dos Generosos (Lisbon) 109, 110, 114–6, 119
Academia dos Ilustrados (Lisbon) 132
Academia Naturae Curiosorum (Schweinfurt) VII, 199–235, *passim*
Academia Portuguesa 109, 114, 116, 118, 120, 121, 131, 132, 135
Academia Real da História Portuguesa 109–13, 116, 130–7
Académie de la Chine 145
Académie des Inscriptions et Belles Lettres 23, 135
Académie Française (Paris) 23, 26, 135, 182, 194
Académie Impériale des sciences de Saint-Pétersbourg 111, 134, 136
Académie Royale de Chirurgie 23
Académie Royale des Sciences (Paris) VII, 66, 67, 68, 78, 79, 84, 109, 110, 139, 140, 142–6, 151, 152, 154, 155, 157, 162, 164–7, 169, 172, 174, 180, 193, 194, 236, 259, 261, 262, 264
Académie Royale des Sciences et Belles-Lettres de Prusse (Berlin) 111, 136
Accademia dei Lincei (Rome) 180
Accademia del Cimento (Florence) VII 56, 68, 83, 84, 88, 90, 91, 94, 96–106, 194, 294
Accademia dell'Arcadia (Rome) 132
Accademia della Crusca (Florence) 120
Accademia Telesiana (Cosenza) 293
Afonso VI, King of Portugal 115, 123
Agarrat, Antoine 177, 178
Alexander VII (Pope)
Almada, André de 111
Apollonius of Perga 86, 101
Argenville, Antoine-Joseph Dezallier d' 251
Argote, Jerónimo Contador de 121
Ashmolean Museum (Oxford) 14
Auzout, Adrien 66, 67, 72, 90, 100, 177, 179, 191, 193
Azevedo, António de Oliveira de 121
Azevedo, Francisco de 120

Bacon, Francis 238, 242, 243, 245, 264
Bailly, Jean-Sylvain 42
Bainbridge, John 13, 15
Barbosa, José 121
Bartholin, Erasmus 95
Bathurst, Ralph 14
Baudelot de Dairval, Charles 47
Bauhin, Caspar 216
Baumé, Antoine 34
Béchet, Jean 177
Bellers, Fettiplace 254
Benedetti, Giovanni Battista 54
Bernard, Edward 15, 16
Bernoulli, Jean 48
Bianchini, Francesco 132, 142, 162–6, 168, 169, 171, 172
Bibliothèque du Roi (Paris) 241, 256–8
Bignon, Jean-Paul 26, 170
Blondel, Nicolas-François 29
Bluteau, Raphael 109, 110, 121, 122
Bonfa, Jean 150
Bontius, Jacob 214
Borelli, Giovanni Alfonso 86, 87, 95, 96, 99–101, 105, 106, 148, 149
Botelho, Lourenço 121
Boulduc (family) 27
Boulliau, Ismaël 55, 56, 64, 65, 69, 72, 79, 88, 92, 96, 100, 103, 108, 177, 179, 183
Bourdelin, Claude 35, 36, 240–6, 248, 256, 258, 260, 261, 264
Bourdelin, Louis-Claude 26, 35
Bourdelot, Pierre Michon dit l'abbé 24, 25, 191
Bourdin, Nicolas de 177
Bourdin, Pierre 177, 179
Bouvet, Joachim 144, 151
Boyle, Robert 4, 175, 176, 189, 190, 193, 240, 243–8, 255–7, 260–2, 264, 265
Bradley, James 14
Brahe, Tycho 4, 54, 55, 70, 125, 128, 129
Breteuil, Louis Auguste Le Tonnelier, baron de 41
Briggs, Henry 13, 15
Brouncker, William 15, 190, 193
Browne, Thomas 220, 225

Brûlart, Pierre   177
Brunetti, Cosimo   100
Bruno, Giordano   129
Buffon, Georges-Louis Leclerc de   30, 38, 40, 263
Buot, Jacques   177
Burg, Johann   212
Butterfield, Michael   149

Cambridge, University   3–19
Camões, Luís de   119, 120
Campos, Manuel de   132
Capasso, Domenico   136
Capell, Rudolf   224, 226
Carbone, Giovanni Battista   136
Carcavi, Pierre de   26
Cardinal de Retz   177
Carvalho, Inácio de   121
Cassini (family)   27, 40
Cassini de Thury, César François   49
Cassini, Jean-Dominique   49
Cassini, Giovanni Domenico   138–42, 144–53, 155–7, 160–73, 191
Castiglione, Baldassare   112
Cavendish, William   184
Cesi, Francesco   180
Chapelain, Jean   56, 92–94, 99, 100, 102, 104, 107, 108, 182, 183, 191, 193
Charles II   189
Charleton, Walter   185, 186–8, 190, 192
Châtelet, Emilie du   38
Christian Albrecht of Schleswig-Holstein   203
Clavius, Christophe   163
Clement XI, Pope   169, 171
Colbert, Jean-Baptiste   25, 31, 56, 66, 138, 139, 143, 146, 147, 179, 184, 193, 194, 259–61
Collège de Boncourt   184
Collège de Clermont   153–5, 177
Collège de Navarre   177
College Louis le Grand   142, 153–6
Commerson, Philibert   30, 38
Comte, Louis Daniel le   144
Condé, Louis II de Bourbon   25, 35
Conferências Eruditas   116, 118, 122
Contador, José   121
Copleston, Edward   5–6
Costa, António Rodrigues da   121
Courcillon, Philippe de   159

Courten, William   252
Cristo, André de, friar (André de Fróis de Macedo)   123
Cunha, António Álvares da   114–16, 118–20, 123, 124
Cunha, Luís da   116, 135
Cureau de la Chambre, Marin   26, 27

Dati, Carlo Roberto   85, 95, 97, 99, 100, 103
Delambre, Jean-Baptiste   49
Delisle, Guillaume   49
Delisle, Joseph-Nicolas   31
Deparcieux, Antoine   34
Desagulliers, John Theophilus   14
Descartes, René   32, 182, 184, 188, 191, 192, 204
Dezalier d'Argenville, Antoine Joseph   48, 251
Digby, Kenelm   107, 108
Divini, Eustachio   95, 96, 99, 105
Dodart, Denis   241–7, 255, 258
Dortous de Mairan, Jean-Jacques   49
Du Bosc, Charles   184
Du Prat, Abraham   98
Duchesne, Antoine-Nicolas   38
Duclos, Samuel Cottereau   240, 245, 246, 248, 258, 260, 261, 264, 265
Dufay, Charles   240, 248, 250–6, 261–4
Duhamel du Monceau, Henri-Louis   35
Duverney, Joseph-Guichard   32

Erasmus, Desiderius   53, 73
Evelyn, John   184, 186–8, 190

Fabri, Honoré   95, 97–99, 101, 1056
Fehr, Johann Michael   211
Feodor III, Tsar   161
Ficino, Marsilio   293
Fogel, Martin   205
Fontaney, Jean de   142–53, 155
Fontenelle, Bernard Le Bouyer de   38, 139, 155, 162, 191, 194
Fortes, Manuel de Azevedo   121, 130, 133
Fouquet, Nicolas   26
Frederick II, King of Denmark   128
Freind, John   14
Frénicle, Bernard   107, 108
Fréret, Nicolas   31
Friedrich Wilhelm of Brandenburg   57, 75
Frankfurt, Univerity   57, 73

INDEX 299

Galilei, Galileo   87, 92, 94, 105, 117
Gallois, Jean   26
Gassendi, Pierre   31, 32, 92, 98, 129, 177, 179, 182, 184
Gaston d'Orléans   177
Gayant, Louis   27
Gaynot, François   177
Geoffroy (family)   27
Gerbillon, Jean-François   144, 147
Gerdil, Hyacinthe Sigismond   5
Gessner, Conrad   204
Godinho, Jerónimo   121
Gonzaga, Maria-Luisa, Queen of Poland   56
Gouyé, Thomas   148, 152, 153
Gray, Stephen   253–6, 263
Greenwich Observatory   68
Gregorian Calendar, Commission   169, 171–2
Gregory, David   14
Gresham College (London)   188, 189, 252
Grew, Nehemiah   258, 259
Grimaldi, Francesco Maria   92
Guericke, Otto von   71, 79
Guettard, Etienne   28
Guisony, Pierre   98, 99, 101, 102, 106, 108

Haak, Theodore   181, 188
Hales, Stephen   253
Halley, Edmond   14, 15, 16
Happel, Eberhard Werner   231–2, 233
Hartlib, Samuel   55
Hauksbee, Francis   253–7, 263
Heinsius, Nicholas   93, 95, 97, 99, 100, 103
Henri II of Savoy   177
Herbert, Edward, 1st Baron of Cherbury   181
Hevelius, Johannes   52, 55–72, 74, 75, 78, 79, 92
Hobbes, Thomas   15–16, 86, 98, 99, 175, 182, 184, 185
Hooke, Robert   11, 15, 175, 190, 257
Huygens, Christiaan   84, 90, 92–108, 182, 183, 191, 192

Innocent XII, Pope   164, 169

Jänisch, Johannes   211, 212, 213
Jan III Sobieski, King of Poland   68
Jardin des Plantes   184
Jardin du Roi (Paris)   241, 243, 250, 258, 263

Jenquel, Kaspar Friedrich   219
João IV, King of Portugal   115
João V, King of Portugal   109, 111, 131, 132, 135–7
Jowett, Benjamin   18–19
Jungius, Joachim   205
Jussieu, Antoine-Laurent   38

Keill, John   14
Kepler, Johannes   31, 55, 128
Kielmansegg, Johann Adolph Kielmann von   203
Kircher, Athanasius   55, 72, 146, 150
Krahmer, Johann   218
Christina, Queen of Sweden   170

La Chaise, François d'Aix de   147, 156
La Hire, Philippe   31, 37, 148, 171, 172
Laplace, Pierre-Simon de   42, 50
Lavoisier, Antoine-Louis   21, 28, 29, 35, 38, 42, 43, 44, 45
Le Gallois, Pierre   47
Le Monnier, Louis-Guillaume   29, 30
Leibniz, Gottfried Wilhelm von   164, 167, 168, 171, 210
Leitão, Francisco   121
Lémery, Nicolas   34
Leopold I, Emperor   201
Lhwyd, Edward   14
Lima, Manuel Dias de   121
Lionne, Artus de   158–60
Lionne, Hugues de   159
Lipsius, Justus   73
Lister, Martin   160, 262
Longomotanus, Christian   126
Longon, Mr.   221
Louis XIV, King of France   56, 66, 68, 111, 138, 139, 141–5, 147, 153, 154, 156–9, 161, 167, 169, 173, 178, 238, 261
Louvois, Marquis de   259, 260
Lubieniecki, Stanisław   52, 55, 56, 64–66, 67, 70, 72–76, 78

Macedo, André de Fróis de (see André de Cristo)   123
Macedo, António de Sousa   118
Machado, Diogo Barbosa de   123
Macquer, Pierre Joseph   34

Magalotti, Lorenzo   83, 87–89, 99–101, 103–105
Malpighi, Marcello   106, 287
Mancini, Antonio   102
Maraldi, Giacomo   169–72
Marchais, Antoine   179
Marchant, Jean   241, 243, 258
Marchant, Nicolas   241, 243, 258
Marolles, Michel de   178
Maupertuis, Pierre-Louis Moreau   40
Major, Johann Daniel   200, 203–8, 213–35
Medici, Cosimo III de'   91
Medici, Leopoldo de'   56, 64, 67, 68, 83, 85–91, 94–97, 99–103, 105–108
Melo, Francisco Manuel de   121
Meneses, Francisco Xavier de   113, 116–18, 122, 129, 130, 132, 134
Mercier, Louis-Sébastien   48
Mersenne, Marin   55, 181, 184, 238
Merz, John   17
Mesmer, Franz-Anton   45
Millington, Thomas   14
Mirabeau, Honoré-Gabriel Riqueti, marquis de   44
Miscellanea Curiosa Medico-Physica Academiae Naturae Curiosorum   199–235, *passim*
Moller, Daniel Wilhelm   218
Moller, Johannes   223–5
Monconys, Balthazar   192
Montmor Academy   83–85, 87, 93, 94, 98–103, 105, 107, 174, 176, 180, 183–5, 191–3
Montmor, Henri Louis Habert (de)   24, 83–85, 90, 93, 94, 100, 182, 183
Moray, Robert   84, 102, 107, 190, 193
Morhof, Daniel Georg   204, 205, 207, 211, 222–3, 224, 227, 234, 235
Morin, Jean-Baptiste   177–9
Morison, Robert   14
Mylon, Claude   177, 182

Necker, Jacques   41
Neile, Paul   190
Newman, John Henry   4–5
Newton, Isaac   17, 28, 134, 239, 263
Nollet, abbé   34, 38
Noris, Enrico   163–5, 168–71
Noyers, Pierre des   56

Observatoire de Pékin   145, 149
Oldenburg, Henry   13, 55, 56, 67, 71, 191, 211, 217
Olearius, Adam   214, 216
Olhoff, Johann Erich   69
Oxford, University   3–19, 257

Pailleur, Jacques Le   182
Pan, Kosa   159
Paris Observatory   31, 57, 68, 138, 140–2, 145, 152, 153, 155, 157, 160, 164, 165
Pascal, Blaise   238, 239
Patin, Guy   31
Peacock, George   7
Pecquet, Jean   27, 191
Pedro II, King of Portugal   115, 116, 118, 119, 122
Perrault, Claude   27, 30, 32, 37
Pestana, José do Couto   121
Peter I, Tsar   111
Petit, Pierre   66, 177–9, 193
Petiver, James   252
Petty, William   184
Pfautz, Christoph   56
Philippe II, Regent of France   257, 259
Phra-Narai   158, 160
Picard, Jean   29, 177
Pierrepont, Henry, marquess of Dorchester   185
Pimentel, Luís Serrão   118, 120, 123
Pimentel, Manuel   121, 123
Placcius, Vincent   205
Placentinus, Johannes   52, 55–64, 69, 70, 72–76, 78, 79
Plot, Robert   14, 257
Pontchartrain, Jérôme Phelypeaux, compte de   167
Pontchartrain, Louis II Phélypeaux de   26, 259

Ray, John   11
Réaumur, René   40, 41, 240, 248–50, 252, 253, 255–7, 260–2, 264
Renaudot, Théophraste   24
Ricci, Michelangelo   84–90, 97, 99–106, 108
Riccioli, Giovanni Battista   72, 79, 92, 150
Roberval, Gilles Personne de   56, 90, 92–94, 177, 182, 183
Rohault, Jacques   191

INDEX

Rhode, Johann   226
Rothmann, Christoph   54, 117, 128, 129
Rouelle, Guillaume-François   43
Royal Society of London VII   17–18, 25, 55, 56, 67, 79, 84, 102, 107, 109, 115, 116, 134, 136, 152, 153, 160, 168, 174, 189–92, 194, 202, 208, 230, 236–8, 248, 252, 253, 257, 259, 261, 262, 264
Rudbeck, Olaus   71
Rudolf II, Holy Roman Emperor   54, 128

Sachs, Philipp Jakob, von Lewenheimb   201, 203, 209, 211, 212, 213, 218, 226
Saporta, Pierre   191
Sarmento, Jacob de Castro   134, 135
Sartine, Antoine de   42
Savile, Henry   15
Schellhammer, David   201, 213–15, 218–28, 231–4
Schelhammer, Günther Christoph   225–6, 228
Schultz, Gottfried   212
Silva, José Soares da   121
Silva, Manuel Teles da   130, 131
Sloane, Hans   252–4, 258
Société des Missions Etrangères   142, 144
Société d'histoire naturelle de Paris   51
Société royale de médecine   23, 24, 26
Sorbière, Samuel   31, 85, 86, 98, 100, 191–3
Sousa, Luís de Vasconcelos e   123
Sousa, Manuel Caetano de   113, 115, 121, 131–3
Sprat, Thomas   192

Tachard, Guy   144
Tellier, Michel François Le   259
Tenneur, Jacques-Alexandre Le   177

Thévenot, Melchisedéch   84–91, 99–104, 106, 107, 148, 191, 193
Thou, Jacques-Auguste II de   177
Thuret, Isaac   149, 150
Thuret, Jacques   149
Tyson, Edward   262

Ursus, Nicolaus Reimarus   54, 55

Valentini, Michael Bernhard   218
Vauban, Sébastien Le Prestre, marquis de   29
Verjus, Antoine   147, 149, 153, 156
Visdelou, Claude de   144
Viviani, Vincenzo   85, 86, 91, 95, 101, 162
Volgnad, Heinrich   211, 212, 213, 216, 218–19, 221, 232
Volgnad, Philip   216

Wadham College, Oxford   181
Wallis, John   13, 15
Ward, Seth   12–13, 15
Webster, John   12–13
Wedel, Georg Wolfgang   232
Wegelius, Erhard   166
Welsch, Georg Hieronymus   224–5
Whiteside, John   14
Wilkins, John   12, 181, 189, 259
Willughby, Francis   11
Wilhelm IV, Landgrave of Hesse-Kassel   54, 117, 128
Woodward, John   252–4, 258
Wren, Christopher   11, 15, 107

Young, Thomas   6, 11

301